SOCIAL PROBLEMS
AND
SOCIAL POLICY:
The American Experience

This is a volume in the Arno Press Series

SOCIAL PROBLEMS AND SOCIAL POLICY:
The American Experience

Advisory Editor
Gerald N. Grob

Editorial Board
Clarke A. Chambers
Blanche D. Coll
Walter I. Trattner

*See last pages of this volume
for a complete list of titles.*

SOCIAL SECURITY
AND PUBLIC POLICY

Eveline M. Burns

ARNO PRESS

A New York Times Company

New York — 1976

Editorial Supervision: SHEILA MEHLMAN

———◆———

Reprint Edition 1976 by Arno Press Inc.

SOCIAL PROBLEMS AND SOCIAL POLICY: The American Experience
ISBN for complete set: 0-405-07474-3
See last pages of this volume for titles.

Manufactured in the United States of America

———◆———

Library of Congress Cataloging in Publication Data

Burns, Eveline Mabel Richardson, 1900-
    Social security and public policy.

    (Social problems and social policy--the American
experience)
    Reprint of the ed. published by McGraw-Hill, New
York, in the Economics handbook series.
    1. Public welfare. 2. Social security.
3. Social security--United States. I. Title.
II. Series.
[HV31.B8 1976] 368.4'00973   75-17211
ISBN 0-405-07483-2

Social Security and Public Policy

46799

ECONOMICS HANDBOOK SERIES

SEYMOUR E. HARRIS, EDITOR

THE BOARD OF ADVISORS

NEIL W. CHAMBERLAIN
Yale University—Labor

JOHN M. CULBERTSON
University of Wisconsin—Monetary Theory

SEYMOUR E. HARRIS
Harvard University—International Economics,
Social Security; all other areas

FRANCO MODIGLIANI
Massachusetts Institute of Technology—Economic Theory

RICHARD A. MUSGRAVE
Princeton University—Public Policy

MARC NERLOVE
Stanford University—Econometrics and Mathematical Economics

Burns · SOCIAL SECURITY AND PUBLIC POLICY
Carlson · ECONOMIC SECURITY IN THE UNITED STATES
Coppock · INTERNATIONAL ECONOMIC INSTABILITY
Duesenberry · BUSINESS CYCLES AND ECONOMIC GROWTH
Hansen · A GUIDE TO KEYNES
Hansen · THE AMERICAN ECONOMY
Hansen · THE DOLLAR AND THE INTERNATIONAL MONETARY SYSTEM
Hansen · ECONOMIC ISSUES OF THE 1960s
Hansen · MONETARY THEORY AND FISCAL POLICY
Harris · INTERNATIONAL AND INTERREGIONAL ECONOMICS
Harrod · THE BRITISH ECONOMY
Henderson and Quandt · MICROECONOMIC THEORY
Hoover · THE LOCATION OF ECONOMIC ACTIVITY
Johnston · STATISTICAL COST ANALYSIS
Kindleberger · ECONOMIC DEVELOPMENT
Lebergott · MANPOWER IN ECONOMIC GROWTH
Lerner · ECONOMICS OF EMPLOYMENT
Taylor · A HISTORY OF ECONOMIC THOUGHT
Tinbergen and Bos · MATHEMATICAL MODELS OF ECONOMIC GROWTH
Valavanis · ECONOMETRICS

SOCIAL SECURITY
AND PUBLIC POLICY

Eveline M. Burns

NEW YORK SCHOOL OF SOCIAL WORK
COLUMBIA UNIVERSITY

New York   Toronto   London

McGRAW-HILL BOOK COMPANY, INC.

1956

SOCIAL SECURITY AND PUBLIC POLICY

Library of Congress Catalog Card Number 55-11558

7 8 9 – M P – 9 8 7

09195

To my husband
ARTHUR ROBERT BURNS

Editor's Introduction

FOR YEARS many teachers of economics and other professional economists have felt the need of a series of books on economic subjects which is not filled by the usual textbook or by the highly technical treatise.

This present series, published under the general title of the Economics Handbook Series, was planned with these needs in mind. Designed first of all for students, the volumes are useful in the ever-growing field of adult education and also are of interest to the informed general reader.

The volumes are not long—they give the essentials of the subject matter within the limits of a few hundred pages; they present a distillate of accepted theory and practice, without the detailed approach of the technical treatise. Each volume is a unit, standing on its own.

The authors are scholars, each writing on an economic subject on which he is an authority. In this series the author's first task was not to make important contributions to knowledge—although many of them do—but so to present his subject matter that his work as a scholar will carry its maximum influence outside as well as inside the classroom. The time has come to redress the balance between the energies spent on the creation of new ideas and on their dissemination. Economic ideas are unproductive if they do not spread beyond the world of scholars. Popularizers without technical competence, unqualified textbook writers, and sometimes even charlatans control too large a part of the market for economic ideas.

In the classroom the Economics Handbook Series will serve, it is hoped, as brief surveys in one-semester courses, as supplementary reading in introductory courses, and in other courses in which the subject is related.

In the current volume of the Economics Handbook Series, Eveline M. Burns, Professor of Social Work at the New York School of Social Work, Columbia University, treats all the important facets of social security. In Part One, Dr. Burns considers the nature and amount of security benefits and the conditions governing their receipt; in Part Two, choices of risks for which social responsibility will be accepted (e.g., old age, unemployment, medical care); in Part Three, the financing of social security programs; and finally, in Part Four, the administrative issues. She does not restrict herself to problems confronting the United States but draws as well on her unusual grasp of social security theory and practice abroad.

Educated in England, Dr. Burns has had a long experience: as an outstanding student and later member of the faculty at the London School of Economics; as a teacher of college and graduate students at Columbia University and elsewhere and in the Seminars of the Social Security Administration; as researcher and writer in the area of social security; as a member of the Federal Advisory council on Employment Security; as advisor of the original Committee on Economic Security, which introduced the national program in this country, and later as a consultant to former Secretary Hobby and many public and private organizations and committees interested in the problems under consideration in this book.

It is difficult, if not impossible, to think of any authority in this field with a richer experience; and her book reflects her concentration over a long period on social security problems. This volume is the product of the mature academic economist intensely interested in this important field; but even more it is the product of one who knows a subject as only one can who interests herself not only in theory but also in the process of legislation and administration.

SEYMOUR E. HARRIS

Preface

THE NECESSITY to write a preface is not the least of the obstacles to be overcome before a book can see the light of day. Not that it is difficult, as a rule, to state what one had hoped to do; the problem is rather to explain why, in the face of the increasingly painful divergence between one's original high objectives and the chapters as written, one nonetheless persisted with so discouraging a task.

My own objectives are fairly easy to state, namely, to discuss the problems of social security policy. I have attempted, first, to identify the major questions about the nature of social security programs which must be answered by every community desiring to assure, through the instrumentalities of government, a measure of economic security to some or all of its members. Second, I have tried to indicate some of the more important considerations which have to be taken into account and evaluated in answering these questions.

Such an approach has both advantages and disadvantages. Prominent among the former is that, if successful, it should equip the reader with a method of analyzing various programs or policies and comparing them by reference to the same characteristics and criteria. For many years, as a member of official and unofficial advisory bodies and committees concerned with social security policies, I have been impressed by the frequency with which differences of opinion stem from a disposition on the part of the protagonists to judge issues by reference to a single criterion or to consider only some of the relevant consequences. Yet specific social security measures, even when there is agreement about the major objective, inevitably have a variety of repercussions. Sound, rational, and democratic policy formation requires that decisions be made with an awareness of at least the more important of these considerations.

The analytical method also avoids the inconveniences of a program-by-program study of social security institutions. As a teacher, I have long been dissatisfied with the typical college or graduate course on social security (including my own), which usually emphasizes the history of legislation and the detailed provisions of individual programs. The history of social legislation is indeed of great importance, but I believe it is most meaningful when related to contemporary problems and when used as an instrument for revealing the forces and environmental conditions that determine specific policy decisions. In this way, the student can

ix

be sensitized to the need for changes in current provisions as these underlying determinants change. But this result presupposes a firm grounding
in the problems common to all social security measures as well as an
ability to distinguish between the essential features of any given program,
and the details and technical provisions which aim to implement broad
policies. This knowledge and analytical capacity, I believe, the program-
by-program approach fails as a rule to impart.

On the one hand, laboriously acquired knowledge of the details of
each program is frequently rendered obsolete by legislative and administrative changes almost before the academic year is over. On the other
hand, the study of program after program tends to involve considerable
repetition, when policies and issues are discussed, because many issues
are, in fact, common to several programs. Frequently, so much time is
devoted to the detailed intricacies of individual programs that the student
loses sight of the basic issues and finds it difficult to apply principles derived from the study of one measure to the analysis of others. Furthermore, the program-by-program approach is apt to lead to a neglect of
those problems which arise out of the coexistence of several social security
institutions.

But the analytical approach carries its own risks. The first of these,
of which I am painfully aware, is the difficulty of developing an orderly
and convenient framework for the analysis of individual measures. Still
greater is the risk of neglecting important groups of considerations affecting policy. I have tried to include those which appear to me to be,
or to have been, most influential, but undoubtedly many users of this
book will disagree or wish to add others. I merely ask them to remember,
as I have had to do, the problem of space: not every influence can be dealt
with, and one must select those which appear most significant. It is at
this point that the danger of bias is greatest and most difficult to avoid.

The necessity to keep the discussion within reasonable limits is, indeed,
the third problem presented by the approach I have chosen. Social security institutions affect, and are affected by, a wide range of economic, social,
cultural, administrative, and political factors. But this is not intended to
be a book on economics, sociology, political science, or social philosophy.
My more modest aim has been to reveal the bearing of some of these
forces on the formation of social security policy, and I fear I have at times
had to simplify and select in a manner that some of my social science
colleagues may find superficial or dogmatic. I shall however be well satisfied if my efforts serve to alert policy makers to the points at which they
would do well to consult experts in these specialized areas.

Considerations of space have similarly enforced a rigid economy in
the use of illustrative material. I have usually had to content myself with
a single illustration of a policy or principle. I have attempted to compen-

sate in part by giving footnote references to sources where more detail, or other examples, can be found, and I trust that these will be of use to teachers in particular. The vast majority of my illustrations are drawn from United States experience during the last twenty years. But it has been necessary from time to time also to utilize foreign experience either because, as in the case of a National Health Service, no corresponding institution exists in this country or because it was important to show how identical legal provisions can have different consequences in different environments. However, the factual focus is primarily on the United States, and this is not a comparative study as such.

In the preparation of this book, I have incurred a number of obligations which I am happy to acknowledge. My first impetus came from my friend Professor Harry Jones of the Columbia Law School, who invited me to prepare for the Third American Assembly, Columbia University, a research paper on the basic issues underlying contemporary proposals for amendment of the American social security system. In fulfilling this task I developed the general frame of analysis used in this book. I wish to thank the American Assembly for permitting me to incorporate some parts of the original document, which appears in the volume entitled *Economic Security for Americans*. I am deeply grateful to Dr. Henry A. Moe and the John Simon Guggenheim Memorial Foundation, for the award of a Guggenheim Fellowship in 1954 which freed me from my usual academic responsibilities and made possible a continuous period of writing. I can only hope that this book, which could not otherwise have been written, will cause them to feel that their confidence in me was justified. I was able to complete the work in Manchester, England, as the holder of the Simon Visiting Professorship in Research, a post which carries no teaching responsibilities, and I wish to record here my appreciation of the generous policy adopted by the University of Manchester.

My thanks are also due to the International Labour Office, Geneva, for the library and other facilities granted me in the winter of 1954; to Mrs. Margaret Otto and her colleagues for unfailing help in the use of the library of the New York School of Social Work, Columbia University; and to Miss Hazel Fraser, my secretary, and Mrs. Marjorie R. Dunn, of Geneva, who struggled with my handwriting.

Professor Richard Titmuss of the London School of Economics helped me more than he probably realized by his interest in my general method of approach and by his penetrating comments on certain chapters. Mrs. Barbara Rodgers, of the Department of Social Administration, University of Manchester, read all of the manuscript, and Mr. Robert J. Myers, Chief Actuary of the Social Security Administration, read parts; this saved me from several factual errors. To that most excellent editor, my friend and colleague Professor Seymour Harris of Harvard, I am indebted for a most careful reading of the manuscript and for many helpful suggestions. Needless to say, I alone am responsible for such errors and shortcomings as remain.

The dedication of this book to my husband, Professor Arthur R. Burns of Columbia University, falls far short of indicating the full extent of my appreciation of his never-failing encouragement and support, in this as in all my previous work.

EVELINE M. BURNS

Contents

Editor's Introduction   **vii**

Preface   ix

Introduction   1

PART ONE. DECISIONS AS TO THE NATURE AND AMOUNT OF SECURITY BENEFITS AND THE CONDITIONS GOVERNING THEIR RECEIPT

Chapter 1. Benefits Related to Need   19

Payments Based on Demonstrated Need   19
Benefits Based on Assumed Average Need   22

Chapter 2. Benefits Related to Contributions   27

Modifications of the Insurance Principle   29
Is Social Insurance "Insurance"?   33

Chapter 3. Benefits Related to Previous Earnings.   38

Modifications of the Principle in the Interest of Security   41
The Method of Determining Previous Earnings   42
The Effect of Price Changes on Benefits   48

Chapter 4. Income Guarantees and Willingness to Work   56

Controls Embodied in the Benefit Provisions   58
Controls through the Conditions Attached to Receipt of Benefit   64
 Deterrent Conditions Attached to Security Payments   64
  Use of the Test of Need   65
  Restriction of the Program to High-income Receivers   67
  Tests of Past Attachment to the Labor Force   67
  Limitation of Benefit Duration   69
  Administrative Controls on Malingering   70
   The Nature of the Controls   70
   The Consequences of the Controls   72
    The Effect upon Malingering and Abuse   73
    The Effect upon Worker Mobility   74
    The Effect upon Income-maintenance Objectives   76

The Effect upon Personal Freedoms 77
The Effect upon Costs 77
The Lack of Precise Information 79

Chapter 5. The Bearing of Social Security Programs on the Family System 80

The Principle of Relatives' Responsibility in Public Assistance 80
The Problem of ADC and the Broken Family 86
Children's Allowances 89

PART TWO. DECISIONS AS TO THE RISKS FOR WHICH
SOCIAL RESPONSIBILITY WILL BE ACCEPTED

Chapter 6. Threats to Continuity of Income: Chronological Age or Retirement 97

Effects upon National Output 98
The Economic Needs and Circumstances of the Aged 101
Cost Considerations 102
The Economic and Social Environment 103
Attitudes to the Claims of the Aged 105
Technical and Administrative Problems 106

Chapter 7. Threats to Continuity of Income: Prolonged Unemployment and Disability 112

Income Loss Due to Long-period Unemployment 112
Income Loss Due to Disability 117

Chapter 8. Threats to Adequacy of Incomes: The Costs of Medical Care 127

Alternative Methods of Financing and Organizing Medical Care 128
Problems Peculiar to Public Medical Services 134
Problems Common to Compulsory Health Insurance and National Medical Services 139
Methods of Remunerating Professional Personnel 139
Maintenance of High Standards of Service 142
Avoiding Overuse of the Service 144
The Determinants of Action 145

PART THREE. DECISIONS ABOUT THE FINANCING OF SOCIAL SECURITY PROGRAMS

Chapter 9. The Types of Taxes to Be Levied 155

Taxes on Workers 156
Payroll Taxes on Employers 160

General Considerations   160
The Special Case of Experience-rating   165
Nonearmarked Taxes   171
Private Underwriting of Social Security Costs   177
A Note on American Experience-rating Systems   184

Chapter 10.   The Distribution of Costs over Time   189

Reserves in Old-age Insurance   190
The Predictability of Long-range Costs and Income   191
The Purposes of Reserve Financing   197
Unemployment Insurance   203

Chapter 11.   The Distribution of Financial Responsibility among Different
              Levels of Government   212

The Technical Nature of the Program   213
The Nature of the Fiscal Resources of Different Levels of Government   215
The Intensity of the Desire to Assure Equality of Access to Minimum Se-
curity   218
The Importance Attached to Free Mobility   219
  Worker Mobility   219
  Business Location and Tax Competition   220
The Importance Attached to Specific Fiscal Policies   221
General Attitudes toward Central and Local Governments   222

Chapter 12.   Methods of Implementing Intergovernmental Cost Sharing   224

Division of the Field on a Program Basis   225
Grants-in-aid   227
  Precise Definition of the Purpose of the Grant   228
  The Terms of the Financial Arrangements   239
    Open- versus Closed-end Grants   239
    The Matching Principle   240
    Equal-matching versus Variable Grants   243

PART FOUR.   DECISIONS REGARDING THE STRUCTURE AND CHARACTER OF
             ADMINISTRATION

Chapter 13.   Administrative Issues   251

Organizational Structure   252
Intergovernmental Cooperation   255
The Adequacy and Quality of Administrative Personnel   259
Bureaucracy and Democratic Administration   262

PART FIVE. CONCLUSION

Chapter 14.   The Choice of Social Security Policies   269

  The Underlying Determinants   269
  The Implications for Policy   276
  The Role of the Social Scientist   279

Name Index   281

Subject Index   283

Introduction

THE NATURE and extent of threats to the economic security of individuals and families depend in large measure upon the methods by which their incomes are normally obtained. The economic security of entrepreneurs and profit makers, for example, not only is dependent upon their own skill and efficiency in competing with others in their own line of business but is also affected by changes in public taste which influence the demand for their products and, perhaps even more importantly, by the general level of economic activity in the community as a whole, which determines income levels and total demand. In addition, the economic security of those entrepreneurs who are engaged in agricultural production is affected by such forces as weather, pests, and other factors lying outside the control of the individual producer.

Threats to the economic security of wage and salary earners, whose incomes are obtained from employment by others, are many. The wages or salary received may, for a variety of reasons, be excessively low in relation to the worker's needs, especially if he has substantial family responsibilities. In addition, salaried workers and others whose terms of employment are fixed for relatively long periods of time are vulnerable to erosion of their standard of living in periods of inflation. But above all, the economic security of both wage and salaried workers depends upon their ability to find and hold a job, and the threats to continuous employment are many. In addition to such personal misfortunes as sickness and accidents or debility and loss of working capacity due to old age, the worker, as employee, is affected by all those threats to security to which employers are liable, for if his employer is incompetent or inefficient, if there is a change in demand for his product or a decline in the general level of economic activity, the worker is likely to find himself unemployed. In addition, the job security of given individuals is affected by prevailing employment discriminations, which may bear little or no relationship to the worker's skill or economic effectiveness, such as compulsory retirement policies at some specified age or prejudices against the employment of individuals on the basis of sex, race, or creed.

The greatest threat to the security of those who are living on pensions of fixed money amounts payable in respect of past employment, or in the form of an annuity purchased from a commercial insurance company, or who derive income from capital invested in fixed-income securities is, of course, the occurrence of inflation. But even when the value of money is stable, some persons receive pensions and income from savings that are meager in the extreme and insufficient to provide alone for the maintenance of the recipients.

Because of the economic functions which are carried by the family, the economic security of by far the largest single group of the population, namely children below working age and the mothers and wives who care for them and/or their husbands, is affected not only by whatever threatens the income security of the family breadwinner but also by another risk, namely that the breadwinner may die or desert the family. In addition, the economic security of the members of all families except the very richest is influenced by the size of the family itself: an income that may be adequate for two or even three persons may fail to yield subsistence if it must be stretched to help support eight or ten.

Finally, the security of all income receivers is subject to the threat of heavy and unavoidable charges upon income. For most families, the most important of these charges are the costs of medical care, including hospitalization.

By the middle of the twentieth century, governments had begun to concern themselves in greater or lesser degree with some or all of these threats to economic security. Many different types of public action can be distinguished. In the first place governments have adopted a series of measures whose object is to reduce the general extent of economic insecurity. Preventive health measures are probably the earliest example of this type of public action. Originally developed on a relatively restrictive basis, concerned primarily with protecting the community as a whole against infectious or contagious diseases, public health activities today tend to emphasize positive health and rehabilitation. As such, they operate to reduce the extent of income loss due to ill health and also to increase incomes from employment by fostering the development of a more alert and vigorous population.

A more recent form of government action looking toward a reduction of economic insecurity for all members of the community is the series of positive measures, and express or implied commitments, of modern governments to promote or maintain full employment. In many countries governments have sought, or have been given, legislative authority to take various steps deemed necessary to maintain a high level of economic activity and employment in general. Although there is great difference between governments in the measures they propose to adopt and in the extent to which they are in fact equipped to take action when needed, the fact that certain types of public action can directly affect the volume

of employment is nowhere seriously questioned, and most highly industrialized nations now appear to hold their governments responsible
for taking such steps as are appropriate and necessary to avoid general
economic breakdowns.[1]

The incidence of economic insecurity in general is also affected by
governmental policies regarding inflation and deflation, and efforts to
assure stability in the value of money are today included among the objectives to which all governments give at least lip service.

Other steps taken by governments, while less far-reaching than the
above, also tend to reduce the extent of economic insecurity. Among
these are the creation of public employment offices and measures aiming
to increase the geographical and occupational mobility of labor, such
as subsidies toward the costs of travel, vocational retraining, and the
like.

A second group of public measures directed toward the enhancement
of the economic security of the citizens takes the form of efforts to ensure
that persons who are in fact employed or gainfully occupied shall receive
what is currently regarded by the community as an adequate or appropriate income in return for their activities. In this category fall minimum-
wage laws and public action in support of labor organization and collective bargaining. Similarly, tariffs on imports operate to protect the
standard of living of the groups (both entrepreneurs and workers)
engaged in the production of the articles thus protected. Many governments have adopted measures to guarantee minimum incomes to some
or all agricultural producers, which may take the form of outright subsidies or of price-support programs. Governments have also developed
crop insurance schemes to protect agricultural producers from the loss

[1] It is significant that a Republican president who has consistently stressed the values
of private initiative and individualism nonetheless stated in transmitting his Economic
Report in 1954, "Government must use its vast power to help maintain employment
and purchasing power as well as to maintain reasonably stable prices. Government
must be alert and sensitive to economic developments, including its own myriad activities. It must be prepared to take preventive as well as remedial action; and
it must be ready to cope with new situations that may arise. This is not a start-and-
stop responsibility but a continuous one.

"The arsenal of weapons at the disposal of Government for maintaining economic
stability is formidable. It includes credit controls administered by the Federal Reserve
System; the debt management policies of the Treasury; authority of the President to
vary the terms of mortgages carrying Federal insurance; flexibility in administration
of the budget; agricultural supports; modification of the tax structure; and public
works." (Letter of Transmittal, *Economic Report of the President*, January 1954.) For
a discussion of the nature of the full-employment obligation and of policies relevant
thereto, see *National and International Measures for Full Employment*, Report by
a Group of Experts Appointed by the Secretary General, United Nations, New York,
December, 1949, *passim*.

or lowering of income due to floods, droughts, crop diseases, and other threats to the harvest, so curiously classified as "acts of God."[2]

In the third place, governments have reacted to the problem of individual and family economic insecurity by actions directed toward encouraging individuals to make provision, through private savings or insurance, against possible interruptions to the flow of income. These efforts have taken such varied forms as compulsory public insurance of bank deposits, stimulation of institutions, such as savings banks and credit unions, which serve more particularly the low-income receivers, and encouragements in the form of tax concessions for individual or group savings.

A fourth category of measures which has become increasingly characteristic of governments all over the world in the last half century now commonly goes by the name of social security. Here, the object of public action is to provide alternative income to persons whose normal private incomes have temporarily or permanently disappeared or to remove from individuals and families the burden of some very generally experienced charges on income. The first of these types of public action are now usually termed income security or income-maintenance measures. They embrace such familiar programs as public assistance or relief, compulsory social insurance, statutory payments and awards to certain categories of persons (such as veterans), income-conditioned pensions, and work relief programs. In all of them the essential circumstance which brings about public action is that the individual has suffered or is likely to suffer some demonstrated or presumed loss of income. The second type of social security measure, whose significance for raising standards of living is equally important, takes the form of arrangements to socialize the costs of some items which enter into normal consumption patterns but whose incidence is experienced differently by different families. Thus many governments have aimed to protect individuals, even while they enjoy normal incomes, from a reduction in their standard of living due to the costs of medical care by instituting health insurance systems or by providing medical care as a public service similar to public education. Similarly, most highly developed countries, except the United States, make payments to all families with children regardless of income levels in recognition of the fact that the standard of living of the family declines as the number of its members increases. Again, many countries provide for payment of all or part of the costs of funeral expenses through some type of compulsory social insurance. Public education and subsidized housing and even rent control are other examples of this type of governmental action.

[2] For a discussion of these and other measures, see Theodore W. Schultz, *The Economic Organization of Agriculture*, McGraw-Hill Book Company, Inc., New York, 1953, part III.

Institutions for these purposes now figure prominently in the social structures of most highly developed countries and significantly affect standards of living. By the mid-century, in five English-speaking countries expenditures for income maintenance and social security services accounted for between 5.52 and 13.18 per cent of net national income,[3] and the beneficiaries embraced either all, or a substantial part of, the populations.

These public social security measures have typically taken two forms: cash payments and benefits in kind. In most countries, the former are today by far the more important.

The traditional social security system, the poor law, as a rule provided assistance in kind, by giving needy persons supplies of the commodities needed to support life (or more recently, by issuing them grocery orders) or by supporting them in an institution. During the last fifty years, outdoor relief (or assistance given in the home) has come to supersede institutional relief, at least for able-bodied persons, while assistance in cash has rather generally taken the place of payments in kind. Nevertheless, even today, in some parts of the United States applicants for general assistance (or general relief, as it is sometimes called) are given grocery orders or supplies of commodities or are supported in the poorhouse.

The policy of giving economic assistance in kind was adopted in part precisely because it was believed to be unpopular with the beneficiaries and would thus serve to deter recourse to publicly assured income. But it was also thought to be a method of meeting the basic needs of the economically insecure with minimum cost to the taxpayer, especially at a time when there was a general presumption that those who sought public aid were almost by definition persons incapable of efficiently managing their own economic affairs. Over the years, however, there has been a growing recognition of the undesirable effects on human personality of this removal from the individual of all freedom in the running of his economic life and of the fact that this system is often administratively costly, especially for large numbers. These considerations, coupled with widespread resentment on the part of the recipients, especially during the depression years when millions of normally independent

[3] The actual percentages were: Australia, 7.30; Canada, 7.99; United Kingdom, 11.87; New Zealand, 13.18; and United States, 5.52. In all countries except the United Kingdom, by far the larger proportion of these expenditures were for income maintenance. In the United Kingdom the expenditures for services (notably health) were almost as large as the income-maintenance figures. (*Social Security Expenditures in Australia, etc., 1949–50: A Comparative Study*, Department of National Health and Welfare, Research Division, Ottawa, February, 1954, p. 18.) Since these estimates are subject to many qualifications and difficulties of interpretation, they should be used in conjunction with the warnings given by the authors.

workers were forced to seek public aid, led to the virtual abandonment of this form of assistance and the search for new approaches that would facilitate the assurance of income security to the unemployed through cash payments.

These efforts have had two consequences: the invention of new social security systems that either replaced the poor law or functioned simultaneously with, but independently of, it, and modifications in the character of the poor law itself. Thus in most highly developed economies today, the typical governmental instrument for ensuring the economic security of individuals or families is some form of social insurance or a statutory cash payment or an income-conditioned pension.[4] And while the poor-law system is found in some degree in most of these countries (frequently under the more modern title of public assistance), its character has been greatly changed. Thus in the United States, by the middle of the twentieth century, the majority of the population was covered by some type of social insurance system against the risk of income loss due to old age, death of a breadwinner, and short-period unemployment, and in a lesser degree against loss of income due to occupationally connected accidents or illnesses or death. Fewer were similarly protected against income threats due to disability not incurred in the course of employment. Nevertheless, all those not protected by such social insurance systems and those for whose needs the social insurance benefits proved inadequate could fall back upon the residual public assistance system, which, however, typically provided payments in cash and in the home. In many other countries, the scope of the non-public-assistance economic security systems is even greater, and the relative importance of public assistance is correspondingly less.

But while the cash payment in the home has thus become the typical form assumed by governmental programs, the issue of cash versus payment in kind is still an important one in certain areas. In the first place it has come to be recognized that the interests of certain categories of beneficiaries may be best served by some type of institutional care. In the United States, for example, in 1935 the public assistance titles of the Social Security Act embodied a number of provisions which aimed to eliminate payments in kind and assistance in the poorhouse. Thus it was provided that the Federal grants-in-aid to the states would be payable only in respect of assistance in cash given in the home. But as such payments thereafter became the normal type of public assistance in the states, it was increasingly recognized that for some recipients, and notably the infirm aged, institutional care might actually be a preferred and more

---

[4] The nature of these various institutions will be discussed in detail in the following chapters.

suitable form of aid.[5] And in fact, the Social Security Act was amended in 1950 to permit Federal reimbursement of grants made to needy persons in certain medical institutions although the ban on Federal aid for grants to persons in other types of institutions remained. The social security systems of other countries, too, contain provisions which reflect a desire to ensure that the use of the cash payment shall be the typical form of public assistance but that recourse to institutional care shall not be eliminated if it is at the request of the individual concerned or in his interests.[6]

In the second place, the issue of cash versus kind has also arisen in countries whose concept of income security has extended beyond the mere assurance of continuity of income, to include a concern about the adequacy of any given average level of incomes to meet the needs of families with children (see Chapter 5). In such countries, two schools of thought are to be found. One has held that the appropriate remedy is to adopt a system of children's allowances, whereby cash payments are made to families in some proportion to the numbers of children in each. Such systems are now very widespread; indeed, the United States is the only country of major importance not including a children's allowance system among its social security programs. The other approach holds that if it is a matter of public policy to prevent children from being economically penalized because they are members of large families dependent upon a single income, then the proper approach is to provide services and benefits in kind, of a nature which is peculiarly appropriate to the needs of the children. Many countries, whether or not they have enacted children's allowance systems, make this kind of provision for children. Free milk in schools, free or subsidized school meals, distribution of free or subsidized special foods or medicaments for children and nursing mothers, payment of vacation expenses of mothers and young children, and subsidized public housing for large families are examples.[7]

The issues at stake in the choice between these two approaches will be

[5] By 1947 both the Social Security Board and the American Public Welfare Association were urging elimination of the so-called "institutional prohibition." (*Annual Report, 1946*, Social Security Board, pp. 506–507; and *Public Welfare*, April, 1947, p. 78.) For a further discussion of the issues involved, see Louis Evans, "Providing Institutional Care for Recipients of Public Assistance," *Public Welfare*, November, 1945, pp. 248–253; and "Should the Social Security Act Be Amended to Allow Payment of Public Assistance to Inmates of Public Institutions? A Symposium," *Public Welfare*, February, 1946, pp. 26–31.

[6] Thus in Great Britain, local authorities providing institutional care for old-age pensioners are reimbursed by the aged person, but the charge made must not equal the full amount of the pension, thereby leaving the pensioner with some "spending money" and emphasizing the voluntary character of entry into the institution.

[7] For further examples of the measures taken in different countries, see *Economic*

discussed in Chapter 5. In fact, however, by the mid-century, while most highly developed countries were providing some kinds of direct serv- ices or payments in kind in respect of children, systems of cash payments through children's allowance systems were growing by leaps and bounds and accounted for more substantial expenditures.

In the third place, the question of cash versus kind is also a lively issue in those countries which have adopted public programs to remove the threat to family living standards of the costs of medical care. Here, countries face a choice between some form of cash indemnity system and the direct provision of needed medical care by government as a public service.[8] The cash payment under indemnity systems may indeed differ somewhat from that made to individuals under most income security systems, for it may be made to the supplier of the medical service, on be- half of the patient, instead of to the patient himself. Many compulsory health insurance systems, for example, permit the patient to consult the doctor of his choice but reimburse the doctor from social insurance funds. No money thus passes through the patient's hands. Other com- pulsory health insurance systems, however, indemnify the patient by paying some defined portion of his medical bills or by paying him a flat sum for specific types of medical care received. Both of these indemnity systems, however, differ in some major aspects from the alternative ap- proach, which has come to be known as the public health or medical service, whereby the government accepts responsibility for operating a system of medical care to which all, or defined groups of the population, have access, either free or at nominal cost. Most countries which make some public provision against the costs of medical care have adopted some form of indemnity system. However, the public medical service is found in many countries, either, as in Great Britain, for the entire popu- lation, or, as in the United States, for certain categories of people, such as veterans.

The appropriateness of the generally prevalent cash payment has also been questioned in yet a fourth area, namely as a method of meeting the income needs of the long-period unemployed. Here, it has been held that the interests of both the individuals concerned and the community as a whole would be better served by the provision of work opportunity, rather than by the continued payment of cash allowances, for which the recipient makes no return in the form of work. There is a considerable body of evidence to support the view that idleness as such, if long con- tinued, is a demoralizing experience for most unemployed persons, espe-

Measures in Favor of the Family, United Nations, Department of Social Affairs, New York, 1952.

[8] For a discussion of the issues involved, see Chap. 8.

cially when they live in a culture which attaches a high value to economic independence and when the inability to obtain employment effectively isolates the individual from the patterns of life and relationships that are common to other members of the community. In this sense it is true that unemployment creates needs that are not met merely by the assurance of an adequate alternative flow of income. It is important that workers' skills should not deteriorate through nonemployment and that those whose skills have become obsolete should be retrained for other employment. Furthermore, it is obviously to the interest of the community as a whole if the payments made to those who are technically unemployed can call forth some addition to output. Nevertheless, most countries, apart from the United States, have made relatively little use of the public provision of work as a technique for assuring economic security.[9] Even in the United States, where this method was extensively employed between 1935 and 1940, the work opportunities given were not in all respects similar to those available in the private economy,[10] while since 1942 public work programs for the unemployed have given way to a system of cash unemployment insurance payments.[11]

Thus by the middle of the twentieth century, the extensive social security systems that had come to be characteristic of most industrialized countries were primarily concerned with the making of cash payments to individuals and families, and it is with these that we shall be mainly concerned in the following pages. Since, however, programs designed to deal with the costs of medical care now also figure prominently among the social institutions of many countries and are under active consideration in the United States, and since the financial, and many of the administrative, problems to which they give rise are similar to those raised by the cash income security programs, attention will be paid to health insurance and public medical services at appropriate points.

The social and economic issues raised by the adoption of these complex public measures are usually formulated, in contemporary America as well as elsewhere, in terms of the individual programs with which the nation had equipped itself by the mid-century [12] and take the form of questions as to what precisely should be done about the modification, expan-

[9] For some of the reasons, see Chap. 7. During the 1930s Australia, New Zealand, and Sweden also experimented with major work programs.

[10] For an account of experience with work programs in the United States, see *Security, Work and Relief Policies*, National Resources Planning Board, Government Printing Office, Washington, D.C., 1942, chaps. 9, 12 and pp. 462–469, 504–513. See also: Donald S. Howard, *The WPA and Federal Relief Policy*, New York, Russell Sage Foundation, 1943.

[11] Occasionally a few communities have developed sporadic work relief programs for able-bodied general relief recipients.

[12] For an account of the main features of the American Social Security System, see

sion, contraction, or reorganization of specific programs or provisions of individual laws.

Thus, for example, such issues as the following have come to the fore. Should the coverage of Old Age and Survivors Insurance (OASI) be extended to include the remaining groups of uncovered workers? Should benefits be made available to persons who have never worked in covered employment by "blanketing-in" all those already over age 65? Should retirement from gainful employment be made a condition of benefit receipt? Should insurance benefits be increased or lowered? Should benefits continue to bear some relationship to the individual's previous earnings, or should there be some uniform minimum income payable to all eligible aged persons? Should there continue to be two systems of old-age security? If not, should a more universal and comprehensive system pay benefits on the basis of demonstrated need, or on passage of some income test, or on some other basis? Should the entire cost of OASI continue to be assessed against employers and workers, or should there be some contribution from the general revenues? If so, at what time and in what degree? Should the costs of old-age insurance be met as they arise each year, or should some longer-range plan be retained involving the building up of reserves against future high annual disbursements? Should the Federal government continue to share in the costs of old-age assistance (the needs-test program for the aged), or should this be a responsibility of the states and localities? If there is to be Federal sharing, what kind of a grant-in-aid system should be used?

Similar questions are posed in regard to the measures which have been adopted to provide against insecurity due to unemployment.

Among the current issues are the following: Should the coverage of unemployment insurance [13] be broadened? Should unemployment benefits be higher or lower than they now are? Should benefits be paid to the dependents of unemployed workers? Should the eligibility conditions be tightened (by requiring longer employment or higher earnings in some previous period), or should they be liberalized? Under what circumstances and for what kinds of conduct should workers be disqualified from receiving benefits? Should benefits be paid for more than the usual twenty- to twenty-six-week maximum duration? Should the program continue to be financed almost exclusively by employers? Should the taxes of employers be reduced if their own employees suffer little unemployment? If so, what

---

Eveline M. Burns, *The American Social Security System*, Houghton Mifflin Company, Boston, 1951.

[13] In the United States the terms "unemployment insurance" and "unemployment compensation" are used almost interchangeably. The former is used throughout this book because it is the older and more generally understood elsewhere. It is also the form used by the Federal government.

is the best formula to use for granting tax reduction? Should the financing of unemployment insurance continue to be essentially a state responsibility (with the Federal government meeting only the costs of administration)? What should be the Federal role if some states are unable to finance benefits at the average level without having to raise taxes far in excess of those levied in the majority of states? If the Federal government comes to the aid of the states, should this take the form of loans or nonrepayable grants? Should the Federal government get out of unemployment insurance altogether? Should any plans be made to provide for the income needs of persons who exhaust unemployment insurance benefits (a problem that would be acute in any depression)?

When we turn to insecurity due to ill health, the questions are posed in slightly different terms because, apart from railroad workers and veterans and persons suffering from occupationally connected accidents or illnesses, there are few programs assuring income in this contingency. But here, too, the issues are posed in specific terms.

Should there be a social insurance program providing benefits for persons unable to work because of disability, however caused? Should there be different insurance systems for those permanently, and for those temporarily, disabled? Should whatever laws are enacted be administered by the Federal government or the states? What tests of eligibility should be adopted? Should the benefit formulas be similar to those of OASI or to those of unemployment insurance laws? How should they be financed? Should employers and workers both contribute or employers alone? Should the financing follow the principles of workmen's compensation, where the liability to pay benefits is regarded as a risk falling on the employer against which he is required to insure (with a private insurance company or with a state fund) or to give guarantees of ability to self-insure, or should it follow the principles of more modern social insurance programs, where the state levies taxes on specific persons (usually employers and workers) and directly administers the program of benefits to workers? Would there be a need for a separate workmen's compensation program if a general disability insurance system were enacted?

Because ill health not only means loss of ability to earn but also usually involves the individual in medical expenses (which for certain families may be disproportionately heavy in relation to income and savings), proposals have been made for socializing these costs also by some method of social insurance (such as existed in England until 1948 and is still in force in most European countries) or of public service (such as is provided for veterans in the United States or for all the population in Britain since 1948 through the National Health Service).

Specific bills proposing one or other of these methods of relieving the individual of the possibly heavy costs of medical care have for many years been before the American Congress. In regard to these, too, specific questions must be answered. If any such attempt is made to extend the range of governmental provision against insecurity, should the program cover all types of illness and medical expense or only "catastrophic" illnesses? Should it be limited to meeting hospital costs? Should the government administer the program itself, or should there be a system of governmental subsidies to private insurance plans? Which government should act in this field? If both the Federal government and the states should be involved, what should be the respective roles of each? Since, unlike the income security programs, such a venture would involve the rendering of services (or the reimbursement of expenditures for services rendered), government would be involved in the problem of quality of service. Can a program be devised which does not lower the quality of service rendered? How should professional personnel be remunerated in a public program? Should the role of government be limited to subsidizing the supply of essential facilities and trained personnel?

Similarly, many policy issues confront America in the field of public assistance. Should relief be payable to people if they have relatives capable of supporting them? If so, which relatives are to be held liable and to what extent? Should the names of relief recipients be made public? Should public assistance payments be made to families where the father has deserted or where the mother has had illegitimate children? Should public assistance be used to supplement incomes of persons in full-time but low-paid employment? Should people on relief be forced to dispose of all their assets before receiving public aid? What should be the standard of public assistance payments? Should they make it possible for relief recipients to enjoy any minor or major luxuries? Should there be five different public assistance programs—Old Age Assistance (OAA), Aid to Dependent Children (ADC), Aid to the Blind (AB), Aid to the Permanently and Totally Disabled (APTD), and General Assistance—or should there be a single category of aid to needy people? What should be the role of different levels of government in the program? Should the Federal government bear any part of the costs? If so, in what proportion and under what formula? What degree of Federal control should accompany Federal financial aid? What should be the financial and administrative relationships between the states and the localities?

The issues at stake are presented to the country in this specific form, program by program, because America, like most other countries, has approached the general problem of income insecurity risk by risk. Various causes of interruption of private income (old age, death of a breadwinner, unemployment, ill health) have been identified, and specific measures to deal with specific risks have been devised. And because the newer social security systems do not give protection against all types of income interruption, while the coverage of none is universal, the country has found it necessary to retain, as a kind of catchall, the traditional instrument of almost all organized communities for dealing with destitution, namely public relief, or public assistance, as it is now usually called.

But while the problems thus present themselves today in the form of concrete proposals for the modification of specific features of one program or another, it is inconvenient and, indeed, highly undesirable to consider each in isolation.

First, many of the issues posed are common to several programs. Thus, many of the questions affecting coverage of social insurance laws are common to all social insurance systems, whatever the risks insured against, and a piecemeal discussion of them, risk by risk, would involve tedious repetition.

Second, whatever may be the situation in terms of rational analysis of causal factors or of administrative convenience, life is in fact not compartmentalized, and what is done in one law or program has repercussions on another. In the last resort these measures are devised in the interests of people and of people who live in families. Logical analysis may suggest the desirability of developing different programs on a risk-by-risk basis, but to the family with an aged father, a sick breadwinner, and an unemployed son, it does not make much sense to have to deal with three sets of administrators all making available benefits of differing amounts on different bases and requiring the fulfillment of vastly different conditions.

The individual who is covered by OASI, unemployment insurance, and disability insurance finds it hard to see why dependents' benefits are payable under OASI and unemployment insurance (if he lives in certain states) but not under disability insurance. The unequal treatment of individuals in similar circumstances by the various public assistance programs gives rise to discontent and pressure for change.[14] In 1950 the fact that old-age assistance payments averaged $43.23 a month whereas OASI benefits, toward the cost of which the beneficiary had contributed, averaged only $22.60 was a powerful argument for liberalization of OASI.[15] Similarly the liberalization of OASI survivor benefits in 1950 led to successful pressure to liberalize the Railroad Retirement program. Thus, the nature of one program will greatly influence policy in another.

Third, the piecemeal approach to social security policies, program by program, leads to the neglect of some serious problems posed by the totality of social policy in this field. Public assistance provides a good

14 In mid-1954 the average monthly payments per recipient were: OAA, $51.39; ADC, $23.81; AB, $55.85; APTD, $53.36. For general assistance, the monthly payment per case averaged $51.13. The differences are especially marked in some states.
15 Figures relate to June, 1950. For beneficiaries newly awarded benefits in that month, the average benefit was slightly higher: $26.30.

illustration. Here the response of America to the fiscal inability of some of the states to provide adequate assistance to their needy residents was to create, under the Social Security Act in 1935, a system of Federal grants-in-aid. But instead of making a single grant for all public assistance purposes there weré several grants for different categories of needy persons: old-age assistance, aid to the blind, and aid to dependent children.

In 1950 a new category was added—aid to the needy permanently and totally disabled. Initially, the terms of the grant, the proportion of Federal aid, and the conditions to be satisfied by the states to secure it all differed for each program. Even by 1956 the grant for ADC differed from the others. Furthermore, over the years, a vast system of Federal grants-in-aid for a variety of purposes has developed (there are around twenty in the field of social welfare alone). What might have been a manageable and defensible system, had there been only one or two grants, becomes unwieldy when, for example, a state has to satisfy a wide variety of different conditions in administering programs with very similar objectives, and the occasions for friction between the two levels of government are multiplied. In other words, the sheer multiplicity of grants gives rise to problems that are not evident when grant policy for each individual purpose or program is considered in isolation.

Similarly, when the different social insurance systems are developed risk by risk, decisions as to the extent to which workers and employers should share in the cost of any given program may well make sense when each program is considered in isolation. But as the range of risks protected against is extended, the total burden falling on wages and payrolls when all social insurance contributions are added together may come to be unduly heavy. If so, other sources of revenue may have to be contemplated, or a decision may have to be made that wage and payroll taxes are more especially valuable for financing some social insurance programs than others.

This book, therefore, will not deal with contemporary issues program by program or risk by risk. Rather, an effort will be made to consider the general and specific problems posed by governmental action in this field and to discuss in this context some of the outstanding social security issues of the day.

In fact, every community that decides to use the instrument of government to assure some minimum of economic security has to answer four major questions, whatever the cause of loss of income and however large or small the group of people to be given this protection.

Decisions have to be made as to (1) the nature of the protection to be afforded and the conditions to be satisfied for its receipt; (2) the specific risks to interruption of income for which public responsibility will be accepted; (3) the financial arrangements to be made, including decisions as to how the burden shall be shared between different sections of the population, what is to be the period of accounting (i.e., whether to aim to cover each year only the actual expenditures incurred in that year or whether to adopt some longer period over which income shall balance outgo), and what shall be the relative financial responsibilities of different levels of government; (4) the allocation of administrative responsibility between private organizations and government and between different levels of government and the determination of convenient administrative structural organizations at any given governmental level.

PART ONE

Decisions as to the Nature and Amount of Security Benefits and the Conditions Governing Their Receipt

BOTH THE levels of cash payments and the conditions governing their receipt vary greatly from one social security system to another. Some make cash payments whose amount depends on the ascertained needs of each individual recipient, and restrict payments to people found to be "in need." But there are wide variations in standards of need, in the extent to which applicants are expected to exhaust their own resources, and in the definition of resources (some communities, for example, hold that income possessed by relatives is a resource for needy people; others do not). Some programs pay a uniform money sum to certain categories of people, who may be defined as those above or below specified ages or those who have paid a specified number of contributions to a social insurance scheme. Other systems pay benefits whose amount reflects the value of contributions paid by, or on behalf of, the beneficiary to a social insurance plan. Yet others, while restricting payments to "insured workers" as defined, provide benefits bearing some specified relationship to the beneficiary's previous earnings.

These different systems answer in different ways certain fundamental questions relating to the mutual rights and responsibilities of the individual and the community. If benefits are to be available as a right rather than as a discretionary allowance, what safeguards for the economic interests of the community should accompany their receipt? What should be the relation between the level of socially provided income (whether discretionary or paid as a right) and that normally secured from employment? How far should government relieve the family of its economic responsibilities? The following five chapters will explore some of the issues at stake.

CHAPTER 1

Benefits Related to Need

EVEN WHEN the policy of cash payments has been decided upon, further choices have to be made. On which of several available principles shall the cash payments be based? Payments can be based on (1) actual need as demonstrated in the individual case, (2) an assumption of average need, (3) the principles of private insurance, in which the payment is related to the contributions paid by the insured person, (4) the past earnings or standard of living of the beneficiary.

PAYMENTS BASED ON DEMONSTRATED NEED

The payment of benefits on the basis of demonstrated individual need is the principle on which public assistance operates and which governs the income of over five million Americans. Here, the applicant is typically visited by a social worker who determines his available income and resources and sets these against his income needs as revealed by her investigations. The difference, or budgetary deficiency, is in principle the amount of relief to be granted.

This basis for the determination of social security income has several advantages. It is said to permit the adjustment of publicly assured income to the precise needs of the individual applicant and to save money to the taxpayer by eliminating payments to persons who are not needy. It is true that all other methods treat individuals suffering loss of income as members of larger or smaller groups. Hence the benefit, as determined by the formula applicable to the group as a whole, may exceed or fall short of the minimum needs of individual families. It is not surprising, therefore, that even such countries as Great Britain and New Zealand, which in principle have aimed to cover the entire population by a social security system with benefits based on some principle other than demonstrated individual need, nonetheless find it necessary to retain this system to supplement the standard benefits payable on the major program when these fail to meet the basic needs of recipients whose special circumstances depart far from the average. This supplementary function of public assistance has come to be so clearly recognized that the adequacy of other types of benefit system is often judged by the proportion of beneficiaries who have to seek supplementation from public assistance.[1]

In practice, however, limits are set to this degree of individualization. First, in some American states and in some areas of others, a shortage of funds prevents the full payment of the budgetary deficit, as determined by this careful investigation.[2] Second, many states set dollar maxima to the public assistance payment to be made in respect of any individual or family, however great the need as revealed by investigation.[3] Third, to an increasing degree, the states, in the case of special public assistance, and/or the localities, in the case of general assistance or relief, tend to lay down standards as to the items which are to be included in the family's budget and as to the precise dollar sum to be allowed for each,[4] although above this standard additional sums can often be granted at the discretion of the administrator for exceptional circumstances. This standardization is likely to be accelerated if the unit of administration is large, in order to secure uniformity of treatment of all applicants within the geographical area covered. But where the process of itemizing the budget and attaching money values to each item is carried very far, the system begins to approximate a benefit system basing payments on

---

[1] Thus in the United States in 1949 to 1950 the OASI program was subject to criticism because, *inter alia*, of the extent to which beneficiaries received supplementary OAA. (Cf. Abraham M. Niessen, "OASI and Its Relation to the State Assistance Plans: Fifteen Years of Developments," *Social Service Review*, September, 1952, pp. 319–333.) Similarly in Great Britain the proponents of an increase in the contributory old-age pension in 1953 to 1954 pointed to the large and growing amount of supplementation of pensions by National Assistance.

[2] In 1952, Mississippi was paying only 65 per cent of the budgetary deficiency except in unusual circumstances, and by 1954 this figure had increased only to 75 per cent. As a rule, when such reductions of payments occur, they are most severe for general assistance and aid to dependent children cases. For policies of other states, see *Analysis of the Social Security System*, Hearings before a Subcommittee of the House Committee on Ways and Means, 83d Cong., 1st Sess., 1953, Appendix I, p. 1161 (hereinafter this report is referred to by title only). For the situation in earlier years, see Eveline M. Burns, *The American Social Security System*, Houghton Mifflin Company, Boston, 1951, pp. 312, 328, 350–351.

[3] By 1953, only sixteen states did not have such maxima. While the dollar limit tended to center around the amount of the Federal matching maximum, the limits ranged from $30 (Mississippi) to $80 and over in Maryland and Washington. Sometimes the maximum may be exceeded for medical and hospital care.

[4] This development has been fostered by the Social Security Administration, which has increasingly urged the states to make the inclusion of specified items in the budgets mandatory, and hence uniform within their political subdivisions, and to indicate additional special items to be provided for and in what circumstances. It has also urged the attaching of dollar values to the specified items. (See *State Responsibility for Definiteness in Assistance Standards*, Social Security Administration, Bureau of Public Assistance, December, 1946; Burns, *op. cit.*, pp. 326–327; and Floyd Bond and Associates, *Our Needy Aged: A California Study of a National Problem*, Henry Holt and Company, Inc., New York, 1954, pp. 158–159.)

an assumption of average need. The only leeway for individual adjustment is then provided by the discretionary allowances for individual circumstances, and there is some tendency to standardize even these.

It is difficult to determine whether or not a system basing benefits on demonstrated need results in a saving of money for those who foot the security bill. On the one hand, there are savings due to the fact that no payments are made to individuals who have adequate resources of their own.[5] But on the other hand, the commitment to meet need as demonstrated means that in many cases higher payments will be made to persons whose needs are great than would be made by any of the other three benefit systems identified above. Moreover, when carefully carried out, the process of determining needs and resources in each individual case is costly to administer and calls for highly skilled personnel. Besides, the investigation cannot be made once and for all since the circumstances of the applicants change. An important current issue is, indeed, how often such reinvestigations should take place. Thus the system may not be very practical when very large numbers of payments have to be made or in programs where the caseload fluctuates sharply from time to time.

As against the advantages claimed for a system making payments on the basis of demonstrated need in the individual case is the fact that inherent in it is the necessity for the applicant to submit to investigation and discuss his personal affairs with an official. Even though in the last twenty years strenuous efforts have been made to administer this process in a manner which damages the self-respect of the individual as little as possible,[6] all the evidence suggests that such a system is greatly disliked by those who are, or might be, subjected to it.[7] Moreover, the greater the efforts made to render the system palatable to applicants (by, for example, using the applicant as the sole or major source of information, or not making inquiries about him from other persons), the more the administrators are vulnerable to attack from those who judge each social security system by its cost to the taxpayer. In fact, most of the attacks on American

[5] See the section of Chap. 4 entitled Controls through the Conditions Attached to Receipt of Benefit for a qualification to this statement due to the tendency to liberalize the test of need.

[6] For an account of the standard procedures recommended by the Federal government, and adopted by most of the states, see *Handbook of Public Assistance Administration*, Social Security Administration, Bureau of Public Assistance, Washington, D.C., 1945–. The sections relating to determination of eligibility and need are reproduced in *Analysis of the Social Security System*, pp. 361–363. For the most comprehensive statement of the professional social worker's attitude to the administration of a needs-test system, see Charlotte Towle, *Common Human Needs*, 2d ed., American Association of Social Workers, New York, 1952, *passim*.

[7] For a fuller discussion of attitudes toward social security systems involving a test of need, see the section of Chap. 4 entitled Controls through the Conditions Attached to Receipt of Benefit.

public assistance administrations in recent years have been based on allegations that the investigating officers took too liberal a view of the applicant's needs or were lacking in zeal in ferreting out all his available resources.

Nor must it be forgotten that a decision to base benefits on demonstrated need in the individual case still leaves many difficult questions open for decision. What is the standard of living which is to be assured by the public payment? What items are to be included? Should the budget cover minor luxuries as well as food, clothing, and shelter? What about medical care? What and whose resources are to be taken into account? Is an applicant to be required to exhaust all his resources (e.g., sell his house or homestead, dispose of his life insurance, reduce his savings to zero, etc.) before any public assistance payment will be made? To what extent is income provided by relatives of the applicant to be regarded as part of the resources of the applicant himself in deciding the amount of his public assistance payment? And which relatives? [8] These are the real policy issues raised by the decision to base benefits on demonstrated need in the individual case, and they will be discussed more fully in Chapters 4 and 5.

Meanwhile, it should be noted that there appear to be no serious proposals to extend this system: indeed, most social security proposals today reflect efforts to substitute some other system of benefit payments for the public assistance principle. In modern social security systems, public assistance tends to be regarded either, as indicated above, as a relatively unimportant but necessary source of supplementation to some other benefit system or as a method of providing, during the period in which this other system is maturing, for persons who for technical reasons are ineligible for its benefits.

BENEFITS BASED ON ASSUMED AVERAGE NEED

The payment of benefits based on an assumption of average need takes one of two forms: the income-conditioned pension and the uniform money sum payable to all persons in defined categories. Both reflect the central idea that all persons in the defined groups are likely to have certain common minimum needs for income and that the function of government is to ensure that none falls below this minimum standard.

Under the income-conditioned pension system (sometimes referred to

---

[8] For an account of the specific provisions in the various state old-age assistance laws in regard to these issues in 1953, see Bond and Associates, *op. cit.*, chaps. V, VI. See also *Characteristics of State Public Assistance Plans*, Social Security Administration, Bureau of Public Assistance Report 21, 1953; and Burns, *op. cit.*, chap. 11.

in public assistance circles as the "flat-grant-minus" system) the law lays down a certain minimum money income, possession of less than which entitles an individual to claim benefits of a specified money amount. For each unit of income in excess of this minimum the benefit falls by some defined sum, until a maximum private income is reached above which no benefit is paid. Furthermore, the law defines with considerable specificity just what kinds of income are to be included in the applicant's qualifying income and the extent to which it may include income from specified relatives.

The income-conditioned pension is the basic system in Australia and New Zealand and is approached in the public assistance laws of a few American states. In New Zealand, in 1950, for example, the standard social security benefit was £130 a year, for which any resident was eligible if his income did not exceed £78. For every £1 of income in excess of this amount, his social security benefit was reduced by £1. Income was defined as that of himself or his spouse only, and certain forms and amounts of property were disregarded. While no American state has formally adopted this benefit system, the old-age assistance laws of a few states achieve the same result. In Massachusetts the budgetary standard, i.e., the assistance payment plus the applicant's resources, must provide not less than a given number of dollars a month ($79 for an applicant living alone in 1953). The system is an income-conditioned pension in all but name. A similar result is achieved in California, where the $80 maximum payment has in fact been administered as a standard payment which will be received unless the individual's resources exceed this sum, and the $80 payment is reduced by the amount of the applicant's income if more than $80.[9]

Several proposals have been made to use the income-conditioned pension as the major American technique for assuring income security. Thus in 1946, Dr. Lewis Meriam of the Brookings Institution proposed that the social insurance system should be replaced by one in which aid would be available to persons whose means (including those of relatives) were insufficient to support "a very strictly defined minimum standard of health and decency" as determined by research. The individual or family would be eligible for assistance when and if the resources, as determined by in-

[9] Actually, the $80 being regarded as the sum necessary for basic or primary needs, the applicant is allowed to use part of his private income for "special needs" as defined and in amounts as specified by regulations. Hence the standard payment may be received by persons with quite considerable private resources. (Bond and Associates, *op. cit.*, pp. 123–125, 157–158, 203–204.) Other states which approach the so-called "flat-grant-minus" system are Colorado, Washington, Louisiana, Nevada, and New Mexico, where the law requires that income and assistance together must equal a specified money sum.

come reports, fell below a sum, or a schedule of sums, set forth in the law.[10] And in 1951 Senator Hugh Butler suggested the adoption of a basic Federal pension of $50 a month payable to all persons with incomes of less than $600 per annum and falling by $1 a month for each $50 of income in excess of $600. Income was to be determined on the basis of income-tax returns.[11]

The second form of benefit based on assumed average need merely provides a uniform money sum for all persons in defined categories. It is found in the United States only in the pensions and awards paid to veterans, but proposals for adoption of a universal free pension for all persons above a certain age have been strongly supported, especially by organizations of the aged, in some of the states. The system was adopted in Canada, in 1951, where pensions of $40 a month are paid to all residents reaching the age of 70. It is the principle underlying the benefits of the social insurance systems (such as the British), which grant flat or uniform benefits to defined categories of insured persons.[12] Finally, the benefit based on assumed average need is the usual principle adopted in children's allowance systems, where uniform money sums are paid to the parents (usually the mother) in respect of each child or each child in excess of a given number. Sometimes the amount of the allowance varies according to the age of the child, but it is still the same sum for all children of any given age.[13]

Both forms of this principle have the advantage of relative simplicity of administration and keep government intervention in the private life of the individual to a minimum, especially in the case of the free pension. And even with the income-conditioned pension, it is possible to use income-tax returns for the determination of eligibility, thus substituting more objective criteria and a less personalized method for the public assistance procedures for testing need. Both, however, are less effective than public assistance in meeting need on an individualized basis and, unless the uniform benefit were relatively high, might give rise to considerable supplementation from public assistance. The free pension also inevitably means that payments are made to some people whose private resources are adequate without social security income.

[10] Lewis Meriam, *Relief and Social Security*, Brookings Institution, Washington, D.C., 1946, chaps. 18, 37.

[11] *Program for a True Pay-as-you-go Full-coverage Social Security System*, Remarks of Senator Butler of Nebraska, in the U.S. Senate, Extension of Remarks June 16, October 20, 1950, and January 17, 1951, Government Printing Office, Washington, D.C., 1951.

[12] In Great Britain the flat benefits vary only by sex, age, number of dependents, and, in the case of married women, whether or not the claimant was employed and insured in her own right.

[13] For a further discussion of children's allowances, see Chap. 5.

Whether or not either system could be an effective substitute for the social security programs now in effect in the United States would depend on whether the dislike of the test of need (which has stimulated recourse to the non-public-assistance types of social security) extends also to the more objective criterion of money income. Even more significantly, it would also depend on the feasibility, in a country as economically diversified as the United States, of defining both the maximum permissible income and the standard benefit in dollar terms which would suffice to meet minimum average needs in the high-income, high-standard-of-living states without being out of line with normal living standards in the poorer states (or parts of states).

Thus, this basis of benefit determination also raises, but does not automatically solve, the question of the minimum level of living to be guaranteed by public income security systems. Some of the considerations bearing on this central issue will be outlined in Chapter 4. Meanwhile it should be noted that when, as in systems of this kind, the minimum level is defined in the law in money terms, the real standard of living guaranteed by the program will change with changes in the general level of prices. Methods of dealing with this problem will be discussed below, since it is not peculiar to benefit systems based on assumed average need.

A more subtle problem concerns the possible inflexibility of such benefit systems in the face of changes in the general levels of national income. For obviously as real incomes in general rise and fall, the relationship between the income assured by the public income security system and that of the rest of the population will change. The evidence seems to suggest both that communities are sensitive to considerations of equity in this respect and that it is not beyond the bounds of human ingenuity to provide on an orderly and systematic basis for this contingency. Thus during the depression of the 1930s, Australia on several occasions reduced the money amount of the flat-rate old-age pensions in order to keep them in line with the general decline in all money incomes. And in Sweden, where national income rose sharply after the flat rates of the old-age benefit system were set in 1946, the law was amended in 1950 to provide a 40 per cent rise in the money pension to enable beneficiaries to share in the increased general productivity.[14] Awareness of this problem is also seen in the provision of the British National Insurance Act of 1946, whereby there are to be periodic, five-yearly reconsiderations of the flat benefit rates in the light of "the circumstances at the time of insured persons . . . including in

[14] Sweden has also an automatic cost-of-living adjustment in its old-age pension system. Between 1946 and 1952 this had increased the money pension by 35 per cent to correspond to a 35 per cent rise in the general price level. But money wages had increased by 90 per cent, and the 40 per cent standard-of-living increase in the pension aimed to bring pensions more closely in line with increased real wages.

particular the expenditure which is necessary for the preservation of health and working capacity and to any change in these circumstances since the rates and amounts of benefits were laid down . . . and to the likelihood of further changes." Since the criteria suggested run in general terms, their interpretation is likely to be much affected by the economic circumstances in which the remainder of the population find themselves when revisions are under consideration.

CHAPTER 2

Benefits Related to Contributions

THE PRINCIPLE of paying benefits that bear a direct or close relationship to the contributions paid by the beneficiary during some previous defined period is derived, of course, from private insurance. It was rather generally adopted in the early social insurance systems in America and elsewhere. The typical old-age security programs provided benefits related to the level of contributions paid by the beneficiary during his working life, and either increased these benefits in proportion to the time over which contributions had been paid, or provided that no benefits would be payable if the claimant had not been making contributions for some long period (often twenty years). Similarly, the unemployment insurance laws often not only related benefits to the claimant's past earnings (on which contributions would have been paid by him or his employer) but also adjusted the duration of benefit to each beneficiary's previous earnings or contributions.[1]

The early insurance-oriented, nondeterrent, non-means-test income security systems also tended to be self-financing in the sense that contributions were paid into special earmarked funds which were separate from the general budget of the government, and in workmen's compensation programs the insurance analogy has been so closely adhered to that in many states employers insure against their benefit liabilities with private insurance companies (see Chapter 9). The whole costs were paid by the beneficiaries and/or their employers. If there was any contribution from the general revenues, it was small or, as in the original British unemployment insurance law, a token amount, to emphasize the fact that while autonomously financed, the program was nonetheless a public one with implications for the general welfare. In continental countries, but not in England nor in the United States (except for the special income security measures for railroad workers), the autonomous character of these systems was further evident in the administrative arrangements. They were, and are, administered not by a regular department of the government but by special bodies whose governing boards usually contain representatives of

---

[1] For the classical statement of the application of the principles of insurance to the determination of the nature of an unemployment insurance program, see A. D. Watson, *The Principles Which Should Govern the Structure and Provisions of a Scheme of Unemployment Insurance,* The Unemployment Insurance Commission, Ottawa, 1948.

beneficiaries and employers.[2] In workmen's compensation even today much of the administration is carried out by commercial insurance companies.

The parallelism with private insurance was everywhere emphasized. Such measures were called social insurance systems. The workers covered were known as "insured workers." When they had acquired the necessary minimum period of coverage, they were spoken of as having "insured status," and, as in OASI, differing periods of coverage ("fully" or "currently" insured) gave the right to different types of benefit. The benefits in turn were called "insurance benefits."

This emphasis on the "insurance" character of the programs was deliberate and served several purposes. The most important was probably to reassure both the beneficiaries and the general public regarding the probable consequences of what was, at the time the social insurance laws were first introduced, a radical departure from the prevailing policies controlling governmental responsibility for income security, namely those embodied in the deterrent poor law.[3] In countries where, as in the United States, recourse to this, the only then available form of public aid, had been accompanied by great loss of social status, it was hoped by emphasizing the "insurance" aspect of social security payments to persuade insured workers that no loss of self-respect was involved in accepting a benefit under the new program. This concern probably accounted for the heavy emphasis on the "insurance character" of OASI when it was inaugurated, a policy which eighteen years later involved the Administrator in many sharp exchanges with members of a congressional committee.[4]

Under an insurance-oriented program it could be emphasized that the beneficiary and his employer had contributed toward the cost of the benefit, i.e., that it was in some measure an earned payment, to which the beneficiary was as morally entitled as he was to an annuity from a private insurance company. To the general public, too, the insurance aspect of the new social insurance measures rendered more palatable some departure from the prevailing public methods of dealing with income loss. By a system relating benefit rights to contributions, the general taxpayer was, it appeared, protected against the danger of ever mounting demands on the public purse from greedy beneficiaries. Fears of the demoralizing

---

[2] Even in the United States the original Social Security Act was administered by a special Board of three members, no more than two of whom could be of the same political party. In 1946, the Board was replaced by a single Social Security Commissioner, to whom the Federal Security Administrator delegated his powers in connection with the administration of the Social Security Act.

[3] Cf. Eveline M. Burns, "Social Insurance in Evolution," *American Economic Review Supplement*, March, 1944.

[4] *Analysis of the Social Security System*, part 6, "First Session on the Legal Status of OASI Benefits."

effects of public handouts were lessened by the parallelism to insurance: the beneficiary of a private insurance contract was not demoralized by receiving his annuity, why then should a worker insured under a public system be demoralized when the time came for him to draw the benefits toward whose cost he had contributed? These ideas were the more persuasive in that all the early social insurance laws provided for something less than universal coverage. The new policy therefore was to be tested in relation to a limited and selected group, in this sense the best risks, for the workers who would qualify as eligible were by definition those fairly regularly employed. The risk of destroying initiative by abandoning the previous policy of harsh treatment of the economically insecure was therefore likely to be minimized.

Modifications of the Insurance Principle

Nevertheless it has become apparent that strict adherence to the principles of private insurance inevitably limits the extent to which a social insurance system can provide the answer to the demand for income security.

In the first place, when eligibility is dependent upon coverage for a substantial period of time, the system cannot solve the problem of those already in need of income at the time the law is enacted, or for some years thereafter. This is a particularly acute problem in old-age security. If, in order to secure a benefit at age 65, a worker has to be insured, say, twenty years, then all those who were over 45 at the time the law was passed can never benefit from it. In Canada, this feature of an insurance-oriented program was one of the considerations which led to a preference for a flat universal pension.[5] Even under the more liberal eligibility provisions of the American OASI program, the failure of the system enacted in 1935 to afford benefits to a substantial proportion of those reaching age 65 in the subsequent fifteen years was a source of much criticism of the program and 'led to demands, notably in the early 1950s, for "blanketing-in" the already aged.[6] By 1953 there were still 2.6 million aged persons dependent

[5] Elizabeth Wallace, "Old Age Security in Canada: Changing Attitudes," *Canadian Journal of Economics and Political Science*, May, 1952, p. 133.

[6] Such a proposal was made by the U.S. Chamber of Commerce. See *Proposed Policy Declaration: Federal Social Security Program for the Aged*, U.S. Chamber of Commerce Referendum 93, Washington, D.C., 1952. For a discussion of the issues involved, see Miriam Civic, "Social Security Reappraised," *Business Record*, National Industrial Conference Board, June, 1953; and Eveline M. Burns, *Comments on the Chamber of Commerce Social Security Proposals*, American Public Welfare Association, Washington, D.C., 1953. See also *Pensions in the United States*, A Study Prepared for the Joint Committee on the Economic Report by the National Planning Association, 82d Cong., 2d Sess., 1952, pp. 64ff.

upon old-age assistance (over half as many as were drawing old-age benefits), in spite of the very liberal eligibility provisions adopted in 1950.

It is therefore understandable that countries with such systems have typically modified eligibility conditions to permit the payment of benefits to those already old when the law was first passed. In the United States, the original minimum requirement of five years of coverage for OASI eligibility was already generous but was greatly liberalized in 1950 after it became increasingly evident that under the rules established in 1935 and 1939, it would be many years before the system would mature. By the 1950 Amendments an individual who could show at least six quarters of coverage became eligible if he had secured at any time quarters of coverage equal in number to half the quarters elapsing between that date and his attainment of age 65.[7] For persons in the upper age brackets this represented, of course, a very large concession, and those who held that social insurance must be judged by the principles governing private commercial insurance could properly point out that it was misleading to hold that the beneficiaries had "paid for the cost of their benefits" and had therefore "earned them."

It is undeniable that tremendous windfall gains are reaped by those already elderly [8] and because for these individuals no claim that they have earned their benefits can be made, the payment of such benefits has been held to destroy the insurance character of the system as a whole. To this general charge we shall return later. Meanwhile it should be noted that private employers when putting into effect private pension plans (which are often insured with private insurance companies) frequently provide for substantial "unearned" benefits for employees already elderly at the time the scheme is initiated. Nor must it be forgotten that the availability of large unearned benefits due to liberalization of the eligibility provisions is essentially a transition phenomenon. Because of the provision that a worker must have been covered for at least half the quarters elapsing since 1950 and the date of his claim for benefits, the absolute number of quarters required to qualify increases steadily year by year for all covered workers. The worker retiring in 1953 could have been eligible with 6

[7] Although the measuring period closes with age 65, quarters of coverage secured before 1951 or after age 65 may be used to meet the requirement.

[8] These windfall gains were the more spectacular because simultaneously the 1 per cent increment for each additional year of coverage was abolished, so that there was no longer any "penalty" in the form of a lower benefit for short periods of coverage, and because workers admitted to benefit status by virtue of these liberal eligibility conditions received not a special (and lower) transitional benefit but a benefit determined by the formula applicable to all other workers, and this formula had in turn been greatly liberalized by the Amendments.

quarters of coverage (half of the 12 quarters since 1950): the worker retiring the following year needs 8 quarters (half of the quarters since 1950). By 1971 all workers will have to possess 40 quarters of coverage, which is the standard eligibility requirement that both before 1950 and thereafter confers full insured status on any worker.[8a]

In the second place, the strict individual equity idea associated with insurance has also been sharply departed from in the formulas governing benefits of modern social insurance systems, and for the same reason, namely the desire to utilize the program as a major instrument for solving the problem of income insecurity. For if the principle of maintaining an actuarial relationship between contributions and benefits is strictly ad-herred to for each individual covered, the lowest benefits will be received by the lowest-paid, who are typically the most insecure. The usual social insurance formula today weights the payment in favor of the lower-paid worker, and the programs usually provide a minimum benefit and very fre-quently also additional payments for persons dependent on the beneficiary, although no differential contribution is charged against workers with family responsibilities.[9]

Similarly, unemployment insurance systems, in addition to these modi-fications of the benefit formulas, have usually found it necessary to depart from strict insurance principles in regard to duration of benefit. The ratio rule, which led to restriction of benefit duration by reference to an individual's total earnings (or contributions) in some previous defined period, will, in a system with relatively liberal eligibility requirements based on earnings, often create a situation in which a worker is declared eligible, but only for two or three weeks of benefit payment.[10] Hence it is not surprising that many unemployment insurance systems, including those of roughly a quarter of the American states, today either provide for uniform periods of benefit duration for all eligible workers or, where the ratio rule is retained, specify a statutory minimum duration (as is done by a handful of American states).

An even more drastic departure from insurance principles as normally

[8a] Special eligibility requirements were adopted for elderly persons newly covered by the 1954 Amendments but applied only to persons reaching age 65 or dying before October, 1958, i.e., their transitional nature was emphasized.

[9] Because these modifications of the benefit provisions are also found in those systems which relate benefits to previous earnings for reasons other than a desire to reflect prin-ciples operating in private insurance, their detailed discussion will be reserved for Chap. 3.

[10] In 1952 the combination of minimum earnings requirements and the method of computing duration meant that an eligible worker might claim benefit for as few as four to six weeks in ten states. For an account of the duration provisions of American laws, see *Comparison of State Unemployment Insurance Laws as of August, 1954*, U.S. Department of Labor, Bureau of Employment Security, 1954, pp. 67–72. See also Chap. 7.

understood has taken the form of upward revision of money benefits after their amount has been determined. Thus in 1950 and again in 1952 and 1954, the benefits of already retired OASI recipients were increased to reflect changes in the cost of living.[11] This responsiveness of public programs to changes in prices is regarded by many as one of the major advantages of public social insurance as a form of old-age security as compared to private insurance, where the individual has no recourse against the progressive erosion of the purchasing power of his annuity in the event of inflation. But it cannot be denied that such adjustments are in sharp opposition to private insurance practice.

In the third place, there has been a modification of a provision found in most social insurance laws that stress the insurance concept. In order to emphasize the relationship between contributions paid and benefits received by the individual, the amount of the benefit typically bore some relation to the length of time over which contributions had been paid. Thus in the United States, until 1950, the basic OASI benefit as determined by a worker's average monthly wage was increased by 1 per cent for each year of coverage.

This partially met the demands of equity: the more contributions a worker had paid, the higher his benefit. It appeared also to be an answer to the problem of the worker who was already elderly when the system was inaugurated, for it was then possible to admit such people to benefit status after fairly short periods of coverage but to pay them lower benefits than would ultimately be received by their younger colleagues, who on attaining age 65 would have paid taxes for a longer period. In fact, however, this type of effort to secure the best of both worlds, namely to solve the contemporary problem of the need for income by those already old and also to maintain the equity concept associated with the insurance idea, faces a major dilemma. If individuals are made eligible after short periods of coverage, but receive a lower benefit adjusted to reflect this fact, then during the first generation of the program the average benefit awarded will be unduly low in relation to assumed needs. This is an especially important consideration in those systems, such as OASI, where the same formula determines benefit amounts both for aged persons and for survivors, because surviving families are most likely to be found in the case of men dying relatively young (i.e., after only short periods of coverage). On the other hand, if it is made high enough to meet the income needs of those qualifying after short periods of coverage, the benefit received by those who have earned more by contributing for an entire working life will be relatively high and for the system as a whole may necessitate a rate of annual contribution much higher than the community thinks it worth while to make in order to solve the problem of need in old age. Hence it

[11] For other examples and a discussion of the issues involved, see Chap. 3.

is not surprising that in 1950 the annual increment for years of coverage was abolished.

Those who are concerned about equity may, however, take some comfort from the fact that, even so, the method of determining the benefit amount still yields relatively larger benefits to the individual with long and continuous coverage.[12]

Is Social Insurance "Insurance"?

There has been much discussion in recent years as to whether or not these departures from the strict actuarial relationship between what an individual pays into a social insurance fund and what he gets out of it render the use of the word "insurance" in the term social insurance inappropriate and misleading.[13] Much depends upon how "insurance" is defined and on what concepts are associated with it. If it merely means a system in which all members of a given group agree to socialize the costs of compensating, on some agreed principle, for a risk to which all are exposed, by sharing the costs among themselves, then modern social insurance systems with all their modified eligibility and benefit provisions can rightly be called insurance. For efforts are made in all of them to calculate on an actuarial basis the costs of the benefits payable for as far ahead as seems feasible and to set rates of contribution that, over this period, will yield revenues adequate to cover these aggregate costs.[14] But on this broad definition of insurance every function of government in a responsible democracy which adopts orderly budgeting procedures could be classified as insurance.

[12] Since benefits are based on average monthly wages and these are determined by, in effect, totaling an individual's earnings between 1950 (or 1937 if more advantageous) and the date he claims benefits and dividing them by the calendar quarters elapsing in this interim, the worker claiming a benefit in, say, 1980 who has worked (and therefore paid contributions) for only half of these quarters will be assigned an average monthly wage that is only half that of his similarly paid fellow who has worked steadily (and paid contributions) for the entire time. The resulting benefit differential is of course reduced by the heavy weighting given to the first $110 of the average monthly wage as so determined, but there is still a differential in favor of the man who has relatively long and continuous periods of coverage. The Amendments of 1954 permitted beneficiaries to disregard the five years of lowest earnings and months of total disability, but absences from covered employment in all other years reduce benefit amounts.

[13] For the view that the term is appropriate, see Nelson H. Cruickshank, "Some Labor Views on the Social Security Problem," in *Annual Proceedings, 1953*, Industrial Relations Research Association, pp. 186–189; and the paper by Arthur Larson in *Economic Security for Americans: Final Edition*, Third American Assembly, Columbia University Press, New York, 1954. For the contrary view, see the sessions on the Legal Status of OASI benefits in *Analysis of the Social Security System*.

[14] For a discussion of the extent to which these costs are predictable so that "old age" or "unemployment" can be regarded as "calculable risks," see Chap. 10.

If insurance be thought of as group insurance of a kind sold by private insurance carriers, it would seem not inappropriate to claim that modern social insurance systems deserve to be classified as insurance. Here, it can be argued, the difference is largely a matter of scale, namely the extent of coverage, the liberality of the benefits, and the range of the risks assumed by private enterprise and by government. For the relatively generous un-earned benefits provided by public social insurance systems and the wide range of risks protected against involve premium rates that would deter the sale of any large volume of such insurance as a profit-making private venture, in which the decision to buy such insurance or not is in the hands of each individual employer and/or worker.

If, however, insurance be thought of as ordinary life insurance, in which the benefits payable in the individual case bear a direct actuarial relation-ship to the premiums paid and in which the principle of risk homogeneity in cost apportionment is strictly adhered to, then modern social insurance systems cannot appropriately be classified as insurance, for as we have seen, there is often little actuarial relationship between the amount of the benefits an individual receives and the contribution he is required to make. Moreover, there is little or no classification of the insured into groups having similar risks, and the cost to the individual is not propor-tionate to the probability of his incurring the risk. To the extent, there-fore, that the term social insurance may be interpreted to mean that the system fully reflects individual equities, its use may give rise to misunder-standing, for, as we have seen, modern social insurance systems tend to subordinate equity to the broader social purpose of the program.

Finally, those to whom the word "insurance" suggests an immutable contract precisely paralleling the binding contract entered into between a commercial insurance company and a private individual will, with justice, assert that social insurance is a misleading term, for the nature of the statutory rights conferred by the program can always be changed by subsequent legislatures.

Some of the dispute as to whether social insurance is or is not "in-surance" is thus a matter of semantics. Even if it is proper to regard so-cial insurance as "insurance," it is clear that it is a very different type of insurance from private commercial insurance. Its compulsory character and the fact that it was invented to deal with a social problem which called for some kind of public action causes the principles governing the coverage and eligibility conditions, the nature of the benefits, and the methods of financing [15] to be very different from those governing the sale of insurance on a competitive profit-making basis. Some have therefore

---

[15] For a discussion of the financial implications, see Chap. 10; and Reinhard A. Ho-haus, "Reserves for National Old Age Pensions," *Transactions of the Actuarial Society of America,* October, 1936, pp. 330–365.

suggested that it should be regarded as an additional and quite clearly identifiable form of insurance and that efforts be made to disseminate a wider understanding of its peculiar characteristics.[16] Others have held that the system itself is a self-destroying institution. Brought into being to achieve certain ends in a specific social and economic environment, its very existence has, it is held, in turn modified that environment and thus opened the way to attainment of the same ends by different methods.[17]

In any case, it seems likely that the term is here to stay, and it will be frequently used in the following chapters. But while fully admitting the valuable historical function which has been served by the linkage of the modern nondiscretionary, nondeterrent income security systems with insurance concepts, it would be unrealistic not to recognize that the persistence of the word "insurance" in the name given to such systems has a number of consequences. For semantics do matter.

First, it is likely to give rise, from time to time, to the kinds of misunderstandings which have just been discussed and to give apparent logical support to those who, for a variety of reasons, may wish to attack these nondiscretionary, nondeterrent systems.[18]

Second, it enables those who, for whatever reason, would prefer a limited public program to invoke "sound insurance principles," such as the concept of "insurable interest," to justify restrictive eligibility and benefit provisions.

Third, it perpetuates and strengthens the importance attached to the idea of equity as between individuals or classes covered by the system. Yet in a program brought into being to deal with a social problem considerations of equity have to be balanced against, and usually subordinated to, considerations of adequacy. As Reinhard A. Hohaus has stated in a masterly analysis of the difference between private and social insurance:

16 Cf. the statement of the Third American Assembly "Unless the essential principles of our social insurance system are widely understood by the American people, the system will be vulnerable to political pressures for unsound changes in the social security structure. To safeguard against this, every effort should be made to carry on an effective and continuing program of public education in this field." (*Economic Security for Americans: Final Edition*, p. 10.) The system was defined as one in which "benefits bear some relation to *aggregate* contributions," and which does not involve a test of need [italics supplied].

17 Cf. Burns, "Social Insurance in Evolution," p. 199; and Eveline M. Burns, *British Unemployment Programs, 1920–38*, Social Science Research Council, Washington, D.C., 1941, pp. 315–332.

18 For an excellent illustration, see the speeches of Congressman Carl Curtis before the U.S. Chamber of Commerce and the National Conference of Social Work in 1953 (*The Social Welfare Forum, 1953*, Columbia University Press, New York, 1953, pp. 71–79); and Sessions on the Legal Status of OASI Benefits of the Curtis Committee, in *Analysis of the Social Security System*, pp. 879–1015.

Because of its voluntary nature . . . private insurance must be built on principles which assure the greatest practicable degree of equity between the various classes insured. . . . Social insurance, on the other hand, is molded to society's need for a minimum of protection against one or more of the limited number of recognized social hazards. . . . Hence, just as considerations of equity of benefits form a natural and vital part of operating private insurance, so should considerations of adequacy of benefits control the pattern of social insurance. . . . The foregoing need not necessarily imply that all considerations of equity should be discarded from a social insurance plan: rather the point is that, of the two principles, adequacy is the more essential and less dispensable.[19]

If this be so, and the progressive abandonment of the strict "insurance" features of social insurance systems strongly supports Mr. Hohaus's position, then the embodiment of the term "insurance" in the name of such systems, by perpetuating an emphasis upon equity, may impede changes which might make such systems more nearly achieve their major social purpose.

Finally, the presence of the word "insurance" may act as an obstacle to the frank recognition of the many social and economic issues which are raised by legislation of this type. For in the very broadest sense it fosters the illusion that questions relating to coverage, eligibility, benefits, and financing can be resolved by formulas derived from commercial insurance practices.

It is easy to see why there is reluctance to abandon insurance analogies as the criteria for answering the central problems raised by a public income security program. . . . It means giving up a nice, simple automatic test, and facing the central and perplexing issues of social policy that arise wherever the public decides to use government to achieve certain ends. . . .

Nor should this conclusion dismay us. Once we are prepared to accept the instrument which happens to be called social insurance for what it is, namely a means of using government to guarantee predictable, nondiscretionary cash payments to some or all members of the community, we are more likely to appreciate the real nature of economic and social issues and conflicts that arise. We shall be less likely to retain specific provisions that do not serve their purpose if we force ourselves to say what that purpose is in each instance. And we shall be more likely to equip ourselves with an instrument that is responsive to changes in social values and in the

[19] Reinhard A. Hohaus, "Equity, Adequacy and Related Factors in Old Age Security," *The Record*, American Institute of Actuaries, June, 1938, pp. 82, 84. For an analysis of the same problem in the field of unemployment insurance, see Eveline M. Burns, *Private and Social Insurance and the Problem of Social Security*, Canadian Welfare Council, Ottawa, 1953, part I.

economic environment. We shall be facing, instead of evading, the central issues of public policy. [20]

In any case, as we shall see in the following chapter and in Part Three, it is possible to develop a rational and theoretical justification for many of the eligibility, benefit, and financial provisions of modern "social insurance" programs without necessarily stressing their analogy to insurance.

[20] Burns, *Private and Social Insurance and the Problem of Social Security,* p. 13.

CHAPTER 3

Benefits Related to Previous Earnings

THE PRINCIPLE that benefits should bear a relationship to the recipient's previous income or earnings, is in fact found, as we have seen, in those countries that have more or less strictly followed the private insurance principle, since such systems typically relate contributions to earnings. But it occurs also in those, like the United States, which have substantially departed from private insurance. Such a method of determining social security benefits has many advantages. In the first place, where the geographical area covered by a social security system is large and characterized by great diversity of price levels or of economic conditions reflected in wide differences in average earnings or incomes, such a system makes it possible to overcome a major dilemma. This is the risk that the payment of benefits that are adequate to meet basic needs or are otherwise acceptable in terms of prevailing standards in those parts of a country where levels of living are high may result, in other sections of the country where lower earnings levels prevail, in the payment of a benefit that is deemed to be dangerously close to, or even in excess of, the earnings of fully employed workers. The fear that assurance of a social security benefit may have an adverse effect on willingness to work by eliminating the penalty for idleness will be discussed more fully in the following chapter. Here it is only necessary to note that a wage-related benefit system is especially well devised for large and economically heterogeneous communities, for it enables them to apply a uniform principle to all citizens wherever they reside and at the same time maintain any desired differential between benefit and normal earnings, as well as occupational differentials.

The United States is one of the countries where these considerations assume importance. Although price levels do not vary substantially from one part of the country to another, wage and income levels do. In 1952, per capita income in Delaware was $2,260; in Mississippi it was $818.[1] The

1 Throughout this book the state income figures used are the old series relating to state income payments as issued by the Department of Commerce prior to September, 1955. For the new series relating to personal income by states and a comparison with the old, see *Survey of Current Business*, U.S. Department of Commerce, September, 1955, pp. 12 ff. For the ranking of states by per capita income payments and changes between 1947 and 1952, see *Analysis of the Social Security System*, pp. 405–408; also see *Survey of*

distribution of incomes within the states also varies, so that the proportion of the population receiving annual incomes below any specified level cannot always be inferred from a state's ranking in terms of average per capita income. Thus in 1950, Alabama and South Carolina were states with roughly the same per capita income, but the proportion of families and unrelated individuals with incomes of less than $2,000 was 78.6 in the former and only 57.2 in the latter. Delaware has a per capita income slightly higher than that of New York. Yet the proportion with incomes of less than $2,000 was 37.1 per cent in Delaware but only 30.5 in New York. For those with incomes of less than $3,000, the corresponding percentages were 55.5 and 48.9. In 1950 the percentage of families and unrelated individuals with incomes of less than $1,000 varied from 15 in New Jersey to 49.3 in Mississippi; those with incomes of less than $3,000 varied from 43.5 per cent (in New Jersey) to 85.5 per cent (in Alabama).[2]

There are also very significant differentials in earnings in different industries. Average gross weekly earnings in 1954 ranged from $94.19 in building construction to $40.10 for workers in laundries. And within any industry occupational differences in earnings are wide. Finally, there are marked differences in earnings as between urban and farm communities, although here the precise difference is more difficult to determine.[3]

In the face of these wide differentials the advantages of a wage-related benefit formula are self-evident. The OASI uniform formula, for example, even with the heavy weighting for the first $110 of monthly earnings, yields average benefits that vary substantially. For male workers at the end of 1954, while the average monthly benefit was $59.14 for the United States as a whole, it ranged from $65.57 in Connecticut to $47.19 in Mississippi. Individual benefits ranged all the way from the minimum of $30 to the maximum of $98.50.[4]

Different communities and individuals appear to attach different importance to the reflection of prior earnings differentials in income security benefits. Obviously, so long as it is deemed essential to maintain incentive

---

Current Business, U.S. Department of Commerce, August, 1954, for state incomes, 1929 to 1953.

[2] For other income brackets and for all states, see Selma J. Mushkin and Beatrice Crowther, *Federal Taxes and the Measurement of State Capacity,* U.S. Public Health Service, May, 1954, Appendix Table A-7.

[3] Official estimates of the income of farm families understate farm income by omitting more of the income in kind of the farm than of the nonfarm group. However, even when allowance is made for this, and for other factors less relevant to the general point now under discussion, farm incomes are in general conceded to be lower than those of nonfarm families. (Elizabeth E. Hoyt, Margaret G. Reed, et al., *American Income and Its Use,* Harper & Brothers, New York, 1954, pp. 109–112.)

[4] For the distribution of beneficiaries by $10 brackets and by state, at the end of 1954, see *Social Security Bulletin,* June, 1955, p. 15.

(see Chapter 4), a country with marked geographical or occupational differences in earnings will favor a wage-related benefit system. But some would urge its adoption for even broader reasons. It has been held, for example, that a free-enterprise society which stresses the rewards of individual initiative should ensure that its social security system also embodies incentive principles: that the higher income secured by the higher-paid (and presumably therefore more enterprising) worker should be reflected in higher social security benefits when he cannot work.[5] Others, however, believe that this is carrying the theory of incentive to an extreme. They would maintain that there are already sufficient incentives in the social environment and in the wage system itself and that a worker who is not influenced by these will hardly respond to the further inducement offered by the knowledge that higher earnings during his working life will add slightly to the amount of his old-age benefit when he retires. Others go so far as to claim that the earnings level of the vast majority of workers typically covered by social security systems is determined by factors among which the degree of enterprise shown by the individual plays a relatively minor role.

The wage-related benefit system is favored by others, including many sections of organized labor, who regard social security income as a kind of "deferred pay."[6] In this view, such payments are merely an extension of the wage contract. The difficulty about this theory is that it may impede the attainment of the security objective, since, unless substantial modifications in the principle are permitted, the lowest-paid worker will receive a benefit which, being only a percentage of already low wages, will almost by definition be inadequate to assure even a modest livelihood. Logically, therefore, a social security system based upon the deferred-pay theory would involve a restricted program, limited to those workers whose wages were sufficiently high to ensure that a fraction thereof would meet the worker's demand for security. This would still leave the community to grapple with the problem of devising an acceptable income security system for those excluded.

In fact most of those who hold the deferred-pay theory of social security benefits have accepted substantial modifications of the principle, including the weighting of benefit formulas in favor of lower-paid workers. But it is significant that the more logical exponents of the principle oppose the

[5] Cf. J. Douglas Brown, "Concepts in OASI," in *Proceedings, 1948,* Industrial Relations Research Association, pp. 100–106.

[6] ". . . employers think of their social security tax payments as part of their wage cost. The law supports this contention, since the employer pays income tax on income *after* the social security tax has been paid, recognizing that it is a kind of deferred wage payment, whereas wage-earners pay income taxes on income including the amount deducted from their pay for social security." (Nelson H. Cruikshank, *Your Stake in the Social Security Trust Fund,* American Federation of Labor, Washington, D.C., n.d.)

payment of dependents' allowances in social security benefits, on the grounds that no such recognition of family responsibilities is to be found in the wage system.

Finally, there may be compelling political considerations in favor of the wage-related benefit system. The workers of a country may distrust their elected representatives and fear that unless benefits are tied to some clearly defined objective measure, such as the specified proportion of earnings, the decision as to the income the mass of workers can look forward to and count upon when they retire or are otherwise unable to earn may become a political football from year to year. In such countries as Great Britain or Sweden, where the average voter feels closer to his government and more certain that his elected assembly will be responsive to the wishes of the vast mass of the voters rather than to the pressures of changing and powerful special-interest lobbies, this political consideration assumes less importance. But in the United States, it is undoubtedly more compelling.

Adoption of the wage-related benefit system, for whatever reason, entails its own problems. Among these, the most important concern the conflict between the benefit-wage principle and the demand for security, the method of determining the beneficiary's past wages for benefit-payment purposes, and the effect of changing price and wage levels on this method of determining benefits.

MODIFICATIONS OF THE PRINCIPLE IN THE INTEREST OF SECURITY

It will have been evident that as a basis for social security benefits the principle of relating benefit to wages has one serious disadvantage, namely that it yields the lowest benefits to those whose earnings are lowest and whose private resources for tiding over periods of nonearning are likely to be least. This problem is intensified by the fact that the typical wage-related benefit formula provides a benefit that is only a fraction of previous earnings.[7] Where earnings were very low, the benefit may then fail to meet even the most elementary needs of the beneficiary.

It is therefore not surprising that all social security systems have modified, in greater or lesser degree, the strict relationship between benefits and earnings. One method is to weight the benefit formulas heavily in favor of the lower-paid workers. Thus in the original Social Security Act benefits were based on each individual's cumulative total earnings prior to age 65 and equalled $\frac{1}{2}$ of 1 per cent of the first $3,000 of such earnings, but only $\frac{1}{12}$ of 1 per cent of the next $45,000 and $\frac{1}{24}$ of 1 per cent of earnings above this total. By 1955, as the result of a series of amendments[8] the

[7] For the reason for this provision, see Chap. 5.

[8] In 1939 the benefit was made equal to 40 per cent of the first $50 of the individual

benefit was equal to 55 per cent of the first $110 of average monthly wages, plus 20 per cent of the next $240. Such a weighted formula means of course that the higher-paid workers secure benefits representing a much smaller proportion of their average wages than do those in the lower-earnings brackets. In 1955 under the formula then prevailing, whereas the benefit of the man with average monthly earnings of $100 or less equalled 55 per cent of his earnings, for the $200 man it was 39.3 per cent, and for the $300 man it was 32.8 per cent, and for the $350 man it was exactly 31 per cent. This is a very substantial departure from the proportionality principle.

A second modification of the wage-related benefit principle has taken the form of statutory minimum money benefits. No matter how low a worker's earnings, if he is eligible at all he cannot receive less than a certain sum. In the United States these minima have generally been set very low. By 1955 the minimum monthly benefit was $30 for an insured retired person. In unemployment insurance the minimum benefits ranged between $5 and (exceptionally) $12.50 a week.[9] Nevertheless the departure from a strict application of the wage-related benefit principle is clear, and the trend of the minimum is upward.

A third and very important modification of the wage-related benefit principle occurs when dependents' benefits are granted. In most countries this concession to the social purpose of a public income security system has been more general than in the United States, where it is found only in OASI, in Workmen's Compensation, and in the unemployment insurance systems of a quarter of the states. Furthermore, apart from OASI the amount of the dependents' benefit is very small and is often not related to the previous wages or the actual benefit of the beneficiary. In all the unemployment insurance laws dependents' benefits take the form of a fixed money amount (usually $2 or $3 per dependent) added to the weekly benefit amount.

THE METHOD OF DETERMINING PREVIOUS EARNINGS

It is one thing to enunciate a principle, it is quite another to translate it into administratively feasible policies and procedures. For, like the private insurance-oriented social security systems, those which base benefits on

---

worker's average monthly wage plus 10 per cent of the next $200. In 1950 and 1952 the heavy weighting in favor of the low paid was still further emphasized. Thereafter until 1954 the formula provided a benefit equal to 55 per cent of the first $100 of average monthly wages, plus 15 per cent of the remainder up to $200.

[9] For the minimum in the individual states, see *Adequacy of Benefits under Unemployment Insurance*, U.S. Department of Labor, Bureau of Employment Security, 1952, Table B1 and *Comparison of State Unemployment Insurance Laws as of August, 1954*, pp. 56–60.

previous wages or earnings must maintain extensive records, often over the entire working life of the covered population. Even if the administration devises and maintains economical and efficient methods, the records will only be as good as the original data furnished by employers and/or workers.

In many countries concern about the administrative feasibility of the wage-related benefit system has led to a limited or gradual application of such systems. Initially, at least, coverage is limited to those groups which appear to present the fewest administrative headaches. From this viewpoint the ideal coverage group would be represented by the employees of a large firm which gave steady employment and employed relatively few occasional or part-time workers. Here the employer can be assumed to be an experienced and reliable record keeper; he can be identified and his record keeping checked if necessary against other returns he makes to the government. Furthermore, if firms are large, the administration does not have to deal with and police so many employers for each million workers covered, and because the workers are steadily employed by one employer, the administrator's task of posting records is simplified. At the other extreme is the worker who shifts from employer to employer (such as the migrant or casual employee) or those working even less than a full day for any one employer (such as domestic servants) or who are employed by individuals who do not typically keep records or make periodic returns to government.[10]

A system relating benefits to previous earnings also experiences difficulties in regard to the self-employed, particularly in the case of those whose incomes from self-employment are small or who are only occasionally self-employed, or part of whose income is secured in kind (such as farmers). In addition to such problems as separating out income attributable to invested capital from that attributable to employment, assuring that deductions for costs are not excessive, and the like, there is a general problem of securing appropriate and adequate records from such groups. Thus it is understandable that the 1935 Social Security Act excluded agricultural workers, domestic servants, and the self-employed from coverage, largely for administrative reasons,[11] while the state unemployment insurance laws still typically exclude employees of small firms.

By 1950 both the Bureau of Old Age and Survivors Insurance and the Bureau of Internal Revenue had gained sufficient experience to feel able to tackle the collection of taxes and the record keeping involved, and

[10] These considerations have also a bearing in the financial realm and affect the feasibility of collecting social security taxes from such employers and workers.

[11] It is also true that at that time there was little demand for coverage from these groups. As the advantages of coverage have been realized, more particularly since the Amendments of 1950, the demand for coverage has been more insistent.

coverage was extended to "regularly employed" agricultural and domestic workers and to all self-employed persons except farmers and some professional groups who specifically desired exclusion. But even after these amendments some 13 per cent of all paid civilian jobs were uncovered. The operation of the legal provisions designed to limit coverage to "regularly employed" workers proved to be both inconvenient and unfair to many workers and by 1953 a committee of experts proposed, after consultation with the departments involved, that coverage be made almost universal by the adoption of certain arrangements designed to overcome the administrative problems.[12] In 1954 these recommendations were carried into effect, except for a few groups of self-employed professional workers, such as doctors and lawyers.

Another response to the administrative difficulties of securing the necessary data for determining benefits in wage-related benefit systems has taken the form of a modification of the benefit formula itself. In 1937, when most American states began to administer an unemployment insurance system that aimed to pay benefits equal to 50 per cent of the beneficiary's weekly wages during some specified previous period, the problem of how to secure the necessary wage records loomed large. Employers were far from ready to accept the obligation to send in periodic wage and hour reports to the government (even pay-as-you-go income tax deductions were unknown at that time), and questions were raised as to the promptness, reliability, and accuracy of the reports likely to be furnished. In addition, the other burden of reporting laid on employers by the OASI sections of the Social Security Act called only for quarterly earnings reports, whereas, logically, the unemployment insurance system needed reports on a weekly basis. Hence one state after another began to devise formulas which would enable them to pay benefits on the basis of data on quarterly, rather than weekly, earnings. By 1954 nine states even based benefits on annual earnings. The initial formulas, namely that benefits would equal $\frac{1}{26}$ of quarterly earnings, would of course result in a benefit equal to 50 per cent of the worker's weekly wage if he had been regularly employed for each of the thirteen weeks in each quarter. But weeks of nonworking would obviously result in a benefit less than this. To counteract this difficulty various devices have been adopted. All the states using the quarterly earn-

---

12 *A Report to the Secretary of Health, Education and Welfare on Extension of Old Age and Survivors Insurance to Additional Groups of Covered Workers*, Consultants on Social Security, Government Printing Office, Washington, D.C., 1953. The Committee also made proposals to overcome the obstacles to coverage of state and local government employees covered by public retirement systems. For a more detailed discussion of these arrangements and of the problems involved in coverage of farmers, and methods of overcoming them, see *Social Security Amendments of 1954*, Hearings before the House Committee on Ways and Means on H.R. 7199, 83d Cong., 2d Sess., 1954, pp. 37–54, 195–225 (hereinafter referred to by title only).

ings formula now base benefits on that quarter in the specified period during which earnings were highest. Many of them, in addition, have increased the fraction of quarterly earnings to make a rough-and-ready allowance for lost time. Thus by 1954, twenty-one states defined the basic benefit as more than $\frac{1}{26}$ of quarterly earnings. In eight of these the fraction was $\frac{1}{20}$. Eleven other states used a weighted schedule which gave a greater proportion of earnings to lower-paid workers than to those earning more.[13]

Such adjustments can, of course, only partly offset some of the anomalies due to the fact that the new formulas necessarily reflect both levels of earnings and patterns of employment. They favor the regularly employed worker, whose benefit will be more than 50 per cent of his normal weekly earnings in any state where the formula defines the benefit as more than $\frac{1}{26}$ of quarterly earnings. They also favor the irregularly employed individual who may have had one complete quarter of earnings as against the man who over the base year might have worked for a larger total number of weeks without securing thirteen weeks of employment in any one quarter. In any case, a benefit formula that utilizes reports of earnings alone, with no data on hours, yields benefits that are less than the assumed 50 per cent of earnings if short time is worked and more than this percentage in periods of high employment and much overtime.

Yet another approach to the administrative problem of securing the necessary data on which to base benefits in a wage-related benefit system is to abandon the requirement for continuous reporting from employers and to rely instead on a "request reporting" made by the employer at the time the worker claims his benefit. This is the system which has always been used in workmen's compensation and has more recently been adopted for unemployment insurance by a number of states. It is obviously not appropriate in long-period risk programs where benefits reflect earnings over a period of many years.

So long as employers are in any case forced to keep records (e.g., for income-tax, withholding-tax, or OASI purposes) the risks that under this system it may be difficult and time-consuming to determine a worker's unemployment benefit will be relatively small. But it must be remembered that this system has been used in unemployment insurance systems only in a period of high employment, when claims have been relatively few. Whether it would prove feasible and sufficiently speedy in periods of mass layoff remains to be seen. This problem of heavy peak loads is not faced by systems providing income security where income loss is due to disability (whether occupationally caused or otherwise) except, of course, in the rare event of a serious epidemic.

A question also arises, more particularly in the long-period risk pro-

[13] *Comparison of State Unemployment Insurance Laws as of August 1954,* pp. 56–60.

grams, as to the period over which earnings are to be taken into account for benefit-determination purposes. The OASI formula, in essence, totals all earnings in covered employment from a specified date up to age 65 [14] or death, if earlier, and divides them by the actual number of calendar quarters elapsing between the specified date and the time the worker dies or reaches age 65.

One consequence of this formula is that workers who have been unable to earn in some years because of sickness or unemployment or who work for some years in uncovered employment will suffer a lowering of benefit amount. To meet this difficulty several modifications of the basic formula have been proposed. One would base benefits on some given number of years (five years has often been suggested) in which earnings are highest rather than on an entire lifetime. This is the principle which, as we have seen, was adopted in many unemployment insurance laws when, for administrative reasons, data on a quarterly basis were used for determining weekly benefits. Benefits were based on the quarter of highest earnings. But in OASI the financial implications of such a change are likely to be particularly serious. For over a working lifetime annual earnings may fluctuate considerably, and the financing of the system may be greatly complicated if individuals receive benefits based on their years of highest earnings, although for the greater part of their lives they pay taxes on much lower amounts. Furthermore, difficult questions of equity may arise. It may be felt "unfair" that a beneficiary who has particularly high earnings in five out of a working life of forty-five years becomes thereby entitled to a benefit much higher than that received by his fellow workers who for all except five of these same years have paid identical social security taxes.

A modification of this proposal (adopted in the Amendments of 1954) would disregard, for benefit-determination purposes, some specified number of years when earnings were lowest. The extent to which this would eliminate the lowering of benefit amounts due to periods of sickness or unemployment would depend on the number of years in which low or zero earnings would be disregarded.

A more effective device is that found in some countries, such as Great Britain, which disregard all periods of unemployment and sickness in determining benefit rights.[15] In the United States this policy was adopted

---

[14] If it is to his advantage, wages earned after age 65 until a worker applies for benefits will also be taken into account.

[15] In Great Britain this is done by "crediting" workers with contributions in respect of such periods. However, this concession does not apply to a minimum of 156 contributions which must be actually paid. In Britain the principle applies only to eligibility, not to amount of benefit, which is at a flat rate. Less-than-standard rate benefits are payable where the claimant has less than the required annual average contributions either paid or credited.

in 1954, limited, however, to periods of extended total disability, and then only for workers with a long wage record. The desirability of adopting such a device will depend in part on the ease with which it is possible to test whether a worker's absence from the OASI system was in fact due to sickness and unemployment. This is less of a problem for countries, such as Great Britain, which have unemployment and sickness insurance systems of almost universal coverage and where therefore the administrators of the old-age pensions system can verify illness or sickness from these records of other administrators. It is more of a problem in the United States, where temporary disability insurance covers only about one-fifth of employed persons and where unemployment insurance laws exclude so many workers. In any case, whether or not the method of completely disregarding periods of sickness and unemployment in determining old-age benefit amounts will be adopted depends upon a country's willingness to shoulder the extra costs involved. For it must not be forgotten that those who benefit by such a provision will be receiving some degree of unearned benefit, whose cost must be met from the incomes of some other groups.

One further difficulty is faced by old-age security systems which base benefits on income during an entire working life. Since no worker could have secured earnings in covered employment prior to the initial establishment of the system, it is usual to provide that earnings will be counted from the time a worker reaches a specified age or from the date of enactment of the original legislation. As we have seen, this has been done in OASI. But real difficulties arise if coverage was not originally universal and if it is subsequently extended to bring in more workers. For then, those newly brought in could not possibly have had any covered earnings prior to the amendment date and would inevitably receive lower benefits because their "average wage" would be lowered by years of noncoverage.

It is for this reason that in 1950, when OASI coverage was greatly broadened, a "new start," namely January, 1951 instead of January, 1937, was enacted. But since this could not in fairness be made available only to those newly covered, all persons with covered earnings subsequent to that date could thereafter have their benefits based either on their entire period of covered employment or only on employment after 1950.

The new start may be an effective answer to the problem of the newly covered worker, but it yields substantial unearned benefits to many people and may offend people's sense of equity even though the windfall gains are essentially a transition phenomenon. Indeed much of the criticism of the OASI system made during the years 1952 to 1954 was directed to the disproportionately large benefits that were received by individuals who had been covered, and therefore paid social security taxes, for as few as six quarters.

THE EFFECT OF PRICE CHANGES ON BENEFITS

Public income security programs which aim to provide benefits that bear some relationship to the previous earnings or wages of the recipient face one further problem: how to maintain the relationship originally decided upon, in the face of changes in the price level. In fact, of course, over recent years the problem has been one of adjustment to a rising price level. At first sight, it might seem that the systems with formulas which take account of an individual's past earnings are less likely to experience this type of difficulty than those which provide flat-rate benefits. For a change in prices is likely to be reflected in money wage levels and therefore, as prices rise or fall, so will social security benefits. So long as the lag between changes in the general price level and in money wages is relatively slight, the wage-related benefit systems are undoubtedly better devised than flat-rate systems for dealing with the problem of changing price levels. The unemployed or disabled worker who draws a benefit based on the wages he received in a recent past period, which is frequently a year and often shorter, has a reasonable chance of receiving a benefit which bears the same proportion to his normal wages as was intended in the original law.

Even in these short-period risks, however, some systems base benefits on earnings in a more distant period, because of the relationship between the so-called "base" and the "benefit" year. Almost all the American unemployment insurance laws, for example, determine a worker's benefit rights on the basis of his record in covered work over a prior year, called the base year or period. These rights remain fixed for a period called the benefit year. As a rule, the date establishing the beginning and end of the base period depends on when the worker first applies for, or begins drawing, benefits, i.e., on the beginning of his benefit year, and most laws provide that the base period is to be the first four of the last five completed calendar quarters prior to the beginning of the benefit year.[16] Thus a worker becoming unemployed any time between April and June in one year would draw a benefit based on his earnings during the twelve months January to December of the preceding year. The lag period would be only between three and six months, and unless there was a sharp change in prices and wages in this short period, his benefit would reflect, pretty exactly, his normal earnings.

In roughly a fifth of the states, however, the beginning and ending

[16] For details of the provisions in the individual state laws, see *Comparison of State Unemployment Insurance Laws, as of August, 1954,* U.S. Department of Labor, Bureau of Employment Security, 1954, pp. 43–47.

dates of the base and benefit years are calendar periods fixed by law and the same for all workers. In such cases a worker may receive benefits based upon earnings received in a much more distant period. If, for example, the fixed benefit year runs from January to December and the base year runs from April to March for all workers, a worker becoming unemployed in the last quarter of 1954 would draw benefits based on the period April, 1952 to March, 1953. Over a period of this length significant changes in wage levels may have occurred.

But in general, it is true that the short-period risk systems that base benefits on previous earnings are comparatively well insulated against price changes except in the case of catastrophic and galloping inflations. As will be seen below, however, such systems often contain other features, such as fixed money maximums on benefits and upper money limits to the level of wages taken into account in determining benefits, which restrict the extent to which changes in prices will be automatically reflected in benefits.

The problem of changes in the price level is, however, much more serious for income security programs dealing with long-period risks, namely old age, permanent disability, and survivorship. In the first place, the benefit, once determined, will be drawn for a long period of time, unlike unemployment or temporary disability payments, which are seldom available for more than six months. Even, therefore, if at the time it was determined, it bore the desired relation to the beneficiary's previous earnings and therefore his prior standard of living, its purchasing power may be eroded by inflation before the beneficiary dies or is no longer eligible (as in the case of surviving children reaching maturity). From this point of view, the wage-related systems are as vulnerable to inflation as the flat-benefit systems. In countries which have experienced drastic inflations the problem of the declining purchasing power of even wage-related benefits has been a major social security issue since World War I.[17] Even in the United States, when in 1950 the benefit formula and the wage base were changed so as more nearly to reflect changes in wages and prices since 1935 in the benefits thereafter payable, it was felt necessary also to increase the benefits of those who had already retired.

In the second place, when, as in OASI, benefits are based upon earnings over a working lifetime (permanent disability insurance benefits would presumably follow the same principle), an upward trend in the level of prices means that the benefit, reflecting in part as it does the lower price level of earlier years, is inadequate to meet the worker's needs at

[17] For some of the ways in which benefits have been adjusted to rising prices, see Carl H. Farman, "Increased Living Costs and Social Security Benefits," *Social Security Bulletin*, January, 1954, pp. 14ff.

the higher level of prices prevailing when he retires. Various proposals have been made to overcome this problem. One would base benefits not on life earnings but on some more recent five- or ten-year period. This is not a very effective protection against the effects of inflation because even over a period of this length major changes in prices can occur. In 1940, the year when OASI benefits were first payable, the consumer price index, calculated for city wage earners and clerical workers' families, stood at 59.9. By 1945, it had risen to 76.9, and by 1950, to 102.8. Furthermore, for many workers, earnings decline during their later years, hence to base benefits on earnings during the last five or ten years before retirement may mean selecting a relatively unfavorable period for benefit determination.

Another suggestion, which, as we have seen, was adopted for other reasons in 1954, is to disregard some specified number of years in which earnings were lowest. This device too can provide only a limited protection against inflation unless the number of years which may be disregarded is very large, in which case the proposal would differ from that previously discussed only in that the relatively short period taken into account in determining benefits would not necessarily be the one immediately preceding a worker's retirement.

In general, it must be admitted that relatively little can be done to eliminate the downward drag on long-period wage-related benefits occasioned by an upward price trend that occurs during the beneficiary's working life. Where the effect upon the benefit rate is serious, about the only available remedy is to provide for an across-the-board increase in benefits, either on a planned or an emergency basis. This happened in the United States in 1950 and again in 1952 and 1954, when blanket increases were made in both current and future OASI benefits. The disadvantage of this "solution" is that if it is necessary to do this frequently, it may destroy some of the values of the contributory system. For the mathematical relationship between benefits and wages (defined as wages over a working lifetime) is then completely changed, and in money, though not in real, terms already retired workers will receive higher benefits than they have paid for. And, as will be shown below, such a drastic adjustment creates financial problems.

Quite apart from the difficulty of ensuring that income security benefits for long-period risks bear a realistic relationship to wages at the time a worker claims them, and thereafter, the wage-related benefit systems face other difficulties when the price level changes sharply, because of certain other features commonly found in the benefit formulas. These are the inclusion in the law of a money maximum to the absolute amount of benefit that any worker can receive, however high his actual earnings, and money limits to the amount of wages that will be taken into account in the benefit formula. These features are found in both long- and short-period income security systems.

The purposes of these limits are not always easy to determine. In systems that limit coverage to persons earning less than a certain sum, presumably as a method of defining the group most obviously in need of the protection of public programs, an upper limit on the earnings to be taken into account for benefit-determination purposes follows automatically. But such limits are also found in systems like the American, which do not restrict coverage by reference to level of earnings. In OASI, for example, all workers in covered employment are subject to the Social Security Act regardless of the level of their earnings but are taxed, and have their benefits computed, only on the first so many dollars ($3,000 to 1950, $3,600 from 1951 to 1954, and $4,200 thereafter). The corresponding limit in unemployment insurance laws is usually $3,000. It seems likely that the earnings limit found in benefit formulas was in part a reflection of a financial decision that taxes should not be imposed on earnings of more than a given sum.[18] The imposition of fixed dollar limits to the benefit any individual can receive was more probably a concession to the social character of the program. Workers in the upper wage brackets would receive less than the normal or average percentage of their previous earnings in order that those at the other end of the wage scale might be given more adequate benefits without increasing the over-all cost of the program. The dollar limit on benefit amount may also reflect public attitudes at the time the system was introduced. In 1935, when the idea of an income security system that carried no stigma was relatively new and by no means generally accepted, it might have been thought that public opinion "would not stand for" benefits higher than the $15 written into all but two of the original laws.

Both the benefit maximum and the money limit to the level of earnings taken into account in benefit determination are, of course, serious qualifications to the general principle that benefits should reflect wage differentials. In fact, in systems using these two types of limit, benefits reflect wage differences only up to a certain degree. Here, we are concerned more directly with their effect in increasing the vulnerability of such systems to changes in the general level of prices. The only effect of a falling price and wage level is to render the dollar limit less and less effective, and if prices fall very far, the limits might in fact never be invoked. Exactly the opposite occurs when prices and wages are rising. More and more workers are then affected by the dollar limits and if these are not changed, the system may approximate a flat-rate benefit system, for an

---

[18] This is not inevitably so, however. Some American unemployment insurance systems have a dollar limit on earnings for taxation purposes but disregard the limit in the benefit formulas.

ever larger proportion of workers will draw benefits at the maximum rate, while for the average worker, the benefit will come to represent an ever smaller proportion of his actual earnings.

The effect of these limits can be seen very clearly in the American unemployment insurance systems. When the laws were first enacted, it was generally intended that benefits should approximate 50 per cent of a worker's weekly wages. The benefit ceilings, which were a feature of all the laws, approximated two-thirds of average weekly wages in most states, so that relatively few workers would have been subject to these limits. In 1939, the ratio of ceilings to average weekly wages was 67 per cent, and less than 25 per cent of workers were affected by them. Between 1936 and 1953, average weekly wages in covered employment tripled, and while dollar benefit ceilings were increased, this happened only after a considerable time lag, and the actual increase was less than twice the original rate. Hence by the end of 1953, all but three states had basic benefit ceilings between 29 per cent and 49 per cent of average weekly earnings in covered employment. Even in nine of the ten states with higher ceilings because of dependent's allowances, the average was only 53 per cent. Such a failure to adjust dollar ceilings to rising money wages had two results. First, it greatly weakened the claims of the system to pay differential, wage-related benefits. By 1944, 58.5 per cent of all beneficiaries drew benefits at the maximum and therefore flat rate, and in the following two years the percentage was over 70. In 1952 over 55 per cent of all weeks of total unemployment were paid at the ceiling rate: in seven states more than 70 per cent of new claimants were eligible for the maximum. By the fall of 1953, the proportion of all insured claimants eligible for the maximum weekly benefit amount was 58.8 per cent: in fifteen states the proportion was between 71.9 per cent and 79.2 per cent, while in one it was 85.4 per cent.[19] It is questionable whether a system which paid anything other than a flat rate to so few as 20 or 30 per cent of eligible workers could reap the advantages claimed for a wage-related benefit system.[20]

Second, the rigid character of the benefit ceilings, coupled in many states with a dollar limit to the amount of earnings creditable for benefit-determination purposes, has depressed the average far below the 50 per cent compensation originally intended. Average weekly benefits for total unemployment declined from 41 per cent of average taxable weekly wages

[19] Detailed figures by state are given in *Employment Security Administrative Financing Act,* Hearings before the Senate Committee on Finance, 83d Cong., 2d Sess., 1954, pp. 89–95.

[20] For further information on benefit ceilings and their effects, see Eveline M. Burns, *The American Social Security System,* Houghton Mifflin Company, Boston, 1951, pp. 146–148.

in the states in 1939 to 33 per cent in 1952.[21] Since the impact on beneficiaries of these provisions is felt primarily by the higher-paid workers, it is not surprising that in 1952 workers making $50 a week or less could count on receiving a benefit at least equal to 50 per cent of weekly wages. But those earning more, who by that date constituted the majority, received a considerably smaller proportion, the average in the majority of states being less than 45 per cent. The $80-a-week worker received less than a third of his wages in most states.[22]

The OASI system contains both a limit on creditable earnings and a dollar maximum to the benefit payable. In 1938, when the $3,000 limit to creditable earnings prevailed, about 6 per cent of covered male full-time workers were earning over the limit. By 1950 the proportion had risen to 57 per cent. Although in that year the dollar limit was raised to $3,600 in the expectation that this would reduce to 36 per cent the proportion of workers not all of whose wages would count toward benefits, this result was not attained. Rising prices and rising wages continued apace, and despite the somewhat higher limit, in 1951 48 per cent, and in 1953, 61 per cent of full-time covered males had earnings in excess of $3,600. In consequence, in 1953, of all recently retired workers no less than 49 per cent drew benefits within $10 of the $85 maximum. So heavy a concentration of beneficiaries in this one bracket reflected not the fact that their earnings had been actually the same but rather that the maximum on creditable earnings was too low to reflect differences in their earnings.[23] The increase in maximum creditable earnings to $4,200 from 1955 onwards still failed to reflect the full effect of the upward trend in average earnings.

Workmen's compensation laws provide another illustration of the problem created by the failure to adjust dollar maxima to changes in the level of money wages. In principle, these laws provide for compensation during disability at a fixed percentage of the weekly wage. This statutory percentage in the case of two out of three workers so protected has usually

---

[21] It has been objected that such comparisons of averages are invalid because in 1952 average wages included much overtime. But although in 1939 average weekly hours in manufacturing were 37.7, while for the last quarter of 1953 they averaged 40, allowance for this factor would not explain away the difference revealed by the comparison. Furthermore, it has been held improper to compare average benefits with the average of all wages: the proper comparison, it is held, should be between benefits and the wages of beneficiaries only. While in principle this is unobjectionable, the comparison given in the text would be invalid only if it could be shown that the difference between the wages of beneficiaries and of all covered workers was greater in 1953 than in the earlier years.

[22] *Adequacy of Benefits under Unemployment Insurance,* p. 16 and Table B9.

[23] For details and a fuller discussion of this problem, see *Social Security Amendments of 1954,* pp. 54–65.

been 66⅔ or more. By 1952 only three states, with less than 2 per cent of covered workers, specified a percentage that was less than 60 per cent of wages. The benefit payments are, however, subject to an overriding dollar maximum.

In 1939 the dollar maxima (which in no case amounted to more than $25 a week and were less than $20 in half the laws) were sufficiently high in relation to average wages to permit the payment of the statutory percentage as compensation in the vast majority of cases. Over the next ten years, such increases in dollar maxima as occurred failed to keep pace with the rising wage levels. In consequence, by 1953 only five states had maxima high enough to permit workers with average wages to be paid the statutory percentages (which in all these states were less than the usual two-thirds of wages). With the maxima effective in mid-1953, a worker in receipt of the average 1952 wage would have been paid a benefit amounting to less than 50 per cent of his wage under more than two-thirds of the laws, while in four states with 6.5 per cent of covered payroll the maximum benefit was less than 35 per cent of the average wage.[24]

The difficulties which have just been discussed arise because the social security systems concerned write certain fixed money sums into the law. In this respect the wage-related benefit systems face essentially the same problem as the flat-rate systems, namely how to maintain whatever benefit-wage or benefit–standard–of–living relationships were established when the original dollar amounts were written into the law, in the face of general price or wage changes that affect everything except this statutory dollar limit. One solution, which has been adopted in some countries, immediately suggests itself, namely to write into the law a provision for varying the dollar limits, minimum and maximum, or flat rates with changes in the general level of prices. In 1950, for example, Sweden introduced an automatic cost-of-living feature into her flat-rate old-age pension system. Whenever the cost of living rises or falls by five points, certain sums are added to, or subtracted from, the money pension as fixed in 1946. Living costs are computed quarterly, and benefit changes are automatic. The same principle could be applied to the benefit limits and dollar maxima to creditable earnings found in so many American income security laws. In fact, it has been adopted in one of the states which spell out in dollars the minimum standard to be assured recipients of public assistance or the maximum payment to any individual. Thus Massachusetts increases or decreases the budget whenever the official state monthly index of the cost of living changes by 5 per cent or more. New York City likewise adjusts the standard assistance budget by reference to

24 Dorothy McCamman and Alfred M. Skolnik, "Workmen's Compensation: Measures of Accomplishment," *Social Security Bulletin*, March, 1954, p. 8.

changes in the cost-of-living index. Similarly, in Illinois and Utah, the legal maximum payment is increased or decreased semiannually with changes in the national cost-of-living index. At one time Utah also applied this principle to unemployment insurance benefits.

This type of adjustment of money benefit amounts written into the law has the great advantage of reducing the lag in adjustment. For it must not be forgotten that if there are substantial price rises, sooner or later the basic law will be amended so as to write in different dollar limits. But, as the American experience has shown, it is often many years before formal legislative changes are made, and in the meantime the system may depart far from its original objectives, whether these were to maintain a particular relationship between benefits and wages or to assure a certain standard of living.

The device would, of course, not be an answer to the difficulties faced by the long-period risk systems in guaranteeing in the face of secular trends in prices a benefit that bears a realistic relationship to the money earnings of a beneficiary over his working life. But it could be applied to the problem of the already retired worker whose benefit, even if accurately reflecting his past earnings when first awarded, loses its purchasing power after he has retired or become permanently disabled. However, in such a case, problems of cost arise which are not present when automatic price adjustments are made in dollar limits to maximum benefits or to creditable earnings. For in the latter case, higher benefits will be paid only to the extent that the beneficiary has actually earned higher wages and paid taxes on them. Hence as the benefit costs rise, the income of the fund increases correspondingly. But where automatic cost-of-living increases are applied to benefits already awarded, no corresponding increase in revenue will be secured. Whatever cost is involved must be carried by current contributors to the fund or, as it is in some countries which have adopted this device, by the general taxpayer. Similarly, where the principle is applied to flat-rate benefit systems, unless corresponding changes are made in the flat rates of contribution, the additional costs will again fall on the general taxpayer.[25]

[25] Cf. Helen Fisher Hohman, "Old-age Security in Postwar Britain: Adjusting Pensions to Rising Prices, 1946–1952," *Social Service Review*, June, 1953, pp. 177–192.

CHAPTER 4

Income Guarantees and
Willingness to Work

IN EVALUATING the relative desirability of the different bases for the determination of social security benefits, it is important to note that all of them come to grips, in different ways, with two central policy issues: what should be the relationship between income assured by government guarantee and the level of income that can normally be secured by participation in production; and to what extent should the community assume responsibilities for economic support that were previously assigned to, and assumed to be carried by, the family? This chapter will deal with the first of these issues; the second will be discussed in Chapter 5.

The problem of the relationship between social security income and privately secured income has plagued social security planners from the first, and the fear that any, or at any rate too liberal, a publicly assured income would, by reducing the economic penalty for not working, discourage initiative and thereby cause a drop in national output has led to a variety of provisions in the laws. These provisions are often favored also by ardent advocates of social security programs because they believe that abuses of the system, if serious enough to attract public attention, may bring the entire program into disrepute. That these fears are not wholly groundless may be seen from the many attacks upon public assistance systems in the United States in recent years arising from allegations that relief was being paid to people who did not need it (e.g., the famous "lady with the mink coat") or to people who could have obtained work had they tried. Similar attacks have been made upon unemployment insurance systems.

It should be emphasized that recognition of this problem does not imply that the sense of personal responsibility is weak in the average citizen. Experience demonstrates that the vast majority of the citizens prefer work, when it is available, to idleness, and are sufficiently influenced by the American mores, by their sense of family responsibility, by belief in the desirability of a high standard of living, and by the lure of contemporary advertising institutions to be unwilling to exist on social security income, especially if more money can be secured by working. Once an individual has developed regular work habits, and more particularly

56

if he has become attached to a specific company, many factors other than the availability of a social security benefit are likely to influence any tendency to prefer benefit status to work. The risk of sacrificing his standing under the increasingly prevalent seniority provisions which affect a worker's vulnerability to layoff, his prospects of promotion within a firm, and in effect also his rights under fringe benefit schemes act as heavy deterrents. Furthermore, most workers need work for social and psychological, as well as economic, reasons. Studies of the unemployed have revealed that the sense of inadequacy experienced by employable individuals who are not participating in the normal work routines of all other members of the society of which they are a part is very acutely felt and will be avoided whenever possible.

But there are marginal groups of whom all this is not true. Workers whose normal incomes are very low and whose economic horizons are very limited may, if social security income is adequate for their modest wants, prefer benefit status to securing an income from employment, particularly if their normal type of employment is arduous or unpleasant, or if they are unmarried with no family responsibilities. Certain categories of workers who do not have a firm attachment to the labor market are also less likely to resist the temptation to prefer idleness on benefit to an earned income. Young workers who have not yet acquired regular work habits are a case in point. Studies of abuses of unemployment and disability insurance systems have revealed that women, especially married women, as a group often present this same general problem. Myers and Schultz, for example, in studying the effects of a partial shutdown of a textile mill, found that most of the people drawing benefits and not looking for work were married women who wished to attend to family responsibilities.[1] Similarly, Dr. Becker found female workers to be relatively numerous (together with some other groups) among those abusing unemployment insurance laws.[2] Among other groups where the problem of the effect of assured social security income on willingness to work may assume serious proportions are irregularly employed workers, such as longshoremen and those shifting constantly from one job to another.

Finally, there is no doubt that an unknown but almost certainly tiny proportion of people are psychologically conditioned to resist acceptance of the normal responsibility for self-support and family maintenance. Whether this deviation from normal attitudes is due to a weakness of character within the control of the individual (the assumption underlying the view that such people should be punished) or whether it is a sign of

[1] Charles A. Myers and George P. Schultz, *The Dynamics of a Labor Market*, Prentice-Hall, Inc., New York, 1951, chap. 6.

[2] Joseph M. Becker, *The Problem of Abuse in Unemployment Benefits, A Study in Limits*, Columbia University Press, New York, 1953, pp. 255–266, 300–307.

severe psychological illness and not within the individual's control (the assumption underlying the view that such people should be regarded as mentally sick and treated accordingly) is at the moment beside the point. The fact remains that individuals so conditioned present a real problem to the planners of social security systems.

Furthermore, studies in the field of unemployment insurance suggest that the volume of abuse will increase if the feeling becomes general that the administration is lax.[3] The real problem is how to devise a social security system which will not expose people to irresistible temptations to profit at the public expense and how to do so without penalizing the vast majority of people of high initiative and strong work attachment in order to protect the system against the marginal malingerers. Contemporary social security systems attempt to deal with this problem in two ways: through the principles on which the amount of the benefit is determined and by attaching certain conditions to the receipt of benefit.

CONTROLS EMBODIED IN THE BENEFIT PROVISIONS

The famous principle of "less eligibility" enunciated by the English Poor Law Commissioners in 1834 expressed the view that publicly assured income should never exceed the earnings of the lowest category of independent worker. Until recent years, the administration of the poor law or public assistance in the United States has continued in principle to reflect this view. During the last half century, however, and notably since the 1930s there has been a significant change, and in many states and communities the view now prevails that public assistance should meet need as demonstrated.

Where there are large families and normal incomes are low, however, this may lead to payments that exceed those which could have been secured by active employment. While this may not be a serious problem in the case of the aged or of widowed mothers of young children, where either for physical reasons the recipient is in any case unable to work, or for social reasons it is deemed undesirable that he or she should work, it may be an important consideration in the payment of allowances to physically fit persons of employable age.

In fact, in the United States as a whole, it can hardly be argued that the public assistance monthly payments provide a standard of living so high as to encourage malingering. The monthly payments on general assistance, the only assistance program which provides for the able-bodied (other than Aid to Dependent Children (ADC) for mothers of dependent children), were averaging around $50 a case at the beginning of 1954.[4]

[3] *Ibid., passim.*

[4] Actually, there has always been great variation from state to state. In January,

While most recipients were likely to have some minor resources of their own, especially in the rural areas, the fact that a typical "case" included more than one person (the last available estimates indicate an average of about 1.8 persons per case) means that except in very low-wage areas or occupations, the differential between what could be earned by employment and what could be secured from public assistance must have been substantial. For during 1953, gross weekly earnings in manufacturing averaged over $71, and even in retail trade they ranged from $53 to $56.

Nevertheless, the higher the standard of minimum adequacy adopted by the community, the more acute becomes the question of the effect of this assured minimum on economic incentive. It is not surprising, therefore, that as public assistance has moved toward basing payments on actual need, there has been a renewed search for controls, other than those embodied in the rules governing the amount of the payment, to ensure that all persons who could be self-supporting do in fact carry out their social obligations (see the following section).

The non-needs-test, nondiscretionary systems meet this major problem in different ways. Those which make payments on the basis of assumed average need may set the assured minimum income, at least in the case of single workers, at a relatively low level in relation to average earnings. Thus in Great Britain the flat rate of benefit for adult men was about 20 per cent of the average wages of males when the Act of 1946 went into effect, and even with the addition of a benefit for a dependent wife it was only around 33 per cent. By 1954, despite an increase of about 25 per cent in benefits in 1952, owing to the considerable rise in money earnings in the interim the proportions were even smaller.[5] In New Zealand, where the flat income-conditioned benefit has been several times increased in view of rising money wages, the benefit by 1953 was a little over 30 per cent for a single man and but a little over 60 per cent for a married couple, of the average award wages of male workers.[6] But in adopting this solution such countries run the risk that the program may need considerable supplementation from some other system if the differ-

---

1954, for example, when the national average monthly payment was $50.30 a case, Tennessee averaged $10.95 and Mississippi and Arkansas only $13.16, while at the other extreme New York averaged $73.50, New Jersey, $70.36, and Rhode Island, $66.58. All figures exclude vendor payments for medical care.

[5] The weekly benefit rate from 1952 to 1955 was 32s. 6d. plus 21s. 6d. for an adult dependent. Average weekly earnings for men were 129s. 2d. in 1947, and 205s. 2d. in 1954. For a discussion of benefits in Britain in relation to earnings and prices, see "Facts about Pensions," *The Economist* [London], Dec. 4, 1954, p. 811.

[6] By 1953 the unemployment benefit was 57s. 6d. for a man and the same sum for a dependent wife. The average award wages (more representative of current wages than the basic wage) ranged around 185s. to 195s. a week in 1952. (See *Year Book of New Zealand, 1953*, Auckland, pp. 164ff., 811ff.)

ential between the guaranteed minimum and average earnings is very wide and if the average level of earnings is not very high.

Others confine the flat or the income-conditioned system to categories of persons, such as the aged, where there is a presumption that the majority of those eligible are in fact incapable of substantial work. Canada, for example, limits its flat universal old-age pension to persons 70 and over: for the aged between 65 and 69, the public income security system is based upon a test of need. This, too, is only a partial solution for it still leaves unresolved the problem of social security policy regarding the excluded groups.

The systems which base income security benefits very closely on the principles of private insurance experience the problem of the effect of security payments on initiative to a much lesser degree. Where benefits are wholly earned by the contributions of the insured, no question of the effect on initiative arises, except in the very broadest sense, in that a society in which everyone aimed to retire at 40 on some modest annuity would be unlikely to enjoy as high a standard of living as it would if everyone capable of work continued in active employment until 65. But this is not a problem peculiar to governmental systems. If all individuals succumbed to the "why not retire at 50" advertisements and purchased annuities from private insurance companies in order to retire early, the effect would be the same.

In any case, as we have seen, most communities have found it necessary to modify the strict actuarial relationship between what an individual contributes and what he gets as a social insurance benefit in order to use the system as a major instrument for dealing with economic insecurity. They then have to face squarely the problem of the proper relationship between benefits and normal earnings, and in this task little help can be derived from efforts to apply standard insurance concepts, such as "insurable interest" and the like.[7]

The typical social security system which bases benefits on some relationship to previous earnings takes account of this problem by limiting benefits to less than 100 per cent of such earnings. The resulting differential between benefits and earnings is expected to operate as bait to encourage people to prefer work and the higher income that can thus be secured.[8] Thus, American unemployment insurance laws aimed originally to provide benefits that were equal only to 50 per cent of wages. In fact,

[7] For a detailed analysis of the applicability of these concepts to a program with a social purpose, see Eveline M. Burns, *Private and Social Insurance and the Problem of Social Security*, Canadian Welfare Council, Ottawa, 1953, especially pp. 5–8.

[8] For a forceful attack upon the theory that some differential is necessary for this purpose, see Nat Weinberg, *Analysis of Some Arguments against the Guaranteed Annual Wage*, a paper presented at the Annual Meeting of the Industrial Relations Research Association, Washington, D.C., Dec. 28, 1954. For a statement of the view that "we

as we have seen, the average benefit has in general represented an even smaller proportion of average earnings. Workmen's compensation laws similarly express benefits as a fraction of prior wages, usually 66⅔ per cent. Even in OASI the total of all benefits paid to the insured worker and/or his dependents cannot exceed 80 per cent of his average monthly wage or self-employment income, although the application of this rule cannot reduce the benefit below a specified dollar sum.

But here too the central conflict between security and other social objectives arises. Where previous incomes were low or where the earner's family is large, a benefit that is deliberately pegged lower than the previous full-time wage will not meet the family's needs, and some supplementary public aid will have to be invoked. Where importance is attached to the use of an income security system to assure the community a flow of purchasing power as a buttress against downward spirals of economic activity, this benefit principle has real disadvantages, for the larger the differential between benefits and wages, the smaller is the impact of the program upon the economy as a whole. It has been estimated, for example, that because of the low percentage of wages which is compensated by unemployment insurance benefits (in addition to coverage limitations and the relatively short duration of benefits), the American unemployment insurance programs can be counted on to make up for no more than 20 to 25 per cent of the decline in national purchasing power due to lost wages in a mild recession, and even less in a long-continued depression.[9] Thus communities which attach importance to the use of public income security systems as "built-in stabilizers" will be reluctant to carry too far the principle of maintaining a sizable differential between benefit and wages. It is significant that in 1954 the Economic Report of the President required by the Employment Act of 1946 stressed the fact that "because the flow of security to the individual has been built primarily on welfare considerations, its contribution to the economic progress of the United States has not been adequately appreciated . . . unemployment payments can help to curb economic decline during an interval of time that allows other stabilizing measures to become effective," and consistently with this

must expect difficulties in getting some unemployed persons to accept work if the take-home pay for not working is attractive," see *The Economics of the Guaranteed Wage*, Report of the Committee on Economic Policy, U.S. Chamber of Commerce, Washington, D.C., 1953.

[9] *Social Security Programs and Economic Stability*, Social Security Administration, Division of Research and Statistics, Note 3, June 28, 1954 (mimeographed). It was estimated that during the 1949 to 1950 recession, benefits on state, railroad, and veterans' unemployment programs above those that would have been paid even at high levels of employment replaced about 25 per cent of the private wages and salaries lost over the period. From October, 1953 through March, 1954, the corresponding figure was 23 per cent.

view of unemployment insurance as a weapon in the fight for full employment the report urged an increase in the size of benefits.[10]

In fact, as we have seen, few countries have been willing to carry the principle of the benefit-wage differential to its logical conclusion. Many of them grant dependents' benefits, so that the differential is larger for the single worker than for the man with a family, a policy which some have defended on the ground that the married man is likely to have a greater sense of responsibility and be less vulnerable to the temptation to malinger. Most wage-related benefit systems provide either for the weighted benefit formula, which in fact gives the lower-paid worker a higher percentage of his previous wage than is received by earners in higher brackets, or have written minimum money benefits into the law. Unless, therefore, extreme care is taken to devise eligibility requirements that eliminate workers whose average earnings would, on the basis of the standard formula, yield a benefit less than this minimum, the recipient of the minimum will draw a benefit in excess of the standard percentage of his previous earnings. Since such eligibility conditions would eliminate the necessity for a minimum benefit, it is not surprising that this safeguard has not been adopted (although, as will be shown below, many systems aim to exclude workers with extremely low earnings for other reasons). In fact, therefore, the minimum does in some cases yield benefits very close to previous earnings.[11]

But this presents the curious result that the differential is likely to be smallest for precisely those groups who, as was shown above, are likely to be most vulnerable to the temptation to prefer benefit to work, namely young workers who have not yet established regular work habits, married women, and casual or intermittent workers. For it is these people whose earnings are likely to be relatively low and who are most likely to be affected by the minimum benefit in the benefit formula that is weighted in favor of the low earner.

There is clearly much difference of opinion as to the precise differential between benefits and earnings that will constitute adequate protection against alleged tendencies to malinger. The use of the differential in income security systems, as Professor Lester has pointed out, rests on the assumption that one can "draw up some kind of schedule of propensity for benefits in relation to the size of the differential between benefit and

10 *Economic Report of the President,* January, 1954, pp. 96–98.

11 In Michigan, in 1952, a low-paid worker earning up to $30 a week could have received a benefit (including dependents' allowances) of over 90 per cent of his previous wage and, even without dependents, of 65 per cent and over, whereas the recipient of the average weekly wage in the state at that time received a benefit equal to only 36 to 46.7 per cent of previous wages. For the situation in this and other states, see *Adequacy of Benefits under Unemployment Insurance,* U.S. Department of Labor, Bureau of Employment Security, 1952, Table B9.

normal pay. Such a relationship would mean that as the differential diminished or disappeared, the propensity, and hence the number of workers preferring a benefit status, would increase."[12] The difficulties of doing this are obvious, and it seems likely that differences of opinion as to the appropriate relationship between benefit and wages will persist. Meanwhile, the fact should not be overlooked that even today the differential in current social security programs varies greatly, not only as between high- and low-paid workers, but as between workers in different states and as between programs compensating for different risks (unemployment insurance and workmen's compensation, for example).[13] Exploration of the precise consequences of these varying differentials provides a fruitful field for research.

In any case, the use of a differential as a control on tendencies to malinger logically requires that benefits should be related not to wages but to take-home pay. For benefits, at least in the United States, are not subject to tax, whereas wages are. In addition, the individual who is working incurs costs (carfare, wear and tear, special clothing, and meals away from home) that are not borne by the unemployed worker on benefit unless he lives in a state which, as a condition of eligibility, requires him actively to seek work by canvassing various employers. Employers have laid great emphasis on take-home pay rather than wages as the basis of comparison, and some labor groups have also conceded the logic of the position.[14] The practical difficulties of applying the concept are, however, considerable, especially in view of the fact that taxes change and that they fall unevenly on families of different incomes and sizes. Hence even some standard differential to allow for the bite which income taxes take

[12] Richard A. Lester, "The Nature and Level of Income Security for a Free Society," in James E. Russell (ed.), *National Policies for Education, Health and Social Services,* Doubleday & Company, Inc., New York, 1955, p. 301.

[13] On the other hand, sometimes the same differential is provided for risks where the probabilities of malingering would seem to be very different; or even greater differentials exist where threats to initiative hardly exist. Speaking of workmen's compensation benefits it has been observed that "Although this [malingering] may be a real problem in the case of temporary and especially permanent-partial cases, the dead do not malinger, nor do the permanent-totally disabled, but benefits in these categories are even less generous than the others." (Herman Miles Somers and Anne Ramsay Somers, *Workmen's Compensation,* John Wiley & Sons, Inc., New York, 1954, p. 83.)

[14] For the employers' view, see "Statement of Employer Members of the Federal Advisory Council on Employment Security, January and March, 1954," reproduced in *Employment Security Administrative Financing Act,* Hearings before the Senate Committee on Finance, 83d Cong., 2d Sess., 1954, pp. 193–196. The Guaranteed Annual Wage plan as proposed by the United Automobile Workers (CIO) in 1954 also asked not for full wages but only for "amounts sufficient to insure take-home pay adequate to maintain the living standards which the worker and his family enjoyed while fully employed." (*Preparing a Guaranteed Employment Plan,* UAW–CIO Education Department, Publication 321, Detroit, Mich., 1954, p. 3.)

from wages (15 per cent has sometimes been suggested) would affect different workers differently.

CONTROLS THROUGH THE CONDITIONS ATTACHED TO RECEIPT OF BENEFIT

In view of the difficulties of trying to avoid encouragements to idleness through safeguards embodied in benefit formulas, the United States, like most other countries, has adopted a second and additional approach. This consists of attaching to the receipt of benefit conditions which are believed to minimize the threats to initiative.

Deterrent Conditions Attached to Security Payments

The earliest of these was to make the receipt of social security income so unpleasant that most people would do anything to avoid having to resort to it. This was the principle which underlay the old poor law and which characterized American public assistance until relatively recently. The recipient was treated in every way as a second-class citizen: in addition to undergoing a rigorous test of destitution, he often was denied various civic rights (such as the right to vote or hold public office), the fact of his destitution and public support was publicized, and frequently he could secure assistance only on condition that he entered a workhouse or other institution. (It is often forgotten how rare was outdoor relief prior to 1930.) By and large the administration reflected the view that relief recipients were *ipso facto* unworthy persons.

This policy no longer appears to commend itself to the American people as a general rule. The experience of the 1930s in particular, when so many millions of previously independent and self-supporting Americans were unable to earn through no fault of their own, challenged the view that all relief recipients were unwilling to support themselves and should be treated accordingly. Several of the requirements written into the Social Security Act in 1935 as a condition for the receipt by the state of Federal assistance grants aimed to make assistance less deterrent in character (e.g., the requirement that assistance must be given in cash not kind, that it be payable in the home, not in an institution, that the names of recipients and the amounts of their grants be kept confidential, and that the applicant be given the right of appeal). In consequence, many of the more deterrent features of the old poor law are no longer found in modern public assistance.

Yet here too there are still differences of opinion, and one of the current issues in public assistance centers around the question of whether or not the names of public-assistance recipients should be made public. In 1951 a rider attached to the Revenue Act permitted states to continue to qualify for Federal aid even if they allowed public access to records of names of recipients and amounts and dates of payments, provided they prohibited the use of any such lists or names for commercial or political purposes.[15] As against the savings due to elimination from the rolls of some who would be discouraged from drawing relief improperly by the publication of names must be set the humiliation of those who are genuinely in need and the feasibility of establishing controls over commercial or political misuse of the relief rolls.[16]

Nor must it be forgotten that while the conditions attached to the receipt of the federally aided categories of assistance (old age, dependent children, the blind, and the totally disabled) have been relaxed in favor of the recipient, the same is by no means true of the non-federally aided assistance program (general assistance or relief). In many sections of the United States treatment of the relief recipient still reflects an attitude that assumes that all persons seeking such aid are suspicious, if not unworthy, characters or at best that their need for public aid is largely their own fault.

Use of the Test of Need

In any case, public assistance continues to embody one condition which is generally regarded as being "deterrent," namely the requirement to undergo a test of need and to be dependent on the discretion of an administrator for decisions as to eligibility and amount of payment. This control relies for its effectiveness on the assumption that to most independent and self-reliant persons the procedures accompanying the application of a needs test will be regarded as so humiliating that every effort will be made to avoid seeking this type of public aid. It is, indeed, this feature which, from the point of view of the potential beneficiary, so sharply distinguishes public assistance from the other three types of social security benefit that have been discussed.

Many people, however, believe that the test of need is itself a deterrent to initiative. If, it is held, the frugal worker who has saved against a rainy day finds that when his private income ceases, he must exhaust all his savings before becoming eligible for public aid and is then treated no differently from his shiftless neighbor who took no thought for the morrow, the inducement to save is thereby weakened. It is not therefore

[15] For the extent to which states have availed themselves of this permission, see *Social Security Bulletin*, January, 1954, pp. 9–10.

[16] For a discussion of the issues involved, see Howard S. Friend, "FSA versus Indiana: The Secrecy Issue," *American Economic Security*, September–October, 1951; "Voluntary Agency Speaks on Current Welfare Issues," *American Economic Security*, January–February, 1952; Arthur J. Altmeyer, "Social Welfare Today," *Social Security Bulletin*, April, 1952; and Hilda C. M. Arndt, "An Appraisal of What Critics Say about Public Assistance," *Social Service Review*, December, 1952, especially pp. 470–473.

surprising that, in partial recognition of this fact, most income security systems which apply a test of need allow a beneficiary to retain a certain proportion of his assets. Thus most American public assistance systems define need in such a way as to allow applicants to retain a small capital sum or certain kinds of property. Often recipients may continue to own and occupy a house or homestead, though in this case the state often takes a lien on the property or claims the right to reimbursement from its sale after the recipient's death. Sometimes these so-called disregarded or exempt items are very large indeed.[17] Most laws permit the applicant to retain certain specified kinds and amounts of personal property, normally of an amount deemed sufficient to cover the cost of emergencies, last illness, and burial. While $300 is the most usual figure, in some states this personal allowance is as high as $1,000.[18]

In Great Britain, concern about the adverse effect of a needs test upon individual initiative, coupled with a strong emotional attitude toward means tests as such, has led to the adoption of a long list of disregarded items in defining "need" when determining eligibility for National Assistance. In addition to very substantial property exemptions (both general and of such specific kinds as war bonds) the applicant is permitted to retain the first so many shillings of friendly society benefit or workmen's compensation payments, and benefits for war injuries.

It is evident that these statutory liberalizations of the concept of "need," while serving to offset detrimental effects upon the individual's willingness to save, also have the effect of greatly weakening the use of the needs or means test as a deterrent to any propensity to prefer publicly provided income to independent self-support. For the more precisely defined in legislation and the more generous the allowances, the less offensive will be the test to the average applicant.

The extent to which the test of need can be utilized as a deterrent in democratic societies in which the mass of low-income receivers constitute the majority of the voters is therefore not easy to forecast. For it must not be forgotten that it has been the urgency of the desire for a predictable and nondiscretionary income guarantee free of the requirement to undergo a test of need that accounts for the increasing pressure to substitute some other social security system for public assistance.

[17] In North Dakota and Oklahoma, old-age assistance recipients have been permitted to own real property up to an assessed valuation of $7,500 and over, while in California, where the limit is $3,500 less encumbrances, the generous allowance for the latter and the great difference between assessed and market valuation mean that an applicant could possess very considerable resources and still remain eligible.

[18] For an excellent account of the relevant provisions in American states in 1953 to 1954 and their detailed operation in California, see Floyd Bond and Associates, *Our Needy Aged: A California Study of a National Problem*, Henry Holt and Company, Inc., New York, 1954, chaps. V, VI.

Thus the Senate Finance Committee in reporting on the Social Security Amendments of 1950 stated:

> We consider the assistance method to have serious disadvantages as a long-run approach to the nation's social security problem. We believe that improvement of the American Social Security System should be in the direction of preventing dependency before it occurs and of providing more effective income protection free from the humiliation of a test of need.[19]

Although these other systems are thus debarred by their very nature from utilizing the control of the test of need and the discretionary payment, their eligibility conditions also reflect an effort to minimize the adverse effects of income guarantees on the economic incentive of the beneficiary.

Restriction of the Program to High-income Receivers

Some social insurance laws, especially those stressing the adequacy of the benefit payment, aim to minimize the adverse effects of high benefits upon the desire to work by restricting eligibility therefor to persons with earnings in excess of a certain level. This can be achieved either by excluding from coverage those earning less than a certain sum or by making a certain minimum amount of credited earnings (or contributions based on earnings) a condition of eligibility. To the extent that very low earners are thereby excluded, the possibility of paying benefits of a reasonably high level and still maintaining a substantial differential between benefits and wages is enhanced. But there are obvious limits to the use of this safeguard. Carried very far, it would exclude the very people most in need of social security income. And in fact, the actual limits found in OASI are extremely low and quite unrealistic in terms of current wage levels. The minimum earnings required for coverage for self-employed persons is only $400 a year, while a quarter of coverage (the vital element in the formula governing eligibility for all employed persons) is defined as a quarter in which $50 or more has been earned.[20]

Tests of Past Attachment to the Labor Force

Most unemployment insurance laws include among their eligibility criteria an "earnings requirement," namely a minimum sum that must have been earned in the recent past if the claimant is to be entitled to any benefits at all. A major purpose of such requirements is to restrict benefit

[19] *Social Security Act Amendments of 1950*, S. Rep. 1669, Calendar no. 1680, 81st Cong., 2d Sess., 1950, p. 2. A similar view was expressed in the House report. For a discussion of this aspect of social security systems, see Eveline M. Burns, *The American Social Security System*, Houghton Mifflin Company, Boston, 1951, chap. 2.

[20] The self-employed worker is automatically credited with four quarters of coverage as soon as he earns the minimum $400.

payments to persons whose past conduct creates a presumption that they are normally members of the labor market, a fact which has two consequences. First, it defines the group for whom there is a real security problem justifying public action: if a worker is normally dependent on earnings, then the consequences to him of a stoppage of earnings are serious. It can hardly be argued, for example, that a worker earning less than $100 or even $400 in a previous year was being wholly or mainly supported by his earnings. His problem, if calling for social action at all, is not one created by the short-term unemployment for which unemployment insurance is an available remedy but something different, calling for other types of support and remedial action. Second, and of more immediate concern in this chapter, the earnings requirement offers some guarantee that the worker is normally a self-reliant, self-supporting individual, whose economic incentive is likely to withstand any temptation to prefer idleness if benefits are available.

But here too the competing pulls of the desire to solve the problem of individual economic insecurity and the desire to protect the economic interests of the community as a whole are evident. The higher the mini- mum is placed, the fewer will be the number of workers whose income security problem is solved by the unemployment insurance system. It is therefore not surprising that most American unemployment insurance systems place the minimum relatively low in relation to average earnings and that the number of workers excluded by this device is correspondingly small. By 1954, the minimum required for any benefit ranged from $150 a year or less in five states to $400 or more in eight states. In only one state was it as high as $600.[21]

Sometimes, too, the normally steady worker who through no fault of his own suffers unemployment in his base year may be debarred from benefits in the following year when, after having again obtained work, he is temporarily laid off, because he is unable to meet the earnings requirement. Moreover, earnings requirements as a condition of eligibility favor the high-level wage earner and penalize the worker whose normal earnings are low. For wherever the money minimum earnings are pegged, it is obviously easier for the high-paid worker to satisfy them by relatively short periods of employment. This unfairness may be in some degree modi- fied by requiring earnings in more than one calendar quarter [22] (as is now

[21] For the development of the earnings requirement in American unemployment in- surance laws and the requirements in the individual states in 1952, see *Adequacy of Benefits under Unemployment Insurance*, pp. 6–7 and Table A1. See also *Comparison of State Unemployment Insurance Laws as of August, 1954*, U.S. Department of Labor, Bureau of Employment Security, 1954, pp. 48–53.

[22] This can be achieved either specifically or, more usually, by eligibility formulas which require a worker to have earned at least thirty times his benefit rate. Since the benefit rate is supposed to equal 50 per cent of the weekly wage, this requirement could not be satisfied by a worker who worked only during one quarter.

done in most American unemployment insurance laws), but as no law calls for earnings in more than two quarters, the relative advantage of the high-paid worker employed for a short period remains.

Furthermore, unless provision is made for adjustment of the minimum in accordance with changes in the level of money wages, the effectiveness of this device as a technique for eliminating from benefit status those who are not normally regular members of the labor market may be only short-lived.

It is evident that the requirement to have earned a minimum money sum during some specified previous period can be only a rough-and-ready test of past attachment to the labor market and is definitely inferior to a test that runs in terms of period of employment. Such an eligibility criterion is embodied in the British national insurance system and is found in a few American unemployment insurance systems. But the use of this test brings its own problems. How much work constitutes a week of employment? American laws use the test of minimum earnings ($8 or $12, or wages of 16 per cent of average wages). How many weeks of work indicate a serious attachment to the labor market? And the administration of such a criterion, which calls for knowledge of time worked in addition to data on wages for benefit-determination purposes, makes greater demands on employers for record keeping and reporting than most American administrators are apparently prepared to contemplate.

Limitation of Benefit Duration

A fifth control on possible adverse effects of income guarantees on initiative is the policy of limiting the duration of benefit payment. This device is used in unemployment insurance, where benefits are usually paid only for twenty, or increasingly, twenty-six weeks, in a benefit year.[23] In terms of the problem here under discussion, this device has two advantages. First, it lessens any inducement to prefer benefit status to employment because the worker knows that after a brief time, benefit will stop, and the odds in favor of holding on to an established job will be greater. Second, it sets a limit to the risk run by society as a whole. Whatever may be the adverse effects of benefit availability on the will to work, they cannot last for more than twenty or twenty-six weeks.

Here too, however, this device cannot be too rigidly used. In periods of recession a large number of workers may "exhaust benefit," and some other provision has to be made for the income needs of such unemployed. There are, however, several other considerations which bear upon decisions regarding the duration of unemployment insurance benefit, and these will be discussed in Chapter 7. In any case, the device of limiting

---

[23] For duration periods in American unemployment insurance laws, see *Adequacy of Benefits under Unemployment Insurance*, pp. 22–24 and Tables C2–C5; and *Comparison of State Unemployment Insurance Laws as of August, 1954*, pp. 67–72.

benefit duration is not appropriate or needed for nondiscretionary, non-deterrent income security programs dealing with long-period risks, such as old age or permanent disability.

Administrative Controls on Malingering

All public income security systems dealing with presumably employable persons pay great attention to tests of the involuntary character of the claimant's alleged inability to earn.[24]

The Nature of the Controls. The typical unemployment insurance system does this in two ways. First the law lays down certain positive conditions which every applicant must satisfy if his claim is to be valid: he must be able to work and available for work. Thus, claimants have to register periodically at an employment office and, so to say, run the risk of being offered a job. Furthermore, it is not easy for an employed worker to attend the office at the required intervals, so this requirement acts also as an obstacle to those who might seek to draw benefits while still holding a job. Second, the law disqualifies workers whose unemployment is due to certain specified causes, the most usual being voluntarily leaving suitable work, discharge for misconduct, and refusal of suitable work. In addition, most laws disqualify a worker whose unemployment is the consequence of a labor dispute in the outcome of which he has an interest. Almost all states disqualify workers for fraudulent misrepresentation.

It will be immediately apparent that the application of such provisions calls for administrative interpretation and discretion and that the effectiveness of these controls will in large measure depend upon the way in which the law is administered. For unlike almost all other controls utilized by the non-needs-test systems, this type does not involve the application of objective criteria (such as amount of earnings) which can be defined with precision in the law. And as will be abundantly clear from the examples given in the following pages, differing interpretations will have widely different social and economic consequences and can operate to raise or depress employment standards.

It is true that efforts have been made by both the Federal government

---

[24] In this chapter the issues are discussed solely in relation to the unemployment risk. Because the feasibility of developing appropriate administrative controls is a crucial issue in proposals to extend government action in the field of disability, they are treated in Part Two, Chap. 7. For a detailed account of the eligibility and disqualification provisions of the various state laws, see *Comparison of State Unemployment Insurance Laws as of August, 1954,* chap. IV; *Unemployment Insurance Legislative Policy: Benefits, Eligibility,* U.S. Department of Labor, Bureau of Employment Security, 1953; *Majority and Minority Reports of the Committee on Benefit Disqualifications,* Federal Advisory Council on Employment Security, October, 1953; "State Unemployment Insurance Legislation, 1953," *Social Security Bulletin,* December, 1953, pp. 19–20. See also: Lee G. Williams, "Eligibility for Benefits," in *A Symposium on Unemployment Insurance, Vanderbilt Law Review,* February, 1955, pp. 286–306.

and the states to limit the realm of administrative discretion in the interpretation of the suitable-work clause by writing certain specific criteria into unemployment insurance laws. The Federal act, for example, requires the states to include in their laws a provision that work is not suitable if (1) the job is available only because of a strike, lockout, or other labor dispute, (2) if the wages, hours, or other conditions of work are substantially less favorable to the claimant than those prevailing for similar work in the locality, (3) if as a condition of being employed the individual would be required to join a company union or to resign from or refrain from joining any bona fide labor organization. And most states add other statutory criteria. These include a claimant's physical fitness for the work, his prior training and experience, his prior earnings, the length of his unemployment, his prospects for obtaining work at his highest skill, his prospects for obtaining local work, and the distance from his residence of the available work.

Yet many of these phrases are necessarily vague: What is "substantially less favorable"? What is "local work"? Some of the criteria are in practice far from easy to apply. (How determine a man's prospects for obtaining work at his highest skill or even the prevailing wage for specific types of work where conditions of employment are not standardized? What is the prior training and experience of a domestic worker who shifted for several years to welding in an aircraft factory?) And many of them, in their application to the individual case, call for the exercise of a high degree of administrative discretion. (How greatly can the wages offered by an available job depart from a man's prior earnings and still be regarded as suitable? How great a distance from a worker's residence renders a job unsuitable? What length of unemployment justifies denial of benefit to a man refusing a job that he regards as unsuitable in view of his prior training and experience?)

Similar difficulties are experienced in administering the disqualification for voluntarily leaving suitable work, statistically one of the most important causes of disqualification. Is every kind of voluntary quit to disqualify a worker or only voluntary leaving without good cause? Is good cause to be limited to causes connected with the work or attributable to the employer, or should it include good personal cause, such as obtaining a better job, illness of the claimant or in his family, or, in the case of a normally employed married woman, removal to some other area because her husband's new job is there? Furthermore, how much of a worker's unemployment subsequent to a voluntary quit should be attributed to this cause and how much to general economic conditions? If a worker voluntarily left suitable work but thereafter complied with all official requirements and vigorously but unsuccessfully sought new work, should he be denied benefit for the entire period of his unemployment or only for a limited period following the disqualifying act, on the theory that thereafter his un-employment was due to general lack of work? What about the worker who, in good faith, leaves one job for a better one, only to find that the new job fails to materialize or is unexpectedly terminated shortly after acceptance? Is he still eligible for benefits?

The disqualification for discharge for misconduct also presents legis-lators and administrators with perplexing problems. Should the miscon-duct be limited to misconduct connected with the work, or include the misconduct of claimants off the job? Where there are differences of opinion between a worker and his employer, the former claiming that his severance was for a voluntary quit for good cause, the latter that it was a discharge for misconduct, the agency is involved in difficult determinations of fact.[24a]

It should be noted too that major policy issues are raised in regard to the penalty to be imposed for specific types of disqualifying behavior. Here, the state laws reflect widely different points of view. Some set out in the law the precise period for which benefit will be denied. Others leave considerable discretion (usually within statutory limits) to the adminis-trator. Some deny benefits only for a fixed period, often six weeks im-mediately following the disqualifying act, but others deny benefit for the entire period of ensuing unemployment however long it lasts. This of course means that the severity of the penalty becomes a matter of chance: the worker who is reemployed within a week of disqualification suffers little or no penalty; the man whose unemployment is long is severely pe-nalized.

Under both these types of penalty, however, the total number of weeks of benefit to which a worker is entitled in any benefit year is unaffected. The penalty is in principle a postponement of benefit payments, and even the worker denied benefit for the duration of his unemployment following a disqualifying act may secure work in time to again qualify in the same benefit year should he again become unemployed. But some laws impose more severe penalties and reduce total benefit rights (usually by the num-ber of weeks of disqualification). Thus a worker normally entitled to twenty weeks of benefit but disqualified for a six-week period would thereafter be entitled only to fourteen weeks of benefit however long he was unemployed in that benefit year. Some states go so far as to cancel all benefit rights in connection with one or more disqualifying acts.

The Consequences of the Controls. The specific provisions written into law and the administrative practices and policies will in the last resort

[24a] For an analysis of the problems of interpreting the various disqualification pro-visions, see Paul H. Sanders, "Disqualification for Unemployment Insurance," and Jerre S. Williams, "The Labor Dispute Disqualification—A Primer and Some Problems," *Vanderbilt Law Review*, February, 1955, pp. 307–375.

reflect contemporary beliefs as to the precise consequences of any given provision and the relative weight that is attached by the community to a variety of fundamental considerations. Among these are the degree of concern about malingering or abuse; the value placed upon worker mobility; the intensity of the desire to use unemployment insurance as a major instrument for assuring income security; the value placed on family obligations and attachments; and the prevailing attitude toward costs.

THE EFFECT UPON MALINGERING AND ABUSE. The eligibility conditions relating to ability to, and availability for, work, together with the disqualification provisions, are undoubtedly important devices for excluding from benefits those who are not involuntarily unemployed. During the period 1947 to 1952, total disqualifications under American state laws ranged from about 1 million to 1.33 million per calendar year, or from 12.0 to 19.4 per 1,000 claimant contacts.[25] Moreover, the extent to which these provisions protected the system from individuals who were unable to work or who had no intention of working is probably understated by these figures, since knowledge of the existence of these tests and controls undoubtedly deterred some such workers from applying for benefits in the first instance. But despite these substantial results, without further evidence it is impossible to say whether or not these administrative controls fully or adequately served the purpose of restricting benefits to persons with a continuing attachment to the labor market. On the one hand, some observers hold that despite these controls benefits are still paid to workers who are not seriously interested in obtaining work and point to the rapidity with which some workers appear to secure work after using up their benefits or to the presence on benefit rolls of some persons clearly on the way out of the labor market (e.g., certain married women) in support of their contention. On the other hand, the increasingly severe disqualifications which most states have imposed in recent years have given rise to the charge that, if anything, the controls are too effective and, in the effort to keep out a few malingerers, result in denying benefit to many genuinely unemployed workers.

Some assert that the requirement that the worker should report periodically at an employment office is an inadequate control, especially when reporting is only at weekly or even biweekly intervals, for it in effect places the onus of finding work on the employment office. Accordingly, it has been suggested, and some states have required, that claimants should demonstrate that they have made efforts on their own behalf. Obviously, however, such requirements cannot reasonably be laid on all claimants: in a one-industry town, or for a worker with a highly specialized type of skill, or in the case of a serious general depression, the requirement that the applicant canvass many employers leads only to a sense of demoralizing

25 Defined as new spells of unemployment plus continued claims.

futility for the worker and unnecessary irritation and perhaps embarrassment for employers.[26] Hence those who oppose this requirement hold that the test of availability for work and willingness to work should take into consideration such facts as business conditions, the coverage and efficiency of the employment service, the nature of the hiring methods in the claimant's normal industry, and his individual circumstances. It has, indeed, become increasingly evident that if major reliance is to be placed on reporting at an employment office as a test of genuineness of unemployment, more attention must be paid to the employment of highly skilled and trained employment service interviewers, who, where no suitable jobs are immediately available, have in effect to evaluate the claimant's state of mind. It is clear, too, that the effectiveness of this test depends on the efficiency of the employment service itself in locating suitable job openings.

Furthermore, it should be noted that none of these controls is very effective in the case of the worker who, in a sense, demonstrates too much initiative, albeit of the wrong kind. This is the worker who succeeds in drawing benefits although he is still working. If his employer is willing to connive, or if his job is on a part-time basis, he may still be able to work and yet report at the employment office as required.

THE EFFECT UPON WORKER MOBILITY. Some types of disqualification provision, or the way in which others have been administered and applied, may adversely affect mobility and initiative. An interpretation which limits good cause for leaving work to causes attributable to the employer will tend to discourage workers from trying to better their economic position, by exposing them to the risk of disqualification for benefit if the new job proves to be of short duration. The same happens if the period of disqualification is long or if it lasts for the whole period of unemployment following the disqualifying act. These considerations are important in a country that attaches a high and perhaps even excessive [27] value to mobility in general, or at times when relocation of industry (and therefore of workers) is a vital national interest.

But mobility has occupational as well as geographical aspects, and the provisions of unemployment insurance laws, and notably the suitable-work clause, affect this type of mobility also. It is clearly to the economic inter-

[26] For an intensive study of the effects of "the genuinely seeking work clause" in Great Britain, see *Report of the Committee on Procedure and Evidence for the Determination of Claims for Unemployment Insurance Benefit*, H. M. Stationery Office, London, Cmd. 3415, 1929; and Eveline M. Burns, *British Unemployment Programs, 1920–38*, Social Science Research Council, Washington, D.C., 1941, pp. 91–95 and chap. IV.

[27] There seems to be some tendency to underestimate not only the human costs of high mobility (disruption of social contacts, interference with the education of children, loosening of civic attachments, and the like) but also the economic costs attributable to the need for additional physical facilities, schools, hospitals, houses, etc., in the area of in-migration.

est of the community as a whole that, once it is clear that there is no further demand for a man's services in some given occupation, he should as speedily as possible move to some other where his services are needed. When the suitable-work clause is liberally interpreted, unemployment insurance benefits have the effect of enabling the worker to hold out against this adjustment, thereby hindering desired interoccupational mobility. If workers are permitted to be highly selective about the work that is "suitable" for them, their period of unemployment may be unduly prolonged, for no jobs of the type and pay desired by the worker may in fact exist.

But it is not always easy or even possible to know at the time a worker loses his job whether his special kind of skill or occupation is likely to be no longer in demand. It may be that industry as a whole is suffering a recession. So long as it is assumed that sooner or later the general employment situation will improve, there may be little to be gained by forcing unemployed workers to take other kinds of jobs than those to which they were accustomed. It may be that the worker's firm is undergoing a periodic but relatively brief shutdown. Many laid-off workers are given to understand by their employers that they will be recalled as soon as operations are resumed. If benefits are denied workers for refusing to take other jobs during this period, they may drift away from their previous attachment to the original company. In any case, new employers, concerned about labor turnover, may not wish to hire such persons, fearing they will return to their old employers as soon as the plant reopens. Many employers favor unemployment insurance precisely for the reason that it keeps their skilled workers available for employment as soon as demand revives, instead of encouraging them to drift to other places or other types of occupation. This of course suggests a further problem: absolute mobility in and of itself is not necessarily a positive economic good, and one of the issues that is raised by the disqualification provisions is precisely how much and what kind of mobility is desired.

Since unemployment insurance operates to increase a worker's reservation price, it may also tend to check short-term mobility by discouraging workers, especially the higher-paid, from accepting certain kinds of low-paid temporary jobs during their period of unemployment. Some would argue that this is not necessarily an economic disadvantage. As one writer has put it,

> To the extent that benefit levels encourage workers to maintain either a higher reservation price or a more restricted classification of acceptable jobs, the supply of labor available for certain kinds of work may be curtailed. Much, of course, depends on the severity with which the agency interprets and applies the "suitable work" provision. Insofar as the benefit level does restrict the available labor supply for low-paying or low-grade

work, it is a force exerting pressure for improvement in the wages, work conditions, or promotion prospects on such jobs. . . .

From a social viewpoint, a good argument can be made for pressure to improve the long-run attractiveness of jobs, where that possibility exists. Of course, for workers only temporarily in the labor market, a temporary type of work may be suitable. Even so, one may be able to make a valid case for mild upward pressure on the lowest paying jobs in manufacturing on the same economic grounds as those used to support a legal minimum wage that directly affects only a small fraction of the work force.[28]

THE EFFECT UPON INCOME-MAINTENANCE OBJECTIVES. One of the less desirable consequences of the disqualification provisions, as applied in many states, is that they result in denying benefits to people who, by any common-sense standard, would be regarded as members of the labor market and lacking income because involuntarily unemployed. Thus whereas most states disqualify a worker only in respect of separations from his most recent work, others, expressly or by interpretation, require the agency to review the work history of each claimant during his base period and to disqualify him if he committed some disqualifying act within that period, even if his most recent employer laid him off for lack of work. This can result in denying benefit to a worker whose current unemployment is solely due to being laid off by his employer.

Similarly, longer periods of disqualification or those which run for the duration of unemployment following the disqualifying act will lead to denial of benefit rights to many genuinely unemployed workers who actively seek, and would accept, suitable work if available, shortly after their disqualifying act was committed. In periods of heavy unemployment such workers may never draw any benefits even though they are demonstrably willing to work. For this reason some have held that the disqualification period should be a uniform limited period, fixed by statute in accordance with the average length of time ordinarily required for an employable worker to find work in a normal labor market.[29] Thereafter, it is argued, the joblessness of the worker should be attributable not to his disqualifying act but to the condition of the labor market and compensated as such.

In an effort to limit the range of official discretion in applying the test of availability for work, some states have by statute declared that certain types of worker are by definition "nonavailable." These have included students, pregnant women, and women who leave work to marry. But not all persons in these categories are in fact unavailable for work, and such an all-inclusive definition results in denial of benefit to some genuinely unemployed persons and hence is a restriction of the effectiveness of unemployment insurance as an income security measure.

[28] Lester, *op. cit.*, p. 305.
[29] Cf. *Unemployment Insurance Legislative Policy: Benefits, Eligibility*, p. 61.

Again, provisions on "suitable work" found in a few state laws, such as that "no work is unsuitable because of distance if it is in substantially the same locality as the claimant's last regular employment," result in denial of benefit to some genuinely unemployed and available workers. Such a provision would disqualify an unemployed woman worker who left one job and locality because her husband's job took him elsewhere and refused a job offered by her ex-employer in her old district. She would be disqualified even though genuinely available for types of work found in the new locality.

THE EFFECT UPON PERSONAL FREEDOMS. In a very broad sense, it is of course true that, as compared with the time when unemployment insurance systems did not exist, an unemployed worker today has greater freedom than before. For however stringent the eligibility requirements and however harsh the disqualification provisions, the worker has at least a choice he did not have before unemployment insurance was enacted, namely to comply with the legal and administrative requirements and thereby draw benefits or not to comply and receive no benefits. Yet this does not deny the fact that the personal circumstances of some workers may be such that it is practically impossible for them to meet the requirements or that they can do so only at the expense of what many would regard as an undue interference with their personal lives.

Thus, systems which contain in the law a requirement that a claimant to be eligible must be available for work "in a locality where his base period wages were earned or in a locality where similar work is available," while apparently a reasonable control on, for example, the highly skilled worker who attempts to "take a holiday on benefit" by moving temporarily to some area where his kind of skill is known not to be in demand, may also penalize workers whose personal circumstances dictate a change of locality. For such a definition of availability could lead to disqualification of, for example, an auto worker who has to move for reasons of family health to another area where, although there is no automobile industry, he may be genuinely available for various types of work performed there by other manufacturing plants. Or he may, under another type of provision, find himself disqualified for "voluntarily leaving" his last employer. The case of the working married woman worker who follows her husband to a new locality has already been referred to.

In these instances there is a clear conflict between two social values: the importance attached to the individual making his maximum contribution to his own support and the high value attached to family cohesion. Many workers are caught in this dilemma, and societies differ in the extent to which they will penalize, by denying benefit, the worker who gives priority to the claims of the family.

THE EFFECT UPON COSTS. The relationships between disqualification pro-

visions and the over-all costs of the program are clear: unless the administrative costs of their application are extremely high, the more severe the
disqualification provisions, the lower will be the over-all costs of the program. In particular, use of the disqualification provisions to limit payments to cases where the unemployment was the employer's fault will
greatly cut down costs by reducing the number of benefit payments.

This aspect of disqualifications has special significance in the United
States, where in all except two states the costs of unemployment insurance
are carried solely by employers and where, because of experience-rating
arrangements, each individual employer has an interest in seeing that as
few benefits as possible are charged against his account.[30] In these circumstances it is perhaps inevitable that employers should be interested in
seeing to it that costs are kept to a minimum by stringent disqualification
provisions and that they can present a good theoretical case for the position that compensable unemployment thus financed should be limited to
unemployment directly attributable to the employer. The employers'
point of view has been well stated by an employer member of the Federal
Advisory Council on Employment Security:

> We regard the unemployment compensation program as a measure to
> impose on the individual employer primarily and, secondarily, on employers
> in general, the responsibility to provide limited support for workers who
> become unemployed because their employers fail to provide work. Only on
> the basis of this public policy can we account for the decision to finance
> the program entirely out of employer contributions based on payrolls.
>
> If these laws had been intended to compensate for all types of unemploy-
> ment—including that caused by personal reasons or for no good reason at
> all—there would have been no justification for singling out employers to pay
> for the program or for selecting payrolls as the tax base.
>
> An individual employer has not the remotest responsibility for unemploy-
> ment which results from acts of misconduct or unjustified quitting by his
> employees. Nor do employers in general have a special responsibility in
> such cases. If there be a social obligation, it should be a burden on the
> general public and not on any special class.[31]

This approach to unemployment insurance inevitably leads to efforts to
prevent the employers' accounts (which greatly influence the rate of tax
payable by the individual employer or employers as a group) from being
debited with the cost of benefits paid to their ex-employees. It explains the
pressure for long periods of disqualification and for provisions which
cancel all benefit rights as a result of voluntary quitting, discharge for

[30] For more detailed discussion of experience-rating formulas and their consequences,
see Chap. 9.

[31] Minority report by George A. Jacoby on *Unemployment Compensation Disqualifications,* U.S. Department of Labor, Federal Advisory Council on Employment Security,
Committee on Disqualifications, Oct. 22, 1953.

misconduct, or refusal of suitable work.[32] As we have seen, however, such provisions can seriously impair the income-maintenance objectives of the program.

The Lack of Precise Information. The problem of societies which rely heavily on economic incentive to call forth productive efforts but which also desire to assure some basic economic security to all their members is thus a difficult one, even though the risk of demoralization is probably a good deal less than some opponents of social security measures often assert. No wholly effective control has as yet been devised. Those which operate through the benefit formulas are of only limited applicability if income-maintenance objectives are to be achieved, because the wider the gap between earnings and benefit, the smaller is the contribution to family security, and because the low level of earnings of many workers precludes the adoption of a very wide gap. The somewhat more flexible and effective controls through the conditions attached to receipt of benefits introduce an element of discretion into the program, and their formulation and application call for a high degree of awareness of all their economic and social effects. Above all, as will have been evident from the preceding pages, it is often necessary, if rational decisions are to be made, to make difficult choices between alternatives (e.g., to maintain a certain degree of labor mobility even if it results in some malingering or to keep abuse to a minimum even if it results in some check to mobility or denial of benefits to genuinely unemployed workers). It is therefore particularly unfortunate that so little is known about the precise effect of these different controls and about the relative numbers of people who are affected one way or another. Relatively little research of a kind that would assist in policy determination has been carried out. Furthermore, such research must be continuous, for the effect of the administrative controls changes with changes in the prevailing social and economic conditions and notably with fluctuations in the general level of employment. Yet only a brief survey of the implications of these controls reveals how widespread are their economic and social consequences. It is not therefore surprising that the problem of disqualifications and administrative controls remains one of the most hotly disputed issues in the field of income security or that, in the absence of precise measures, it is one so highly tinged with emotion.

[32] Or the provision for cancellation of benefit rights based on employment with the employer in connection with whom the disqualifying act occurred, in the case of states which charge each base-period employer with a share of the costs of a worker's benefits when a worker had two or more employers in his base period. For an illustration of the lengths to which some would carry these restrictive provisions, see the bill introduced by Senator Teacher in the Michigan Legislature, 1954, reproduced in *Unemployment Insurance,* Hearings before the House Committee on Ways and Means, 83d Cong., 2d Sess., June, 1954, pp. 278–280.

CHAPTER 5

The Bearing of Social Security Programs on the Family System

A SECOND major concern of communities which establish public social security systems has been the effect of these arrangements on the functioning and cohesion of the family as such. In principle, the family has been expected to support its own members. Over the years, the community has increasingly taken over some of this responsibility. Thus it is no longer assumed that the family can and will educate its younger members, at least through high school age, and most American states provide free college education also.

The care and support of those members of the family who are insane or feeble-minded has long been accepted by the public authorities, and in most states this is also true of those suffering from tuberculosis and certain other diseases. With the development and liberalization of social security programs, the economic responsibilities of the family have again been narrowed, and fears have been expressed that these measures will seriously weaken the sense of family responsibility and may even destroy the cohesion of one of society's most important institutions. Hence it is not surprising that some of the contemporary issues in public income security policy involve decisions as to the economic role of the family and that the provisions as to benefits and the conditions governing their receipt reflect this concern.

The issues at stake can be most clearly seen by a consideration of three current problem areas: the operation of the principle of relatives' responsibility in public assistance laws, the problem of the broken family in connection with the ADC program, and proposals for the adoption of a system of children's allowances.

THE PRINCIPLE OF RELATIVES' RESPONSIBILITY IN PUBLIC ASSISTANCE

The old poor law adopted a firm attitude toward relatives' responsibility: public aid was not given if there were relatives who were capable of supporting the needy family members, and the span of the family for this purpose was very wide. Modern public assistance has greatly narrowed this concept of the family: in many American states today, as elsewhere, brothers and sisters, uncles, aunts, cousins, and grandchildren are not typically expected to contribute to the support of needy relatives. But the laws still generally reflect the view that adult children should be responsible for the support of their parents and that parents should be responsible for minor children.[1] In keeping with this position many old-age assistance programs include financial support from children among the resources available to an applicant, which must be deducted from his needs in determining his eligibility or the amount of his payments. A few states go so far as to deny aid to an individual whose relatives have been found capable of supporting him, even if the children in fact refuse to accept the responsibility. Yet others claim the right to recover from the legally responsible relative the costs of assistance given to an aged person or to do so from any estate he may leave. In some cases the state may take a lien on the property of the OAA recipient, although usually he and his wife may be permitted to enjoy its use during their lifetime.[2]

This effort to enforce the principle of mutual family support raises very difficult problems in its practical application. The first of these concerns the action to be taken if relatives refuse to accept their responsibility. The denial of any aid to a needy aged person in the hope that rather than see him starve the delinquent relatives will carry out their legal obligations is an extremely drastic sanction and one which in general public opinion appears to condemn. The alternative is to resort to legal action. In some states an aged person, as a condition of eligibility, may be required to sue his relatives for support, or at least to cooperate with the administrative agency in doing so. But quite apart from the fact that many parents appear to be very reluctant to sue their children, and rather than do so may even prefer to eke out a miserable existence on whatever slender resources they can muster, legal action is a time-consuming process and one whose costs may largely offset the payments relatives are finally compelled to make. Furthermore, experience has shown that convictions are not easy to secure. Cases for prosecution have frequently to be approved by boards of supervisors or welfare committees who may be personally acquainted with the defaulting relatives; they must be

[1] In addition, a husband is liable for the support of his wife, and in some states the obligation is mutual. For an account of the situation in the different states, at the end of 1953, see *Summary of Basic Duties of Support Imposed by State Law,* Council of State Governments, Chicago, 1953, reprinted in *Analysis of the Social Security System,* pp. 308–316.

[2] For an account of the provisions in the various state laws, see Elizabeth Epler, "Old Age Assistance: Main Provisions on Children's Responsibility for Parents," *Social Security Bulletin,* April, 1944, pp. 3–12; and *Analysis of the Social Security System,* pp. 352–353, 434.

prepared and presented by a district attorney who is usually an elected official and therefore not anxious to offend influential personalities; and they are tried before judges who may or may not be in sympathy with the purposes of the relatives' responsibility requirements and who often tend to be more lenient with relatives than a strict interpretation of the law would require.[3]

Even if a relative complies with the law under pressure, the determination of how much he or she should be required to contribute presents problems of policy and of execution which have plagued administrators and judges for over a century. While the maximum would usually be set at the amount of the applicant's needs as determined by investigation, not all are able to put up this sum. The relative held liable must report income and, since most systems today vary the amount of the contribution according to the relative's needs and circumstances, he must also give a detailed account of his living arrangements and financial needs. In effect, therefore, relatives are submitted to a test of need, which is often strongly resented, even by those who are able to prove inability to contribute. Only about half of the states use formal income scales for determining the "base sums" to be allowed for the needs of the supporting relative and his family and the precise dollar contribution to be required if income is in excess of this amount.[4] Elsewhere the decision is a matter of agency policy or is even left to the individual caseworker. The determination of the "base sum" raises difficult issues. In some cases the standard has been that of the public assistance scale, and any income of children above this amount has been held to be available for support of the needy relative. The obvious undesirability of forcing an entire family down to this low standard of living and the deterrent effect upon initiative of so doing have led many legislators or administrators to adopt a higher standard. In fact, the standard of the City Worker's Family Budget as compiled by the Bureau of Labor Statistics appears to be very commonly used. Even then, allowances have to be made in the interests of equity for what a judge struggling with this same problem a hundred years ago referred to as "divers circumstances perpetually varying," [5] such as sickness, debts, and the like. While these

[3] For an account of the problems of administering and enforcing the relatives' responsibility requirement, see Epler, *op. cit.*; and Floyd Bond and Associates, *Our Needy Aged: A California Study of a National Problem*, Henry Holt and Company, Inc., New York, 1954, pp. 199–201, 256–259, 315–320. See also *Report of the Senate Interim Committee on Social Welfare*, part V, Sacramento, Calif., May, 1953; and *Minnesota's Aging Citizens*, Minnesota Commission on Aging, St. Paul, Minn., January, 1953.

[4] For an account of the methods used in 1952, see Elizabeth Epler, "Old Age Assistance: Determining the Extent of Children's Ability to Support," *Social Security Bulletin*, May, 1954.

[5] See opinion of Chief Justice Richardson of the Supreme Court of New Hampshire

administrative arrangements may go far toward securing greater equity of treatment of families in different circumstances, they have two serious disadvantages. First, they greatly extend the degree of official intervention and even control over the private lives of people who are not themselves applicants for public aid. Second, the more liberal they are, the fewer will be the individuals found liable to support needy parents, and the smaller will be the sums required of those held liable.[6]

There is little doubt that the relatives' responsibility requirement is one of the most controversial, and probably also the most unpopular, of the many eligibility requirements for public assistance. For differing reasons, it is disliked by applicants, by their children, and by many administrators and legal officials. But decisions to abolish or retain it involve the balancing of a number of considerations, regarding many of which far too little precise information is as yet available.

Obviously, much will depend upon the extent of the financial savings due to retention of the requirement. These may not be as great as is sometimes assumed, for a very large proportion of the old-age assistance recipients come from relatively low-income groups, where the ability of children to contribute to their parents' support is limited or non-existent. And against any contributions received must be set the costs of administration and enforcement, which are admittedly considerable. Nevertheless, the scattered evidence suggests that with vigorous enforcement some net savings may be obtained for the taxpayer in the form of denial of eligibility to some applicants or payment of less than full cost of maintenance to others whose relatives can contribute partial support.[7] And to these must be added an unknown amount of further savings due to the fact that knowledge of the existence of such a legal requirement undoubtedly causes some children, who would otherwise not do so, to give financial aid to their parents, thereby keeping down the numbers of applicants. Small as these savings may be, the taxpayers may think them worth while.

In favor of retention, too, are the arguments of those who see in enforcement of the legal requirement to support parents a necessary instru-

---

in 1827 when considering the question of whether a son should be charged with the support of his father. The full remarks of the judge could be quoted today with perfect relevance. (*Dover v. McMurphy*, 4 N.H. 158.)

[6] In California, for example, even in a county outstanding for the vigor with which it administered its relatives' responsibility requirement only 15 per cent of relatives were found to have some measure of legal liability according to the contribution scale in 1953. For the state as a whole in 1944 and in 1953, about 12 per cent of OAA recipients were receiving some aid from relatives, amounting in all to between 3 and 4 per cent of total OAA costs. (Bond and Associates, *op. cit.*, pp. 201, 258.)

[7] W. R. Brown, "Family Responsibility and Recovery Laws in Public Welfare Administration," *American Economic Security*, May–June, 1952.

ment for offsetting any tendency to a weakening of the sense of mutual family responsibility. The growth in old-age assistance rolls in certain states which have abolished the requirement is frequently cited in support of this view.[8] While not denying that, for reasons to be discussed below, the sense of family economic solidarity may be less strong than it once was, those who would abolish relatives' responsibility argue that, in fact, the practical administration of the requirement tends to penalize only the truthful and the more conscientious and that those legally liable relatives who are prepared to lie about their incomes, to take advantage of the many loopholes in the law, or to disregard inquiries or warning notices and await a prosecution that seldom eventuates can still evade their obligations in most communities. They point too to the fact that the typical state makes little or no effort to enforce support from relatives living outside the state, thereby discriminating between different children.

Even, however, were the requirement enforced more vigorously and in a more equitable manner, many would abandon it because they believe that enforcement of the obligation for financial support damages interpersonal family relationships. Holding that the ultimate moral and social justification for mutual financial support lies in the bonds of affection uniting members of the family, exponents of this view hold that a law which requires one member of a family to sue another, or which forces parents who have long been independent into a position of humiliating financial dependence on their reluctant children, or which causes sons and daughters to lower their own and their children's standard of living in order to support a parent is likely to create frictions and tensions within the family which will undermine its very stability and cohesion. Others point to the adverse effect on the initiative of the younger generation of a situation in which additional income serves only to increase the recipient's liability to support an aged relative with whom he may or may not have been on affectionate terms.

It is evident that the two major functions of the family, the economic and the social, cannot always be reconciled.[9] Nor can it be denied that certain broader social and economic developments have tended to weaken the sense of mutual financial responsibility within the family, especially in regard to the responsibility which children feel for the support of their parents and the extent to which parents themselves expect such support.[10]

[8] Cf. *Analysis of the Social Security System,* pp. 348–359.

[9] It is also apparent that many individuals are caught between conflicting loyalties to the family and to the state, as witness the objections of many old people to giving the state a lien on their property because they feel a sense of obligation to "leave something" to their sons and daughters.

[10] In an opinion survey in California in 1953, only 40 per cent of OAA recipients and 45 per cent of aged nonrecipients stated that they would be willing to accept help from

The smaller size of families during the first half of this century has meant that there are fewer children to share a burden which may be very heavy if concentrated on one or two children instead of shared by several and which has become all the heavier because of the increasing span of human life. The fact that today many children not only marry and start families of their own at younger ages but also make their own homes independently tends to loosen the sense of closeness to parents and to create a psychological barrier to acceptance of the duty to support. Furthermore, the range of economic responsibilities which parents are expected to assume for their minor children raises the question whether it is reasonable to require the adult also to support his needy parents.[11] There is considerable evidence that the aged themselves tend to assume that the claims of grandchildren are paramount. Finally, the more mobile the society, both spatially (in that the children tend to live in different geographical areas from their parents) and socially (in that they tend to occupy jobs at higher income levels than those of their parents), the looser are likely to be the bonds of common interest and even affection, and the less willingly will children accept the burden of supporting needy parents. Nor can it be denied that if there proves to be growing acceptance of the idea that receipt of socially provided income involves no stigma, the pressure to remove the relatives' responsibility requirement may prove irresistible.

Some communities and some states appear to have already decided that the effort to maintain the principle is unrealistic in the light of changes in social attitudes and in the economic and social environment. All social insurance laws, of course, have no such requirement, for need is not a condition of eligibility. But even the income-conditioned pension typically, as in New Zealand or Great Britain, expressly limits resources of aged applicants to those possessed by the applicant and his spouse. And a quarter of the American states have no legislation of any kind establishing the duty of children to support their parents, while half a dozen others, although having some type of general support legislation, do not apply it in the administration of old-age assistance. Great Britain has probably gone farther than any other country in that for all public assistance applicants (and not merely the aged) the resources taken into account are only those of the applicant and spouse, while

---

their children; only 29 per cent of the former and 40 per cent of the latter believed that children should be required by law to help support aged parents. Somewhat surprisingly, those reared in cities were rather more willing to accept support (48 per cent) than those reared in a rural background (41 per cent). (Bond and Associates, *op. cit.*, pp. 296–300.)

[11] Cf. Alton A. Linford, "Which Way Public Assistance Administration?" *Social Service Review*, July, 1952.

children of 16 or over, even when living with the family, are treated as separate applicants.

THE PROBLEM OF ADC AND THE BROKEN FAMILY

The Aid to Dependent Children program also raises controversial issues which turn around theories of the social and economic role of the family system.[12] Originally ADC was planned as a program to enable young children in families deprived of a breadwinner because of death, disability, or absence from home of a parent, to continue to enjoy a normal home life with the mother, by ensuring the family an income. Many people still tend to envisage ADC as a program for widowed mothers. But with the expansion of OASI an ever larger proportion of survivor families is provided for on OASI, and the proportion of ADC families in which the father has left the home has steadily increased.[13] Especially in communities where the ADC payments are relatively generous, this has given rise to the charge that the program makes desertion all too easy for fathers in whom the sense of family responsibility is weak, for they will know that their family will nonetheless be taken care of. Similarly it has been charged that the program encourages illegitimacy by providing an assured income to unmarried mothers and their children. Furthermore, the growth in the number of ADC families of all types [14] has occasioned proposals that mothers should be required to work if they can possibly do so.

Far too little is known about the influence of the ADC program on

[12] For an account of the ADC program, see Phyllis R. Osborn, "Aid to Dependent Children—Realities and Possibilities," *Social Service Review*, June, 1954, pp. 153–172.

[13] By 1952 only about a fifth of the children receiving ADC were in families where the father was dead, as against about 38 per cent in the early 1940s. In about half of the cases the need of the child was due to the fact that the father had deserted the mother, was not married to her, or was otherwise absent from the family. For a detailed study of the characteristics of ADC families, see G. Blackwell and R. F. Gould, *Future Citizens All,* American Public Welfare Association, Chicago, 1952; and *Analysis of the Social Security System*, pp. 297ff. By 1953 the father had deserted the family in 17 per cent of the cases, the father was divorced or separated in another 17 per cent and in 20 per cent of the cases the mother was not married. (Wilbur J. Cohen, "Current and Future Trends in Public Welfare," *Social Service Review*, September, 1955, p. 255.)

[14] The number of children receiving ADC grew from 404,000 in 1936 to 941,000 in 1941. With the expanding employment opportunities of the war years, there was a decline to 639,000 in 1944, but thereafter the number grew rapidly to a peak of 1,661,000 in 1950. By the beginning of 1954 the number of child recipients had fallen to a little over 1.5 million. (The corresponding figures for the number of ADC families are: 162,000, 390,000, 254,000, 651,000, and 560,000.) For trends in ADC, see Ellen J. Perkins, "Old Age Assistance and Aid to Dependent Children, 1940–50," *Social Security Bulletin,* November, 1951. In 1954 the numbers again increased and by June, 1955, a new peak of 1,691,733 recipient children had been reached.

desertion and illegitimacy. Although the number of cases of this type (as well as the proportion they form of the total caseload) has undoubtedly increased sharply as compared with previous decades, comparisons are to some extent vitiated by the fact that prior to 1940 not all states operated such programs, or had them in existence in all political subdivisions, while some children who would by 1950 have been cared for on ADC were being supported in 1940 by other programs no longer in existence (such as the Civilian Conservation Corps and the National Youth Administration). In any case, some substantial increase in recipients would be expected in view of the increase in the population at risk (the population under 18 increased 26.8 per cent in the period 1940 to 1953). Furthermore, during and following World War II there was a general increase in the numbers of broken families and illegitimacy, a substantial part of which must be attributed to the social dislocations of the period.[15]

The precise extent, therefore, to which the growth in the numbers of children benefiting from ADC means that the program operates as a stimulus to antisocial behavior or instead reflects merely the fact that the community is now meeting more adequately a need for income that existed much earlier and is discovering for the first time how important is family breakup as a cause of income loss—this question must remain a matter of speculation pending the outcome of further research.

Yet even if it could be shown that the availability of ADC, by reducing the financial penalty for desertion or illegitimacy, makes such action more likely on the part of some people,[16] appropriate remedies are not easy to find. Few would probably be willing to penalize the children in such families by denying all aid.[17] To remove illegitimate children from their mothers frequently involves merely more costly foster child care or maintenance in an institution, and often enough such facilities are inadequate, even for present needs. Furthermore, influential schools of thought hold that the interests of the child may be better served by permitting him to retain the emotional security of living with a mother who may not live up to certain moral or cultural standards than by placing him in an approved foster home or institution.

[15] Families broken by divorce or desertion increased by about 80 per cent over the period 1940 to 1952. The number of illegitimate live births increased by 58 per cent between 1940 and 1950. (*Analysis of the Social Security System*, p. 303.)

[16] It is even possible that a parent who took very seriously his financial obligations to his family might find that if he is in a low-paid occupation, has a large family, and lives in a community paying relatively generous ADC allowances, he could secure a higher standard of living for his family by deserting than by remaining at home on his job.

[17] "While it must be granted that some ADC homes are far from ideal, it must be also accepted that a poor home will not become a good home because needed financial aid is withheld." (Osborn, *op. cit.*, p. 162.)

In recent years efforts have been made to invoke legal penalties to force deserting parents to carry out their family responsibilities. The Amendment to the Social Security Act in 1950, requiring states, after 1952, to include in their laws a provision that notice must be given to the appropriate law-enforcement officers when assistance is paid on behalf of children who have been abandoned or deserted by a parent, is a case in point.

But this remedy, like the similar resort to legal pressure for enforcement of the relatives' responsibility requirements, is not always simple to apply. Although most people would probably agree that a deserting father should be compelled to support his family to the extent of his means, by legal pressure if necessary, the deserted wife who hopes for eventual reconciliation may refuse to collaborate with the authorities in supplying information or taking necessary legal action, even at the risk of loss of her ADC payments. The father may have, and very probably has, moved to a different state and will be difficult to find. While in recent years fifty jurisdictions in the United States have agreed to reciprocal legislation to enforce the support of dependents, many technical difficulties still face the state which endeavors to bring legal action against a parent who has deserted to another part of the country. And in any case there remains the problem of determining the precise amount of the contribution, with all the difficulties discussed in the preceding section, frequently aggravated by the necessity to adjudicate the relative claims of two families: the one deserted and the new family elsewhere.

Those who hold that such unsocial behavior as desertion or the bearing of illegitimate children is a problem that exists independently of any income security system (even though in some cases it may be aggravated thereby) maintain that it must be attacked in other ways, notably by remedial and therapeutic measures, such as casework services on an individual basis and by broader educational measures.[18] In the last resort, indeed, the problem of desertion and illegitimacy, like that of the work-shy and the malingerer, raises the unresolved issue of punishment versus treatment. To the extent that communities are unwilling to use the threat of family starvation as a punishing weapon and are unable to devise satisfactory safeguards in the benefit and eligibility clauses of their social security programs, they are increasingly compelled to come to grips with the problem of finding other appropriate social measures for dealing with these types of antisocial behavior.

18 Cf. Hilda C. M. Arndt, "An Appraisal of What Critics Say about Public Assistance," *Social Service Review*, December, 1952; Albert Deutsch, "Our Neediest Children," *Woman's Home Companion*, January, 1952; Kermit T. Wiltze, "Social Casework Services in the Aid to Dependent Children Program," *Social Service Review*, June, 1954, pp. 173–185; and "The Salt Lake County ADC Program," *Public Assistance in Utah*, February, 1952, p. 1ff.

The suggestion, made with increasing frequency as the total ADC rolls have increased in a period of high employment, that mothers of dependent children should be encouraged or even forced to take paid employment raises somewhat different issues. Its adoption would clearly involve an abandonment of the original conception of the program, namely that it was socially desirable to ensure the presence of the mother in the home while the children are still young. The increasing tendency of mothers of young children to take paid employment appears to have led to some questioning of this conception, more especially in communities with adequate day-care facilities. In any case, the proposal involves a decision as to whether a child's growth and development is likely to be harmed less by having a working mother in a society where this is becoming increasingly common than by spending his childhood with his mother in the home but in a dependent status which often carries considerable stigma among his peers and probably involves a low standard of living. Here again, only more extensive research can supply the answer.

Children's Allowances

Up to this point we have considered the bearing on the family system only of those measures which are concerned with interruptions to the flow of private income. As we have seen, many income security systems grant benefits for dependent children. However, as a distinguished English economist has observed, "Children do not spring into existence when their father falls sick or out of work and vanish when he returns to work: to provide for them in emergencies is only to call attention to the absurdity of ignoring their existence at other times." [19] In fact, concern about the major weakness of the family system as an instrument for providing economic support for the citizens of the future, due to the adverse effect of sizable numbers of children on the per capita standard of living of members of the family unit, has given rise to a variety of governmental measures.

The most common of these is the practice of permitting deductions from income for income-tax purposes in some relation to the number of dependents supported by the taxpayer. But as a method of dealing with the income inadequacies of members of large families, it has obvious disadvantages. It puts no additional money into the hands of the submarginal families, and it gives relatively the least amount of tax remission to those who need it most, namely to those whose incomes are so small that they are not liable to tax or are taxed only at the lowest rates.

19 Barbara Wootton, "The Impact of Income Security upon Individual Freedom," in James E. Russell (ed.), *National Policies for Education, Health and Social Services,* Doubleday and Company, Inc., New York, 1955, p. 392.

Until recently, few suggestions have been made that the United States should follow the example of some thirty other countries in which, through some system of children's allowances, the burden of child rearing is to some extent removed from parents. Under these plans, a periodic payment is made, usually to the mother, for each child below a certain age without any test of need or income. The funds come either from general taxation or from social insurance contributions. In Canadâ, for example, any child under 16 born in the country or resident there for one year is eligible for a children's allowance regardless of the income of its parents. These allowances, which in 1954 ranged from $5 to $8 monthly, are normally paid to the mother and are financed by the Dominion from general revenues.[20] In Great Britain the system is similar except that no payment is made for the first child, and the amount of the allowance does not vary with the child's age.

There is evidence of some growth of interest in the United States in such measures today, and with increasing frequency the suggestion is made that the United States should follow the example of Canada and Great Britain. Here again, the final outcome will depend on the weight attached to a variety of considerations.

The first of these consists in the importance attached to securing for all children some agreed minimum standard of living, regardless of the size of the family into which they are born and the income of their parents. In most countries which have introduced children's allowances, the stimulus to this major change in social policy has come from observation of two simple statistical facts: first, that if a given income has to be shared among several people, each will enjoy a lower standard of living as a result; second, that as there is great variation in the numbers of children per family and as the largest families typically occur at the lower income levels, many children are condemned to a relatively low standard of living merely because of the size of the family into which they were born.[21] The object of the children's allowance system, therefore, is to equalize in some degree the economic opportunities of all children.[22]

[20] For a brief account of the Canadian System, see R. B. Curry, "Family Allowances in Canada," *Public Welfare*, March, 1948, pp. 50–55.

[21] In the United States, in 1939, the median family unit income (in which adults were counted as a unit and children as half a unit) for all nonfarm families with only wage or salary income averaged $474. But for families with no children (47 per cent of all families), it averaged $592, while for those with three children or more (14 per cent of all families) it fell to $281. Furthermore, about one-third of all children were in families with unit incomes of $150 to $299, and about 70 per cent of all children were in families whose unit income fell below the national average. (T. J. Woofter, Jr., "Children and Family Income," *Social Security Bulletin*, January, 1945.)

[22] This argument in support of children's allowances among others was forcibly made

Children's allowances, however, are a costly program. In times of good or high employment they typically represent the second highest item in the social security budget (old age being the first). Unless, therefore, there is a willingness to accept some substantial measure of income redistribution from the childless to those with young families and, if the program is financed from a progressive general tax system, also from high to low income classes, children's allowance systems will hardly be favored. By deliberately making the payments free of any income test, in order to ensure their widest utilization, some payments are inevitably made to families that could have gotten along well without them. Countries with such systems have been prepared to pay this price in order to ensure that no child is deprived of an allowance because his parents are reluctant to submit to a needs test. In any case, it is frequently argued that the richer recipient will be paying a higher rate of income tax, so that, with uniform allowances for all recipients, a net redistribution of income nonetheless results. Some have adjusted the income-tax system of deductions for dependents to ensure that above a certain income level no net advantage accrues to the family from the receipt of children's allowances.

A system which places publicly supplied funds in the hands of all parents obviously implies considerable faith in the integrity of parents and in their devotion to the well-being of their offspring. In fact, such sparse studies as are available suggest that in the vast majority of cases this confidence is not misplaced and that most parents use the additional income as it was intended they should, namely for the benefit of their children. Concern about the proper use of the allowance is evident, however, in the provision found in most countries that the allowance is normally payable to the mother, presumably on the theory that she is less likely to use the money for her own enjoyment.

Even so, there are some who hold that this degree of confidence in the sense of parental responsibility may be misplaced in a significant proportion of cases. It has also been pointed out that the large sums involved in children's allowances raise serious questions of competing priorities. Since in many recipient families the additional income yielded by the children's allowance will be used for meeting marginal needs of children, it is argued that more effective and economical use could be made of the sums expended by providing free, or on a subsidized basis,

---

by Lord Beveridge in the famous Beveridge Report. For an account of the objectives of children's allowance systems and their nature in the different countries, see *Economic Measures in Favor of the Family*, United Nations, Department of Social Affairs, New York, 1952; also "Family Allowance Schemes in 1947; Parts I and II," *International Labour Review*, April–May, 1948; and *Family Allowances*, Report II, Eleventh General Meeting, International Social Security Association, Geneva, 1954.

goods and services of which many children are badly in need and which carry a high priority. If, it is held, the taxpayers as a whole have to foot the bill, then there should be some definite assurance that their sacrifice will in fact result in a meeting of what the community deems the most urgent needs.[23] This view is opposed by those who mistrust the substitution of the parents' judgment of what is best for children by decisions made by the state or by some welfare agency.[24]

Even more broadly, a concern about the effect on family responsibility in general motivates some of those who oppose children's allowances. The system does, of course, represent a major redrawing of the limits of the economic responsibilities of the family. The extent of the removal of financial responsibility for the upkeep of children must not, however, be exaggerated. Most children's allowance systems pay allowances which, except for the very largest families, are relatively low in relation to the normal income of the breadwinner, even in the lowest income brackets, and with one or two exceptions the amount per child is far from sufficient to meet the full costs of maintenance. They aim, in other words, merely to supplement, not to substitute for, the resources which the family devotes to the support of children. In this connection it is perhaps significant that one group that has traditionally been the spokesman for the principle of mutual family responsibility and family cohesion, namely the Catholic group, has in general strongly favored children's allowances.

Attitudes toward the population problem may also influence attitudes toward children's allowances. If sufficiently high allowances are paid, the program might, of course, have an impact upon the birth rate. In fact only two or three countries have adopted children's allowances as part of a deliberate population policy, and only in the French system, and perhaps also the Italian, are the payments sufficiently high to be likely to exert any direct influence. Even in France, the relation of family allowances to the rising birth rate, which France, like many other countries with and without family allowance systems, has experienced in recent years, has not as yet been determined. In any case, all other systems, as we have seen, aim only to remove part of the costs of child rearing, not to make it a profitable occupation.

Such fragmentary evidence as is available from Canada and elsewhere suggests that the major population influence of children's allowance systems is exerted through the death rate rather than the birth rate.

[23] For a vigorous statement of the case in favor of expansion of "social utilities" rather than cash allowances, see Charlotte Whitton, *The Dawn of Ampler Life,* The Macmillan Co. of Canada, Ltd., Toronto, 1943, *passim.* See also Alva Myrdal, *Nation and Family,* Kegan Paul, Trench, Trubner & Co., London, 1945, chap. 9.

[24] In defending the payment of cash children's allowances to mothers one Canadian legislator described the mother as "the best and most efficient Canadian child welfare institution."

More of the children that are born are kept alive. It seems, however, safe to say that countries which are concerned about declining populations or rates of population increase will be more likely to favor children's allowances than those which regard themselves as overpopulated, and it is perhaps significant that the tremendous expansion of children's allowance systems, which has been one of the most striking social developments of the years following World War II, has taken place in a period of generally high demand for labor.

Organized labor in some countries has sometimes initially opposed the children's allowance system on the ground that it would operate to keep wages down and has often held that a more appropriate remedy for the poverty of members of large families is action to raise wages. In fact, it is doubtful whether it is seriously maintained that wages in general could be raised sufficiently to provide an acceptable living standard for members of the very largest families. In any case, however high the average wage, the relatively disadvantageous position of the child in the unusually large family will still remain. It is also questionable whether humanitarian considerations play a major role in the determination of wages. The evidence regarding the effect on wages of paying children's allowances suggests that a more important influence on wage trends is the general level of productivity and the strength of organized labor. Where, as in Canada and England, labor is strong and productivity high, the payment of children's allowances does not seem to have had any noticeably depressive effect on wages: where, as in France, labor is weak and productivity low, children's allowances have undoubtedly functioned as an alternative to general wage increases.

An important incidental advantage of a children's allowance system for countries with extensive social security systems that aim to provide social insurance types of benefits adequate for maintenance is that it greatly simplifies the problem of the relationship of benefits to earnings. If all families, whether or not drawing social security income, receive allowances proportional to the number of children, the social security benefit does not have to be increased to take account of family responsibilities (other than the wife), and the possibility of maintaining a substantial differential between benefit and earnings is thereby greater.[25] It also avoids or minimizes the necessity of supplementing low wages by public assistance.

[25] This point was strongly made by Dr. L. C. Marsh, who regarded children's allowances as "the key to consistency" in planning a comprehensive social security program for Canada. (Report on Social Security for Canada, prepared by Dr. L. C. Marsh, for the Advisory Committee on Reconstruction, Ottawa, King's Printer, 1943, p. 30.) Similarly, Lord Beveridge regarded children's allowances as an integral and necessary part of his social security proposals. Cf. Eveline M. Burns, British Unemployment Programs, 1920–38, Social Science Research Council, Washington, D.C., 1942, pp. 255–263.

PART TWO

Decisions as to the Risks for Which Social Responsibility Will Be Accepted

A SECOND major group of social security issues concerns the selection of risks to income against which some public provision will be made. So long as public assistance is the sole public income security system, this question assumes less importance, for, with one major exception, most public assistance systems are, in principle at least, all-inclusive as to risk. That is to say, they provide some measure of alternative income for needy people whether the cause of need is unemployment, old age, death of a breadwinner, or disability, etc. The exception, as was clear from the preceding pages, is where the lack of income can be traced to the individual's own actual or presumed unwillingness to contribute to his own support.[1] Even this exclusion is hard to adhere to, for most communities are unwilling to allow the individual's dependent family to starve, and unless relief is given in an institution, it is difficult to prevent the family from sharing with the father whatever public income is provided.

Once the public assistance principle is departed from, or even when a less deterrent form of public assistance is envisaged, the question of risk selection arises. Some countries, it is true, have made the nondeterrent, nondiscretionary form of income security available to the whole population for all causes of income loss (this is the case in Great Britain and New Zealand), but most others, including the United States, have limited the preferred forms of social security to specified risks to continuity of income. Some of the most perplexing issues today concern the extent to which the non-needs-test, nondeterrent types of income security should be used to meet additional risks to income.

By 1956 the United States had limited this type of security to a pre-

[1] In some parts of the United States relief is still denied to employable men even though their unemployment may be entirely involuntary. In others, relief is denied to workers on strike.

sumed income loss at age 72, to loss of income due to retirement from work between the ages of 65 and 71, to death of a breadwinner, to short-period unemployment, and, in a very limited degree, to disability. Among the proposals on which future decisions may have to be made are those which suggest extending the social insurance approach to provide benefits (1) on the mere attainment of age 65 or even a lower age, without any requirement to have retired, (2) for a larger number of weeks of unemployment than is usual under the typical unemployment insurance law (i.e., to cover long- as well as short-period unemployment), (3) for loss of income due to disability however caused and for however long the disability lasts, and (4) to cover the costs of medical care.

It will be noted that the first three of these proposals involve an extension of public responsibility in an area where in principle government action to assure continuity of income by non-means-test, nondiscretionary methods has already been accepted in some degree in the United States. On the other hand, the last breaks new ground in that it involves public action not to meet the problem of interruptions of private income but to relieve individuals and families of part of the costs they incur even when normal incomes are secured. With minor exceptions such proposals involve the acceptance of new areas of public responsibility. In principle, of course, proposals to introduce systems of children's allowances also involve decisions as to the extension of public responsibility for family security, in this case the threat to the family standard of living caused by the presence of several children in the home. The issues raised by such proposals have, however, already been discussed in Chapter 5 because they relate so directly to prevailing theories regarding the social and economic roles of the family. In the following three chapters, therefore, we shall be concerned only with the extension or contraction of public programs dealing with risks to continuity of income and with the possible extension of public action to an area new for America, although not for many other countries, namely the threat to family security attributable to the costs of medical care.

CHAPTER 6

Threats to Continuity of Income: Chronological Age or Retirement

PUBLIC INCOME SECURITY PROGRAMS dealing with the risk of old age differ according to whether the event which is held to justify public action is the mere attainment of some chronological age or whether it is voluntary or enforced retirement from the labor market after some defined age. Thus in Canada and several other countries the non-means-test, nondiscretionary type of old-age benefit is available automatically when individuals reach a specified age; in some other countries, such as the United States, the benefit can be claimed, at a certain age, only if the individual substantially retires from the labor market (i.e., it contains a retirement test); in income-conditioned pension systems, where the benefit is reduced in some degree as income (including that from employment) increases, a retirement test is indirectly applied; and some systems, such as Great Britain's, build into their old-age security systems positive inducements not to retire by awarding a higher benefit if the individual keeps on working beyond the minimum retirement age. By the 1950s, some of the most acute differences of opinion turned around the question of whether an old-age security system should pay benefits automatically on attainment of some specific age or should be conditioned on age plus retirement from the labor market.

Before the major economic and social issues at stake are dealt with, one argument in support of the use of chronological age alone as the criterion calls for consideration. This is the assertion which has frequently been made in the United States that to make payment of social security benefits dependent upon retirement is inconsistent with the alleged "insurance character" of the OASI program. If, it is held, a worker has paid contributions for "old-age insurance," he should be entitled to receive benefits on reaching age 65, with no strings attached. This objection, however, has little validity. First, the level premium contribution rate of the OASI system is based upon the assumption that the system is a retirement, not an old-age, benefit program. Much higher contributions would have to be paid if the actuarial calculations were to be based on the assumption that benefits would be automatically payable at age 65. Second, the program is not an insurance, but a social insurance, system. It does not provide benefits which have been wholly earned by the beneficiary: it is a social program paying to all beneficiaries, over the next generation, benefits larger than can possibly have been earned by their own contributions. Every person who was older than 21 when he was first covered will draw an "unearned" benefit, because he cannot possibly have paid contributions for the full period up to age 65. This is most obvious in the case of those already in the upper age brackets by the time they were first covered, for the liberal eligibility conditions introduced in 1950 admitted such persons to full benefit rights after extremely short periods of coverage. In addition, since the full rate of tax (8 per cent) is not to be imposed until 1975, everyone entering the system prior to that date will in some measure have failed to "earn" his benefit.[1]

While these provisions in the law may be defensible in terms of its broad social purpose, as we have seen in Chapter 2, they cause the system to depart sharply from an ordinary commercial insurance or annuity system. The rights of persons covered by it differ from those of people who have made a contract with a private insurance company, and the validity of a retirement test must be judged not by whether or not it is consistent with "insurance principles" but by its objectives and its economic and social consequences.

EFFECTS UPON NATIONAL OUTPUT

To the extent that income security programs either make it possible for people to retire from the labor market prior to the age at which their effective productivity declines to zero, or near zero, or contain provisions which force or encourage them to do so, the community as a whole suffers a loss of potential output. How large or how small this loss will be depends upon a number of factors.

Among these is the age at which the payment is available and its relationship to the age at which, in fact, the majority of workers prove to be incapable of making further contributions to output. In most countries old age, for the purposes of benefit eligibility, has been set at 65. Thus in the United States attainment of age 65 is a basic eligibility condition for both OASI and OAA, and it is very commonly found also in private pension plans. There is, however, nothing sacred about this particular age. Some countries have set a higher limit to the age at which public responsibility for income maintenance is accepted. In Sweden, for

---

[1] Strictly speaking the date is somewhat earlier than this, for the ultimate contribution rate is swollen by the loading for the cost of unearned benefits. But even if these increase the ultimate rate by 2 per cent, the 6 per cent rate is not payable until 1965, and all entrants to the system prior to that date will not "earn" their benefit.

instance, people are not eligible for old-age pensions until they have reached age 67. Other countries have different age limits for different types of social security programs. The Canadian national universal pension is payable from age 70, while the Dominion-provincial old-age pension (similar to OAA) is payable to otherwise eligible people from age 65. On the other hand, some social security systems regard old age as beginning earlier. In some countries (e.g., Czechoslovakia and Turkey) it is 60, and this age has been selected for women in several countries (such as Great Britain) in which the pensionable age for men is 65. From time to time proposals have been made in the United States for lowering the pensionable age for both sexes or for women alone to this level. In some countries "old age" begins earlier for some types of workers (e.g., miners) than for others and may be as low as 50 or 55.[1a]

To what extent these countries are depriving themselves of output by making it possible for individuals to retire at these ages depends of course on the capacity for work of people at these ages and the extent to which the countries are fully using the rest of their labor supply. It is known that economic efficiency and capacity to work decline with age, but there is much difference of opinion as to the nature and extent of the decline, the age at which it occurs, and the significance of the aging process for efficiency in different employments and occupations.[2] Certainly not all persons in these older age groups are incapable of work. In the United States, for example, it has been estimated that in June, 1954, over 3 million out of 13.7 million persons aged 65 and over had income from employment.[3] In March, 1952, 58 per cent of all men 65 to 69, 22 per cent of those 70 to 74, and 18 per cent of men 75 and over were still in the labor force. The corresponding figures for women were 15 per cent, 6 per cent, and 3 per cent. And such evidence as is available suggests that if the age group 65 to 69 could be broken down still further, the proportion continuing to work in the two or three years immediately following age 65 would be even more impressive. Furthermore, these figures clearly underestimated the proportions capable of work, since some persons drawing OASI benefits were undoubtedly capable of work but had chosen instead to retire on benefit.

It is highly probable that developments in the field of health will in the future, even more than in the past, prolong vigor as well as life, thereby expanding the employment potential of the old. The more this

[1a] For the practice of various countries and some of the considerations affecting their policies, see *The Age of Retirement*, Agenda Report IV, International Labour Organisation, European Regional Conference, 1955. Geneva, 1954.

[2] John J. Corson and John W. McConnell, *Economic Needs of Older Workers,* The Twentieth Century Fund, Inc., New York, 1956, chaps. 2, 3.

[3] *Social Security Bulletin*, December, 1954, p. 16. A later study revealed that during 1953, 1.76 million worked full time the year round.

happens, the greater will be the possible additions to national output foregone by those countries which, through their social security systems, make it possible for (or even encourage) people to retire at a relatively early age. And obviously, the larger the percentage of the population of the "pensionable age," the greater will be the economic loss to the community as a whole.[4] Nevertheless, the extent of the economic loss must not be overemphasized. So long as the community has a general labor surplus and is unable to ensure full employment, there is little to be gained by adding still further to the number of work seekers. Furthermore, many would hold that, in view of the difficulty all too frequently experienced by the older worker, once unemployed, in securing new employment (in part because of the discrimination by employers against older workers as such), countries would do better to absorb the existing supply of work-seeking aged before adding to their number by social security policies that discourage retirement.

These considerations do not negate the economic fact that the worker who retires before his economic usefulness has disappeared represents a loss of potential output. But it is clear that community attitudes to encouragement, through social security systems, of early or late retirement will be influenced by changes in the general employment situation, as well as by long-term trends in the employability of the aged. When there is heavy unemployment, the net loss to the community through the non-employment of people beyond a certain age will appear unimportant relatively to the losses due to the unemployment of workers at lower ages, and arguments for rationing job opportunities in favor of the young may prevail. Thus the inclusion of a retirement clause in the original Social Security Act was an obvious reflection of the economic conditions of the time. It was hoped to encourage retirement at age 65 because in 1934 to 1935 there was much unemployment, and it was felt desirable to reserve for young workers such jobs as were available.

The desire to encourage retirement was shown even more clearly in the provisions of the original Railroad Retirement legislation. Here, in addition to a concern about general unemployment, much was made of the argument that it was in the interests of public safety in a railroad system operating under seniority rules to encourage retirement of elderly workers. But as economic conditions have changed, the wisdom of thus discouraging the aged from participating in production has been increasingly questioned, for so long as an aged person is capable of work, the loss of his contribution to production in a period of high demand for labor means a sensible loss of national output.

Periods of general unemployment are likely to intensify the fears of those who hold that, in the absence of a retirement test, beneficiaries will

[4] See below for data on demographic trends.

"compete unfairly" with other workers for available jobs and tend to depress wages because they can afford to accept work at less than prevailing rates. The validity of the fear, often expressed by labor unions, of the wage-depressive influence of certain "subsidized groups" (such as pensioners or married women) is, however, difficult to determine. It might be argued with equal cogency that precisely because such persons have a measure of economic security, they would be more independent and discriminating about the jobs it would be worth their while to accept. Valid or not, however, the fear of this type of subsidized labor supply furnishes part of the support for the view that the risk justifying public action is retirement from the labor market, rather than mere attainment of some specific age.

THE ECONOMIC NEEDS AND CIRCUMSTANCES OF THE AGED

The desirability of making payment of old-age pensions or benefits dependent upon a retirement test will also be affected by the conditions and needs of the aged themselves. There appears to be a growing conviction that, provided they enjoy reasonable health, older people have more satisfying lives if they continue to participate normally in production than if they withdraw entirely from the labor market. This view fosters a critical attitude not only toward provisions (such as are often found in private pension plans) for compulsory retirement at some specific age but also toward certain types of retirement test in public programs which in effect place a premium upon not working.

Where these considerations lead to an abandonment of any retirement test, other social considerations come into play, for the community then has to decide at what age the old-age benefit shall become automatically payable. Here the actual severity and incidence of the risk of loss of income will play a role, since in the last resort the development of income security programs has been motivated by a concern for people who are economically insecure. The proportion of the members of any age cohort who are at any time in fact incapable of earning for physical or other reasons, and who prove to possess on the average savings inadequate to provide what the community regards as an acceptable living standard, will play an important part in determining where the automatic pensionable age shall be set. The larger the proportion, the greater is the probability that the community will be prepared to countenance the payment of pensions to some who are not in need of them in order not to penalize those who are.[5] In some countries, for example, concern about the plight

---

[5] For an account of the situation of the aged in the United States, see *Economic Problems of an Aging Population,* part II of Report of the Joint Committee on Railroad Retirement Legislation, 83d Cong., 1st Sess., 1953; and *Man and His Years,* an account

of older widows has led to the setting of a lower pensionable age for women than for men. However, where the system contains a retirement test, this has deprived the community of the productive work of some older employed women who exercise their option to retire at an earlier age than their male fellow employees.

These social considerations will have different force at different times. Where, for example, employer attitudes toward employment of the aged are highly discriminatory, it is likely that there will be a greater disposition on the part of the public to minimize the loss due to induced early retirement and to show increased concern for the income needs of the aged as a group. Even so, it would not necessarily follow that the only course would be use of a retirement test or a lowering of the pensionable age to the point where discrimination against, or substantial unemployment among, the age cohort comes into play. For an alternative remedy might be to set the pensionable age at whatever is judged to be the point at which unemployment becomes, for physiological or other reasons, a general characteristic of the group, and to treat as a problem of unemployment, or disability, the failure of older persons below that age to secure work. At least one country (Ireland) has adopted this solution. However, it would involve providing unemployment benefit for longer duration than is usual (i.e., beyond a certain age unemployment benefit would be payable until the pensionable age is reached), and, since the presumption would be that the condition was permanent, benefits might have to be higher than standard unemployment insurance rates.

COST CONSIDERATIONS

Even if general economic considerations and the facts regarding the economic circumstances and needs of the aged fail to point to any very evident decision as between old age as such (however defined) and retirement as the risk against which governmental action is appropriate, the scales may yet be tipped by considerations of cost. For obviously to pay benefits automatically on attainment of some specified age instead of on the basis of age plus retirement is likely to increase the proportion of the national income which is channeled to the beneficiary group. And the lower the minimum pensionable age, the greater will be the income transfer.[6]

---

of the First National Conference of Aging, sponsored by the Federal Security Agency, Health Publications Institute, 1951.

[6] This would explain, for instance, the action of the American Congress, in 1954, in eliminating the retirement test for persons 72 and over but retaining it for those between the ages of 65 and 71. However, this action could also be justified by social and economic considerations; the loss in output due to the possible nonemployment of persons

It has been estimated by the actuary of the Social Security Administration that to pay benefits automatically on attainment of age 65 would increase the long-range costs of the program by approximately 1.4 per cent of payrolls. As of the beginning of 1955, abolition of the test would have added more than 2 million people to those currently on the beneficiary rolls and increased total annual disbursements by $1.9 billion, a rise in current cost of about 40 per cent or of 1.15 per cent of taxable payroll.[7] People may feel that there are better uses for this money (including increasing the benefits of those who can no longer earn) than paying benefits immediately on reaching age 65 to aged persons, many of whom are still quite capable of supporting themselves.

Even, therefore, if broader economic and social considerations are not decisive, many would argue that public programs should aim to provide against the risk of loss of income due to retirement and age rather than age alone, solely because by so doing the over-all cost of the program can be kept to more modest proportions. At the same time, it must not be forgotten that the higher the age set for retirement and the nearer it is set to the age at which physical inability to work is a common characteristic of the members of the eligible group, the less significant will be the savings due to adoption of a retirement test.

THE ECONOMIC AND SOCIAL ENVIRONMENT

The weight attached to the factors hitherto discussed, even if precise quantitative information were available (which unfortunately is far too rarely the case), will be affected by economic conditions and social attitudes prevailing at the time policy is determined and by demographic developments.

In the first place, other things being equal, the higher the level of national income, the more is it likely that chronological age will be favored over age plus retirement. The richer society is likely to attach less importance to any given loss of potential output than is the community operating at a very low level of output. When average incomes are high, the taxpayer will more readily accede to more substantial income transfers in favor of some specific age groups, for even after tax, his disposable income will be sizable in real terms. Furthermore, when national income is increasing, his disposable income may increase despite growing taxes,

---

age 72 and over is relatively small. And socially, since relatively few are capable of employment, the need for alternative income is correspondingly great.

[7] Robert J. Myers, "Old Age and Survivors Insurance: Retirement Test under the 1954 Amendments," *Social Security Bulletin*, December, 1954, p. 15. See also Robert J. Myers, "Bases and Background of the Retirement Test," *Social Security Bulletin*, March, 1954, p. 14.

and the disparity between his increasing welfare and that of the income-less aged person may cause him to be more willing to run the risk of making payments to some who may not be in need, in order to avoid penalizing any who are in fact needy.

Second, the choice between the two objectives will be affected by pre-vailing attitudes toward retirement as such in the community as a whole. If the average man regards early retirement as a desirable life pattern for himself, he will be more disposed to support legislation which makes this possible for other people as well, i.e., which defines "old age" as be-ginning chronologically relatively early, and which leaves the individual free to retire or not as he pleases.

A third important influence is the number of the aged (however de-fined) in relation to the size of the working population. For at any given time additions to the income of any age group over and above what its members secure by their own productive activity, either work or savings, must come from the incomes of the rest of the population which is cur-rently engaged in production.

In the United States estimates of the population in the upper age brackets can be made with reasonable accuracy for considerable periods ahead on the basis of age groups already born. Even over a twenty-year period they suggest two sets of facts likely to influence social security policy.[8]

First, the numbers of aged persons, whether defined as those over 60, over 65, or over 70, will increase by fifty per cent from 1955 to 1975. Second, the numbers in the 60 to 64 age group are almost half the size of the group 65 and over. These facts suggest that any policy which per-mits or encourages retirement before it is physically necessary may well involve a sizable sacrifice of potential output, more particularly if the age of retirement were set at 60 instead of 65. However, the effect of the rising numbers in the older age groups on the real burden of an old-age security program (i.e., the future economic drain on the incomes of those still producing as compared with that experienced in 1950) de-pends upon the probable size of the population of working age in these future years. And here projections are far less reliable, largely because of the influence exerted by changes in the birth rate (and to a lesser extent

[8] The following tabulation shows the projected total population of the United States, aged 60 and over, 1955 to 1975, and the enumerated population, 1950 (in millions):

Age	1950	1955	1960	1965	1970	1975
60–64 years	6.1	6.7	7.3	7.8	8.6	9.4
65–69 years	5.0	5.3	5.9	6.4	6.8	7.6
70 years or over	7.3	8.7	9.8	11.0	12.1	13.1
Total, 60 or over	18.4	20.7	23.0	25.2	27.5	30.1

(Analysis of the Social Security System, part I, Tables 7, 11, pp. 10, 18. Projections are based on the population 20 years of age and over alive on July 1, 1950.)

by immigration). Already the great increase in the birth rate which accompanied the end of World War II and the ensuing period of high employment has rendered obsolete the official population predictions made
as late as 1950.[9] One estimate made in 1954 suggests that persons 65 and
over will increase from 11.8 per cent of the population 18 and over in
1950, to 14.2 per cent in 1970, but any such estimates must be accepted
with caution. All that can be said with certainty is that there will be
many more persons in the productive age groups over the next quarter
century than appeared likely a few years ago to share the burden of
supporting the certain increase in the numbers of the elderly and aged.
But although the precise ratio in future years cannot be stated with certainty, and may well change very sharply over a relatively short period
of time, it is improbable that decisions as to pension policy will not be
influenced in the future by what this ratio turns out to be.

Thus, for example, since by the mid-1950s this growth in numbers,
and very frequently also in the proportion of the aged in the total population, was characteristic of the demographic picture in many countries,
it is understandable that to an increasing degree public policy in old-age
security systems has simultaneously been subjected to reconsideration.
In those systems where complete retirement from the labor market is
not a condition of eligibility, suggestions for raising the pensionable age
or for the introduction of a retirement test have been made with growing
frequency.[10] And in those which applied a rigid test of retirement there
were renewed efforts to discover some more flexible system which would
protect the interests of the taxpayer without depriving the community of
such productive efforts as the aged were capable of.

ATTITUDES TO THE CLAIMS OF THE AGED

A further influence affecting the weight a community will attach to
economic, social, and cost factors at any given time is the sensitivity of
the community to the claims of the aged as against those of other groups
who have to be supported by the working population. Many countries,
and notably the United States in recent years, have witnessed a pronounced growth of public concern about the welfare of the aged, an
interest to which their growing numbers and capacity for organization
and exertion of political pressure have contributed not a little. Indeed,
in America it would be difficult to explain some aspects of public policy in

[9] For a discussion of population developments and a critique of past projections, see
Joseph S. Davis, "Our Changed Population Outlook and Its Significance," *American
Economic Review*, vol. 42, no. 3, June, 1953; see also testimony of Dr. Henry S. Shyrock,
of the Census Bureau, in *Analysis of the Social Security System*, part I, pp. 4–52.

[10] Thus in 1954 a British official committee (the Philipps Committee) proposed a gradual
raising of the pensionable age from 65 to 68.

regard to the aged without taking into account the influence of powerful political lobbies of the aged.

But they are not the only groups making claims upon national income: veterans and users of roads are vociferous in many countries. The very fact which, in the long run, will increase the numbers in the productive age groups, namely an increase in the birth rate, involves in the short run a heavy burden on current earners of support and education until children enter the labor market. People may feel less generous toward the aged if they have to carry heavy costs of child rearing and be more likely to insist that public action be limited to provision for persons who are presumptively in need, i.e., who have retired from the labor market, and to frown upon proposals to pay automatic pensions at some specified age, especially if this is set relatively low.

Even more broadly, the sum total of all other demands (such as defense and other tax-financed expenditures) which cut into the freely disposable income of current earners will have an influence on the community's willingness to shoulder an additional burden in the form of a lowering of the pensionable age or complete abolition of a retirement test.

Attitudes to the claims of the aged as compared with other groups will also affect the community's response to the undeniable loss of output occasioned by retirement of the elderly prior to the time when their economic effectiveness falls to zero. For even if there is a general labor shortage, a favorable sentiment toward the aged as such may foster efforts to utilize other available labor reserves (such as employment of married women or recourse to overtime) rather than to raise the retirement age of public social security systems.

TECHNICAL AND ADMINISTRATIVE PROBLEMS

Finally, whatever the policy objectives desired, the actual program adopted will be influenced by the success with which human ingenuity can devise techniques to implement them. From this point of view there are many problems still to be solved, and many of the devices adopted have had unexpected repercussions.

First of all, it is necessary to devise some test of retirement. No country has been prepared to insist that beneficiaries perform no paid work at all, for such a fiat would outrage prevailing mores. Hence, as we have seen, efforts are made only to prevent the beneficiary from continuing in his customary employment, or from undertaking full-time, or substantially full-time, work. Thus in the American Railroad Retirement system, retirement annuities are awarded only after termination of all employment, whether in or out of the railroad industry. However, once awarded an annuity, the beneficiary can continue to draw it even though he is later employed, as long as he does not work for a railroad or for the last nonrailroad employer for whom he worked before his retirement. These provisions effectively discourage employment because workers severed from a job at age 65 or later are unlikely as a rule again to secure full-time paid employment.

The extent to which these provisions encouraged total retirement from the labor market, or merely a substitution of railroad by other forms of employment, is not known. In any case, such an occupational measure of retirement is likely to prove acceptable only in schemes limited to a single industry or a relatively small number of industries.[11]

A different measure of retirement was adopted in the Social Security Act from 1939 onwards, namely a definition that tested the fact of retirement by reference to a defined volume of earnings. Under the 1954 Amendments, benefits are withheld when a beneficiary under age 72 earns more than a specified sum ($1,200 in a calendar year). For each additional $80 or fraction thereof one month's benefits are withheld; however, no benefits are withheld for months in which the claimant can show that he did not render services for wages in excess of $80 or substantial services in a trade or business.

The use of a money sum as the measure of retirement or substantial retirement has, however, several disadvantages. First, its significance is affected by changing price and wage levels, and if the upper limit to earnings is to be meaningful, it must be raised from time to time. In fact, the original 1939 limit of $14.99 a month became highly restrictive due to rising wage levels long before it was raised to $50 in 1950, and within two years it was increased to $75 a month and two years later to $1,200 a year.

Second, a test that runs in terms of an absolute money sum discriminates against the higher-paid worker for whom a relatively slight amount of even part-time employment may lead to a withholding of benefit, whereas

11 In fact, between 1939 and 1955 a similar differentiation between types of employment occurred under the Social Security Act and gave rise to great criticism. Here, benefits were withheld only in respect of earnings in employments covered by the Act; those who could secure work in uncovered employment could continue to draw benefits however high their earnings. This definition of employment, which made for considerable inequity, was originally adopted for administrative reasons, since the Bureau of OASI could police the retirement clause by matching records of earnings with the benefit claims but would, of course, have records only of earnings in covered employment. Obviously, every extension of coverage reduced the extent of unreported earnings and made less necessary a distinction between covered and uncovered employment. It is not surprising, therefore, that simultaneously with the great extension of coverage brought about in 1954, the retirement test applied thereafter to earnings from any kind of work, covered or uncovered.

the worker whose monthly or annual rates are lower may not have to give up employment to a similar degree. It thus tends to approach a needs test instead of a test of extent of employment.

Third, the use of money earnings as a test of retirement gives rise to considerable misunderstanding. Thus the American retirement test has been attacked on the ground that it nullifies the objectives of an essentially social insurance type of program by introducing a test of need into the eligibility conditions. This however was not its intent. The limit applies only to income from work: a beneficiary can receive any amount of income from other sources and still continue to draw benefits. In fact, the dollar limit represents an effort to define by law, and therefore to remove from the realm of administrative discretion, what constitutes "retirement from the labor market." [12] Any earnings less than the amount set out in the law are regarded as derived from casual, and not regular, employment. Thus the dollar limit to earnings is a test of retirement, not of individual needs, and is comparable in intent to other such measures in similar retirement benefit systems.

In any case, the policing of a retirement test creates many administrative problems, and the effort to resolve them, or even to develop a system that is administratively feasible, may lead to the adoption of formulas which, while simplifying the problem of the administrator, create inequities as between persons with different patterns of normal employment.[13]

Another technical difficulty has to be faced if the operation of a retirement clause is not to act as a prohibition upon any kind of economic activity on the part of old-age security beneficiaries. As was pointed out

[12] The original Social Security Act withheld benefits from anyone in receipt of wages from "a regular employment" but did not indicate how regular employment was to be defined.

[13] A notable example is the discrimination against the wage earner as compared to the self-employed worker which prevailed in the United States under the 1952 Act, and which was wholly attributable to administrative considerations. Because earnings from self-employment were computed and reported on a taxable *year*, rather than a *quarterly* basis, deductions from benefits were, for administrative reasons, imposed only if the beneficiary earned more than (at that time) $900 (12 times $75) for the taxable year, and for each $75 in excess of this sum he lost one month's benefits up to 12 in all. Thus while a wage earner who earned over $75 in any one month in the course of a year lost one month's benefit, a self-employed person could earn in the same year $900 and still draw full benefits. Indeed, if the latter could prove that earnings, even greatly in excess of that sum, were earned only in a few months of the year, he would still draw full benefits for the other months in which he was not "substantially" engaged in self-employment. In addition, for persons having both wages and self-employment income, the retirement test was applied independently, so that a person with self-employment income of $900 and wages of exactly $75 a month could receive benefits for all 12 months of the year. Under the 1954 Amendments an annual basis was adopted for both groups and the test applied to wages and self-employment income combined.

above, almost all public systems aim at most to prohibit full-time or "substantial" employment. Indeed, public opinion appears generally to be averse to efforts to enforce complete idleness. But a provision like that operating in the United States, whereby any earnings in excess of the statutory maximum amount result in the denial of the entire benefit for the month in question, will discourage employment unless it yields substantially more than the benefit plus the permitted amount of earnings.[14] Efforts to avoid this difficulty by, as in the United States, continually raising the amount of exempt earnings, would, if carried far, destroy the effectiveness of the retirement clause for substantial numbers of beneficiaries. The alternative solution would be to abandon the "all or nothing" type of retirement test and substitute for it a sliding scale whereby specified amounts of earnings would lead to a somewhat smaller reduction of the benefit. In this way, within the limits of some defined total monthly income the beneficiary would always be better off by some degree of employment. The administration of such a sliding scale of adjustments would, however, not be easy. Until these problems are resolved, such a proposal may well remain impracticable, even though the remarkable skill with which administrative technicians have solved the many other awkward problems associated with the operation of complicated social security systems justifies the hope that in the end this problem too will yield to human ingenuity.

Where it is desired to use the social security system as a positive encouragement to retirement, consideration has to be given to the relationship between the benefit offered and the income which an aged person could hope to secure from employment. From this point of view the retirement clauses in the Social Security Act have scarcely served as a stimulus to retirement. The benefits were originally so low as to offer no real alternative to continuing in employment if this was possible, and even in later years when substantial increases had been given, the benefits barely sufficed for minimum maintenance,[15] and in any case, the rise of earnings

14 Thus up to 1955 in the United States earnings of $76 or more a month involved a loss of the entire benefit for that month. Hence if a man's primary benefit was $60 and he had an eligible wife, the benefit for the couple would have been $90. If his earnings were only $75, his total monthly income would have been $165. If he earned $80, he lost both his own and his wife's benefit, and his total income would have been only $80. In addition, he would have had to pay income tax on his earnings, whereas his social security income would have been tax-free.

15 A study of the living conditions of retired beneficiaries in 1951 showed that even for the two-fifths who were receiving the highest benefits, among those drawing $50 to $59 a month "the majority did not have enough retirement resources of their own to be economically independent for the rest of their lives at what might be characterized as a public assistance level, and even in the group with benefits of $60 to $68.50 a significant proportion was similarly situated." (Edna C. Wentworth, "Economic Situation of Aged Beneficiaries: An Evaluation," *Social Security Bulletin,* April, 1954, p. 26.)

was still more pronounced so that the economic sacrifice of retiring was very considerable. In fact, very large numbers of eligible workers refrain from claiming benefits on reaching age 65 or return to work for longer or shorter periods after they have been awarded benefits.[16]

Even the more generous Railroad Retirement system, whose object was initially frankly stated to be the encouragement of earlier retirement, has been little more successful, and in 1953 the Board reported that both the number and the proportion of aged workers in railroad employment was higher than in any year since the system began.[17]

Moreover, to secure the desired effect the amount of the benefit would need to be changed from time to time. Economic conditions which have favored the accumulation of past savings with which to supplement benefits could markedly affect the retirement-inducing power of any given level of benefits. So too will the wage levels and the opportunities for employment of the aged at the time retirement age is attained.

Some countries, as was indicated above, have attempted to use their social security systems to implement an opposite policy, namely to encourage postponement of retirement. Thus Great Britain, while retaining a modified or partial retirement test, offers a positive inducement to continue at work, in the form of payment of higher pensions when retirement does occur.[18]

The potentialities of this device depend on two factors: how much importance the community attaches to purely financial considerations as against the gain in output to be secured from longer employment of the aged, and the attitude of aged persons toward additions to ultimate

[16] In 1940, on the average, retirement age under OASI was 68.2 for men and 67.6 for women. This rose to 69.6 for men and 68.7 for women in 1946 and had fallen to 68.5 (68.1 for women) by 1952. In December, 1952 the benefits of over a quarter million beneficiaries (8 per cent of the total) were suspended because they were earning more than the permitted amount. For a detailed analysis of retirement experience under OASI, see Robert J. Myers, "OASI: Retirement Test Experience," *Social Security Bulletin*, November, 1953, pp. 14–18.

[17] *Annual Report, 1953*, Railroad Retirement Board, Government Printing Office, Washington, D.C., 1954, pp. 19–21. The average age of retirement in 1952 for those drawing full annuities was 68.1, and only about 3 per cent took advantage of the possibility of retiring below age 65 at a reduced pension. For a discussion of retirement ages in this industry and the probable effect of the size of the benefit thereon, see "The Older Railroad Force in 1952," *The Monthly Review*, February, 1954, pp. 23–27; and "Immediate and Deferred Retirements," *The Monthly Review*, April, 1954, pp. 63–68.

[18] The weekly pension (since 1951) is increased by 1s. 6d. for each six months of employment after age 65 (men) or 60 (women). But after age 70 (men) or 65 (women) pensions are payable regardless of earnings. The same result is achieved in principle (though the absolute amount of the additional pension may be smaller) in those systems where the benefit reflects the total years of covered employment and where earnings after the pensionable age are creditable for this purpose.

pension as an inducement to keep on working beyond the minimum pensionable age.

The financial implications of the device arise from the fact that if it is necessary to offer a substantial inducement, the cost of the additional pensions payable when finally claimed may be more than the saving due to the fact that some aged persons who continue working will die before drawing pensions while those who do draw them will clearly do so for a shorter period. Even so, some communities, if their demand for labor is very intense, may be prepared to pay this money price in order to secure an increase in the total labor supply.

As yet far too little appears to be known about the influence of offers of additional postretirement income, as compared with other factors, on the willingness to work beyond the minimum retirement age.[19] Here again is an area where more research into incentives, motivations, and values of the group concerned is a prerequisite to effective social action.

[19] For a discussion of the probable effects of this provision in Great Britain, see *First Interim Report by the Government Actuary for the Period 5th July, 1949 to 31st March, 1950,* London, 1951 (H.C. Paper 103); *First Report,* National Advisory Committee on the Employment of Older Men and Women, October, 1953, H. M. Stationery Office, London, Cmd. 8963; and *Report of the Ministry of Pensions and National Insurance, 1953,* H. M. Stationery Office, London, p. 29. In the quarter ended September, 1953, 41 per cent of pensions were awarded to men who had retired at or by the age of 65, and 19 per cent of men were still working at the age of 69¾. But the influence of the pension increment for delayed retirement on these figures is not known, and the government actuary in estimating future income and expenditure in 1954 assumed that 35 per cent of men would claim pension immediately on attaining age 65 and that 25 per cent of those attaining age 70 would still be at work. (*Report by the Government Actuary on the First Quinquennial Review,* H. M. Stationery Office, London, 1954, p. 44.) See also *Reasons Given for Retiring or Continuing at Work,* Report of an Enquiry by the Ministry of Pensions and National Insurance, H. M. Stationery Office, London, 1954.

CHAPTER 7

Threats to Continuity of Income: Prolonged Unemployment and Disability

TWO OTHER types of threat to continuity of income have given rise to differences of opinion as to the appropriate extent of public responsibility. Although many countries have developed special measures for providing alternative income during relatively short periods of unemployment, special and organized provision against the risk of long-period unemployment is much less usual. And while almost all countries today have enacted workmen's compensation legislation protecting some or all workers against loss of income due to industrially caused or connected injuries and illnesses, not all of them, and notably the United States, have similar measures to deal with interruptions to earning due to disability, however caused.

INCOME LOSS DUE TO LONG-PERIOD UNEMPLOYMENT

Most unemployment insurance laws pay benefits for only a limited period, usually for a specified number of weeks during some twelve-month period. In other words, they aim to deal only with short-period unemployment.

The American laws follow the same pattern. The maximum number of weeks of benefit that could be drawn by any worker varied, by 1953, from 16 to 26½ weeks.[1] In three-quarters of the states, however, only workers who have had a specified amount of earnings in a given period

---

[1] In 5 states the maximum was less than 20 weeks, in 16 it was 20, and in 29 it was between 2 and 26. One state had a maximum duration of 26½ weeks. ("Duration of Benefits under Unemployment Insurance in 1953," *The Labor Market and Employment Security*, May, 1954, pp. 29ff.). For an account of duration in earlier years, see *Comparison of State Unemployment Insurance Laws as of December, 1951*, U.S. Department of Labor, Bureau of Employment Security, 1952, pp. 65–70. The maximum duration is usually expressed in terms of the number of weeks of total unemployment times the weekly benefit amount. Thus a claimant entitled to $200 in benefits at the weekly rate of $20, within his benefit year, is said to have a maximum potential duration of 10 weeks of full unemployment (or more than this if partially unemployed).

can qualify for these maxima, the rest drawing benefits for shorter periods depending on the amount of their previous earnings, i.e., there is variable, rather than uniform, duration.[2] As a result, since some claimants do not meet the earnings or employment qualification for maximum benefit, the effective maximum in most states with variable duration is lower than the overriding legal maximum.[3] For the country as a whole, insured claimants in all states were entitled to 22.1 weeks of benefit on the average during 1953, although the average for those who exhausted benefit rights was only 19 weeks. Since the inception of the system, the limits to duration have been steadily raised in almost all the states, but many groups, notably organized labor, feel that the average duration is still too short.

Whether or not unemployment insurance should be used to meet the risks of longer-period unemployment depends on a number of factors. One consideration, however, appears to carry less weight than was once the case. This is the argument that in accordance with "insurance" requirements duration must be limited not only to short periods but must also be in some ratio to the contributions paid in the past by the beneficiary.[4] Once, however, it is granted that unemployment insurance is a social insurance rather than an ordinary insurance program,[5] it is clear that the selection of appropriate duration periods must be determined by broader economic and social considerations and in particular by the function which the community desires the program to fulfill, and this fact has been recognized by many systems.

Some countries, however, have applied a modified form of the ratio rule and grant days of benefit in excess of the normal duration to workers with a past record of steady employment.[6]

Much more important in influencing decisions as to duration of unemployment benefits has been (and is likely to be) the incidence and severity of the risk of unemployment. So long as high employment prevails, the number of workers who are still unemployed after they have exhausted all benefits to which they are entitled is not likely to be very large. Even so, in the United States in 1953, a year of high employment and produc-

---

[2] The most common provision restricts the total amount of a claimant's benefit to a fraction of wages in covered employment earned during the base year, subject, of course, to the overriding maximum.

[3] Average potential duration varied in 1953 from 14.2 weeks in Florida to 24.5 weeks in California, although the overriding maxima in these states were 16 and 26 respectively. In 1953, 72.5 per cent of all claimants were eligible for maximum duration, the percentages in the individual states varying from 40 to 88.6 per cent.

[4] The Canadian system adopts the ratio rule to determine benefit duration on this theory. It is less certain how far the similar American variable-duration provisions were consciously adopted in response to the supposed demands of insurance principles.

[5] See Chap. 2.

[6] Thus in Great Britain since 1953 workers who have had a record of steady employment in the past may be able to draw benefit for up to 492 days (19 months).

tion levels, 20.8 per cent of all beneficiaries drew all the benefits to which they were entitled, and in twelve states the percentage was over 30, while in three it exceeded 40.[7] In states with uniform duration the exhaustion ratios were generally lower (13.2 to 35.2 per cent) than in those with variable duration (14.1 to 41.7 per cent), and, as might be expected, the ratios were lower for the states with the higher limits to maximum duration. Decisions as to whether or not this percentage is "unduly high," indicating that there is a failure to make full use of the instrument of unemployment insurance for meeting income loss due to lack of work even in periods of high employment, require perhaps more detailed information about the characteristics and subsequent history of those who exhausted benefits rights than is generally available. Some have held, for example, that the proportion securing employment as soon as benefit rights lapse is sufficiently high to give rise to a suspicion that no very vigorous search for work was undertaken so long as benefits were available. And others have held that married women with no real intention of continuing in the labor market form a disproportionate share of the exhaustees.

It is, however, notable that in a period of the highest employment levels America had known one-fifth of all beneficiaries on the average, and double that proportion in some states, exhausted benefit rights. Were there a serious depression, the country would have to meet a substantial problem of income loss due to unemployment, toward which the instrument of unemployment insurance, with its current duration features, would contribute relatively little.[8] Even in 1950 the exhaustion ratio rose to 30.5 per cent for the United States as a whole, and this was in no sense a year of serious depression. The choice between using this system (by an extension of duration) or some other instrument to assure income to the long-period unemployed can be looked at from the viewpoints of both the unemployed and of the larger community.

For the unemployed workers, unemployment insurance has the advantage, as compared with an income security system based on need, of being

[7] It was estimated by the Department of Labor that an extension of maximum duration of benefit to 39 weeks would have reduced the number of exhaustions in 1953 from 764,500 to 275,000. (*Unemployment Insurance,* Hearings before the House Committee on Ways and Means, 1954, p. 92.) In 1951 to 1952, when some 20 per cent of all beneficiaries exhausted all benefits to which they were entitled, the exhaustees drew benefits for an average of 18.5 weeks.

[8] It is significant that those concerned with the actuarial soundness of unemployment insurance systems always take into account a so-called "automatic cutoff" to the liabilities of the system, in that in a prolonged depression benefit outgo is assumed to fall off rapidly after the first year of recession because benefit rights will have been exhausted, and many of the beneficiaries in subsequent years will have earnings records lower than normal because they will have experienced some unemployment and will therefore have more limited benefit rights, if indeed they are eligible at all.

paid "as a right" and free of much administrative discretion. However, the benefits are relatively low, averaging around a third of previous earnings. While during short spells of unemployment the worker may be able to supplement these from his own savings, the longer he is unemployed, the less is this possible. Thus a decision to use unemployment insurance as the major instrument for long-period as well as short-period unemployment implies a reconsideration of benefit rates, by reference to some criterion of adequacy for maintenance.[9] Furthermore, while short periods of unemployment, if suitably compensated, may not react too adversely on the morale of the worker, long periods without work tend to be depressing and demoralizing (the more so the more naturally independent the worker) and to occasion a loss of skills. For this reason, many have urged that for the long-period unemployed, a public work program is a more suitable answer to loss of income due to unemployment than indefinite duration of unemployment benefit.[10]

To the community, unemployment insurance, as the instrument for dealing with long-period unemployment, also brings both advantages and disadvantages. It permits the utilization of existing administrative machinery for the payment of benefits and thus offers a method whereby income can automatically be channeled to the unemployed. It is likely to cost less (in immediate tax assessments, though allowance should be made for the resultant increase in national assets) than a large public work program. It also involves no difficult decisions about the appropriate spheres of government activity, as does the latter.

For the public provision of work initially involves the allocation of larger funds for the relief of the unemployed than do either social insurance payments or public assistance. If the objectives are to be attained, and the worker is to be made to feel that he has a "real job," prevailing rates of wages must be paid for the work done, whereas the other types of income security program typically make payments that are pegged below normal wage levels. The types of employment must not be too dissimilar to those on which the workers were previously engaged, if their skills are to be maintained, and this may present a formidable task if the system is to be utilized for large numbers of unemployed. Furthermore, efficient production will normally require provision of appropriate materials, machinery and equipment, and technical supervision, another costly item. While this greater investment of public funds

[9] For the impact on benefit levels of the policy of using unemployment insurance as the major income-maintenance instrument in prolonged and general unemployment, see Eveline M. Burns, *British Unemployment Programs, 1920–38,* Social Science Research Council, Washington, D.C., 1941, pp. 64–68.

[10] See, for example, the arguments of the Committee on Long Range Work and Relief Policies in *Security, Work and Relief Policies,* National Resources Planning Board, Government Printing Office, Washington, D.C., 1942, chap. 17 and pp. 504–513.

may bring forth corresponding additions to the volume of output, this consideration may well carry little weight in a period of heavy unemployment when taxpayers are already suffering from reduced incomes and anxious to keep to a minimum the financial burden of supporting the unemployed. Furthermore, the types of products yielded by such publicly created work are, because of prevailing attitudes toward governmental enterprise, likely to be either marginal by reference to values prevailing in the open market or of a nature on which a money value is not easily placed. Private producers are unwilling to countenance what they regard as dangerous incursions by government into the spheres of private enterprise and resist public projects producing commodities which might narrow their own markets.[11] The one area of activity which has commonly been accepted as appropriate for government, namely public works construction, gives employment of too dissimilar a character to utilize the skills and experience of the vast majority of the unemployed, especially at the very time when the need for publicly provided work is most generally recognized, namely during a general and prolonged depression.

Nevertheless, if unemployment insurance is to be utilized as the major instrument for providing income to the long-period unemployed, by paying benefits indefinitely, or for a longer period than the current half a year maximum, the community abandons the limit it had set to the risk of making payments to persons whose unemployment is not wholly outside their own control. Here, as was pointed out in Chapter 4, much will depend on the effectiveness of administrative controls on malingering and in depressions the most useful of these, namely the offer of employment, is least likely to be available. However, by the same token, at such times the actual economic loss to the community due to individual malingerers is also at a minimum since the surplus of supply over demand for labor is then at a maximum. The major economic risk to the community as a whole, interested in minimizing the risk of involuntary unemployment but granting benefits for long duration, occurs in periods of reasonably high employment. For, especially if the system provides benefits of uniform as well as long duration and eligibility requirements are liberal, workers may, through relatively short periods of past employment, establish rights to extensive benefits. The attempt to overcome this situation by providing for higher minimum earnings or employment requirements as a condition of eligibility is not a complete answer because of the danger that relatively high eligibility requirements may

---

[11] For attitudes toward governmental work programs, see Peter Bachrach, "The Right to Work: Emergence of the Idea in the United States," *Social Service Review,* June, 1952, pp. 153–164.

eliminate from benefit rights many individuals for whom unemployment insurance would seem to be an appropriate source of income.[12]

Another method of combining unlimited duration of unemployment insurance benefit with protection of the community against the malingerer was found in Great Britain from 1947 to 1953. Here, nondiscretionary benefits were payable for a limited period (normally thirty weeks), but to attain the right to draw benefits thereafter, the claimant had to appear before a committee which analyzed his work experience in the light of general employment conditions and those in his own occupation and explored possibilities of retraining or otherwise increasing his employment prospects.[13] If he refused to take suggested steps to increase his employment prospects, he could be denied benefit. In some systems with long benefit duration, the freedom of the claimant to refuse work in other than his usual occupation may similarly be limited to a designated number of weeks following his unemployment. Thereafter he may be disqualified if he refuses work in other than his usual occupation.

Finally, as unemployment insurance pays benefits without a test of need, the community may find itself paying benefits indefinitely to some long-period unemployed who are not in need as judged by prevailing standards. Especially if unemployment is severe, and the burden of support heavy, the voters may wish at some point to limit social security income to those who are defined as needy.

INCOME LOSS DUE TO DISABILITY

In most countries possessing fairly extensive social security systems, measures to provide alternative income for workers prevented by disability from earning have not only figured prominently but have often been among the first types of program to be developed. In the United States, on the other hand, public provision against income loss due to disability was, by the mid-1950s, still very limited. It is true that in most parts of the country the needy sick or disabled might hope to secure some economic support from the public assistance system, and three categories of persons, the permanently and totally disabled, the blind, and disabled persons responsible for young children, might be eligible for assistance from one of the three relevant special public assistances

---

[12] This does not mean, however, that consideration should not be given to earnings requirements when duration is changed. Some of the earnings requirements of certain American states appear to be excessively liberal in view of the amount of benefits for which a worker satisfying them is eligible.

[13] Significantly, however, the committee was prohibited by statute from giving any consideration to the applicant's economic circumstances, i.e., further payment of benefit was in no sense conditional upon a means test.

(APTD, AB, or ADC). But the non-needs test, nondeterrent types of social security program designed to meet income loss due to disability were limited to veterans, to railroad workers, and to cases where the disability was occupational in origin.[14] In addition, in four states there were laws providing social insurance payments for a limited period when earnings were interrupted by disability, however caused.[15] A major issue in contemporary America is raised by proposals to cover the risk of income loss due to both long- and short-period physical disability by social insurance or similar non-means-test systems.

At first sight it might seem curious that in a country which had accepted the general idea of public action based on other than public assistance principles there should be any issue to debate. There can be little dispute as to the severity of the risk of income loss due to disability, for a long series of inquiries over the last twenty years has established the facts. Furthermore, it would seem as if, unlike payments made to able-bodied persons, a system of disability insurance would involve no risk to national output, since sick or disabled recipients would be unable to produce in any case. In fact, however, some of the main doubts about such proposals concern the feasibility of restricting cash payments to persons who are genuinely disabled (i.e., how administratively to test the actual occurrence of the risk) and the effect of assured payments on the beneficiary.[16]

The obvious method of determining the existence of disability would

14 Even so, the workmen's compensation laws by no means covered all employed workers and often failed to cover all occupational diseases. Cf. Herman Miles Somers and Anne Ramsay Somers, *Workmen's Compensation,* John Wiley & Sons, Inc., New York, 1954, pp. 38–59.

15 For an account of these systems see Alfred M. Skolnik, "Temporary Disability Insurance Laws in the United States," *Social Security Bulletin,* October, 1952, pp. 11–22; Margaret M. Dahm, "Temporary Disability Insurance: The California Program," *Social Security Bulletin,* February, 1953, pp. 15ff.; *Rhode Island Disability Insurance Program,* U.S. Department of Labor, Bureau of Employment Security, July, 1954, and Eveline M. Burns, *The American Social Security System,* Houghton Mifflin Company, Boston, 1951, chap. 8.

16 In the United States there are also differences of opinion as to methods of financing and the appropriate administrative arrangements, including the respective responsibilities of the Federal government and the states and the question of whether there should be a single combined permanent and temporary disability program or whether permanent disability should be linked administratively to OASI, with temporary disability, treated as a separate program or linked to unemployment insurance. These problems will be dealt with in the chapters on financing and administration. Cf. A. D. Marshall, "Some Basic Issues in Compulsory Temporary Disability Insurance," *American Economic Security,* September–October, 1949; and Margaret Greenfield, *Permanent and Total Disability,* University of California Bureau of Public Administration, 1953 Legislative Problems, no. 4, Berkeley, Calif., 1953.

appear to be to rely on certification by the patient's attendant physician, and this device is in fact found, alone or with additional controls, in all disability insurance systems. It is, however, disliked by some members of the medical profession as introducing a new element into the patient-doctor relationship, since it appears to make the doctor's judgment the determining influence on the patient's rights to secure benefit. Other professions, such as teachers and clergy, may find very strange the medical profession's fear that good professional-client relationships will be disturbed if the professional renders a decision dictated by his scientific knowledge and judgment but which is disliked by his client. Nevertheless, the experience of certain disability insurance systems suggests that the pressure from patients for improper certifications may prove to be more than some members of the medical profession can resist, and that some additional controls are called for.

These in turn have been criticized by the medical profession as leading to third-party intervention between them and their patients and as involving a grave risk of lay control of professional judgments. In fact, however, the problems do not seem to be insuperable, provided the administration is prepared to use professional personnel to operate the controls and provided the profession is prepared to cooperate with the administration. Some agencies, for example, develop statistical and administrative tests to reveal cases of undue liberality in certification (by comparing each doctor's record with the average) or set up, with medical advice, standards as to the normal duration of various illnesses and scrutinize only the certifications of those doctors whose patients persistently remain "unable to resume employment" for longer than the normal period. Such methods leave the vast majority of medical men undisturbed by controlling authorities. Typically too, where the validity of certifications is questioned the agency relies on the judgment of professional personnel employed on either a salary or fee basis. And similarly, if it appears necessary to require the patient to appear for examination, it is always provided that such impartial examinations shall be conducted by medical personnel.[17]

Hence, although not all disability insurance systems have been sufficiently scrupulous to call upon medical personnel in every case for what are essentially technical medical issues, the experience of many systems, including some of those found in America, demonstrates that with good will on both sides, the determination of the occurrence of the risk can

---

[17] Cf. the methods used by the Railroad Retirement Board, which also uses the home visit by a member of the Board's staff in questionable temporary disability cases. ("Checking for Irregularities in Unemployment and Sickness Benefit Claims," *The Monthly Review*, October, 1954, pp. 192–194.)

be solved with a minimum of lay control of the medical profession and a reasonable protection of the taxpayers' interests.[18]

A further problem which has greatly exercised the medical profession in Europe, although it appears as yet to have caused less concern in the United States, relates to the impact of programs of this type on medical secrecy. Two considerations point to the desirability, if not the necessity, of giving the administration information concerning the specific illness from which a claimant for benefit is suffering. The first is the operation of controls to ensure that benefits are paid only in respect of genuine disability, in the interest of those who foot the bill and the wider community which has a stake in maximizing economic output. The second is the general desirability of obtaining as a valuable by-product from a disability insurance system, a tabulation and analysis and a distribution of morbidity data to health and other interested agencies. Yet here too, experience shows that the problem is not insoluble, through the use of such devices as the adoption of codes or symbols intelligible only to the initiated or by laying upon all those who process the raw data the same duties of professional secrecy and confidentiality as are common to medical personnel.[19]

The technical difficulty of certifications in cases where psychosomatic factors appear to be involved is admittedly a challenging problem, whose resolution is likely to await further developments in medical science and skill. Meanwhile, the danger that some payments may be made to persons whose disability, in the judgment of lay persons at least, is within their own control, has caused some advocates of permanent disability insurance systems to exclude such types of illness from the risks recognized as justifying public action.[20]

[18] Cf. summary of attitudes of the Rhode Island Medical Society in 1954. "In actual operation the medical administration of the program is now working smoothly. Cooperation between the agency and the Society is described as excellent. The Society is satisfied with the procedures for medical certification, and for the most part with those relating to impartial examinations. It believes that the forms which doctors fill out have been simplified as far as possible. The Society has made every effort to educate its members to the importance of returning medical certifications to the agency promptly to expedite the payment of benefits to claimants." (*Rhode Island Disability Insurance Program*, p. 58.)

[19] For a fuller discussion of this issue, see Dr. Charles Berlioz, "Medical Secrecy under Social Insurance Legislation," in *Reports of the Permanent Committees*, I, Medico-Social Committee, International Social Security Association, Geneva, 1954, pp. 11–21.

[20] This was presumably the intent of the Senate Advisory Council of 1948, which proposed a limited permanent and total disability insurance system, in which, to be eligible, a worker "would have to be unable, by reason of a disability *medically demonstrable by objective tests* to perform any substantially gainful activity" [italics supplied]. *Permanent and Total Disability Insurance*, A Report to the Senate Committee on Finance from the Advisory Council on Social Security, S. Doc. 162, 80th Cong., 2d Sess., 1948, pp. 2–3 (hereinafter referred to by title only).

But quite apart from these problems which cause especial concern to the medical profession and some of which arise because of a possible conflict of interests between the representatives of medicine and the social security institutions financed by, and answerable to, the citizens, other difficulties are presented by public disability insurance systems, particularly those concerned with permanent or long-period disability. For short-period disability the problems are less serious, since the limited duration of benefit sets a term to the risk run by society as a whole that some "not genuinely disabled persons" may receive benefits. In fact, in such programs the main problem additional to those already discussed has concerned not the genuineness of disability but the genuineness of attachment of the claimant to the labor market and has arisen notably in connection with the payment of pregnancy benefits.[21]

Payments for permanent disability present more difficulties, and since there are no time limits to duration [22] improper or undesirable payments may have serious consequences both for those footing the bill and for the beneficiaries themselves. In many respects the effects upon the beneficiary are those which give rise to most concern. On the one hand, it is argued, the psychological effect of a decision that an individual is permanently and totally disabled (a necessary administrative step in determining eligibility) cannot be otherwise than harmful. As is indicated below the impressive achievements of modern rehabilitation programs suggest that relatively few persons are "permanently" totally disabled. Hence such a ruling is held to raise unnecessary psychological obstacles to rehabilitative efforts.

In some countries this difficulty has in part been met by the use of different language, "long-period disability" or "invalidity insurance," for example, and efforts have been made to define in more or less objective terms the degree of incapacity that gives a right to a pension payable so long as the incapacity or loss of earning power persists. However, even where the criteria relate to capacity to obtain employment, decisions have to be made as to the precise departure from normalcy, i.e., what percentage of loss of normal earning power shall confer eligibility, and whether the loss of income to be compensated refers to inability to work in one's normal employment or in any employment at all.[23] These deter-

---

[21] For a discussion of this problem see *Rhode Island Disability Insurance Program,* pp. 21–23, 40–46.

[22] In workmen's compensation systems in the United States, the existence of maximum dollar limits to total compensation payable often sets a limit to duration. (Cf. Somers and Somers, *op. cit.,* pp. 69–70.) In the normal permanent disability or invalidity insurance system, however, payment usually continues until the recipient reaches the age qualifying for an old-age pension or dies.

[23] The Federal Advisory Council, for example, adopted the most restrictive criterion. Eligibility was to be based on inability "to perform any substantially gainful activity."

minations, moreover, cannot always be made regardless of the state of the labor market, for the disabled person, as a general rule, is a marginal worker whose prospects of employment are very sensitive to changes in the general level of the demand for labor.

On the other hand, difficult questions arise as to the action to be taken if a beneficiary, as a result either of his own efforts or of rehabilitative measures, increases his earning capacity above the limit which defines eligibility. Thus if a reduction of earning capacity to less than one-third of normal confers eligibility, and if a benefit of 50 per cent of previous earnings is payable, the beneficiary whose earning power is raised above $33\frac{1}{3}$ per cent but less than 50 per cent will have worsened his economic position as a result of his efforts. This situation has even wider ramifications. In recent years increasing emphasis has been placed by the medical profession and others on the possibilities of rehabilitation, so that "it is becoming more and more risky to maintain that this or that complaint is no longer capable of cure, in view of the progress in methods of medical and surgical treatment and of the ever more exact and more efficient resources of physical conditioning and ego therapy." [24] The distinction between "temporary" and "permanent" incapacity for work is indeed becoming outmoded; one between short- and long-period disability appears more fitting in the present state of medical and rehabilitative knowledge.

However, the return to complete or almost complete earning capacity, i.e., to economic independence, deprives the worker of the right to an invalidity pension, at least in those systems where the disability insurance system is envisaged as a protection against loss or reduction of earning capacity.[25] But this means that the rehabilitated person abandons the security of a pension, however modest, in return for presumably higher earnings which are, however, subject to all the uncertainties of the labor market. Many people have felt therefore that the fear of losing long-period or permanent disability benefits acts as a psychological obstacle to undergoing rehabilitation, especially in periods of less than full employment.[26]

---

[24] Report on the meeting of experts, by Dr. Jerome Dejardin, *The Evaluation of Invalidity*, Report III, Eleventh General Meeting, International Social Security Association, Geneva, 1954, p. 11 (hereinafter referred to by title only). This volume contains valuable information on the policies and methods of a large number of countries. For an account of the accomplishments, actual and potential, of rehabilitation in the United States, see Somers and Somers, *op. cit.*, chap. 7; and Henry H. Kessler, M.D., *Rehabilitation of the Physically Handicapped*, Columbia University Press, New York, 1953.

[25] For the position in workmen's compensation and veterans' legislation, see below.

[26] For a discussion of this general problem and the practice of various countries, see *Rehabilitation and Assessment of Benefit*, Report IV, Tenth General Meeting, International Social Security Association, Geneva, 1951, *passim*.

Some countries have tried to meet this difficulty by permitting the rehabilitated individual to revert to his beneficiary status with a minimum of delay and formality if his earning power substantially declines. In other cases (e.g., the post-1948 British Industrial Injuries Scheme) the disabled worker continues to receive some fraction of his benefit even if his earning power is wholly or substantially restored. This, however, may raise difficulties with other, noninjured workers, and, apart from its possibly favorable influence on the attitude to rehabilitation (which all agree is necessary if the process is to have a successful outcome), this type of adjustment can be defended only on the theory that injury as such calls for some compensation.

The question whether the occasion which justifies public action is loss of earning capacity or the need to make reparation for physical injury regardless of its effect on earning capacity is, indeed, a major policy issue that has to be decided in devising non-means-test, nondiscretionary disability programs. It is particularly acute in workmen's compensation and measures for veterans. Here, the benefit provisions consist of an amalgam of both objectives. Workmen's compensation systems typically provide benefits (of limited or unlimited duration) which aim to compensate for income loss. But they also provide permanent partial disability payments which are payable by reference to specific types of disability or disablement and which are often paid regardless of the effect upon earning power.[27] Similarly, the Veterans' program in the United States assesses disabilities by reference to physical criteria and makes payments for disabilities of specific degrees, regardless of the effect upon capacity to earn.[28]

The rationale for such payments appears to lie either in a desire to reward the victims for injury or personal discomfort received in the service of the community (an obvious element in veterans' payments and perhaps figuring somewhat in workmen's compensation) or a desire to penalize those who are held responsible for causing the injury (the idea of employer fault is still reflected in many of the provisions of workmen's compensation). The importance of these attitudes will presumably condition in the future, as in the past, the extent to which reparation for physical or mental injury will find a place side by side with measures to compensate for loss or reduction of income. Meanwhile, in many systems the haphazard admixture of the two types of benefit seems to have led to unexpected anomalies, sometimes to a failure fully to attain either

[27] They will continue to be paid even if the worker returns to full wages at his old occupation, either indefinitely or for some fixed period or as a lump sum.

[28] For an account of the veterans' system, see Burns, *The American Social Security System,* chap. 10.

objective and sometimes to extremely generous treatment of the persons covered by such systems as compared with those whose earning power has been reduced for other reasons.

In any case, the problem of assessment of degrees of injury is administratively highly troublesome, and the device of more or less elaborate schedules or invalidity tables has not proved very satisfactory.[29] And the attaching of a money sum to specific disabilities or degrees of invalidity is likely to be a more or less arbitrary matter, unless weight is given to the concept of loss of earning power. But if this is done, the value of a schedule is much reduced, since specific disabilities have different economic consequences for workers in different occupations.[30]

From this brief account of some of the problems presented by the decision to provide assured income in cases of income loss due to disability two conclusions are inescapable. First, the administration of such programs, and especially long-period disability, involves a high degree of individualization. If proper determinations are to be made of the applicant's physical and mental condition, if the effect on his earning power is to be correctly assessed, and if appropriate rehabilitation and retraining measures are to be taken, these objectives can only be secured by a careful consideration of all the circumstances affecting each individual case.[31] Nor can a decision, once rendered, stand for all time. Changes in the beneficiary's condition, or in medical knowledge which might be utilized for his benefit, point to the undesirability of regarding any decision regarding eligibility and amount of benefit as final.

Second, the administration of such programs calls for the cooperation of a variety of experts. Not merely medical men but experts on occupational characteristics and requirements and on the supply and demand situation in various occupations, as well as vocational rehabilitation experts and social workers, are involved in the process.

But while it is evident that the successful administration of a disability income program (especially long-term disability) makes administrative demands that are far more difficult, and in the short run more costly, than are made by such a risk system as old-age insurance, it does not follow that the problems are insoluble or that public action would have

---

[29] Cf. *The Evaluation of Invalidity, passim.*

[30] Thus the loss of a finger means something very different to a pianist and to a manual worker. For the nature of these schedules in workmen's compensation in the United States, see Somers and Somers, *op. cit.*, pp. 70–74.

[31] Cf. Dr. Dejardin, "It [the method of determining invalidity] has as a consequence like all human problems, the individualization of every case, since it allows the assignment of a different degree of invalidity to persons suffering from the same injury, but who, on account of different age, different vocational training, residence in regions offering different possibilities of employment, may nevertheless possess a quite different earning capacity." (*The Evaluation of Invalidity*, p. 5.)

to await the resolution of all of them. Most modern countries have for decades operated disability insurance systems (both short- and long-period). In the United States the Railroad Retirement Board has for many years operated disability insurance programs for both long- and short-period disability, while short-term disability insurance programs have proved their feasibility and viability in four states.[32] Since 1950, moreover, almost all the American states have administered permanent total disability assistance programs, where the technical problems of determining the extent of disability are precisely similar to those in disability insurance systems.

The decision that has to be made, therefore, by the people of America is whether some measure of failure successfully to solve all the administrative problems of operating a disability social insurance program (including securing the maximum gains from rehabilitation possibilities) is too large or too small a price to pay for removing from the mass of the citizens the fear of income loss due to disability. Furthermore, a truly constructive program with major emphasis, in the case of long-period disability, on rehabilitation demands a willingness on the part of the community to invest a more substantial sum in the disabled person than would be required in a program limited to income maintenance. And despite the evidence that such an investment can yield substantial returns,[33] other claims on the taxpayer's money may prevail. Finally, the form of disability program adopted will be influenced by whether the

[32] The poor performance under American workmen's compensation laws, in terms of benefits accruing to workers, costs of the program, administrative simplicity and speed, and extent to which rehabilitation is seen as a major objective, preclude the citing of these systems in support of the view that acceptable solutions of the various problems are to hand. However, the successful experience of workmen's compensation systems in Canada, and notably in Ontario, indicates that the weaknesses of this program in the United States are due to peculiarities of the laws and administrations in that country and are not inherent in the system. Similarly far too little is known about the administration of the Veterans' program, and notably of the extent to which a desirable balance is maintained between the interests of the taxpayer and the wider community and the veteran body, to permit citation of this program as proof that the problems discussed in this section are capable of solution.

[33] Cf. *Brass Tacks*, Federal Security Agency, Office of Vocational Rehabilitation, 1949, pp. 18–19; K. Pohlmann, "Rehabilitation of the Severely Disabled: UMWA Welfare and Retirement Fund Experience," *American Journal of Public Health*, April, 1953, pp. 445–451; and Mary E. Switzer, "Disability and Dollars: An Investment Prospectus," *Employment Security Review*, October, 1953, pp. 16ff. See especially *Characteristics of the Low-Income Population and Related Federal Programs*, a Report prepared for the Sub-Committee on Low-Income Families of the Joint Committee on the Economic Report, Joint Committee Print., 84th Cong., 1st Sess., Government Printing Office, Washington, D.C., 1955, Section 2. The Disabled: The Role of Vocational Rehabilitation in Improving the Economic Condition of Low-Income Families, *passim*. This report is hereinafter referred to by title only.

community desires to protect its members against loss of income or desires also, or instead, to pay some special gratuity to the individual who has suffered some disablement, regardless of its effect upon his earning power.

In view of the admittedly real problems associated with the determination of disability for benefit-payment purposes, some groups in the United States (and notably the medical profession and private insurance companies) have held that the wiser approach is for government to foster preventive and rehabilitative measures. But hitherto the experience with the one major public rehabilitation program, namely the federally aided Vocational Rehabilitation system, gives little ground for optimism. As late as 1950 to 1951, after the program had been in operation twenty-three years, only some 66,000 persons were being rehabilitated annually despite the known fact of 250,000 otherwise employable persons being disabled each year. Nor has the progress of rehabilitation under workmen's compensation given much ground for encouragement.[34]

Whether the rehabilitation program could be stepped up sufficiently to have a real impact upon the extent of present disability and whether preventive measures could lessen the incidence of disability in the future are the questions that must be answered if preventive and rehabilitative measures are to be thought of as an alternative to, rather than as an integral part of, a program for assuring income during inability to earn because of illness.

In any case, no one seriously argues that such measures could be expected to eliminate the need for alternative income for a large proportion of those disabled over the next ten or fifteen years. And there will always be some people whom no therapeutic treatment or retraining can return to complete self-support. This problem is especially acute for those in the older years and the extent of inability to earn on account of disability as old age approaches is one of the most powerful arguments of those who press for a lowering of the present age limit (65) of OASI.[35]

[34] Cf. Somers and Somers, *op. cit.*, chap. VII.

[35] It is significant that in 1948 the Senate Advisory Council on Social Security, while greatly impressed by the problems of operating a permanent disability insurance program, nonetheless urged enactment of such a measure to pay benefits to disabled persons.

CHAPTER 8

Threats to Adequacy of Incomes: The Costs of Medical Care

IN MANY COUNTRIES public action has removed the costs of necessary medical care from three categories of individuals (and sometimes their families). These three groups are military forces and veterans; persons whose disability arises out of, and in connection with, their employment; and persons whose resources are so meager that they have been found eligible for receipt of income from public assistance. Most countries with substantial income security systems, other than the United States, have also developed other public programs whereby workers, and sometimes all citizens, receive medical care free, or at reduced cost, unaccompanied by any requirement to undergo a test of need.

These programs have taken three major forms: public subsidies to voluntary insurance organizations, most usually mutual benefit societies or clubs, or trade unions organized to provide medical care for their members; compulsory social insurance systems, whereby workers who have paid the necessary number of contributions are entitled to secure all, or specified types, of medical care free or at reduced cost; and national health systems under which medical care (of all or specified types) becomes a free commodity, like roads or public education, which is supplied by the state.[1]

By 1955 governments in the United States had accepted a responsibility for medical care costs in the case of veterans (for all service-connected, and in some cases for non-service-connected, disabilities), for some, but not all, workers injured (and in some cases incurring diseases) as a result of their employment and for needy or (more rarely) "medically indigent" persons held to be eligible under the public assistance laws.[2] The

[1] For a convenient summary of legislation see Carl H. Farman, *Health and Maternity Insurance throughout the World, Principal Legislative Provisions*, reprint of part 8 of Hearings before the House Committee on Interstate and Foreign Commerce, Social Security Administration, Division of Research and Statistics, 1954. For more detail on selected countries, see *Relations between Social Security Institutions and the Medical Profession*, Report IV, Eleventh General Meeting, International Social Security Association, Geneva, 1953 (hereinafter referred to by title only). For developments in the United States, see Michael M. Davis, *Medical Care for Tomorrow*, Harper and Brothers, New York, 1955, *passim*.

[2] In addition, in one state, workers were compulsorily insured under the temporary

public also bears the cost in varying degree in the different states for medical care in the case of certain illnesses, such as mental illness, tuberculosis, and the like. In addition, tax funds are used to support an increasing proportion of medical research and play an important role in hospital construction. Many proposals have been made in recent years in the United States for some public action to socialize the costs of medical care, either of all kinds or for some unusually costly types of care (such as hospitalization or treatment of certain types of illness).[3] This socialization could take the form of one, or some combination, of the types of public program found in other countries.

ALTERNATIVE METHODS OF FINANCING AND ORGANIZING MEDICAL CARE

Because the decision to add the costs of medical care to the range of risks for which public responsibility is accepted implies a knowledge of alternative ways of financing and organizing the supply of medical care, the nature of the three most common forms of public program calls for description.

The method of subsidizing voluntary health insurance plans is the oldest but is also the one which has been least favored in recent years, although many proposals for the adoption of this method have been made in the United States. Under this system, as it has developed in a number

---

disability insurance law for up to eight weeks of hospital care. The provisions for medical care under public assistance laws varied greatly from state to state and within states and, in general, were far from adequate. As late as 1953, in a small number of states neither state nor local public assistance funds were used for medical care, while in some others where local funds only were used, the programs were very limited. Reporting on the situation as a whole, the American Public Welfare Association declared, "When only 15 state public assistance agencies are able to aid localities in the financing of all medical requirements of recipients, when only 13 states have organized medical units responsible for the development and administration or supervision of a medical assistance program, when only 15 states have formally constituted advisory committees in the health field and when only 8 states have established quantity-quality-cost standards for all essential medical care items, it is certainly obvious that there is much yet to be done by state assistance agencies." (Pearl Bierman, "General Aspects of Medical Assistance," part I of a series of reports on *The Role of the State Public Assistance Agency in Medical Care,* American Public Welfare Association, Chicago, 1953 *et seq.,* p. 8. The later reports analyze the nature and methods of administering these programs in more detail.) For a state-by-state study of the nature and extent of public medical care of assistance recipients as of 1946, see *Medical Care in Public Assistance, 1946,* Social Security Administration, Bureau of Public Assistance Report 16, 1948. See also "Tax-supported Medical Care for the Needy," *Public Welfare,* October, 1952.

[3] For details see Maurice B. Hamovitch, "History of the Movement for Compulsory Health Insurance in the United States," *Social Service Review,* September, 1953, pp. 381–399; Davis, *op. cit.,* and references to congressional hearings given later in this chapter.

of European countries, certain types of nonprofit health insurance plans receive a subsidy from public funds provided they meet specified conditions which usually relate to membership, minimum benefits to be provided, and financial stability. No country has achieved one hundred per cent coverage of the population, or even of all workers, by this method, for the obvious reason that the incomes of some persons are too small to permit them to pay the premiums even when lowered by the public subsidy, while, so long as membership is voluntary, there are always some people who could afford the premiums but who refuse to insure. Furthermore, experience has shown that in the effort to reduce premiums so as to make such insurance available to lower-income groups, public subsidies have increased in proportion to income from contributions or premiums, and with this increasing subsidization has gone, understandably enough, an increase in public control. Inevitably at some point the question has been raised whether such a system differs in any major respect from a wholly public program, except in the complexity of its organization. The urge to substitute a wholly public program has been strengthened by the fact that under the system of subsidized voluntary plans, levels of service vary not only with the efficiency of management of the individual funds but also with the character of their membership and notably its occupational composition and economic level and its geographical location. Hence the general tendency has been either to introduce indirect methods of compulsion [4] or to transform the system into one of the other two types of public medical care program.

Systems of compulsory health insurance are in general form closely similar to compulsory social insurance plans for income security. Certain categories of persons (either workers and the self-employed or workers and their employers) are required to pay contributions (or taxes) on the basis of which an insured worker is entitled to benefits. But the benefit takes the form either, as in Germany or the earlier British health insurance system, for example, of free access to certain defined types of medical services, or, as in the French and other systems, of indemnifying the patient for all, or a part, of the fees he has paid the doctor, hospital, or pharmacist. The insured person usually has free choice of doctor or at least of those doctors who have indicated their willingness to practice under the system. Sometimes the insurance funds own their own hospitals and clinics, but more usually service is supplied by other public or private health agencies, who are reimbursed directly or via the patient from the insurance funds.

Under a public medical service the defined categories of persons who are eligible obtain medical care as needed from physicians and other

[4] Thus, in Denmark, the right to old-age pensions is dependent on membership in a voluntary health insurance fund.

medical personnel and receive treatment in institutions which are financed by public funds and are usually publicly owned and operated. The suppliers of professional services may be remunerated in a variety of ways which are often identical with those found in compulsory health insurance systems. However, usually no direct financial transactions occur between the recipient and the donor of medical care. For the persons covered, who in some countries, such as Great Britain, may be the whole population,[5] the system is in all respects similar in operation to the public educational service, for access to the service is conditional neither on the passage of a test of need or income nor on the prior payment of contributions.

The different methods whereby government has sought to remove the burden of costs of medical care from individuals and families have many similarities but also some fundamental differences. The extent of the medical services offered, or reimbursable, for example, can be wide or narrow under any method. Some health insurance systems offer only a limited range of care. The British health insurance system, for example, was essentially a general-practitioner service. Other types of medical care were available, if at all, only as additional benefits offered by those Approved Societies (the administrative bodies), which by reason of good management or low incidence of illness among their members were in an unusually favorable financial position. Other schemes, such as the French and some other European systems, have been more ambitious, offering a complete range of medical services including specialist service, hospitalization, dental care, and rehabilitation.

On the other hand, while some national health services, such as the British, remove from the patient the costs of an almost unlimited variety and extent of medical care, there are others that offer a very narrow range of care. In the American states, for example, a public medical and dental service for the inspection of all school children is very common, but this public service does not typically extend to the treatment of all children found by such inspection to be in need of remedial care. Similarly, some countries provide for complete health service under public auspices for sufferers from tuberculosis although they do not take a similar responsibility for other types of illness.

Similarly under any type of system the range of persons covered may be wide or narrow. There are some public medical service programs that are limited to defined categories of people. Medical and health care for veterans as provided in the United States and elsewhere is an example of a wholly public medical care program of this type. On the other hand,

[5] For the most comprehensive and balanced account of the British Health Service, see James Sterling Ross, *The National Health Service in Great Britain,* Oxford University Press, New York, 1952.

some national health services, such as those of Great Britain and New Zealand, cover the entire population. Some compulsory health insurance systems (such as the British between 1913 and 1948) have provided care only for the covered worker and make no provision for the medical needs of the dependent family, while others (such as the French and German systems) cover the family as well. Some insurance systems are limited to certain categories of wage earners, while others have covered almost an entire population, though it would admittedly be difficult to cover everyone if eligibility for the service is conditional upon the prior payment of contributions by the sick individual or on his behalf. Even here, however, universal coverage could be secured on an insurance basis if some other public authority, e.g., a public assistance agency, were prepared to pay the premiums for such persons. From this point of view, a public medical service would merely be a less complicated method of achieving universal coverage.

Nor is there a major difference between the various systems in the extent to which they involve the government in negotiations with the appropriate professions regarding the terms of remuneration. Under any system, if the burdens of medical costs are to be effectively removed from the patient, or their incidence is to be substantially lightened, the public authorities become concerned with the methods of remuneration and the nature of the charges of the medical profession. This is obvious under a public medical service. Here the government must be able to attract and retain the services of such medical personnel as are needed to provide the promised medical benefits to the eligible population. Whatever the method of remuneration adopted (and, as will be shown below, a variety of methods including salary, fee-for-service, and the capitation system is available), the economic return to the members of the professions concerned must prove sufficiently attractive to assure the desired supply. But under an indemnity system, too, a government becomes involved in the economics of the medical profession. For the amount of the indemnity must clearly be related to the normal charges of the physician. If, as has been the case in New Zealand, for example, the government scheme reimburses the patient by a fixed payment for each visit of the doctor but leaves the medical man free to charge a total fee as much above this sum as he thinks the traffic will bear, the only effect of such a plan may be to offer an income guarantee to all doctors, and the patient may still find himself burdened with a heavy cost. If there is then pressure on the government to raise the level of the indemnity, the total costs of the service may vastly increase and give rise to pressure on both government and the medical profession to reach some agreement about acceptable charges. Such a settlement might take the form of drawing up approved schedules for charges for different types of service or an agreement on the part of the profession to accept the public indemnity in full settlement of their bill to the patient, in which case the amount of the indemnity becomes a vital issue. In either event, government becomes involved in problems of the proper remuneration of a profession.[6]

Finally, as we have seen, not even the subsidized voluntary insurance schemes can eliminate the necessity for standard setting by government, although here the degree of public intervention in the rendering of service is admittedly less than under a compulsory health insurance system and very much less than under a public medical service.

It is doubtful, too, whether the distinction between compulsory health insurance and a public medical or health service lies in the form in which the patient receives his benefit, that is to say whether the plan offers merely an indemnification of all or part of medical costs incurred, or provides benefits in the form of direct medical services. The indemnity system, as we have seen, occurs in voluntary health insurance systems, where it is very usual, in compulsory health insurance systems, and in at least one national health service (that of New Zealand). While changing to the minimum degree the basis of organizing and financing medical care, it has been rejected by many systems for the reasons that:

> The system of direct provision of benefits is the more appropriate system where the full cost, with few exceptions, is borne by the state. It is more convenient for the patient, to the professions involved, to the hospitals and other institutions, and is simpler administratively. It does not require the patient to have money available before seeking treatment and avoids any financial barrier between patient and treatment.[7]

On the other hand, the strength of the organized professions has ensured its retention in many systems, of which the French and New Zealand systems are notable examples. For to the professions, the indemnity system serves as a guarantee of minimum income since it assures the collection of fees up to the amount of the public reimbursement, and where physicians have been able successfully to charge fees over and above the amount reimbursed, the system offers them every advantage. For the community, however, the indemnity system merely increases the effective demand for medical care but offers no guarantee either that

---

[6] A major feature of the operation of the American Emergency Maternity and Infant Care program for meeting the costs of medical care before, during, and after delivery, of the wives of certain grades of servicemen during World War II, for example, was the dispute between the medical profession and the government regarding the latter's insistence that the standard payment to the doctor was to be in full settlement of his claims against the patient.

[7] "Memorandum submitted by the Ministry of Pensions and National Insurance, United Kingdom," in *Relations between Social Security Institutions and the Medical Profession*, p. 247. For a fuller statement of the case against the indemnity system, see the Austrian report in *ibid.*, pp. 107–108; see also the German reply in *ibid.*, p. 223.

there will be any expansion of preventive health services or even that the supply of personnel and facilities will be expanded in response to the increased demand for curative services. At least one country has rejected the indemnity system in favor of direct provision of service by the insurance funds on the ground that the latter is more economical.[8]

The major differences between the various public systems hitherto developed would seem to relate to two characteristics: whether the right to benefit is or is not conditional upon the prior payment of a specified number of contributions; and whether government, in developing the program, accepts responsibility for assuring the availability of adequate personnel and facilities for meeting all types of health needs.

The presence or absence of a contributory requirement as a condition of eligibility is a very important differentiating characteristic of the various available public systems. Under a public medical service, the right of the patient to receive services (or occasionally reimbursement) is not, as it is under health insurance systems, dependent on the prior payment of contributions, or for that matter on any other test.[9] This overcomes one of the disadvantages of compulsory health insurance, namely that the system of requiring prior contributions as a condition of eligibility inevitably bars some individuals from access to the service. While, as was shown in Chapter 4, a case may be made for this kind of barrier in income security programs, no public interest can be invoked for denying medical care and rehabilitation to persons in need of such services. At the same time, national health systems differ from systems of public medical care available under public assistance laws in that eligibility is not conditional upon passing a needs test.

In the second place, the systems differ according to the range and scope of the responsibilities accepted by the government. Under a public medical service the government not only removes all or part of the cost of medical care from those covered by the plan but also itself accepts responsibility for ensuring a supply of services and facilities to the extent called for by the health needs of the eligible group. Thus in the Veteran's health program in the United States it is the Federal government which builds hospitals and other facilities, which hires the needed medical personnel (by salary or other arrangements), and which sets the standards of service. Similarly, in Great Britain, where in 1946 the people authorized their government "to promote the establishment . . . of a comprehensive health service designed to secure the improvement in the physical and mental health of the people . . . and the prevention, diagnosis and treatment of illness," it was inevitable that the relevant Act should add

[8] See reply of the Austrian Federation of Social Insurance Institutions in *ibid.*, p. 108.

[9] The British system even extends this right to foreigners who may find themselves in need of care while in the country.

"and to provide, or secure the effective provision, of services in accordance with the foregoing provisions." Since in Britain the coverage of the Service is universal and embraces all kinds of health service, this has meant in fact that the government, through the Ministry of Health, has to assure that adequate personnel and facilities are available everywhere, that acceptable standards of service are rendered, that appropriate provision is made for research and training, and that these requirements are met with a maximum of economy.

This is perhaps the feature of a national health service that distinguishes it most sharply from an indemnity health insurance system, however wide the scope and coverage of the latter. In the typical health insurance plan all the government does, in effect, is to remove the economic barrier to access to whatever medical services of the defined types may be available. If the patient cannot find a hospital in his community, that is no concern of the program. If certain necessary specialists are not available, the sick person has no complaint against the government, which offers only to meet his costs if he can find a specialist to care for him. If there are too few doctors in his community, or if the general level of professional practice is low, this too is no responsibility of the government. Under a public medical service, however, all these become matters for which government has accepted responsibility and for which it is held accountable.

Problems Peculiar to Public Medical Services

A government administering a public medical service, particularly if its scope is wide, thus faces a number of difficult problems, additional to those which it has in common with compulsory health insurance systems and which will be discussed in the following section. First, and most obvious of these is the necessity of finding an acceptable compromise between the demand of the citizens for a high-grade medical and health service and their reluctance to devote to this purpose the necessary proportion of the national income.[10] It does not yet seem possible to say whether or not in the long run a comprehensive national health service requires a nation to devote a larger proportion of the national income than hitherto to health maintenance and promotion. It is true that, to some extent, a public medical service (or for that matter a compulsory health insurance system) represents merely another way of paying for health services (i.e., by averaging costs over the entire covered group and paying them through insurance contributions or taxes). But the experience of all countries that have instituted such measures indicates that when first enacted, the demands on medical facilities (human and institutional)

[10] See especially Ross, *op. cit.*, chap. 32.

increase very greatly once the economic barrier to their use is removed, and if these are to be met, a larger share of the national income must be devoted to health services.

To some extent this increased demand for medical service is to be expected and even hoped for, since one of the objects of such a program is to ensure that people get medical care as and when they need it, regardless of their ability to pay. But against this initial and often heavy demand for the allocation of increased resources to meet medical needs must be set the possibility that early treatment in cases now too often allowed to run their course will, in time, reduce the need for much care previously given. It has also been held that greater emphasis on preventive medicine will in the long run tend to reduce the proportion of the national income devoted to curative services.[11]

It remains to be seen whether these influences will offset the general upward trend in the costs of medical care due to scientific developments in medicine itself and to the consumer's demand for a higher standard of health.[12]

In the short run, however, there is no doubt that governments instituting such systems are under great pressure to devote larger resources to the service, because of the heavy backlog of previously unmet needs. In a very rich country this may present no insuperable difficulties. But the securing of a proper balance between the health services and other services which make demands upon the taxpayer's income has been an acute problem even in Great Britain, which instituted the National Health Service at the very moment when the nation faced the necessity of making good from limited national resources the attritions and obsolescences in its capital equipment occasioned by World War II.

In view of the heavy and mounting costs of high-standard medical care and the inadequacy of medical personnel and facilities in relation to accumulated needs in the initial stages of such programs, it is not surprising that those responsible for the development and administration of comprehensive health services have to make difficult choices, for priorities must be established, and these always expose the administrator to pressures from interested groups and to criticism when a choice has been made. Thus the British government has been criticized by the medical profession and others for regarding the construction of health centers as a postponable item during the first years of the program, and the hospital authorities have constantly complained that inadequate funds

11 For an estimate of cost ranges in the United States see I. S. Falk, "Cost Estimates for National Health Insurance," *Social Security Bulletin,* August, 1949, pp. 4–10.

12 On the influences making for mounting costs of health services, regardless of how they are financed, see Ffrangcon Roberts, *The Cost of Health,* Turnstile Press, London, 1952, chaps. 2–8.

have been granted for essential improvements and construction. Nor is it always easy to implement the priorities decided upon.[13]

In any case, if the disproportion is very great between needs, augmented by a substantial backlog, and medical resources, an immediate lowering of the standards of care is likely to result. For if the price of medical service is reduced to zero or almost zero, it will then be necessary to spread these supplies very thin over all who wish to make use of them. Some hold that even so, it is arguable whether this method of rationing resources that are inadequate for total health needs is any worse than the previous system of rationing them, i.e., by the price system, whereby some are able to buy all the medical care they need, while others, because of limited incomes, go short. However poor the standard of care under the public program, it may well be an improvement over that previously received by those who formerly went short or who necessarily judge standards of quality by the service customarily received by the poor rather than by the rich.

Inevitably, therefore, any socialization of the costs of medical care, however achieved, brings to the fore the problem of adequacy of facilities and personnel. Some countries, such as Canada, have decided that before adopting even a health insurance system steps must be taken to increase the supply, and improve the geographical distribution, of medical facilities and personnel, and public funds are currently being used for that purpose. Others, such as Great Britain, have first instituted a free health service and then grappled with the problem of supplies. Which course is preferable, assuming the existence of a desire for public action, would seem to depend upon which one would most speedily bring supply in relation to demand. A public and a medical profession that were prepared to accept some temporary inadequacies but to continue to press for expanded supplies might find the British sequence preferable to the Canadian. Where, however, there is a hostile medical profession or a public poorly informed as to the underlying facts, the lowering of service or even failure of the plan to make good on all kinds of care promised in the early years until supplies catch up with demand might endanger the continuation of the service since it would permit the medical profession to claim that all their worst fears were realized.

Almost inevitably, too, a government caught between the pressure of the consumer for more or higher standards of service and the resistance of the taxpayer to further levies on his income tends to seek ways and

---

[13] Thus despite the statutory priority in the National Health Service Act for dental care for young children and nursing mothers, the administrative arrangements for the supply of this service coupled with the terms of remuneration provided for dentists practicing in the general dental service resulted in a shortage of personnel for the priority services.

means of cutting costs, and these efforts often bring it into conflict with the suppliers of the service. Far too little is known about the effect of these efforts to keep costs to a minimum. On the one hand, it has to be admitted that all professional groups tend to set their requirements for necessary equipment and facilities by reference to criteria which emphasize rather the attainment of the highest possible professional standards than the economic cost of meeting these requirements. They also tend to resist the allocation to auxiliary personnel of functions once peculiar to the fully trained practitioner. On the other hand, unless the lay administrator succeeds in working closely and constructively with his medical advisers and unless the profession is willing to cooperate in keeping costs to a realistic minimum, these enforced economies may lead to an undesirable and even an unnecessary lowering of the standards of service.

In the second place, operation of such a service is likely to cause the government to invade some spheres traditionally held to be the preserve of private enterprise or private philanthropy. Thus the necessity of making the most economical and effective use of hospital resources led the British government in 1948 to take over the existing voluntary hospital system, since it could not undertake the costly task of constructing adequate public hospitals for its own clientele, and the country was in no position to afford the unused bed capacity that would have resulted from two competing hospital systems.[14] The need to ensure adequate coverage of the country as a whole by a well-integrated system of essential health facilities (general and special hospitals, clinics, and the like) also pointed to the desirability of combining existing voluntary and public facilities, by compulsion if necessary. Thus the pressures both of economics and of effective planning for adequate service broadened the sphere of public activity.

Similarly, under a public medical service it is impossible for government not to concern itself with the supply and distribution of medical personnel. Quite apart from the difficult problems of estimating future demand for medical personnel, and more particularly avoiding a future surplus in an effort to meet the heavy backlog of demand typically experienced at the inception of national health services, a government which attempts to ensure an adequate and appropriate supply of trained professional medical personnel is likely to come into conflict with the organized professions. For in many cases the monopoly position of the profession and the level of incomes of its members are maintained by a policy of restriction of entry to the medical schools, and it is hardly likely that

---

[14] The necessity for economy in the use of hospital facilities was finally brought home to the country during World War II; Cf. Richard M. Titmuss, *Problems of Social Policy*, H. M. Stationery Office, London, 1950, especially chaps. 22–24.

the profession and the government will hold the same views regarding the need for an increase in the supply of trainees and training facilities.

Most countries are familiar with the problem of the maldistribution of medical personnel, who tend to concentrate in urban and higher-income centers, where medical facilities such as hospitals abound, to the neglect of rural and poorer areas. The methods adopted by governments to remedy this situation may well lead to actions which the professions concerned regard as limitations of individual freedom, or at least as undue intervention in matters which have hitherto been regarded as of purely professional concern. Thus, in Britain, one of the most bitter disputes between the medical profession and the government during the formative period of the National Health Service concerned the machinery set up by the government to prevent new doctors practicing under the Service from entering areas classified as "overdoctored." [15] More recently the evidence suggests that these arrangements are working smoothly and have been generally accepted by the profession. The alternative solution proposed by medical men, that doctors should be attracted to the "underdoctored areas" by the offer of higher rates of remuneration, would have increased the cost of the service. The rejection by the government of this proposal in favor of the device of negative control accompanied by a system of "inducement payments," limited to the first three years of practice in heavily underdoctored areas, illustrates the different considerations that necessarily govern the public authority and the profession in grappling with a common problem.

Thirdly, under a system of public medical care, government cannot evade ultimate responsibility for the quality of medical care in the broadest sense. This involves much more than assuring that the financial and administrative arrangements adopted do not disturb existing patient-doctor relationships or cause a general lowering of the professional standards of the medical personnel, a problem which the national health service has in common with compulsory health insurance systems. It embraces also such questions as whether the system as a whole devotes the proper relative attention to preventive, as contrasted to curative, services; whether adequate provision is made for convalescent or rehabilitative services; whether adequate stimulus is given to research; whether the mental health services are appropriately developed; and the like. These are, of course, not questions that can properly be asked only about a public service; they are in fact often asked in countries which rely almost wholly on private enterprise for the provision of health and medical services. But under a public program, for the first time the facts are a matter of public record, and some one authority is held answerable for

[15] Doctors in independent private practice were, of course, free to set up in practice wherever they wished.

failures to reach desired standards for the country as a whole. It might indeed be said that a much higher standard is required of government than of private enterprise in this respect, and the resulting greatly increased vulnerability to criticism may be one of the considerations which have led to some reluctance on the part of governments to select the alternative of the national health or medical service.

PROBLEMS COMMON TO COMPULSORY HEALTH INSURANCE AND NATIONAL MEDICAL SERVICES

Among the many organizational and administrative problems that are faced alike by health insurance systems and national health or medical services three call for special emphasis, namely the development of appropriate methods of remunerating professional and technical personnel; the development of a plan whose over-all effects will tend to improve rather than lower the standards of medical care; and the invention and operation of devices for avoiding overuse of the service.

Methods of Remunerating Professional Personnel

Both compulsory health insurance systems and national health services have to resolve the problem of devising methods of remunerating professional personnel which will attract and retain an adequate supply of practitioners and which will foster, rather than impede, the rendering of service of high quality. The selection of appropriate methods of remuneration has, in fact, been a major cause of controversy between governments and the professions involved.

A variety of methods has been developed of which the best known are the fee-for-service, payment by salary, and the capitation systems. The fee-for-service system is found, for example, in the French and New Zealand general systems and applies to dental practitioners in Great Britain. Here the insurance fund or the national administration either reimburses the doctor directly in accordance with the services he has rendered or reimburses the patient for all or part of his medical bills. Sometimes it is provided that the attending physician must accept the sum paid by the state in full settlement of his claim. In other cases, he may be allowed to charge what the traffic will bear, over and above the reimbursable sum. As a rule, especially where the public institution pays the patient a percentage of the doctor's bill, detailed schedules of permitted charges are developed by the public authority, usually in consultation with the medical profession.

The fee-for-service system has the advantage of being most similar to that prevailing in private practice and is the one generally favored by medical practitioners. It allows the evaluations of the market place, as expressed by the actions of patients, the widest scope. The popular doctor will have many patients and a larger income than his less popular colleague, and if the judgment of patients reflects a true evaluation of the relative professional skill of the two men, then the fee-for-service system operates to reward efficiency and promotes high standards. This condition is, however, not always satisfied. And on the other hand, the fee-for-service system has several disadvantages. It is highly cumbersome, requiring as it does that doctors and/or patients keep detailed records of the services received. It is likely to require the development of elaborate schedules of fees for different types of service, and quite apart from the technical difficulties of this task, the relative money values attached to different services may influence the types of care or treatment given. If, for example, in dentistry, the price set for extractions exceeds that for preventive treatment, some practitioners may be tempted to neglect the latter. In any case, the use of the fee-for-service system is expensive, for it tempts those members of the profession whose desire for economic rewards exceeds their sense of professional responsibility to increase their incomes by unnecessary services. Nor is it easy under a complicated schedule to devise a series of fees that will ensure any desired average level of incomes to the members of the profession.[16]

The method of employing medical personnel on salary avoids some of these difficulties. It is found in the United States in the Veterans Administration and in Sweden and in some Canadian provinces where municipal doctors are employed, and it is utilized in Great Britain for specialists and hospital staffs. It is true that the problem of setting a level of incomes which the profession regards as fair and reasonable and which the public feels is not out of line with the economic rewards of other highly trained professional persons still remains.[17] But it avoids the difficulties of schedule making and the temptations to the weaker members of the profession to allow the nature and frequency of service rendered to be influenced by economic considerations. It also avoids the detailed record keeping characteristic of the fee-for-service system. On the other hand, medical

---

16 Thus the original fee scale devised for dentists practicing under the British National Health Service yielded in fact incomes that were much greater than intended and far out of line with incomes of doctors practicing under the Service. (Ross, *op. cit.*, pp. 232–264.)

17 For an interesting discussion of the principles which might be adopted in deciding upon appropriate income levels for professional workers (however remunerated), see the reports of the three committees under the chairmanship of Sir Will Spens, which dealt with the problems of remunerating general practitioners, consultants and specialists, and dentists under the British Health Service. (*Reports of the Interdepartmental Committee on the Remuneration of Consultants and Specialists* (1948); *Reports of the Interdepartmental Committee on the Remuneration of General Dental Practitioners* (1948), etc., H. M. Stationery Office, London.)

men object that the salaried service offers no rewards to the more skillful or assiduous practitioner. Although this is not wholly true, since salaried services frequently provide for increments according to degrees of skill or experience,[18] there is no doubt that a salaried system would hardly yield the very high incomes that are received by some highly successful practitioners in private practice. There seems less validity in the claim, sometimes made by the spokesmen for organized medicine, at least by implication, that work of high quality cannot be expected if remuneration is on a salaried basis and that only the prospect of high economic rewards stimulates the medical man to his highest professional efforts. However, the administration of a salaried system with rewards for superior performance would necessarily require some members of the profession to sit in judgment upon others. Although this kind of evaluation is common enough in academic circles and is found in other professions that work for salary, it appears to be resisted by the American medical profession, who in the past have demonstrated some reluctance to act as a body in judgment on the competence of a colleague.

The capitation system, which is found in Great Britain and some other countries, endeavors to avoid some of the disadvantages of both fee-for-service and payment by salary. Under this arrangement, which is feasible only for general practice, the patient selects a physician and is enrolled on his panel. The doctor is paid at a fixed annual rate per head for each person on his panel,[19] regardless of whether or not service is required during the year. Typically, a maximum limit is set to the number of patients, or potential patients, who can be enrolled with any doctor.

In support of this system it is urged that it retains some of the incentives of the fee-for-service system. The doctor who is unpopular with his patients will lose them to his competitors, and his panel being smaller, his income will fall. There will thus be an incentive to give good service, and the doctor who works harder because he has more patients will receive a larger income, but there will be no temptation to give unnecessary service. Indeed, it is alleged that under this system it will be to the interest of the doctor by preventive measures to try to keep his patients healthy. Here, too, record keeping for reimbursement purposes is avoided. On the other hand, the determination of appropriate capitation rates presents difficulties. A sum must be fixed such that for the doctor with an average panel and with an average incidence of need for care among his patients and giving service of average quality, the income yielded will again be one that the profession regards as fair and reasonable and

[18] See for instance the scale adopted in Great Britain for hospital medical and dental staffs (Ross, op. cit., pp. 151–153).

[19] The fee per patient enrolled sometimes varies according to the number of persons on the panel.

the public feels is not too out of line with incomes of persons of a similar degree of training and experience. Furthermore, appropriate allowance has to be made in setting the capitation fee for necessary expenses incurred by the doctor in maintaining his office and equipment.

Where the supply of doctors is limited in relation to the total number of patients, the maximum limits on the size of individual panels may be so high that standards of service suffer. This, however, is not a weakness of the capitation system as such, as has sometimes been argued, but would occur under any method of payment if access to medical service is not restricted by the price system and if supply is short in relation to demand.

Maintenance of High Standards of Service

The problem of operating a public or a publicly controlled medical care system in such a way as to maintain high standards of service has concerned those who have formulated or administered these measures from the first. Some types of safeguard have been relatively easy to introduce. Thus most systems operating by the mid-century permitted the patient free choice of any doctor admitted to practice under the scheme. As these public programs have come to be well established and accepted by the community and the profession alike, the proportion of all doctors and specialists practicing under the schemes has steadily increased and in some countries (e.g., Great Britain) approaches 100 per cent. It can therefore be argued with some cogency that, since the doctors' probable fees are no longer a consideration, the patients' choice is actually much wider than under a nongovernmental system.

In most systems, too, medical men are free to practice under the public program or not as they wish and to accept or refuse patients who desire their services, subject to normal professional limitations. However, in the case of a national medical service, such as the British, where over 90 per cent of the population has indicated a preference for care through the Service, the market for the privately practicing doctor is so narrowed that the average practitioner has in reality little choice but to enter the system.

Medical men have frequently expressed fears that the intervention of government will inevitably interfere with the relationships of doctor and patient and result in a lowering of the quality of care. On the former charge, it has, however, been pointed out that it is by no means certain that patient-doctor relationships, especially where financial transactions are involved, are even now so satisfactory to the patient that the latter would not welcome some changes. And some doctors who have practiced under compulsory health insurance or national health services have held that the removal of direct financial dealings between patient and doctor has made for an improvement of patient-doctor relationships. Many doctors have held, too, that better professional service can be given when the treatment prescribed need no longer be influenced by consideration of the ability of the patient to meet the costs.

The fear that public programs would involve the interposition of third parties between the attending physician and his patient may under certain circumstances be justified, although it is likely to occur only when questions are raised about the appropriateness of treatment given.[20] In reality, most systems prohibit any doctor employed by the fund or agency in a supervisory or controlling capacity from giving treatment to patients. It has been pointed out, too, that the increasing specialization of medical practice has tended to loosen the bonds between the general practitioner and his patients, who in many cases even under private practice receive treatment simultaneously from several medical personnel. This situation, which has been fostered by technical or scientific developments, has indeed strengthened a movement toward group practice, which quite apart from any public medical service, may change the nature of the earlier relationship of doctor and patient, and not necessarily for the worse.

More disturbing to the professional man's normal methods of practice are the controls, embodied in some health insurance or health service systems, whereby prior authority has to be obtained from some committee or official appointed by the administration if certain types of expensive treatment or medicaments are to be prescribed.[20a] This is, of course, a real limitation on the complete independence of professional judgment of the individual physician. On the other hand, unless a high standard of professional competence and a lively sense of responsibility as to the use of public funds can be relied on in all but a minority of cases, some type of safeguard for the interests of the taxpayer is essential in a system where the public foots the entire bill. The problem of the mounting costs of pharmaceutical expenditures (to be discussed below) indicates that this problem is very real. The practical problem facing those who devise public programs is whether such controlling bodies can be so staffed as to give preponderant representation to professional personnel and yet retain a concern for the interest of the taxpayer.[21]

[20] This type of third-party intervention is perhaps more likely to occur when the doctor functions as a certifying agent for a cash disability insurance system (see Chap. 7).

[20a] This limitation applies, of course, only to those prescribed under the public system. Such medicaments can always be prescribed and purchased at the patients' own expense.

[21] For an illuminating discussion of the effects of different types of organizational and other arrangements upon the nature of service rendered and the impact upon the physician, see *Relations between Social Security Institutions and the Medical Profession*, especially pp. 9–43.

The effect of methods of remunerating physicians on standards of service has already been touched upon in the preceding section. It would seem that neither capitation nor the salaried service *of necessity* gives rise to poor professional performance unless the sense of professional responsibility is dormant throughout the profession as a whole. And as we have seen, the system of remuneration by fee for service involves no real change for the doctor (except by giving him a guarantee on collections). Many of the unsatisfactory effects on standards of practice which are often charged against the methods of remunerating professional personnel under public insurance or health service systems are in fact rather the consequence of a sudden increase in the demand for medical services, unaccompanied by a corresponding increase in the supply of trained personnel.

The fear that a public service will be unduly vulnerable to political pressures and manipulations has often been expressed by organized medicine in the United States. The experience of other countries, however, seems to suggest that the extent to which this will happen is in large measure within the control of the profession itself. Admittedly, if political pressures (such as influencing appointments or the volume and geographical distribution of physical facilities and the like) are to be resisted, the profession as a whole has to be on the alert, and the leaders who carry weight with the public have to devote time to influencing public opinion and serving on the many advisory and negotiating committees whose existence appears unavoidable if the viewpoint and the interests of the medical profession, scientific as well as economic, are to exert a proper influence.

Avoiding Overuse of the Service

The experience of all public systems, whether health insurance or public medical service (and indeed of privately organized comprehensive medical care insurance systems), suggests that there is a third problem of major importance, namely the danger of overuse of facilities and medical resources. This overuse may take the form of unnecessary calls upon the time of doctors for trivial complaints; excessive use of hospital facilities where no real need for in-patient care exists; overuse or careless use of medical appliances; or excessively high expenditures on pharmaceuticals. Of these, the last has perhaps been the most dramatic and highly publicized, in the experience of many countries having public programs in recent years,[22] although the rising costs of hospitalization are everywhere causing concern, in public, as in private, systems.

[22] Studies made by the British Ministry of Health and other authorities have shown that the mounting costs of pharmaceutical benefits are attributable to prescribing pro-

In part, the problem is one for which the medical profession itself is responsible. Unless overprescribing is checked by vigorous pressure from within the ranks of organized medicine, the lay administrators have been forced to adopt controlling measures which have varied from the requirement that the doctor secure prior approval for certain types of costly treatment or drugs to the application of ex post facto administrative controls and impositions of penalties.[23]

In part the problem is attributable to the demands of the consumers of medical care, a commodity on which people in general seem inclined to spend less of their own incomes than is socially desirable but which they will use in great quantities if they get it free. Efforts to check overuse have taken various forms: charging a minimal fee for each visit to the physician or for each unit of service or prescription has been found useful in some systems (e.g., in the British system, for dentures or for renewal of spectacles or other appliances when renewal is occasioned by negligence). Obviously, however, there are limits to the extent to which this control can be used, since a fee that acts as an effective deterrent to frivolous or irresponsible use of the system may deter some low-income groups from using the service in cases of genuine need.[24] Public education has also been relied upon, with varying success.

It is probably true to say that the promotion of responsible use by the citizenry of freely available social services is the most crucial of all problems faced by those who favor public action to remove the costs of medical care from the average citizen.

THE DETERMINANTS OF ACTION

Whether or not a community will decide to invoke the powers of government in the field of medical care, for which population categories and for which types of treatment and care it will develop public pro-

---

prietary remedies where similar and cheaper nonproprietary medicaments were available, prescribing excessive quantities, too free prescription of new or expensive drugs, and finally some prescriptions for items that are not really drugs. (Cf. Ross, *op. cit.*, chap. 21; and *Annual Report of the Ministry of Health, 1953*, H. M. Stationery Office, London, 1954, *passim*.) For an account of the problem as experienced in other countries, see Dr. Emil Tuchmann, "The Prescription of Medicaments and the Amount Used," in *Reports of the Permanent Committees*, I, Medico-Social Committee, International Social Security Association, Geneva, 1954, pp. 22–42.

[23] For an account of the administrative controls developed in Great Britain, see *Bulletin of the International Social Security Association*, June–July, 1954, pp. 226–228.

[24] However, in countries with an adequately financed and publicly acceptable general assistance program this difficulty can be overcome, as in Great Britain, by permitting those for whom this payment would be a hardship to secure reimbursement from the assistance agency.

grams, and which type of program will be favored will therefore depend upon a number of variables.[25]

The first of these is the degree of dissatisfaction with existing methods of organizing and financing medical care, as judged by the extent of unmet health needs and by the severity of the economic burden of medical costs upon individuals or families. The greater the importance attached by the public to universal access to comprehensive health services of all types, undeterred by any income barrier, the less will be the weight attached to some of the shortcomings of public programs due to failure to solve, or to solve completely, the problems discussed in the preceding sections.

Even when allowance is made for the pricing system customarily practiced by the medical profession, which aims to adjust charges to income, the burden of medical costs, especially when hospital and other care is included,[26] remains heavy for certain families and individuals. There is evidence that many patients, even among those who benefit from reduced rates, resent the type of means-test relationship which is involved in the method of setting fees in private practice. And the other adjustment to the high costs of medical care very commonly found, namely providing through public assistance for the care of needy or medically needy persons, is unpopular and of little help to the vast middle class.

There appears to be agreement that only by some form of insurance can the uneven incidence of medical costs be prevented from overburdening individual families.[27] On the other hand, opinions differ as to

[25] For the attitudes of different groups in America toward proposals for public action, see *National Health Programs,* Hearings before the Senate Committee on Education and Labor on S. 1606, 79th Cong., 2d Sess., 1946, *passim.* See also *America's Health, Official Report of the National Health Assembly,* Harper & Brothers, New York, 1949, *passim; Building America's Health,* President's Commission on the Health Needs of the Nation, Government Printing Office, Washington, D.C., 1952, vol. II; R. R. Campbell and W. W. Campbell, "Compulsory Health Insurance: The Economic Issues," *Quarterly Journal of Economics,* February, 1952; and Davis, *op. cit.*

[26] On the mounting costs of hospital care, see John H. Hayes, *Factors Affecting the Costs of Hospital Care,* vol. I of *Report on Financing Hospital Care in the United States,* Blakiston Division, McGraw-Hill Book Company, Inc., New York, 1954. For the incidence of medical costs on families in 1953, see Odin W. Anderson, *National Family Survey of Medical Care Costs and Voluntary Health Insurance; Preliminary Report,* Health Information Foundation, Chicago, 1954. This report is partially reprinted in *Characteristics of the Low-income Population and Related Federal Programs.*

[27] For an account of the various plans, see *Health Insurance Plans in the United States,* Senate Committee on Labor and Public Welfare, S. Rept. 359, 82d Cong., 1st Sess., 1951, vols. 1–3; Frank G. Dickinson and I. S. Falk, "Medical Care Insurance: Lessons from Voluntary and Compulsory Plans," *American Journal of Public Health,* May, 1951 (two articles); the articles by Emerson P. Schmidt, Helen Hall, William S. McNary, Charles G. Hayden, and John H. Miller in *Building America's Health,* A Report to the President's Commission on the Health Needs of the Nation, vol. IV, *Financing a Health*

whether the average family could afford to pay the premiums necessary to cover the costs of a comprehensive medical care insurance system, and it is generally admitted that the very lowest income groups could hardly buy this kind of protection without seriously depressing their current standard of living. In any case, the American voluntary health insurance plans meet only a part of medical costs, the percentage being estimated at 17.4 in 1952 and 19.5 in 1953.[28] There is also difference of opinion as to how far, even among the groups that are held to be able to afford the premiums, people would be willing, or could be induced, voluntarily to set aside the necessary funds. Some argue that human nature being what it is, nothing short of the compulsion of the tax collector would bring about the desired result.[29]

Existing methods of financing and organizing medical services are also judged by criteria other than their effect on the economic security of individuals and families. Public action in the field of health has thus been stimulated by prevailing dissatisfaction with the over-all results of purely private provision, as measured by mortality and morbidity statistics,[30] the limited extent of constructive services, such as rehabilitative and preventive programs, and the nonavailability of some types of high-quality care in certain geographical areas. The more strongly deficiencies of this type are felt by the voters to be unnecessary and undesirable, the greater will be the pressure for public action and action of a character that is more comprehensive than a mere indemnity system.

A second influential force is the attitude to government activity as such: a country like the United States with its strong tradition of free enterprise and fear of government activity may well regard proposals to extend the role of government in the field of medical care with greater reservation than Britain, where a substantial measure of public activity is already accepted and where the citizens as a whole appear to have more confidence in their own powers to control the actions of their governments.

The attitudes and traditions of the medical profession itself are a third

---

Program for America, Government Printing Office, Washington, D.C., 1952; and A Look at Modern Health Insurance, U.S. Chamber of Commerce, Washington, D.C., 1954.

[28] "Voluntary Insurance against Sickness: 1948–53 Estimates," Social Security Bulletin, December, 1954, p. 7. The survey of the Health Information Foundation (see note 26 above) suggests that only 15 per cent of charges incurred by families was covered by insurance in 1953.

[29] For a succinct evaluation of voluntary health insurance in America, see Franz Goldmann, "Voluntary Medical Care Insurance: Achievements and Shortcomings," Journal of the National Medical Association, July, 1954, pp. 223–232.

[30] For an evaluation of progress in regard to some of the more prominent serious diseases, see Health Inquiry, Preliminary Report of the Committee on Interstate and Foreign Commerce, Union Calendar 499, 83d Cong., 2d Sess., H. Rept. 1338, 1954.

major determinant. For governmental programs that aim to meet the costs of specific services rendered by recognized professions, such as education or health, or to supply these services directly obviously involve more complex problems than do those which aim merely to provide alternative income, precisely because they require the enlistment of the full participation and cooperation of the professions involved. To some degree government itself can influence the extent of this cooperation, by providing more or less adequately in its administrative structures and organization for appropriate professional representation in, and control of, those aspects of the program which are properly of professional concern. Experience has shown that in formulating programs too much attention cannot be directed to this matter. On the other hand, it is evident that the effective operation of such plans makes heavy demands on a profession that has hitherto functioned as an uncontrolled and self-governing monopoly, answerable to no one for the over-all effectiveness of its operations. These demands are in essence that the profession should recognize that a public interest attaches to some aspects of its methods of organization and remuneration and should be prepared to subordinate purely professional interests to the wider public welfare.

For the adjustments that the medical profession has to make to the new public policies affecting the organization, remuneration, and supply of medical services are many. The individual practitioner may have to face a change in his methods of remuneration which, while probably increasing the total income of the profession, may significantly alter the total incomes of individual physicians, either upwards or downwards. He will have to devote more time than formerly to certain civic responsibilities, such as serving as a certifying officer for various social or medical services, from which he has hitherto been mercifully spared. He will have to learn, as the teacher has already learned, how to maintain a good relationship with his clients even though he denies their requests for improper service, supplies, or certifications. The profession as a group may be forced to take stock of the effectiveness of some of its methods of operating since it will be under greater pressure than hitherto to show that results are achieved with a maximum of economy in the use of scarce resources. Above all, the leaders of the profession will find themselves called upon to take time from their specifically professional activities to represent their fellows on the many negotiating, standard-setting, and controlling committees and organizations which are inevitable if the purely professional aspects of the service are to be under medical control and if the economic interests of the practitioners are to be properly protected.

In many countries, and notably perhaps in Great Britain, the physicians and other medical personnel have already demonstrated an ability to accept the implications of the public interest inherent in the functioning of their professions. In the United States, another profession, the teachers, have long adapted themselves to the problems of professional functioning in a publicly controlled service. The willingness of the medical profession in America to come to grips with the problem of how to render professionally acceptable service under a system of organization that is not of their choosing but may be demanded by the public will in the last resort determine not whether such a system will be brought into effect (for no profession can long withstand the demands of the wider community) but rather whether that system, if adopted, will result in a raising or a lowering of the standards of medical care and the general state of health of all the people.

Finally, the nature and viability of public programs concerned with health and medical care will depend upon the character of the citizenry, their capacity to exercise self-restraint in the utilization of freely available goods and services, their preparedness to countenance shortcomings when these are attributable to forces beyond the control of the administrator, their determination to initiate action to remedy unjustifiable or inexplicable deficiencies, and their willingness to pay, in taxes, the price of a comprehensive service of high quality.

PART THREE

Decisions about the Financing of Social Security Programs

ALL COUNTRIES which enact public social security measures, regardless of the number of risks covered or the type of benefit assured, have to tackle three financial questions: What kind of taxes should be levied? How should the costs be spread over time? What levels of government should share in the financial burden?

These issues become increasingly complex as the number of programs increases. The principle that workers should carry all or the lion's share of a social insurance program may be a feasible solution if only one risk program is in existence but may become impractical if ultimately all risks are covered, because the resulting cost may constitute an unbearably large proportion of the incomes of low wage earners. Similarly, a particular type of grant-in-aid may appear highly rational and appropriate when applied to a single program, but when similar grants are made available for many other programs, a highly complicated and almost unworkable system of financial relationships between governments may result. The nature of these issues changes, too, as the coverage of governmental protection becomes more nearly universal. Thus the question whether to finance an old-age security program on a pay-as-you-go basis or by accumulating reserves assumes very different aspects according as the program is one of universal coverage or is limited to a section only of the population. Furthermore, the answers to these questions are affected by decisions as to the type of social security benefit it is wished to guarantee. A social insurance type of security program may lend itself to certain methods of financing which would not be held appropriate for public assistance.

The question may be asked why consideration of the burden of the total costs of social security programs has not been listed among the financial problems calling for solution. The answer is that this is not essentially a financial question. The decision as to what proportion of the national income shall be distributed on the basis of market criteria (i.e., by reference to value of contribution to output) and what proportion by reference to some other criterion, such as family status or satisfaction of the requirements of some social security system, is one which is decided by reference to a wide range of social and economic criteria with value judgments playing a decisive role. The total amount of money involved in these distributions is merely one method of expressing the sum total of the decisions arrived at. It is sometimes claimed that it is a method of expression which assists in reaching specific decisions, for it measures the extent of income transfer between persons at any one time or as compared with one period and another (in the case of systems where the potential beneficiary accepts a lower income when at work or young or healthy in order to have the right to income when he is unemployed or old or sick). But the experience of all countries has demonstrated that at different times and under different circumstances the reaction of any given community to a transfer of any specific order of magnitude will be very different. Thus even when we are able to measure and compare, within certain limits, the proportion which social security expenditures form of the national income (or some other criterion), in different countries, or for the same country over a given period of time,[1] these indices enable no inferences to be drawn as to whether there is "too much" or "too little" social security, or whether the volume of the transfers is unduly heavy or unduly light.

Probably the greatest use of indices of social security expenditures expressed as a percentage of national income is to serve as a healthy corrective to apprehensions regarding the secular growth of absolute money totals.

For in fact it is extremely difficult to attach any concrete meaning to the frequently posed question "How much social security can a country afford?" At any given moment, of course, the extreme limit is set by the level of average per capita incomes. In this very broad sense it is true that the maximum benefit which could be assured to the members of any society is determined by the total economic output of that community divided equally among them. To this extent, it is meaningful to say that a rich country like the United States "can afford" a higher standard of social security than a poor country like India. But this does not carry us very far. No responsible community could fail to take account of the longer-run consequences of so drastic a policy of income redistribution. Judgments of the ability of a country "to afford" any given degree of income redistribution have to weigh in the balance also the impact upon economic output of the redistributive process. These effects are of two

---

[1] For the most comprehensive of such studies see *The Cost of Social Security 1949–51*, International Enquiry Prepared by the International Labor Office, International Social Security Association, Geneva, 1955. See also *Social Security Expenditures in Australia . . . , 1949–50: A Comparative Study*, Department of National Health and Welfare, Research Division, Ottawa, February, 1954; and for the United States, Ida C. Merriam, "Social Welfare Programs in the United States," *Social Security Bulletin*, February, 1953.

kinds. On the one hand, in a society that operates on the principle of economic incentive the redistributive process may lower the future volume of output both of those from whom income is taken, because their economic rewards are lessened, and of those who benefit from the redistribution, by weakening the pressures upon them to participate in production. On the other hand, income transfers may have favorable economic effects by ensuring greater stability of operation of the economy as a whole or by improving the health, vitality, and educational equipment, and therefore the potential productivity, of those who benefit from them.

But even if it could be shown that any given social security measure had certain adverse or positive effects on the level of national output, it is impossible to say, without further information, whether any given community would feel that it "could afford" the program. It is not merely that there seems to be a rather general tendency to underestimate the favorable impact of these measures on output, perhaps because the results are evident in the long, rather than the short, run or because of the difficulty of establishing a causal relationship. Much more important and vital is the fact that the decision whether or not a given social security system with all its consequences can be "afforded" involves the application of social priorities, and here there are no absolutes. In determining these priorities the effect upon economic output is only one of the considerations to which contemporary societies attach importance. Of equal significance is the concern of the mass of taxpayers and voters about the risk of income loss for themselves, or for other sections of the community for whom they may, for a variety of reasons, have developed some sensitivity, and the extent to which they regard the elimination of this condition as more important than other uses of current income. As these social attitudes change, a community will find its social security expenditures accounting for a larger or a smaller proportion of its national income, and it will regard a burden of any given size as heavy or light, excessive or bearable.[2]

Obviously the decision will be affected by the absolute magnitude of the gains and losses: it is important to know by how much economic insecurity can be reduced by any proposed measure as well as the precise extent to which it will affect national output and the incomes of current producers. And here again, it is probable that the higher the per capita income, the more is a society likely to feel that it can "afford" a social

[2] Cf. Eveline M. Burns, "How Much Social Welfare Can America Afford?" *Proceedings of the National Conference of Social Work*, Columbia University Press, New York, 1949; and "The Financing of Social Welfare," in Cora Kasius (ed.), *New Directions in Social Work*, Harper & Brothers, New York, 1954. See also Seymour E. Harris, "Current Issues in Financing Income Security," in James E. Russell (ed.), *National Policies for Education, Health and Social Services*, Doubleday & Company, Inc., New York, 1955.

security system which accounts for a sizable proportion of its national income and which may even check initiative to some degree. For the consequences of some diminution in its rate of economic expansion (if this should be the cost of the program) are less serious in a wealthy country, and with high average per capita incomes the disposable incomes of those who lose by the transfers will still be substantial.

We have seen in previous chapters that the economic and social effects of social security measures are greatly influenced by the precise conditions laid down for the receipt of benefits and by the types and levels of the benefits payable. But they are also affected by the specific policies applied in the financial realm, i.e., by the particular types of taxes levied, by the methods of accounting used, and by the distribution of financial responsibilities among the different levels of government. The following four chapters will be concerned with these strictly financial questions.

CHAPTER 9

The Types of Taxes to Be Levied

THE SELECTION OF TAXES to finance governmental social security measures involves the search for a compromise between a number of not wholly compatible objectives. Obviously a major purpose is to secure assured revenues of the amount called for by the anticipated expenditures. But this is not the whole story. Different types of taxes fall unevenly upon different sections of the population. Not only, therefore, does weight have to be given to considerations of equity as between individual taxpayers in roughly similar economic circumstances, but also deference has to be paid to prevailing attitudes regarding equity in a broader social sense. A country which accepts as a general public policy the principle that the richer should pay more than their proportionate share of the costs of governmental operations will look askance at a proposal to finance social security systems that results in throwing a disproportionately heavy share of the cost on low-paid workers or will at least require that this disadvantage be outweighed by other positive consequences of such a tax.

Taxes not only bring forth revenues and cast burdens upon various sections of the community: they also have economic consequences by affecting the attitude of the taxpayer toward the desirability of further productive effort. Hence some types of taxes (or levels of tax rates) may be abandoned even though they yield adequate revenue and meet prevailing standards of individual and social equity, because they would discourage the enterprise of businessmen or the willingness of workers to put forth additional efforts, thereby lowering the total national output or at least checking its growth.

Finally some types of taxes result, or are believed to result, in specific types of social behavior, desirable or undesirable. Thus it may be held that a tax levied on beneficiaries to finance a particular social security program will bring home to them the costs of the service and cause them to be more responsible in its use, and this consideration may prevail despite the fact that such a tax may run counter to contemporary concepts of social equity. Or again, it may be believed that by charging employers with the costs of certain social security programs and remitting all or part of the tax by reference to the individual employer's risk experience, they will be induced to take action which reduces the severity of the risk.

On the other hand, it may be believed that to concentrate the costs of a social program on a relatively small section of taxpayers is to give them an undue interest in the nature of the program and one which they can make very effective because, as compared with other categories of taxpayers, they are more easily organized and can exert influence with legislatures.

As we shall see in the following discussion, all these considerations have played a role in determining the types of taxes to be used in the financing of social security programs.

TAXES ON WORKERS

Almost all social insurance programs collect at least part of the costs from workers, in the form of either a percentage levy on all or part of their wages or income or the requirement that all beneficiaries pay a uniform money sum. However, in the United States, in workmen's compensation and in all but two of the state unemployment insurance laws, the taxes are paid wholly by the employer, who also bears the entire cost of the Railroad unemployment insurance and temporary disability insurance programs. But even in the United States, the costs of the most important social security program in terms of coverage and expenditures (OASI) are financed by taxes levied equally on workers and employers, as are those of the Railroad retirement and permanent disability systems. And in Rhode Island and California temporary disability is financed solely by employees,[1] while in New Jersey and New York it is a shared responsibility, with the employee paying the lion's share.

In a very broad sense, this assessment of all or part of the costs of social security programs against workers is a form of taxation by reference to benefit received, a principle which is also found in other parts of the tax structure of some governments.

Payment of the costs by the beneficiary is, of course, the inevitable consequence of those systems which pay benefits on the basis of past contributions. But even when this benefit principle is greatly modified or abandoned, a case can be made for throwing at least some of the costs on the potential beneficiary group. Thus in those benefit systems which relate benefits to past earnings (for whatever reason) it has been felt that the payment of differential benefits could be justified only if differential taxes were paid, i.e., a contribution from the beneficiary was essential. Most countries have held that by establishing a fixed legal relation-

---

[1] It is possible that some of the private plans authorized under the California law may include some contribution from the employer toward the basic benefits as well as for benefits additional to those called for by the state law. But the evidence suggests that such cases are few.

ship between benefits received and taxes paid, the sense of social responsibility is enhanced.[2] Thus Lord Beveridge argued in support of the contributory principle that "The citizens as insured persons should realize that they cannot get more than certain benefits for certain contributions, should have a motive to support measures for economic administration, should not be taught to regard the State as the dispenser of gifts for which no one need pay." [3] This argument has been reiterated both before and since the Beveridge Report. In fact, far too little is known of the responsibility-inducing effect of the requirement of a contribution by the beneficiary. It is true that there is some evidence to suggest that at least when the unit of administration is small, so that excessive utilization of the program results directly and immediately in increased assessments against the members, all will be vigilant to keep costs to an acceptable minimum. This seems to have been the case with some of the early subsidized voluntary social insurance systems which were modeled upon the plans of trade union friendly or mutual-benefit societies. But where schemes are national in scope and administration and where the contribution rate for many risks is combined in a single weekly or monthly deduction from wages, the restraining influence of the worker's contribution seems more doubtful.[4]

Nor must it be forgotten that one of the arguments, frequently heard in the early days, in favor of a social insurance system that required contributions from the beneficiary was precisely that if he paid a contribution, a worker would feel entitled to his benefit as a right. The belief that he has paid for whatever benefits he gets may thus work in the opposite direction from that intended by those who view the contributory requirement as a brake upon unreasonable benefit increases or extensions.[5] The

---

[2] This was one of the reasons why those who supported the principles embodied in OASI deplored the failure to increase the payroll tax as originally scheduled, and notably at the time the system was liberalized in 1939.

[3] *Social Insurance and Allied Services*, Report by Sir William Beveridge, H. M. Stationery Office, London, 1942, p. 108.

[4] There is some evidence that many American workers are under the impression that their OASI tax is a general social security contribution which is used not only for OASI but for unemployment insurance also.

[5] Railroad workers in the United States, for example, frequently defend the highly favorable character of their social security programs and their efforts still further to improve their position vis-à-vis workers in general by the argument that they are paying higher social security taxes than the rest of the employed population—which they are, but so are their employers. Similarly it has been pointed out that the average English worker who as part of his combined weekly social security tax makes a small contribution towards the costs of the health service (accounting for less than 10 per cent of the costs thereof) appears to be under the impression that the service is wholly financed by contributions and that he is entitled to extensive benefits free of any charge "because he has paid for them."

restraining influence of the worker's contribution is even more question-able when, as is true of most social insurance systems, some other groups (employers or general taxpayers) carry part of the costs.[6]

And yet with all these qualifications the experience of countries which have utilized the worker's contribution seems to suggest that the device has some value in inducing some degree of responsibility toward public programs conferring benefits on private individuals. The very nature of a formal contributory program requires legislatures to discuss revenues and expenditures simultaneously and to solicit the views of the potential taxpayers as to their preparedness to purchase additional benefits by pay-ment of additional taxes. It is significant that in both England and, with one exception, America, major extensions or liberalizations of con-tributory insurance systems have always been accompanied by increases in contributions and that these have been accepted by workers.[7]

The possible effect of the contributory system in inducing restraint on the demands made on the public purse is, however, not the only reason why the system of taxing beneficiaries has been favored. Some who feel that the principle cannot be applied one hundred per cent still believe that it is undemocratic to have any section of the population receiving substantial cash benefits with no obligation to pay taxes.

Finally, there is the pragmatic fiscal argument that, with the rising demands of the tax collector on the freely disposable incomes of the population, it is necessary to tax low-income receivers (of whom the beneficiary group is primarily comprised) in order to secure the necessary revenues. It has also been held that this tax is one which it is relatively easy to collect, since the potential taxpayer knows that if he has not paid his taxes, he will lose benefit rights. In fact, it was, of course, the social insurance laws that paved the way for the principle of the with-holding tax and for the taxation of small-income receivers. As treasuries have gained more experience with the techniques for collecting taxes for all purposes from these groups, the special fiscal advantage of the social security tax as a benefit tax has become less significant, and some countries no longer feel it necessary to use the social security systems in this way to reinforce tax compliance. In such countries while an individual may be required to pay a special social security tax or an earmarked percentage

[6] Even Sir William Beveridge tried to reconcile workers to the higher contributions involved in his plan by the argument that these would call forth still higher contribu-tions from other parties. "The Plan for Social Security for the employee represents not 9d. for 4d., but 1s. for 3d." (*Social Insurance and Allied Services*, p. 116.)

[7] The exception to the rule in the United States at the time of the 1939 Amendments can probably be explained by the very novelty of the program and the fact that the sys-tem had not yet begun to pay any benefits.

of his income tax for this purpose, his claim for benefit is not normally checked against his tax record.

But there are also considerations which must be weighed against the alleged advantages of a tax on beneficiaries. The tax on wages and self-employment is a regressive tax: there are no exceptions by reference to any minimum income or to extent of family responsibilities. Also, the rate is uniform whatever the level of earnings, up to the taxable maximum. Hence it has been held that to require the beneficiaries as a class to pay for their own security, especially when the tax is levied only on the first so many dollars of income ($4,200 in OASI), is to require the relatively poor to pay for current security guarantees and is contrary to prevailing theories of social equity. Although in some systems where benefits are weighted in favor of the lower-wage earners the nonprogressive character of the system as a whole may be somewhat modified, it still remains true that the method of financing, as such, is regressive.

The same issue arises in the financing of children's allowance systems. Where they are financed out of social insurance contributions, a horizontal redistribution of incomes results, limited to transfers from childless wage earners to those with children. Only where they are financed from general revenues secured from progressive taxes does a vertical redistribution of incomes from the richer to the poorer classes result.

One further consequence of the principle of assessing the costs against the beneficiaries must be noted. Its strict application involving allocation of 100 per cent of the costs would greatly limit the scope of the programs thus financed. It would be possible to cover only those persons whose current incomes are high enough to permit them to pay the necessary taxes and yet retain an acceptable standard of living. The difficulty of the low-paid agricultural worker or the self-employed person who has no employer with whom to share the contribution has often led to exclusion of such persons from coverage for this very reason. For obviously it makes no sense to levy taxes which force individuals down to an unduly low standard of living when they are young, employed, and active, in order that they may enjoy an adequate social security income when they are 65 or unemployed or sick.

The more extensive and liberal the social security systems and the wider the range of risks covered, the more difficult it becomes to assess all costs against beneficiaries as a group. It is not surprising, therefore, that the United States, like most other countries which have extensive social security systems, has found it necessary to modify the application of this principle in two ways: by relaxing the requirement in the case of certain covered workers and by calling on other sections of the population to contribute to the costs of the program.

PAYROLL TAXES ON EMPLOYERS

Most countries, including the United States, levy taxes on employers as well as on workers to meet the costs of their social security systems. Everywhere, except in Great Britain, employers alone carry the costs of workmen's compensation. In some countries (notably Russia and those which base their social security systems on the Russian model) all social security costs are charged to the employer. In France the cost of children's allowances is carried solely by the employer, who also bears the major share of the cost of other social security programs. And, as we have seen, in the United States employers alone pay taxes for unemployment insurance (except in two states) and also for the Railroad unemployment and disability insurance systems and share equally with workers in the costs of OASI. The employer contribution usually takes the form of a percentage levy on payrolls, although in some countries, such as Great Britain, the employer pays a uniform money sum per employee.

General Considerations

Support for an employer contribution originally came from those who believed that the employer was morally obligated to bear the costs of social security programs, either because in general employers were regarded as being better off than workers,[8] or because the employer was held to be responsible for the occurrence of the risk. The theory that the employer is responsible for interruptions of employment was at one point strongly held by labor unions and perhaps had some validity in regard to occupational injuries and diseases. Its extension to the risk of unemployment is, however, more questionable. Undoubtedly, in some, but not all, industries short-period fluctuations in levels of employment may be eliminated or substantially reduced by stabilizing activities, such as more orderly personnel policies, more carefully planned organization of work within the plant, manufacturing for stock, or efforts to induce the consumer to spread his purchases more evenly over the year by the offer of discounts and the like. But it is doubtful whether employers, individually or as a group, can substantially control the most serious form of unemployment, namely a general depression, or even the kind of unemployment that affects one industry because of a change of consumer taste or the invention of new competitive products. Similarly, old established employers in one geographical area may be powerless to compete with those in a newly opened area where costs are substantially lower, in part

---

[8] There seems little doubt that acceptance by workers of the newly imposed social security taxes was secured more readily by emphasizing the point that the employer had also to pay for a program whose benefits would go solely to the workers.

because of the lower labor costs in the new area. In fact, in recent years, the attitude of labor toward the theory that the employer is responsible for unemployment has become more ambivalent, in part because of the use that employers themselves have made of this theory in the development of experience-rating systems [9] (see below).

In any case, the theory that the employer is responsible for the occurrence of the risk and should therefore be required to foot the bill cannot be applied to the risk of general disability or old age. Those who seek "moral" justifications for cost allocations have therefore substituted another theory to justify the employer contribution to old-age security programs. This takes the form of drawing a parallel between the obsolescence of men (considered as part of the productive enterprise) and of machinery. Just as the employer regards what he has to set aside for depreciation and obsolescence of his plant as part of the costs of doing business, so too, it is argued, should he provide, as part of business costs, against the obsolescence of his working force. Human beings, it is held, should not be treated less favorably than machinery.

Yet even if, for whatever reason, an effort is made to force the employer to contribute to the costs of social security, the question may be asked whether this objective is achieved by requiring an employer to pay a tax based upon the size of his payroll. The theory of the incidence of this tax has given rise to an extensive literature and is still a matter of dispute.[10] The weight of economic opinion seems to be that it is in fact ultimately passed on in large measure to consumers (via higher prices) and to wage earners (in the form of withholding of wage increases that might otherwise have been given) but that some part under noncompetitive conditions falls on profits. The exact proportion borne by these three groups is held to be much influenced by the economic conditions prevailing at the time the tax was first levied and shortly thereafter and by the characteristics of the individual industry. If money incomes are rising at the time the tax is imposed, producers will find it easier to pass the increase to consumers in the form of higher prices. If its imposition coincides with a falling level of money incomes and rising unemployment, it

---

[9] Organized labor originally opposed any worker contribution to unemployment insurance on the ground that unemployment was an employer's responsibility. Later, much of labor's opposition to experience-rating cited the fact that the employer was not responsible, at least for the more important types of unemployment. More recently, however, the guaranteed annual wage policies of the powerful CIO-organized automobile workers appear to be framed largely on the assumption that the employer is, in fact, primarily responsible for unemployment.

[10] For a discussion of tax incidence, see Carl Shoup, *The Prospects for a Study of the Economic Effects of Payroll Taxes,* Committee on Social Security of the Social Science Research Council Pamphlet 9, Washington, D.C., 1941; and Seymour E. Harris, *The Economics of Social Security,* McGraw-Hill Book Company, Inc., New York, 1941.

is more likely to be absorbed by wage earners, whose bargaining power will be gravely weakened at such times.

It should be noted too that the incidence of the payroll tax will be different in the case of OASI, where all employers pay the same rate of tax, and in unemployment insurance, where, due to the frequent exclusion of small employers and because of the operation of experience-rating arrangements (see below), different employers, even in the same lines of business, pay very different rates of tax. Here, the probability is greater that the tax (at least the differential above the minimum rate payable by any employer) will fall upon profits and not be shifted. In fact, students of public finance who have had to allocate the payroll tax for the purpose of estimating tax burdens have adopted different assumptions as to its incidence.[11]

Furthermore, the ability of an individual employer to shift the tax will vary in some measure with the elasticity of demand for his product,[12] its amenability to concealed price increases (in the form of a lowering of quality), the structure of the pricing system (in terms both of the units by which it is feasible to advance prices and the extent of public or institutional controls over prices charged), the degree of organization of his labor force, the feasibility of substituting machinery for labor, the ratio of wages to all costs (there is a range of from 10 to 90 per cent), and similar matters.

[11] The California State Board of Equalization study in 1946 and the Michigan Department of Administration in 1953 assumed its incidence was wholly on the consumer (using as the measure all retail sales and a combination of Michigan's share of national consumption and of retail sales, respectively). Dr. Newcomer in a 1940 study, made for the Treasury of the United States, assumed that all payroll taxes were divided equally between consumers (measured by total retail sales) and profits (measured by income payments for dividends and interest). Mushkin and Crowther in 1954 differentiated between OASI and Railroad payroll taxes on the one hand and unemployment insurance taxes on the other, allocating the former half to consumers and half to workers and the latter wholly to profits. (*The Incidence of Federal Taxes in California,* California State Board of Equalization, Sacramento, Calif., 1946; *The Incidence of Federal Taxes in Michigan,* Michigan Department of Administration Special Report no. 1, May, 1953; *Federal, State and Local Government Fiscal Relations,* U.S. Treasury Department, Committee on Intergovernmental Fiscal Relations, S. Doc. 69, 78th Cong., 1st Sess., 1943, pp. 207ff.; Selma J. Mushkin and Beatrice Crowther, *Federal Taxes and the Measurement of State Capacity,* U.S. Public Health Service, May, 1954.) For a discussion of assumptions as to tax incidence, see the exchange between Rufus Tucker, R. A. Musgrave, and others in *National Tax Journal,* March, 1951, pp. 1ff., September, 1951, pp. 269ff., and March, 1952, pp. 1ff.

[12] A special case of elasticity is presented by production for foreign markets. It has often been argued that payroll taxes are an especially undesirable method of financing social security in a country heavily dependent upon the export trade, as efforts by producers to shift the tax to buyers will lead to a loss of foreign business, while their inability to shift will tend to direct investment and enterprise toward the domestic market.

To the extent that the payroll tax is passed on to workers via the wage structure, the economic effect is, of course, the same as if workers paid the whole costs of the program in the first instance. Some of those who hold firmly to the view that the beneficiaries should carry the costs of social security would defend the employer's contribution for this very reason, namely as being a more palatable way of achieving the desired objective since most workers are not versed in the refinements of the theory of tax incidence. Those, however, who, for some of the many reasons discussed in the preceding section, hold that beneficiaries should not pay the whole cost criticize the employer payroll tax precisely because they believe that its incidence falls on wages.

To the extent that the incidence of the tax falls on consumers, financing by a payroll tax means that the cost is shared by others than the beneficiaries (unless the system is universal in coverage and relates to a risk to which the entire population is equally exposed). Whether this is a good plan or not depends on who these other persons are and on the theories held as to the desirability of income redistribution. Since lower-income receivers account for the bulk of consumption, it has generally been held that a tax which falls on consumers is a regressive tax. Even if the ultimate burden of the employer's tax falls on rich and poor consumers alike, this may be a socially undesirable method of financing, for it is again making the poor help to pay for the poor.

Other critics of the employer's social security tax point to its uneven, unpredictable, and unfair incidence as between different types of employers (some of whom, as was indicated above, can, and others cannot, pass it on) and to the fact that it influences employer decisions as to the allocation of resources between manpower and machinery.

In any case, it should be noted that since, apart from the differential unemployment insurance payroll taxes, no school of thought holds that the whole, or even the major part, of the incidence of the tax falls on profits, the payroll tax is a poor instrument for implementing the policy of casting the burden on employers as such. At least one country (New Zealand) collects contributions from employers in the form of a tax not on payrolls but on business profits. This has the further advantage of not interfering with the processes of production, for it leaves unchanged the relative costs to the employer of labor and of machinery.

As against these objections to continued reliance on the employer's payroll tax for all or a substantial part of the costs of social security programs, the pragmatic argument can be urged that this tax is a richly yielding one and that its capture for these programs has given them a secure financial basis that they would not otherwise have had, in view of the pressure for additional sources of revenue for all governmental purposes.

A further argument very frequently advanced in favor of a contribution from the employer is that if employers are made wholly or partially responsible for the costs of the program, they will cooperate with the administration in keeping costs to a minimum. There is, of course, considerable leeway for employer cooperation in these programs where benefit rights are influenced by employment relationships (as is the case in unemployment insurance). For such a program as OASI, however, the need for this kind of employer cooperation is almost zero, and the case for an employer contribution in this program must rest on other grounds. Even in unemployment insurance, moreover, as was seen in the discussion of controls and disqualifications in Chapter 4, employer interest in keeping costs to a minimum sometimes hinders achievement of the income security objectives of the system. Others, again, believe that to finance a program largely or, as in the case of unemployment insurance, wholly, by employers gives the latter an undesirably powerful influence over the legislatures, which are bound to pay primary attention to the wishes of those who can claim to be paying the costs of the program, to the disregard of broader social considerations.[13]

Finally it has been held by some schools of thought, notably in the United States, that the employer's tax is advantageous because it lends itself to socially desirable ends. By varying the tax paid by individual employers so that they are encouraged to take action directed to reducing the risks run by their own employees, it is urged that a net social gain will result, since prevention is always preferable to cure.

The policy of charging employers taxes at rates varying in some proportion to the benefits drawn by their own workers has been applied in workmen's compensation, in unemployment insurance, and in the general disability insurance system in at least one state, and also presumably in two other states for employers who exercise their option to insure with a private insurance company. Where accidents and illnesses arise directly in connection with employment, it can be argued with some cogency that they are to a substantial degree within the employer's control and that inducements to employers to install safety devices and otherwise organize their methods of production so as to keep illness and accident to a minimum are likely to achieve some success. But where the risk is general disability, however caused, this argument cannot apply.

Even in the realm of industrial accidents and diseases students of workmen's compensation have raised doubts about the efficacy of variable charges on employers in fostering preventive action. While conceding that the decline in industrial injuries owes much in past years to the in-

[13] This was one of the considerations which led the Senate Advisory Council in 1948 to urge a worker's contribution for unemployment insurance. (*Unemployment Insurance,* A Report to the Senate Committee on Finance from the Advisory Council on Social Security, S. Doc. 205, 80th Cong., 2d Sess., 1948, p. 28.)

stitution of systems of compensation, Somers and Somers conclude that "compensation has had a marked initial effect upon prevention activity but that it eventually spends itself and other motivations must replace it," and that although the cost of compensation may still constitute some incentive to prevention activities, it is now clear that the potential savings in compensation premiums are minor as compared to other economies, in part because limited benefits have led to low average premiums which give little leeway for differential rates. They conclude the program "appears to have contributed little to the safety problems of some very hazardous industries" and has been notably ineffective in regard to the small employers who have a much higher frequency rate of accidents but are in general neglected by the insurance carriers. They stress, too, the fact that an effective preventive program depends upon the cooperation of health and other authorities concerned with safety and industrial hygiene with the compensation system and question whether in America, at least, "the majority of . . . states, with their archaic administrative structures and practices and the majority of the private carriers too small for effectiveness in this complex domain, can or will bridge the gap." [14]

The Special Case of Experience-rating

In unemployment insurance, the appropriateness of incentive taxation, through systems of experience-rating, is a major issue in the United States and is one on which labor and management are sharply divided. The dispute has given rise to an extensive literature [15] and has very wide repercussions.[16]

Under experience-rating systems as they operate in all American unemployment insurance laws (and which, indeed, appear to be a unique

[14] Herman Miles Somers and Anne Ramsay Somers, *Workmen's Compensation*, John Wiley & Sons, Inc., New York, 1954, chap. VI. See also the opinions of C. A. Kulp, "The Rate-making Process in Property and Casualty Insurance—Goal, Technics, and Limits," *Law and Contemporary Problems*, Autumn, 1950, pp. 494–495.

[15] For a list of some of the more important sources, see Eveline M. Burns, *The American Social Security System*, Houghton Mifflin Company, Boston, 1951, pp. 156–169; Ida C. Merriam, *Social Security Financing*, Federal Security Agency, Social Security Administration, Division of Research and Statistics, Bureau Report No. 17, 1952, chap. III and pp. 201–212. Many of the recent issues of *American Economic Security* have contained important articles on experience-rating. For a detailed account of state experience-rating formulas and practices, see *Comparison of State Unemployment Insurance Laws as of August, 1954*, U.S. Department of Labor, Bureau of Employment Security, 1954, pp. 17–41. See also Edwin R. Teple and Charles G. Nowacek, "Experience Rating: its Objectives, Problems and Economic Implications," *Vanderbilt Law Review*, February, 1955, pp. 376–410.

[16] Thus in recent years it has affected employer attitudes toward federalization of unemployment insurance and all proposals to strengthen the role of the Federal government in the program, for the Federal administration was believed to be strongly opposed to experience-rating.

American institution) the rate of tax paid by an individual employer may be less or more than the standard rate (usually 2.7 per cent of covered payroll). The original purpose of these arrangements was to give employers an incentive, in the form of reduced taxes, to prevent or minimize unemployment and/or to allocate the costs of benefits among employers in accordance with their responsibility for causing unemployment. It should be noted that such arrangements directly affect only the financing of the program. Workers can still draw their benefits from the pool of all employer contributions and their rights to benefits do not depend on the size of the reserves of their own employers. The charging of employer accounts and determination of their reserve ratios is a bookkeeping device for the purpose of deciding how much each employer must contribute to the common pool.[17]

The practical implementation of this attempt to combine incentive taxation with a system intended to provide benefits for unemployed workers has, however, presented many difficulties. Three major problems have had to be resolved: how to measure the relative experience of different employers; the determination of which employer's account to charge in the case of an unemployed worker with several employers in his base year; and the selection of an appropriate range of tax rates. In grappling with these problems the states have developed a variety of formulas and practices of ever increasing complexity. In fact the precise effect of experience-rating depends on which formula is used. A detailed discussion of these complex measures would be out of place in this book, and attention will be drawn only to some of the broader consequences common to the most typical systems. A more detailed account of some of the typical formulas will be found in the Note appended to this chapter.

In principle, most of the states use as their measure of employer experience the benefits drawn by workers previously employed by the employer in question. Such a system is fairly well calculated to attain the second of the two objectives mentioned above, namely to allocate costs among employers in accordance with the extent of unemployment they "cause," more particularly since most such systems cumulate an employer's total contributions and benefits received by his workers since the system began. Even so, although an employer whose account has suffered heavy drains will have to continue paying taxes at the maximum rate until his reserve ratio [18] has again been built up to the required amount, the

---

[17] At one time some states made the workers' benefit rights depend on the balances in their own employers' accounts, but only two had such a system by the mid-1950s, and both provided for a partial pool.

[18] The reserve ratio is usually equal to the difference between the taxes paid by an employer minus the benefits paid in respect of his workers divided by his total payroll in some specified period.

firm that goes out of business after heavy benefit payments to its workers will not, of course, have carried the full burden of the unemployment legally attributable to it.

But this measure of employer experience has a major disadvantage. The essential item in determining an employer's prospects of securing a lower rate is *compensable* unemployment, rather than unemployment itself, and the stimulus given by experience-rating can operate as powerfully to motivate employers to reduce the extent to which unemployed workers are compensated as to induce them to eliminate unemployment, i.e., the occasion for compensation. With such a criterion, in other words, an employer can improve his prospects for a lower rate in one of three ways: stabilizing his own labor force, opposing improper claims and payments, or bringing pressure to modify the law and its interpretation so as to reduce the chance that if a worker becomes unemployed he will be entitled to a benefit, or if so entitled, that the benefit is not too high or (in all save the benefit-wage and compensable-separations plans [19]) the duration too long.

All such systems, especially the reserve-ratio type, give the individual employer an interest in seeing that his unemployed workers do not receive benefits and inevitably give employers as a group a direct stake in the provisions of the law, since the more liberal the law, the greater will be the charges against their accounts if their workers become unemployed. Where, as is the case in many states, this concern takes the form of providing that employers' accounts shall not be charged with benefits paid to their workers under certain circumstances (e.g., benefits paid after penalty waiting periods to workers who were discharged for misconduct or voluntarily quit) the only consequence is that some minimum rate must be paid by all employers to cover the costs of such benefits.[20] And where, as in some states, noncharging is applied to benefits drawn during the "slack season," the stabilizing objectives of experience-rating would seem to have been frankly abandoned. In practice, the desire to have as wide a spread in rates as possible (at least in the downward direction) has, as we saw in the section on disqualifications in Chapter 4, turned attention to the substantive provisions of the law, which, if made more restrictive, would protect employers' accounts.

Undoubtedly many employers place major emphasis upon securing reduced rates by stabilizing their own operations, although it must also be admitted that the years during which experience-rating has been in operation have been years of high employment and thus peculiarly favorable to stability of employment even without any special effort on the

19 See Note at end of chapter.

20 Unless, of course, the reserve is so excessive that payments can be made from that source.

employer's part. Unfortunately, far too little is known of the precise ways in which employers as a whole have responded to the experience-rating formulas. Such indices as the general levels of unemployment and the actual tax rates paid by employers as a whole or classified by groups supply no clues because of the overriding influence of the employment conditions of the time and because the states have changed the details of their formulas so frequently.

Efforts to develop formulas for measuring experience which do not give the employer so direct an interest in contesting or minimizing his workers' rights to benefit have not been notably successful or, as in the Payroll Variations plan,[21] have purchased success at the cost of gravely weakening the incentives to employers to stabilize.

A second major practical difficulty faced by all experience-rating systems, other than those using the payroll variations plan is the determination of which employer's account is to be charged with the benefits paid to a given worker. The attempt to avoid penalizing the employer who had given short-period employment to workers laid off from their normal job has created a situation in which a given employer's tax rate may be determined not by his own actions but by those of some other firm which employed one of his workers during the relevant base period.

The third major problem in the application of experience-rating principles concerns the range of taxes to be assigned. Obviously, the greatest stimulus to regularity will be given by that system which offers the widest range of tax rates. In fact, most systems provide for a quite narrow spread downwards from 2.7 per cent of payroll, and in no state does the maximum penalty rate exceed 4 per cent. This relatively limited range for the play of incentive taxation is further restricted by the steps taken by the states to protect the solvency of the state fund as a whole (see Note at end of chapter), which may cause an individual employer's tax rate to be influenced more by the employment experience of all employers in his state than by his own employment record.

Employers, who in general strongly favor experience-rating, continue to maintain that the assessment of costs against employers alone must rest in large measure on the theory that unemployment is a responsibility of the employer. Hence, if an individual so organizes his business that his workers suffer little unemployment, he should not have to pay such high taxes as his careless competitor. In this view, payment of unemployment insurance benefits is a liability thrown on the individual employer against which he is, in effect, able to insure, and his insurance rates should reflect his risk experience. Carried to its logical conclusion, this theory opposes any socializing of the costs of unemployment.

Employers also lay great stress on the argument that if an employer

21 See Note at end of chapter.

has a financial stake in the benefits paid to his workers, he will more willingly cooperate with the administration to prevent abuses of the system. Finally it is employers (and some public-finance experts) who support the view that there will be a more desirable allocation of the real costs of irregularity of operation if employers are charged higher rates when their employment experience is bad, and if these costs are then passed on to the final consumers.

Labor, on the other hand, as we have seen, while in general violently opposing experience-rating (some AFL unions have been somewhat ambivalent), has not adopted any consistent theory as to the employer's responsibility for unemployment. Labor's opposition to experience-rating has been based largely on the alleged consequences of this financial device, and notably on the importance which current formulas attach to *compensable* unemployment. In support of the view that this emphasis has adversely affected the benefit-paying objectives of unemployment insurance, opponents of experience-rating point to the increasingly severe disqualifications, which, it is alleged, have been enacted at employer insistence: to the opposition of employer groups in general to any liberalization of the laws which would increase their benefit liability and to the growing employer efforts to inculcate the view that only that unemployment which can clearly be shown to be the employer's fault should be compensated under the unemployment compensation laws.

All opponents of experience-rating challenge the view that the costs, even of such short-period unemployment as is now provided for, should not be socialized. The only consequence of limiting unemployment insurance to that unemployment for which the individual employer can be held responsible, it is alleged, will be the creation of some other public system acceptable to workers to provide for the security of those whose unemployment is otherwise caused. Some support for this contention is given by the demands of certain organized workers (notably the steel and automobile unions) for a guaranteed annual wage as part of a collectively bargained contract. It has been held by some observers that interest in the guaranteed annual wage would not have been so intense if the unemployment insurance system in the states had been more adequate.[22]

[22] The view that the guaranteed annual wage is in reality a demand for a better unemployment insurance system has also been held by employers. Cf. Thomas F. Johnson and Leonard J. Calhoun, "The Guaranteed Annual Wage in Collective Bargaining—Some Problems," *American Economic Security*, January–February, 1954, p. 22. For an account of the nature and some of the problems raised by guaranteed annual wage proposals and their relation to unemployment insurance, see *Preparing a Guaranteed Employment Plan*, UAW-CIO Education Department Publication, Detroit, Mich., 1954; *The Economics of the Guaranteed Wage*, Report of the Committee on Economic Policy, U.S. Chamber of Commerce, Washington, D.C., 1953; *Guaranteed Annual Wage Pay-*

Organized labor is also joined by other groups in laying stress upon other alleged undesirable consequences of experience-rating. Since in many states employers get tax reductions not because they have reduced unemployment but because their state laws are illiberal and have restricted benefit payments, there has developed, it is asserted, an undesirable competition between the states to keep taxes low by maintaining highly restrictive unemployment insurance systems so that the purposes of the Federal tax-offset have been undermined. For if employers of one state pay low rates because their state law is much less liberal than the average, a competitive advantage is thereby secured,[23] and all other states will be under pressure from their employers to keep liberalizing amendments to a minimum. Yet the purpose of the Federal tax-offset had been to make it possible for any state to enact a supposedly adequate unemployment insurance law without exposing its employers to the competition of employers from states which did not have such laws and therefore paid no taxes.

Furthermore, because the formulas do not in general distinguish between that unemployment which may be held to be clearly within the control of the employer and that which reflects the general state of the labor market, experience-rating systems in the past have resulted in a cutting of taxes when employment is high and their raising when unemployment is heavy.[24] Such an outcome is the direct opposite to what sound fiscal principles would indicate and negates one of the original objectives of unemployment insurance financing. This was to levy a uniform and predictable tax which would automatically yield a surplus in high employment periods and thus provide a reserve for depressions, so that heavy benefit payments could be financed without having to raise taxes at the psychologically most undesirable time. Whether or not, as some employers claim, experience-rating formulas can be devised which will not have this unfortunate effect is still a matter of dispute.

---

ments and Related Employer Payments under State Unemployment Insurance Systems, U.S. Department of Labor, Bureau of Employment Security, October, 1953; Miriam Civic, "Guaranteed Wages and Unemployment Insurance," The Business Record, National Industrial Conference Board, New York, January, 1954; William Haber, "The Guaranteed Annual Wage," Business Review [Ann Arbor], January, 1954; and Guaranteed Wages: Report to the President by the Advisory Board, Office of War Mobilization and Reconversion, Washington, D.C., January, 1947. See also, Ernest J. Eberling, "The Guaranteed Annual Wage and Unemployment Compensation," Vanderbilt Law Review, February, 1955, pp. 458–477.

[23] It is important to recall in this connection that under the additional credits provision of the Federal tax-offset system an employer who is paying less than 2.7 per cent to his state because he has qualified under his state's experience-rating formula may nonetheless claim the full 2.7 per cent offset against the 3 per cent he owes the Federal government.

[24] For further discussion of this aspect of experience-rating, see Chap. 10.

Even this brief discussion of experience-rating is sufficient to indicate the difficulties of discovering a formula which will at one and the same time achieve the twin objectives of offering inducements to individual employers to stabilize operations and of assigning the costs of unemployment to those who are responsible for causing it. It seems likely that the two objectives are not wholly compatible and that in some plans the one has consciously or unconsciously been substituted for the other, while generally both have been subordinated to a search for a formula that would result in cutting tax rates to the detriment of security objectives. Important, too, are the different economic consequences of different formulas and rate structures and the varying gains or losses they bring to individual employers, especially as general employment conditions change.

In view of the wide and differing repercussions of these provisions on employer practices and on the competitive position of different types of employers, the adverse effect on the nature of the benefit provisions, and, in a period when employment conditions are less favorable than they have been during the early years of experience-rating, on the solvency of the funds, it is unfortunate that so little intensive research has been devoted to the positive effects of experience-rating. Until more factual data are available, it is impossible for the responsible citizen to decide whether, on balance, the social and economic advantages of experience-rating outweigh its very evident disadvantages. Meanwhile, the system gives rise to the most acute differences of opinion.

Nonearmarked Taxes

Both wage and payroll taxes have in common the fact that they are sources of revenue earmarked for social security. Financing by means of nonearmarked general revenues is typically found in public assistance programs, although in certain states some or all of the funds for one or more public assistance programs are supplied by earmarked taxes, such as sales taxes or taxes on amusements. It is also evident that where a specific "poor rate" is levied on property owners (as was characteristic of poor-law financing in earlier days and is still found in some localities), this also constitutes a form of earmarking. But in general, the lion's share of the public assistance funds at the state level in the United States comes from the proceeds of such taxes as the state relies on for its general purposes,[25] and the Federal share is derived wholly from the general revenues.

[25] *Sources of Revenue for the State Share of Public Assistance, Fiscal Years 1949–51,* Social Security Administration, Bureau of Public Assistance, February, 1953. In the period studied five-sixths of the total state public assistance funds came from general rather than earmarked revenues.

Most income-conditioned pensions are also financed in the same manner, as are the systems of statutory cash payments. In all countries, for example, pensions and awards to veterans are financed from the general revenues. To an increasing degree the same is true of the newer children's allowance systems. However, instances in which the income-conditioned pension and the statutory cash payment are financed by earmarked taxes are not unknown. Thus New Zealand levies an earmarked percentage tax on incomes to provide part of the funds for her social security system, and Sweden does the same for her practically universal old-age pension program. Canada, in 1951, aimed to provide the revenues for her universal old-age pension system by earmarking 2 per cent of taxable personal income up to a maximum specified dollar amount, a 2 per cent tax on corporate income and a 2 per cent sales tax.

As the number of persons covered, and the scope of risks embraced, by social insurance or other nondiscretionary, nondeterrent systems has expanded, there has been a pronounced tendency to abandon sole reliance on earmarked taxes paid by employers and workers. Subsidies from the general taxpayer have come to account for an increasing proportion of the revenues. These subsidies may take the form of a government contribution made at the same time and on the same basis as the contributions of the wage and payroll taxpayer (e.g., the British unemployment insurance system adopts the principle of "equal thirds"); or the government may underwrite the difference between the yield of specified earmarked taxes and the actual expenditures (e.g., the New Zealand social security system, or the Swedish old-age pension program, or the British Health Service); or the government may accept financial responsibility for certain types of benefits (e.g., in many countries children's allowances are financed 100 per cent from the general revenues, although other risks are financed in whole or in part by earmarked contributions). Sometimes, as in Great Britain, the government accepts financial responsibility for certain types of unearned benefits, such as those paid to persons who were already elderly when the old-age insurance program was inaugurated. Similarly, in Britain the insurance funds were not charged with the cost of benefits paid during 1948 to 1953 to unemployed workers beyond the normal or standard period.

The use of general revenues as opposed to earmarked taxes of any kind (either social insurance taxes or other types of earmarked tax) has been caused by a variety of influences. It can perhaps be said that in general the arguments for and against the use of general revenues are the obverse of the arguments discussed in the two previous sections dealing with taxes on workers and taxes on employers.[26]

[26] For a discussion of contributory (earmarked) financing versus financing from the general revenues as applied to Great Britain, see Alan T. Peacock, *Economics of Na-*

From the point of view of fiscal adequacy appropriations from the general revenues have both advantages and disadvantages as compared to earmarked taxes. General revenues afford a much wider base and a yield that fluctuates less sharply over time than certain types of earmarked taxes; appropriations from the general revenues are also more flexible. With earmarking it is impossible to ensure that any given priority of need will have a priority claim on all available financial resources. For one of the disadvantages of the earmarked tax is that its yield may prove to be less or more than was anticipated, thereby causing curtailment of service or stimulating extravagance.[27] The difficulty of diverting to other uses the unexpected surplus of an earmarked fund is one with which treasuries have long been familiar. On the other hand, particularly when programs are new, or have not been accorded general acceptance, the earmarked tax has seemed to be a method of assuring at least some minimum revenue for social security purposes, and it has often been felt that taxpayer resistance may be reduced by identifying a service having popular appeal with a specific and appropriate type of tax. Thus on occasion some states have financed their aid to the blind programs by taxes on amusements, for psychological reasons, and the practice of others of using an earmarked tax on meals in restaurants to finance old-age assistance probably relies on the same kind of emotional appeal to the taxpayer.

Yet it seems likely that decisions as to the use or nonuse of general revenues have been less affected by these broader fiscal considerations than by other factors. Notable among these are prevailing concepts of social equity and attitudes toward the desirability of income redistribution. By and large, financing by appropriations from the general revenues means that the costs of benefits are not paid wholly, or in some cases, even mainly, by the beneficiaries themselves,[28] because, since income and inheritance taxes tend to figure prominently among the revenue sources of many governments, the general tax system as a whole is more progressive than the types of taxes most usually earmarked for social security purposes. This

---

tional Insurance, William Hodge and Co., Ltd., London, 1952, pp. 99–104; and *The Welfare State,* The Labor Party Policy Discussion Pamphlet 46, London, September, 1952. For a more general discussion, see Paul Durand, *La Politique contemporaine de sécurité sociale,* Librarie Dalloz, Paris, 1953, pp. 280–305.

[27] The best-known example in the United States is provided by Colorado, which for many years financed its old-age pension program by earmarked taxes and distributed a sizable "jackpot" at the end of the year among all recipients because of the surplus of the earmarked funds over normal annual expenditures. On the other hand, even the diversified earmarked taxes relied on by Canada for financing the universal old-age pension have failed to yield sufficient revenues, and loans advanced by the Dominion government were necessary in 1953 and 1954.

[28] One exception occurs in those public assistance administrations which stringently enforce recovery provisions, requiring the recipient of relief subsequently to pay back

is notably the case, as was seen above, with wage and payroll taxes, especially when these are levied only on the first so many dollars of wages or income. But even when the earmarked tax is a sales tax, the weight of expert opinion seems to be that such a tax is regressive. With general tax systems that are predominantly progressive in character, however, a double form of redistribution occurs, for the lower-income receivers pay less than their proportionate share of total costs of the social security system but obtain all, or the lion's share, of the benefits. Even with systems of universal coverage, the richer receive back in benefits far less than they contribute in taxes.

Where, therefore, a government relies largely for its general revenues on sales taxes, the substitution of earmarked for general revenues is not necessarily a shift from a regressive to a progressive method of financing. Since such taxes figure prominently in American state revenue systems, many of the supporters of progressive tax policies regard this fact as an additional reason for preferring Federal to state financing (see Chapter 11). Nor can it always be assumed that the largest unit of government has highly progressive tax policies. In Great Britain, for example, the increasing resort by the central government to indirect taxation, especially taxes on beer and tobacco, which figure prominently in working-class consumption, has considerably modified the redistributive effects of the so-called government contribution to the costs of the social insurance and related welfare programs. It is more doubtful whether this has caused the low-income group to pay for its own social benefits and resulted in a horizontal redistribution within the group rather than a net vertical redistribution of incomes, as has sometimes been claimed.[29] However, there is no doubt that substantial reliance on consumption taxes for financing social security benefits means that the ultimate burden of cost is influenced by consump-

---

from future income, if any, the relief he has received, or in states which place liens on the property of OAA recipients and take over the estates of deceased recipients. The question whether public assistance is in principle a loan or an outright grant has assumed considerable significance in some states.

[29] Cf. Findley Weaver, "Taxation and Redistribution in the United Kingdom," *Review of Economics and Statistics*, August, 1950, pp. 201–213. This is the case only if all direct and indirect taxes paid by the lower-income classes are compared merely with the total income security and welfare benefits estimated to be received by that group. But this disregards the fact that all other government expenditures (on armaments, police, justice, etc., and other public ends) have then to be financed wholly by other income groups. Unless it can be argued that the low-income receivers obtain no civic benefits from this type of expenditure, which is surely doubtful, the tax system as a whole remains progressive. (Cf. Alan T. Peacock and P. R. Browning, "The Social Services in Great Britain and the Redistribution of Income," in Alan T. Peacock (ed.), *Income Redistribution and Social Policy*, Jonathan Cape, Ltd., London, 1954.)

tion habits and that those who do not consume the taxed items benefit from an income redistribution.[30]

As against those who favor whole or partial financing from the general revenues, it has been objected that the use of the earmarked tax has the great advantage of bringing home to the beneficiary (or to the community as a whole, in the case of an earmarked sales or income tax) the cost of the service supported. As was shown above, there may be some validity to this argument, although the precise extent of the influence is still unknown. In those systems where the costs are shared in some proportion between the worker, the employer, and the general taxpayer, the restraining tendency of the earmarked tax can at best be partial. Indeed, it is for this reason that some would oppose even fractional financing of social insurance programs by appropriations from the general revenues, since this, they fear, would be the thin edge of the wedge: whenever additional funds were needed, it would be all too easy to increase the share of the general taxpayer. Certainly in those systems (such as the New Zealand comprehensive social security system or the British National Health Service) where the general taxpayer undertakes to meet the difference between the yield of certain earmarked taxes and the annual expenditures, the proportion contributed from the general revenues has steadily increased.[31]

Given the propensity of most voters to disregard the costs involved when supporting legislation conferring benefits on some or all sections of the population, it may well be thought unwise to abandon any devices or safeguards, however frail, which might conduce to a heightened sense of financial responsibility. Yet social and economic forces have conspired to cause the general taxpayer, as opposed to the wage and payroll taxpayer, to play an important role in financing social security measures. Even in the United States, where this trend is generally thought to be less pronounced, by 1950 to 1951, the general taxpayer (Federal, state, and local) was carrying 55 per cent of all income security expenditures. A government contribution to the social insurance systems was avoided in part because it was being made to other types of social security program.[32] And while the relative importance of public assistance can be expected to decline with the maturing of the OASI system, bringing a corresponding decline of the

[30] "Those who do not smoke or drink, but who live in a government owned house, wear utility clothing, use utility furniture and have a large family, enjoy the maximum of benefits and pay the minimum of taxes." (Weaver, *op. cit.*, p. 201.)

[31] In 1952 the British Government attempted to arrest this trend by setting a maximum (£400 million) to the amount of the contribution from the general revenues to the Health Service.

[32] Of a total of $6,036.9 million only $2,717.4 million was from social insurance funds. The remainder was accounted for by public assistance ($1,187.7 million) and payments to veterans ($2,131.8 million). (Ida C. Merriam, "Social Welfare Programs in the United States," *Social Security Bulletin,* February, 1953, p. 8.)

burden on the general taxpayer at the expense of wage and payroll taxpayers, the long-range costs of Veterans programs show an upward trend,
particularly at the time when World War II veterans reach late middle
age. Even more important is the fact that the range of risks covered by
social insurance systems is still relatively narrow in the United States as
compared to many other countries of an equally advanced stage of economic development. Were more risks to be covered, and this type of protection extended to all or almost all the population, it seems likely that
in America too there would be an irresistible demand for a contribution
from the general revenues to the social insurance programs.

For the powerful force which elsewhere has led to the use of "the government subsidy" has been the economic impossibility of meeting the
popular demand for a minimum of economic security in the event of
all types of risk by assessing the whole costs of the measures adopted
against the beneficiaries directly or indirectly. The relatively low income
level of the mass of the beneficiaries, even in universal systems, would
make these costs an intolerable burden on relatively low earners, and subsidies from those in the higher income brackets have been inevitable.

Some people who would oppose any contribution from the general
revenues to the normal ongoing costs of an income security system would
nonetheless favor assumption by the general taxpayer of the costs of unearned benefits, especially those which arise during the period when a
social insurance system is less than fully mature. Such policies have been
adopted in a number of countries.[33] As was seen in Chapters 2 and 3, the
desire to utilize a particular type of income security system, in this case
social insurance, as a major instrument for meeting contemporary needs
has occasioned a relaxing of eligibility requirements in contributory old-
age programs which has conferred substantial unearned benefits on those
already elderly. In addition, in some countries, such as the United States,
the old-age security system provides a variety of other unearned benefits.[34]

[33] Thus in England, the contribution rates for contributory old-age pensions were
fixed at a level which, on an actuarial basis, would ensure that the taxes paid in respect of an entrant at age 16 in 1956 and thereafter would pay approximately for the
whole of his or her benefits. But the cost of unearned benefits payable to those
who in fact entered the system above this age (notably, of course, the group already
in the upper age brackets when the system was inaugurated in 1925) was assumed by
the general taxpayer.

[34] It will be recalled that the main types of such benefits in OASI arise from the
heavy weighting of the benefit formula in favor of the low earner; the grant to veterans of credits toward benefits and eligibility status; the payment of tax rates until
1975 of less than the full-level premium rate; the disregard of years of low earnings
in calculating benefits; and the disregard of periods of total disability in determining
both eligibility and benefit amount. Proposals to base benefits on certain years of high
earnings, or to disregard absence from the system during periods of involuntary unemployment or temporary illness, would add still further to the volume of unearned

Under the OASI system the cost of these unearned benefits is thrown in the first instance on present and future wage and payroll taxpayers. Since the financing and benefit formulas have been so devised that each beneficiary will draw out at least as much as his own contributions (exclusive of those of his employer) would purchase on a private insurance basis, the higher-paid, longer-covered employees do not get a proportionate advantage from the contributions paid by their employers on their behalf. But because at least a substantial part of the employers' tax, as we have seen, falls on workers or low-income consumers, this arrangement means that in the last resort it is these groups that bear the costs of unearned benefits. Many people feel that this is socially inequitable since they hold that the financial burden of meeting the income needs of those who would fail to benefit from a system granting no unearned benefits is one that should fall on society as a whole. It is, of course, true that once broad public responsibility for assuring a minimum income to the aged has been accepted, as it has in the United States through the OAA laws and residual general assistance, any extension of unearned benefits under the social insurance system reduces the financial responsibility of those who finance OAA and general assistance and transfers the cost to the OASI Fund. This fact was a major reason for opposition of labor and other groups to the proposals of the Chamber of Commerce in 1953 to blanket-in to OASI the existing OAA caseload and charge the costs against the Fund. This was felt to be a retrogressive step since it involved shifting the burden of a cost that had to be met anyway from general taxpayers to wage and payroll taxpayers.

PRIVATE UNDERWRITING OF SOCIAL SECURITY COSTS

A wholly different principle for raising the funds for social security payments is found in many countries in workmen's compensation [35] and, in the United States, also in state temporary disability insurance plans. Here, the payment of benefits is treated, in effect, as a liability on the employer against which he may voluntarily or compulsorily insure, and the worker's

---

benefits. One of the most costly items would be enactment of proposals (made in 1953 and 1954) to blanket-in all persons then aged. It has been estimated that to admit such persons to benefit at the minimum $25 rate would have added $700 million to costs in 1953, while the cost of giving them a $35 minimum would be $1.4 billion. The estimated disbursements for 1953, under the law as it then was without this amendment, were $1,498 million. It should, however, be noted that this particular annual unearned burden would decrease sharply over the next ten or fifteen years.

[35] In Great Britain, however, since 1948 workmen's compensation, like other social insurance programs, is financed by contributions from employers and workers with a small state subsidy.

claim is against his employer or the insurer. In some workmen's compensation systems such insurance may be written only with a state insurance agency; very frequently, however, the employer has the option of insuring with a private insurance company. Thus in the United States by 1955 only roughly one-sixth of the jurisdictions had exclusive state funds, while in almost a quarter there was a state fund which competed with private insurance companies for compensation business. The remaining systems were financed by insurance written by private carriers. In addition, in all save seven jurisdictions, self-insurance was permitted under varying conditions, although this type of coverage was relatively unimportant.

Similarly, three of the four American states with temporary disability insurance systems permitted private insurance carriers to participate in financing the program, either by competing with the state fund through a financial arrangement which paralleled that applicable to workmen's compensation, or (in two states) by allowing employers, in effect, to substitute a benefit plan insured with a private carrier for the payment of premiums or contributions to the state fund.[36]

The desirability of thus opening up social insurance financing to private enterprise has given rise to much difference of opinion. Since to many people the very idea that a private profit should be made out of what is essentially a public service is repugnant, and since the necessity to supervise in some degree through public authority the activities of private carriers inevitably involves additional administrative costs, the adoption of such methods, where their existence is not merely a historical survival, must reflect a belief that there are countervailing social advantages. Yet the extent of these is not easy to determine.

One possible justification for this method of financing which might at first sight appear to have considerable validity proves to be less convincing on examination. This is the argument that since, in workmen's compensation at least, the moral, as apart from the formal, legal, justification for charging costs against employers only must be the belief that the employer is at fault or ultimately responsible for the injury, the charge paid by the employer should reflect his own experience. This type of adjustment of charges, it is held, is one that has been perfected by private insurance carriers who are equipped to carry on such business with a maximum of economy. Yet even if such adjustment of charges is desired, experience has shown that public authorities can do the job either on an insurance basis through a state insurance fund precisely paralleling the forms of commercial insuring companies or through levying social insurance taxes and

---

[36] It will be recalled that in one state the contributions are paid wholly by the worker and in two others the employer's share is less than that of the worker.

developing systems of experience-rating.[37] Furthermore, it is believed by some authorities that the advantages of efficient large-scale operation by private insurance have not been reaped and that costs are kept high by the unlimited and excessive competition of an unduly large number of carriers, many of whom are small or inefficient but are kept in business by a system of rate making that reflects average costs rather than those of the most efficient firms.[38]

Furthermore, the costs of raising funds by opening the field to private commercial insurance are inevitably higher than when a similar sum is raised through the tax-collecting powers of the state. Although the costs of securing business are somewhat reduced by the fact that once the law has imposed legal liabilities on employers, insurance companies as a whole no longer have to cultivate an atmosphere favorable to insurance as such, for all covered employers will be "insurance-minded," the companies still have to compete against each other and against the state fund. In fact, the costs of securing business account for a substantial proportion of the premium dollar paid to private insurance companies doing this type of business.[39]

There seems little evidence that the other administrative costs in connection with the adjudication of claims and the like are lower for private insurance companies than for state agencies. Yet since in a public program some state agency has to supervise, at least in a general way, the operation of private agencies financing and administering a public program, an additional administrative cost, which may or may not be chargeable against the private carriers, is created.

As a result of all these factors the proportion of the premium dollar that is actually paid out in benefits is substantially less than 100 per cent. Although for various reasons the exact percentage cannot be known, careful estimates suggest that in the United States the range lies somewhere between 47 and 64 per cent and in recent years may have averaged 55 per cent.[40] While workmen's compensation is admittedly of greater complexity than other income security programs, there is a striking difference between this figure and the corresponding percentages for OASI (where administrative costs, including those of tax collection, amounted to around 2.5 per cent of benefits paid in 1954) and for the Railroad unemployment and

[37] Many of the difficulties of determining employer experience in unemployment compensation systems would not arise in assessing responsibility for occupational injury.

[38] Cf. Somers and Somers, op. cit., pp. 102ff.

[39] In 1953 acquisition costs of workmen's compensation business accounted for approximately 17.5 per cent of the typical gross manual rates in the United States. (Ibid., p. 104.)

[40] Ibid., pp. 119–120, 279–281.

temporary disability insurance system (where the corresponding figure for 1953–54 was 4.7 per cent).

But although financing by private insurance cannot be justified on the grounds of comparative costs, other reasons for its use require examination. It is held, for example, that much greater flexibility is possible: the benefits can be more nearly tailored to the needs and circumstances of those, whether employers or workers, who are affected by the legislation. Thus, for example, in workmen's compensation systems it is possible for employers to insure with private companies against liability to suits from injured workers (a service not offered by the public authorities), and it is obviously convenient to arrange for insurance against workmen's compensation liabilities with the same insurer. Similarly, in disability insurance, it has been held a great convenience for both employers and workers, in concerns providing fringe medical and disability benefits, to integrate these with those provided by the public program. Among other advantages claimed for such integration is the simplification of administration for both workers and employers operating such schemes. Trade unions, which have administered health and medical care programs, financed by the union or jointly with employers under collectively bargained plans, have often favored the merging of public disability benefits with these privately insured (or self-insured) systems because it permits them to retain control over, or participation in, administration. It is also urged that the use of private underwriting permits the payment of benefits above the legally required minimum to certain categories of workers— either because the employees of a given firm constitute risks more favorable than the average, or because the employer may be induced to make some additional contribution [41] to the basic benefits in a plan tailored to the needs of his firm and under his control. However, to the extent that the more favorable risk experience of a group of employees is due to such factors as its age, sex, economic level, or occupational composition, the granting of additional benefits for the statutory amount of contribution or the payment of the minimum legal benefits in return for a lowered premium means only that the advantages of pooling of risks are sacrificed and the public fund is left with the worst risks. This consideration is especially important in disability insurance.

Efforts to ensure that there is no selection of risks on a basis adverse to

[41] The experience of California suggests that this is the least prevalent alternative. Among the recommendations of a study directed to discovering ways in which insurance companies could maintain, or secure, a larger proportion of this type of business, was the suggestion that greater efforts should be made to obtain an employer contribution. (John S. Bickley, *The Impact of a State Disability Act on Insurance Companies,* Ohio State University Bureau of Business Research, Research Monograph 71, Columbus, Ohio, 1954, pp. 34–35.)

the state fund have not proved notably successful, and the more successful they are, the narrower are the opportunities for private insurers to divert business away from the state fund by offering net advantages to employers.[42] Some laws moreover do not even attempt to include such safeguards.[43]

Furthermore, where, in order to assure that workers receive some net advantages from contracting-out, it is required that any privately insured plan must offer benefits superior to the legal benefits in at least some respects, a new and not always happy situation develops. Each liberalization of the legal benefit tends to increase the costs of the privately insured plans and intensifies the resistance of buyers. In consequence, such arrangements tend to enlist the interests of sellers of private insurance as a body against further liberalization of state disability laws since it narrows their profit margin and may even cause a substantial retrenchment of their market.[44] Thus the greater benefits secured by some workers may be purchased at the cost of lower average benefits for workers as a whole.

In any case, as the experience of private insurance companies in relation to OASI has shown, if a firm desires to provide benefits for its employees, over and above those required by the law, it is possible to develop supplementary plans which take account of the legal benefits and are integrated with them in principle, although the arrangements for financing and administering the two plans are separate.[45]

A major question raised by the use of private underwriting of social security benefits concerns the effect of these arrangements on the security of the workers. Where, as is usual in workmen's compensation, the worker's claim is not against a pooled state fund but against the individual employer or his insurer, his chances of collecting clearly depend upon whether his employer has complied with the law or, if not, has financial resources adequate to pay the benefits due. Although all American states except one require employers to give assurance of their ability to meet compensation obligations, compliance with this requirement is far from

[42] Cf. *ibid.,* pp. 28–29, 36.

[43] Thus in New York, for example, the employer may even have a plan covering a section only of his workers. The California law goes further than any in attempting to protect the state fund, but the effectiveness of the measures used has been questioned. For an account of the protective devices in the California law, see Margaret M. Dahm, "Temporary Disability Insurance: The California Program," *Social Security Bulletin,* February, 1953, pp. 15–20; and Bickley, *op. cit.,* chaps. I, II.

[44] Cf. Bickley, *op. cit.,* pp. 20–25.

[45] It seems likely that the reluctance of the insurance companies to concentrate attention on this approach has been due to the accidental fact that the early disability insurance systems levied taxes which proved to be excessive in relation to the costs of the benefits provided for in the law. Hence, there was a considerable margin which enabled the private insurers to offer higher benefits for the same premiums.

complete, in part due to the weakness of the state administrations charged with compliance. Since it is apt to be the marginal or least financially secure employers who neglect to insure, the alternative remedy available to a worker, namely to sue his employer, is of little value, and each year a number of workers fail to receive the compensation to which they are entitled.[46]

The disability insurance systems which permit contracting out through privately insured plans do not expose the worker to the same risk of loss of benefit rights, since if not covered by a private plan, the worker is automatically covered by the state fund. But in such systems new problems arise, such as questions of financial responsibility for workers becoming sick after a period of qualifying employment under a private fund though no longer employed by such a firm or for unemployed workers previously covered by a private plan. Although various arrangements have been developed for dealing with such cases, they add to the complications of financing and administration.

In workmen's compensation systems too, the principle of private underwriting creates the need for a multiplicity of special adjustment funds if the rights of all workers are to be protected. And the frequency of such funds is increasing.[47] Second Injury Funds (developed to prevent discrimination against employment of disabled workers), Assigned Risk plans (to secure agreement among the companies to assume a specified proportion of the poor risks), Funds for Reopened Cases, for Foreign Resident Claimants, or for Vocational Rehabilitation are examples of the efforts made to secure for workers, under a privately insured public income security system, the certainty of benefit payment, equal treatment, and absence of discrimination in employment that is secured much more simply or economically under the modern social insurance plans which have developed since the workmen's compensation pattern was established.

Two further disadvantages of this method of financing are cited by its opponents. It is held that it is socially undesirable to inject considerations of private profit into determinations of benefit eligibility and rights. Where, as has been the case at least until recently, the economic resources and therefore the legal talent available to the insurers vastly exceed those of the individual claimant, it is obvious that the beneficiary is at a grave disadvantage, which, because of the political weakness of many of the state administrations in relation to their powerful competitive rivals, is not offset by the possibilities of appeal to the state supervising agency. And even where the relative position of the contesting parties is less unequal because of the growing strength of unions and the development of

[46] Cf. Somers and Somers, *op. cit.*, pp. 93–95.

[47] For an account of these funds and the problems they were created to solve, see *ibid.*, pp. 130–137.

legal specialists concentrating on serving claimants, it is still held that the situation whereby the worker has to press his claim against the employer or his insurer is conducive to disputed claims. Certainly all observers are agreed as to the highly litigious character of workmen's compensation, although there is some difference of opinion as to how far this excessive resort to legalistic procedures is attributable to the entry of private insurance as such into the financing picture.[48]

In any case, in a system whose object is to make income payments (and also to provide medical care) to injured workers, this introduction of adversary procedures into administration has two unfortunate consequences. It practically compels claimants to employ lawyers, so that a substantial part of the benefits awarded go not to the claimant but to his lawyer in fees.[49] And many observers have called attention to the often disastrous effect upon the injured worker and his prospects for recovery or rehabilitation of a system which makes his physical condition a crucial subject of dispute on which testimony is given at the hearing in his presence by medical witnesses called by the opposing parties.[50]

One final disadvantage of financing by private underwriting remains: the general lack of public accountability to which it gives rise. Less is known about the operation of workmen's compensation than of any other social security system despite the fact that this is the oldest of public income security measures. Even the total volume of money paid as benefits has to be a matter of estimate, and detailed breakdowns by type of benefit or estimates of the numbers of beneficiaries at any given time are so hazardous that experts hesitate to commit themselves. Still less is known about the extent to which the taxpayer or the employer or the worker gets value for money for the payments made as taxes or as premiums. Even in disability insurance, statistics relating to aspects of the system in operation other than the total volume of payments are not available for that part of the program operating under private plans.

As against these many disadvantages, the system of financing a public program through private underwriting has in the eyes of its supporters one

[48] For a convenient account of litigation in workmen's compensation administration, see *ibid.*, chap. V.

[49] In states where the amount of legal fees payable by the claimant is fixed by statute the percentage varies from 10 to 33 per cent of the award, sometimes subject to a maximum dollar limit or on a sliding scale relating to the amount of the award. By 1954 it was reported that attorneys' fees were becoming standardized in the United States at around 20 per cent. No legal control is exercised over the fees for counsel of employers or carriers, the costs of which are, of course, included in the insurance premiums.

[50] Cf. Henry H. Kessler, M.D., *Rehabilitation of the Physically Handicapped*, Columbia University Press, New York, 1953, pp. 50ff.; and Marshall Dawson, *Problems of Workmen's Compensation Administration*, U.S. Bureau of Labor Statistics Bulletin 672, 1940, p. 127.

major advantage. It reserves for private enterprise a field that would otherwise be monopolized by government. Where there is a disposition to fear extensions of government operation, these views may prevail despite the many disadvantages of this method of financing. Nor must it be forgotten that to the private insurance company, underwriting the public program, even if not very profitable in itself, may establish contracts which lead to other more remunerative business.[51]

A NOTE ON AMERICAN EXPERIENCE-RATING SYSTEMS

The first problem in experience-rating is the question of what measure of stability or instability of employment to use, i.e., how to measure the relative experience of different employers. The majority of state systems use, in effect, the benefits drawn by unemployed workers previously employed by the employer in question. Under the so-called "reserve-ratio" formula the benefits paid in respect of his workers are deducted from the contributions an employer has paid, and the resulting balance is divided by his total payroll. The employer must accumulate and maintain a reserve of a specified size before he is entitled to a reduction in his tax rate, the amount of his actual tax being determined by a schedule which assigns specific tax rates for specified ranges of reserve ratios, the highest reserve ratios corresponding to the lowest tax rates.[52]

It has been objected that it is unfair to charge employers with the whole amount of the unemployment suffered by their workers, since the duration of a worker's unemployment may be outside the employer's control. Of two workers, discharged by two employers, one may find another job at the end of two weeks, while the other may remain unemployed until he has exhausted twenty-six weeks of benefit. For this, and other reasons, a few states use as the measure of "unemployment caused by employers" not the product of a worker's benefit rate and the duration of his unemployment but the fact of separation from employment. Under this "benefit-wage" formula, the relative experience of employers is measured by the separations of workers which result in benefit payments, but no account is taken of duration. The index which establishes the relative experience

[51] Cf. Bickley, op. cit., p. 28: "If an insurer protects against the UDC [California's disability plan] exposure, it is in a strategic position to sell him group accident and health insurance."

[52] The so-called "benefit-ratio" formula, used by a handful of states, is similar in principle except that it eliminates contributions from the formula and uses as its measure the ratio of benefits to payrolls on the theory that if each employer pays a rate which approximates his benefit ratio, the program will be adequately financed. Unlike the reserve-ratio systems, the benefit-ratio formulas do not cumulate benefits over a long period but use benefits paid in the last three years.

of an employer is then the total wages which had been earned during the base year by such workers as become unemployed (his benefit wages) expressed as a percentage of his total payroll. Only one separation per beneficiary is recorded for any one employer.

Since this formula aims to levy variable rates which will raise for the state as a whole the total amount paid out as benefits, the percentage relationship between total benefit payments and total benefit wages in the state (during three years) is determined. This shows how much in benefits was paid out for every dollar of benefit wages paid, and hence what tax rate per dollar of benefit wages is needed to replenish the fund. An individual employer's rates are determined by multiplying the employer's experience factor (the ratio of his benefit wages to his total taxable payroll) by the corresponding measure for the state. The higher the ratio, the higher the rate he pays.[53]

Recognition of the disadvantage of using benefits paid as a criterion of stability or instability has led to a search for other measures which would not give the employer so direct an interest in contesting or minimizing his own employees' benefit rights. One such measure, which has been adopted alone or in combination with other measures by a very few states, is payroll variations.[54] Under this system, the difference between the total payroll in one quarter (or year) and the succeeding quarter (or year) is expressed as a percentage of payrolls. Employers whose payrolls show no decrease, or only a small percentage decrease (over a three- to five-year period), are eligible for the greatest relative tax reductions. The tax rate corresponding to any given payroll decline often varies with the size of the reserve ratio of the state fund.

The theory underlying the use of payroll variations as a measure of stability is that payrolls reflect the volume of employment given or not given. However, it has been objected that payrolls also reflect wage levels and rapidity of expansion of industry. A firm which had increased wages in a payroll period immediately preceding a period of substantial layoff

[53] The "compensable-separations" formula, used by one state, is similar in principle in that it uses compensable separations (with no regard to duration of unemployment) as the measure of the employer's experience. But a worker's separation is weighted by his weekly benefit amount, not the wages earned with the employer in question during the base year. The employer's aggregate payroll for three years is then divided by the total of such separations and weekly benefit amounts over the period, to establish his merit-rating index. Rates are assigned by schedule, on the basis of an array of payrolls in the order of the indices, the lowest rates being received by those with the highest indices.

[54] At least one state uses also the age of the business, on the theory that the risk of unemployment is greatest in the first few years of the life of a business. While this may be appropriate if the purpose of experience-rating is to assign financial responsibility in some proportion to costs incurred, it tends to weaken its effectiveness as a stimulus to stabilizing activities by the individual employer.

would pay a higher rate of tax than one which laid off the same proportion of workers but had not thus increased wages. In this respect, those systems which use quarterly rather than annual declines as a measure are less subject to criticism, since it can be argued that changes in wage levels will be minimized because comparisons are made only with the most recent quarter rather than with a more remote period. The payroll variations plan also inevitably reflects trends in employment. The firm which is continuously expanding in terms of volume of employment given may be a highly irregular employer in the sense that it may have high turnover, but it may still qualify for a tax reduction. If the objective of experience-rating is merely to allocate financial responsibility for costs of benefits paid, this would not be an objection to the payroll variations plan, for the total volume of unemployment might remain unchanged as a result of such personnel policies. But if the objective of experience-rating is to minimize the disadvantage to the worker of instability of employment, then the payroll variations formula must be held to offer an inadequate stimulus to eliminate such practices.

The plan has other shortcomings. It would penalize the employer who introduced new methods which cut his labor costs, such as substitution of new machinery or less labor-intensive processes. The annual payroll variations plan provides no penalty for the employer who every year has a seasonal drop in employment but whose total annual payroll is unchanged from year to year. And the quarterly plan may treat differently two employers each of whose workers in a given year draw the same amount of benefits, if the one concentrates all his layoffs in one quarter, while the other spreads them gradually over the four quarters.

However, the use of payroll declines as a measure of the employer's experience does overcome two difficulties that accompany the use of benefits (or compensable unemployment) as a measure of employer experience. First, it eliminates the direct interest of the employer in the amount of benefits paid to his own workers. Indeed, some employers would oppose this system for this very reason. However, it does not eliminate the interest of employers as a group in the benefit provision of the law, since the extent of tax reduction that is granted for any given quarterly percentage decline depends on the condition of the state fund, and this is clearly affected by the liberality or otherwise of the law itself. Second, it avoids the awkward problem of determining which employer is to be held responsible for the unemployment of a given worker.

At first sight it might seem as if the obvious account to charge was that of the worker's most recent employer. But it might be that he had given short-period employment to a worker who had been laid off by his regular employer, and in these circumstances it is held both that it is unfair to charge him with the costs of the worker's unemployment and that it is economically undesirable to do so, since it would deter such employers from offering temporary jobs to workers laid off by their normal employers. In fact, only a handful of states charge the most recent employer, and these usually relieve the employer who has given employment for only a few weeks.

About half the states charge benefits against all base-period employers (i.e., employers with whom the worker earned wages in the period on which his benefit rights are based) in proportion to the wages earned by the beneficiary with each employer.[55] This policy can be defended only on the theory that liability for benefits is a risk inherent in the payment of wages. It is difficult to see how such a theory can be consistent with the objective of rewarding by tax reductions the employer who maintains steady employment, since under such a system employers may find their accounts charged with a fraction of the benefit costs of workers who had left them voluntarily to take work with other employers or who secured work with other employers immediately after being discharged and before becoming eligible for benefits. In a sense, this system makes the liability to charges of all employers depend upon the action of the most recent employer of workers who had been on their payroll at some time during the base year in question. The theory that liability for benefit payments inheres in the very payment of wages also underlies the charging methods of another quarter of the states, which adopt the system of charging base-period employers in reverse chronological order, apparently on the theory that responsibility for unemployment is presumed to lessen with time. Since a maximum limit is placed on the amount that may be charged to any one employer, in many cases the effect on the employer most distant in time may not be very different from that of the system of charging in proportion to base-period wages.

The range of possible tax rates is narrow, and most states set minimum and maximum rates. Employer opposition to severe penalty rates had by 1955 led all but a small minority to fix a maximum rate of 2.7 per cent, and in no state did the maximum rate exceed 4.1 per cent of payroll. And because of a concern for solvency, and the need for a fund to meet the cost of "noncharged" benefits, only about a quarter of the states permitted taxes to fall to zero per cent, although in many cases the minimum was as low as 0.1 per cent.

In any case, the range is small. Some exponents of experience-rating have complained that the existence of these minima and maxima gravely impedes attainment of the objectives of the institution. The irregular employer, once he is assigned the maximum rate, has nothing more to

---

[55] A couple of states charge all benefits to the principal employer during the base period, using as a measure the payment of the largest amount of base-period wages earned by the worker.

fear: the stabilization-conscious employer, once assigned the minimum rate, can rest on his oars for he has nothing more to hope for.[56]

The determination of specific rates applicable to individual employers is further complicated by the fact that however wide or narrow the range of tax rates, the total yield of all taxes must suffice to keep the state fund solvent. Hence most states have either provided for alternative schedules which assign different tax rates for given indices of employer experience according to the condition of the state fund or have modified the experience-ratio requirement for specified rates according as their state reserve fund increases or decreases. By 1955 three-quarters of the states in which the maximum tax rate was legally limited to 2.7 per cent of taxable payrolls further provided for the suspension of experience-rating when the state fund fell below a specified danger point. From the point of view of ensuring adequate resources for the system as a whole such provisions are logical enough. But such arrangements may work havoc with the employment-stabilizing objectives of experience-rating. For in effect they mean that a major influence on the precise rate an employer will be charged is the condition of his state's fund, and from one year to another an employer might find that despite substantial stabilization of his own work force, his assigned tax rate had increased. While the regular employer will (except in the case where experience-rating is suspended) be charged relatively less than his irregular competitors, the size of the differential will steadily decrease as the condition of his state's fund worsens, since most states set the maximum tax at 2.7 per cent.

[56] Russell L. Hibbard, "Minimizing State Unemployment Compensation Taxes," *American Economic Security*, January–February, 1954, pp. 29–31.

CHAPTER 10

The Distribution of Costs over Time

A SECOND major financial question concerns the relative desirability of meeting social security disbursements each year as they arise or spreading the costs over a longer period by the accumulation of reserves or the incurring of deficits to be paid off later. Not all social security systems lend themselves to long-period financing. The forecasting of future costs is feasible only in relation to social security systems where the law defines with considerable precision the amount of the benefits and their duration and where the eligibility conditions are based on objective, nondiscretionary criteria. Thus it would hardly be possible to finance a program based on public assistance principles on a reserve basis. The commitment to meet need in full, the indefinite duration of public assistance payments as long as need persists, the absence of uniform standards as to amount of payment and tests of need, plus the fact that public assistance is a residual program which bears the onus of meeting such needs for income as are not provided for by the other income security systems—all these characteristics make it impossible to forecast what expenditures will be required for many years ahead. In an unemployment insurance program, however, the problem becomes somewhat more manageable, for an arbitrary time limit is set in the law as to the duration of such payments, so that however prolonged a general depression, there is an automatic limit to the effect it can have on unemployment insurance disbursements. Furthermore, the fact that benefits are set in relation to previous wage levels makes some realistic approximations of benefit costs possible.

Similarly, in old-age insurance or in systems based on assumed average need the legal precision of the definitions both of who is eligible and of benefit levels enables the framers of such systems to make some forecasts as to the long-run costs of the program, though, as we shall see below, these forecasts are subject to a wide margin of error.

On the other hand, the advantages of long-period financing are apparent only in regard to risks whose occurrence fluctuates markedly but within predictable limits, from one year to another, or where a long-term trend in the level of annual disbursements can be predicted. These conditions are met in some degree in unemployment and old-age programs, although here too there are very real limits to predictability. Disability and health insurance systems relate to risks whose incidence, apart from

189

occasional epidemics on the one hand and very long-period changes in morbidity due to medical progress and other factors on the other, varies only slightly from one year to another, while the factor which vitally affects the cost of health service programs, namely the use made of available services, has proved to be extremely difficult to predict. Such systems typically embody provisions only for a contingency reserve to cover minor errors in estimates and in fluctuations in tax yields and to allow for the occasional epidemic.

Finally it should be noted that both the feasibility and the worth-whileness of adopting a long period of account for financing income security programs are conditional upon stability in the value of money. Over the last half century progressive inflation has greatly weakened the case for reserve financing, and many countries have moved over to pay-as-you-go financing, modified only by provision for a relatively small contingency reserve. As was shown in earlier chapters, the general social purpose of the long-term risk programs makes it impossible to disregard the effect of inflation on the purchasing power of benefits, and their public character makes it possible to take some effective action. As inflation has proceeded, one country after another has increased the money amount, not merely of all benefits to be awarded thereafter but also of those previously awarded. But since the reserves of these programs are typically wholly or in large measure invested in fixed-income securities (or in assets, such as housing or hospital facilities, where earnings respond only slowly to rising prices and are often controlled), they tend to become progressively less and less significant as sources of income in relation to the greatly enlarged current money disbursements.[1]

RESERVES IN OLD-AGE INSURANCE

No issue in OASI financing has received more attention from the first than the question of the desirability of reserve financing.[2] The final answer will depend upon the extent to which costs are predictable, the purposes it is sought to achieve by the reserve, and the probabilities that actual or proposed reserve arrangements will in fact achieve them. These in turn, must be balanced against any undesirable effects of the existence of large reserves.[3]

[1] Cf. Paul Durand, *La Politique contemporaine de sécurité sociale,* Libraire Dalloz, Paris, 1953, pp. 306–312.

[2] For recent statements of the opposing views, see Nelson Cruickshank, *Your Stake in the Social Security Trust Fund,* American Federation of Labor, Washington, D.C., 1953; and Charles A. Siegfried, "Why Pay-as-you-go?" *American Economic Security,* Conference Issue, 1953.

[3] For an account of the policies actually followed in the United States, see Robert J. Myers, "Actuarial Aspects of Financing O.A.S.I.," *Social Security Bulletin,* June, 1953;

The Predictability of Long-range Costs and Income

The feasibility of predicting future costs and income of long-period risk programs is, as indicated above, vitally influenced by the nature of the income security program itself. Where benefits are of a fixed and uniform money amount payable to all persons reaching a defined age, the problem is presented in its simplest form. Here, it is necessary primarily to utilize demographic projections, for the population of pensionable age will determine future levels of expenditure, and the population in the productive ages will affect the income to be secured from any selected types of taxes. But even in population estimates, as was shown in Chapter 6, there is a wide margin of error, particularly for very long-range forecasts.[4] Furthermore, unless the income of the system is to be derived from a poll tax, further estimates regarding the numbers of people in the selected taxpaying groups and the probable yield of such taxes are called for.

As soon as the system departs from this simple form, the task of developing estimates of benefit outgo and anticipated income becomes infinitely more complex, as can be seen from a brief consideration of the problems of the actuary in regard to OASI.[5] Here, in addition to developing population estimates, the actuary must take account of a wide range of economic and social data. Benefit disbursements will depend upon the number of eligible workers who actually decide to claim benefits and upon the amount of the benefit payment to each. In consequence he must make

James S. Parker, "Financial Policy in O.A.S.I., 1935–50," *Social Security Bulletin*, June, 1951; and Robert M. Ball, "What Contribution Rate for O.A.S.I.?" *Social Security Bulletin*, July, 1949. For further discussion of the issues and references to the different viewpoints, see Eveline M. Burns, *The American Social Security System*, Houghton Mifflin Company, Boston, 1951, pp. 105–121, and Ida S. Merriam, *Social Security Financing*, Federal Security Agency, Social Security Administration, Division of Research and Statistics, Bureau Report no. 17, 1952, chap. II and pp. 200–201.

[4] The estimates of the population 65 and over made by the actuaries in 1953 in connection with OASI ranged from 18 to 19 million persons for 1970, from 22 to 23 million for 1980, and for 38 to 42 million for 2050. Even more important is the range in the relationship between the over-65 age group and the rest of the population. By 2050 the estimates for total population ranged from 239 to 371 million. Under low-cost assumptions those aged 65 and over would represent 11.4 per cent of the total population as against 16.1 per cent for high-cost assumptions, or an increase, as compared with the 8 per cent figure of the 1950 census, of 42 per cent in the one case and 100 per cent in the other. (Robert J. Myers and Eugene A. Rasor, *Long Range Cost Estimates for OASI*, Social Security Administration, Division of the Actuary, Actuarial Study 36, June, 1953, pp. 3–4 and Table I.)

[5] For a detailed account of these problems, see *ibid., passim*, and the series of Actuarial Studies issued by the Social Security Administration, Division of the Actuary, notably Studies 14, 17, 19, 23, and 33.

estimates as to the proportion of the total population in covered employment in each year by age and sex (since, because of the provisions of the
law, this will affect the numbers eligible as well as the yield of the payroll
tax) and the amount of benefits. Vital to these estimates are the assumptions regarding the general level of employment,[6] and until 1954 two
sets of estimates were always presented, the so-called low-employment and
high-employment assumptions.[7]

In addition, estimates of the proportion of the total population in
covered employment are affected by changes in the extent to which women
(and notably married women) customarily engage in paid employment [8]
and changes in the age at which children start working. Because there is
a retirement test, assumptions must be made as to the extent to which
people will continue to work after reaching pensionable age. Furthermore,
since the OASI system is not universal in coverage, and both eligibility
and amount of benefit are affected by work in noncovered employment,
the extent of movement between covered and uncovered employment also
must be estimated.[9] Since the coverage amendments of 1950 and 1954 this
problem has of course become less serious.

Because the conditions of eligibility for dependents' and survivors'
benefits relate to family relationships and in some cases to dependency on
the primary beneficiary, assumptions have to be made as to marital status,
differential mortality by marital status, remarriage rates (for widows' and
mothers' benefits cease upon remarriage), marriage and mortality of child
beneficiaries, the number of surviving aged parents who are "chiefly dependent" on a primary beneficiary, the proportion of survivor beneficiaries

[6] The difference made by the set of employment assumptions used can be appreciated
from the fact that for both 1975 and 2000 the resulting assumed ratios to total population of males 40 to 49 with wage credits was 81 for the low-employment and 88 for the
high-employment assumption. For males 60 to 64 the estimated ratios were 59 and 70
for 1975 and 2000.

[7] In 1954, only high-employment assumptions were used "since current conditions are
more closely approximated thereby. In fact current conditions tend to be somewhat
above the high-employment assumptions." (Robert J. Myers and Eugene A. Rasor,
Long Range Estimates for Changes Proposed in the OASI System by H.R. 7199, with
Supplementary Estimates for Universal Coverage, Social Security Administration, Division of the Actuary, Actuarial Study 38, March, 1954, p. 2.) The low-employment
assumption corresponds roughly to the employment level of 1940 to 1941, while high-
employment corresponds to virtually full employment.

[8] Between 1940 and 1952 the number of married women who were in the labor force
increased by 105.4 per cent but the married female population 14 years and over
increased by only 28.5 per cent. The increased employment of women was especially
marked among those living with their husbands. (Analysis of the Social Security System, p. 840.)

[9] Even this does not exhaust the items which must be taken into account in determining eligibility, for estimates have also to be made of the distribution of earnings over
the four quarters of the year.

who will lose benefits by employment, and even the proportion of married women who will receive benefits in their own right rather than by virtue of their husband's eligibility.[10]

In systems which rely for part of their income on the interest earned by an accumulated fund (as is the case in OASI) further assumptions must be made as to the level of interest rates in future years.[11] A higher interest rate naturally increases income (lowers costs in the actuarial sense).[12] In fact, the assumed rates of interest have changed from time to time as interest rates have risen.[13]

The assumptions made as to the trend of wages are obviously of vital importance in determining benefit disbursements, since benefits are related to wages. Even though the effect of rising wages is held within limits by the weighting of the benefit formula [14] and by the fact that the benefits in force in any year are based on weighted composite earnings of all previous years, it is clear that very different estimates of benefit disbursements will be arrived at according as the actuary assumes rising, falling, or unchanged levels of money wages. Furthermore, these changes affect not merely the future annual money benefit payments, but also the income of the Fund. Rising levels of money wages are a financial gain to the system, because as more people have earnings falling within the monthly wage

[10] For a discussion of the problems of estimating these items and the assumptions used in 1953, see Myers and Rasor, Actuarial Study 36, pp. 6–10 and relevant tables.

[11] Actually, this was not necessary in OASI until 1940, for the original act had provided for a fixed rate of interest (3 per cent). If the market rate fell below this figure, special government bonds yielding 3 per cent were to be issued to the Fund. This arrangement, which of course involved a small public subsidy to the system whenever the market rates fell below 3 per cent, simplified one of the actuary's problems.

[12] In 1953 a differential of $\frac{1}{2}$ of 1 per cent of the interest rate would have had a net effect on the level premium of about $\frac{1}{4}$ of 1 per cent of payroll under the low-cost assumptions and of about $\frac{1}{2}$ of 1 per cent of payroll under the high-cost assumptions.

[13] In 1947 the OASI estimates were based on a 2 per cent rate. In the calculations made for the Congress when considering the 1952 Amendments the assumed rate was $2\frac{1}{4}$ per cent. Since interest rates appeared to be still rising, the long-range cost estimates of the actuary prepared in 1953 and thereafter presented estimates of the relationship between benefit payments and income (as determined by contribution rates and interest earnings) on separate sets of assumptions as to interest rates. In 1953 four alternative estimates were presented based on interest rates of 2, $2\frac{1}{4}$, $2\frac{1}{2}$, and $2\frac{3}{4}$ per cent. (See Myers and Rasor, Actuarial Study 36, Table 16.) From 1954, estimates have been presented on three bases ($2\frac{1}{4}$, 2.4, and $2\frac{1}{2}$ per cent). (See Myers and Rasor, Actuarial Study 39, Table 16.) For the 1954 Amendments and proposed amendments in 1955, Congress assumed a 2.4 per cent interest rate.

[14] Under the benefit formula in force in 1954 benefits were determined by the average monthly wage up to a maximum of $350, 55 per cent being paid in respect to the first $110 and 20 per cent on that part above $110. As more persons approach or reach the $350 maximum, a larger proportion of their earnings falls in the bracket to which 20 per cent rather than 55 per cent applies.

bracket of over $110 but less than $350, a larger proportion of beneficiaries draw benefits which are smaller in relation to contributions (i.e., are more nearly earned), and fewer draw benefits that contain a heavy "unearned" component. In other words, rising payrolls increase the income of the Fund more than they increase its outgo. It was this differential impact of rising wages on benefits and tax yields which accounted for the fact that although cost estimates for the 1939 Act had suggested that the system would not be self-supporting, those made after World War II indicated that the system was then probably on a self-supporting basis. Similarly the actuarial balance of the program under the liberalizing Amendments of 1952 was virtually the same as under the 1950 Act, the reason being that the rise in earnings levels in the interval was taken into account in preparing the estimates of the cost of the 1952 Amendments.

In fact, at any given time, the estimates for the cost and income of the OASI system assume an unchanged level of wages.[15] But it is noteworthy that the average wage assumed for the estimates for all future years has changed from time to time. After the war, for example, the figure was revised and based upon 1947 experience, and in 1952 the assumed average was again increased (by about 20 per cent) to correspond to the 1951 experience. In 1955 the estimates for the cost of the system on the basis of the amendments then proposed were based on earnings at about the level prevailing in 1954 which were about 10 per cent above the previous estimates based on 1951–1952 levels.[15a]

Critics of the estimates on which the system is based have pointed to the great increase in credited wages which has occurred even during the short life of the OASI system [16] and have held that not to take account of this trend in projecting benefit disbursements is to present a highly misleading picture.[17] In reply, the defenders of the present approach point to the fact that since costs and income needs of the Fund are expressed in terms of a percentage of payroll, wage trends affect both sides of the equation in the same direction though not in the same degree and claim in particular that no underestimate of the required income is in-

[15] In the 1953 estimates for male workers employed in covered employment for all four quarters this figure was $2,980 (for females $2,030). For a creditable earnings limit of $4,200 the corresponding figures would have been $3,200 and $2,050. Had there been no limit on taxable wages, the corresponding figures would have been $3,975 and $2,130. For assumptions as to the level wage for workers employed less than 4 quarters, see Myers and Rasor, Actuarial Study 36, pp. 6–7.

[15a] *Social Security Amendments of 1955*, Report of Committee on Ways and Means, H. Rept. No. 1189, 84th Cong., 1st Sess., 1955, p. 13.

[16] Average taxable earnings per worker increased from $900 in 1937 to $932 in 1940 and $2,230 (estimated) in 1954. (*Social Security Bulletin*, September, 1955, p. 36.)

[17] Charles C. Killingworth and Gertrude Schroeder, "Long-range Cost Estimates for Old-age Insurance," *Quarterly Journal of Economics*, vol. 65, 1951, pp. 199–213.

volved because of the above-mentioned limits on the extent to which rising earnings are reflected in rising benefits. Furthermore, the advocates of retention of the "level-wage assumption" urge that it is the only realistic assumption to make in a public program put into effect to meet a specific social need. If, it is held, there were a pronounced upward trend in money wages,

> it is likely that from the long-range point of view the present benefit formula would not be maintained. Rather, revisions would probably be made by the Congress (perhaps with some delay) which would make average benefits as adequate relative to the then-existing earnings level as average benefits under the present formula are in relation to the level prevailing when the 1952 Amendments were enacted.[18]

Because financial estimates for OASI are influenced by such a wide range of economic and social phenomena, it is not surprising that the actuaries have been increasingly modest in the claims they make for their estimates. Typically they present their results not as a single figure but as a range. Thus the OASI actuaries not only presented until recently two sets of figures for low- and high-employment conditions, respectively, but have also always offered a further pair of alternative sets of figures, namely the so-called "low-cost" and "high-cost" estimates. The former uses assumptions as to fertility, mortality, retirement, and remarriage rates, and the like which would result in low cost relative to payroll; the latter are based on assumptions which would lead to high costs as thus defined. It is claimed that efforts are made to select assumptions in each case which are consistent with the actual operating data and with the other assumptions [19] and at the same time to represent a "reasonable range" for the item under consideration. Thus the figures "do not represent the widest possible range that could reasonably be anticipated, but rather our studied opinions as to a plausible range." [20] However, legislative bodies, in deciding between alternative benefit proposals with varying cost implications and in setting tax schedules which are expected to cover the costs need, not a wide range, but a single set of estimates. The actuaries have therefore developed a third series of cost estimates, the so-called "intermediate" cost estimates, which have been used as the basis for congressional action. These estimates are merely an average of the low- and high-cost estimates and are not intended to represent "most probable" figures.

In view of the wide margin of error necessarily attendant upon predicting the costs of a system such as OASI for many years ahead, many per-

---

[18] Myers and Rasor, Actuarial Study 36, p. 20.
[19] This claim has been disputed (see Killingworth and Schroeder, loc. cit.).
[20] Myers and Rasor, Actuarial Study 36, p. 3.

sons have questioned the usefulness of any effort to finance the program on a long-term basis. In support of their position they cite the very wide range in costs as presented at any one time,[21] which, it is alleged, in fact provide very little practical help to legislators. Furthermore, they point to the many revisions of the estimates which the actuaries have been forced to make in less than twenty years and to the very large differences in estimated costs and tax yields which have resulted from relatively small changes in the basic assumptions.[22] Certainly it can hardly be denied that the average citizen who lacks knowledge of how the estimates are produced, and notably of the assumptions made and their reasonableness and validity, must be confused by assertions that the system is or is not in balance at any given time or that a tax schedule which at the time it was set (as in 1939) was inadequate to keep the system in financial balance subsequently became more than sufficient.

Nevertheless, it is still true that while the ranges of cost presented are relatively wide, they are limited. And whether or not it is decided to use the cost estimates as a basis for setting tax rates that will keep the system in balance over long periods, it is undeniable that at any given time long-range estimates of the probable cost of any actual or proposed income security benefits foster more responsible decision making. In choosing between different types and levels of benefits, or between more or less liberal eligibility conditions, an important consideration is the relative effect of the alternatives upon costs currently and in the future. Even though future economic or social conditions may prove to differ from those assumed in the estimates, it is still important, if responsible choices are to be made at any given time between alternatives, to compare relative costs on the basis of the best estimates as to future developments available when policy changes are contemplated. Furthermore, the publication of these estimates, with their assumptions as to trends in demographic or economic conditions, acts as a stimulus to progressive refinement and improvement of the relevant data. In the two decades since the Social Security Act was passed the statistical basis for estimating future costs and revenues has vastly improved, and constant evaluations of experience under the Act itself make possible further refinement of assumptions as to the behavior patterns of beneficiaries and their economic circumstances, and therefore of the costs of some of the provisions of the Act. For this reason, it has been often suggested that, even if no changes in the benefit and eligibility conditions are contemplated, there should be a periodic revision of the

[21] The high and low estimates for the year 2020 under the 1954 Amendments were $23.3 billion and $18.4 billion (contributions) and $23.4 billion and $28.0 billion (benefit payments). For ranges as a percentage of payrolls, see footnote 23.

[22] For a comparison of the 1953 estimates with those of previous years, see Myers and Rasor, Actuarial Study 36, pp. 23 and 54.

cost and revenue estimates. At least one country, Great Britain, legally requires such a reassessment every five years.

The Purposes of Reserve Financing

Even were a society to decide that the actuarial calculations of long-range costs were sufficiently reliable to serve as the basis for long-period financing, whether or not it would be thought worth while to adopt such a financial arrangement would depend upon the importance attached to the various objectives which might be served by the accumulation of reserves.

The purpose of the OASI reserve is simple even though it is not generally understood. It is to make it possible to finance the system wholly by taxes on particular categories of taxpayers (i.e., workers and employers) without ever having to raise the combined tax above a given percentage of payroll even though present estimates indicate that ultimately the benefit disbursements will rise to the equivalent of a higher percentage.[23] This purpose is to be achieved by collecting in the early years of the program more than is necessary to meet current benefit costs and putting the excess in a reserve, the interest on which will be used to meet the annual deficit when, as anticipated, annual disbursements exceed the yield of the maximum rate of tax it is felt practical to levy.[24] This being the objective

[23] Thus in 1935, it was estimated that annual disbursements under OASI would ultimately amount to more than 9 per cent of covered payrolls, although the maximum rate of tax provided for in the Act was only 6 per cent. The gap in income was to be made up by interest on a fund which was to be accumulated to a total of $49 billion by 1980. The Amendments of 1950 and 1952 were estimated to involve an ultimate cost of between 7 per cent and 11 per cent of payroll, or an "intermediate" estimate of 8½ per cent, although the maximum contribution rate provided for was only 6½ per cent. The ultimate cost in 2020 of benefit payments under the 1954 Amendments was estimated at 9.50 per cent of payroll at the time of enactment, although the maximum rate of tax was 8 per cent.

[24] In fact, in recent years the actuarial estimates suggest that the level of contributions provided for will not provide in perpetuity for a reserve which will yield sufficient interest completely to fill the gap. Revised actuarial calculations indicated that the contribution schedule under the 1952 Amendments was insufficient to support the benefit payments by a level premium equivalent of about 0.66 per cent under a 2¼ per cent interest rate and by 0.52 per cent under a 2½ per cent interest rate. Hence, on the intermediate cost estimates the reserve would be drawn upon some time after 1985 and be exhausted by about 2030. The Amendments of 1954, which increased benefit costs to a level premium equivalent of 7.50 per cent (as against 6.62 per cent for the 1952 Amendments) but also raised contributions to a level premium equivalent of 7.12 per cent (as against 6.05 per cent in 1952), reduced the deficiency from 0.57 to 0.38 per cent on the intermediate-cost basis. Assuming a 2.4 per cent interest rate, the Trust Fund would grow more or less steadily to a maximum of $70 billion in 2011 and then decrease until 2031, when it would be exhausted. (Myers and Rasor, Actuarial Study 38, pp. 6–8; and Wilbur J. Cohen, Robert M. Ball et al., "Social Se-

of long-period financing, any failure to allow the fund to grow to the amount calculated to yield the necessary interest means that some other source of revenue will ultimately have to be tapped to make up the difference if the claims of future beneficiaries are to continue to be met. The revenue might be secured by raising the combined employer-worker tax above the previously envisaged maximum rate, or by a contribution from the general taxpayer. Thus in the United States between 1939 and 1949, although the 1939 Amendments had provided a tax schedule which included a periodic step-up of the rate of tax, the Congress continually postponed the date of the tax increase. Since the actuarial calculations had included an item for interest from a fund whose size was determined by the progressively increased rates of tax as set out in the Act, the effect of this postponement of the step-up was to cause the Reserve to grow more slowly and ultimately to reach a lower level than was necessary if the system was to remain in balance.[25] In 1943, the Congress faced up to the consequences of its action and amended the Act to provide for appropriations from the general revenues when needed in the future. This provision was eliminated by the Amendments of 1950.

The claim is sometimes made that these arrangements do not protect the general taxpayer who, it is alleged, contributes anyway because it is he who pays the interest on the Old-age Reserve. But this is to confuse a payment made for a service rendered (in this case, the loan of money by the contributors which has enabled the general taxpayer in past years to enjoy government services without paying their full cost) with a payment made without any *quid pro quo,* i.e., a subsidy. Had the contributors not been in effect compelled each year to buy up a certain proportion of the national debt (i.e., the securities in the Reserve), the general taxpayer would have found himself compelled in future years to raise enough money to finance interest on the national debt *plus* the OASI deficit. Under the present plan he pays the interest on the national debt only, and, part of this being "owned" by the contributors (i.e., the Fund), he at one and the same time pays what he owes for money borrowed in the past and also provides income to the OASI system.

It is important, too, to note that if the sole objective of the Reserve Fund is to fill an actuarial gap occasioned by the deliberate pegging of the ultimate rate of tax at a level calculated to yield income less than

---

curity Act Amendments of 1954: A Summary and Legislative History," *Social Security Bulletin,* September, 1954, pp. 12–15.) See also *Social Security Amendments of 1955,* Report of the Committee on Ways and Means, H.R. Report no. 1189, 84th Cong., 1st Sess., 1955, pp. 11–19.

[25] Toward the end of the period the effect upon the Reserve of the postponed tax increase was obscured because of the gains to the Fund resulting from rising wage levels.

anticipated disbursements in future years, the only relevant question as to the way in which the Reserve is invested concerns the predictability of the yield in money terms. In other words, the test is whether the investments made will yield the rate of interest assumed by the actuary in his calculations. For this purpose, the ideal investment is national government bonds. Unless it can be held that future taxpayers will refuse to pay interest on the national debt, no charge of "endangering the security" of the contributors to the fund because the funds are invested in government bonds can be made.

Even if it was not desired to use reserve financing as a method of making palatable a particular cost-distribution policy, there might still be a case for the accumulation of reserves. Some people, pointing to the growing proportion of the aged in the population, believe that the present generation should do something to ease the heavy burden of support of the aged which will fall upon their successors.

It should be noted that the wider the coverage, and the more the system grants benefit for short periods of coverage (blanketing-in being the limiting case), the nearer is it to covering 100 per cent of the aged in the present, and the smaller is the gap between present and future benefit loads. It has indeed sometimes been held that universal coverage and early maturing of an old-age insurance system would eliminate the need for reserve financing. But this argument overlooks the forecastable upward trend in the absolute numbers of the aged which will still lead to an increase in dollar expenditures on benefits in future years.

The burden on future generations, it is held, can be lightened by making present contributors (employers and workers, alone or in combination with the general taxpayer) pay more than the current cost of present benefits and by putting the surplus in a Reserve Fund. It is true that if this Reserve is invested productively and represents a net addition to the volume of savings and investment which the community would otherwise have made, the ability of a future generation to support a growing number of nonproductive aged persons will in fact be increased. For, since in any year what is consumed by nonproducers must, apart from capital consumption, come out of the current output of these who are producing (i.e., from the current national income), the only way one generation can "lighten the burden" on its successors is to take action now which will increase future productivity. Whether or not this result will in fact be attained by the accumulation of an Old-age Reserve depends on the use made of the reserve funds, and here the nature of the investments is crucial. Unless the community is willing to take steps to ensure that sums equivalent to the annual additions to the Old-age Fund are productively invested, future generations will gain no advantage. Clearly when as now the OASI reserves are borrowed by the government of the day and used for current government purposes, their only effect is to lighten the burden on current general taxpayers by an equivalent amount or to shift the owner- ship of part of the national debt to those who have paid social security taxes. Only if general taxpayers invest rather than spend the money they would otherwise have paid in taxes, or if those who would otherwise have bought public bonds invest an equivalent sum in other types of invest- ment, will there be any net addition to investment and any increase in the productivity of future generations.

How far this takes place is not known. But unless a community can be certain that net investment on the part of the general taxpaying public and/or the potential bondholders is thus increased, the only way to en- sure that the old-age reserves will, in fact, help future generations to carry an anticipated heavy old-age burden is for the government to use the annual additions to the Reserve for new investment purposes. Many coun- tries require their governments to use the funds productively (i.e., for low- cost housing, hospitals, and even undertakings that compete with private enterprises). But it seems doubtful whether the American people would be willing to see government take so active a part in the economic life of the nation. Furthermore, an investment policy dominated by the desire to increase the productivity of future generations might involve the making of investments which would have this result but which would not yield a money profit to the Fund. The productive capacity of future generations would, for example, undoubtedly be enhanced if the present generation were to use the annual additions to the Old-age Reserve for a major health and rehabilitation program. But this would yield no money interest to the Fund, and if the financing of the program includes income from invest- ments as part of its revenues, the system will appear to operate "in the red." [26]

If, for whatever reason, people are not willing to countenance steps which assure that the Fund will represent a net addition to investment, they must abandon hope of easing the burden on the future by reserve accumulations.

In any case, many people hold that the present generation is already making a substantial contribution to the welfare of the future and that no further action is necessary. They point to the investment in human and material resources, current and in the past, which has increased the real volume of national output approximately $2\frac{3}{4}$ per cent annually and seems likely to continue to do so in the future; to the heavy burden on the current generation of training and educating a phenomenally large num- ber of children (due to the high postwar birth rate), who will provide a broader productive base over which to spread the support of the aged

[26] A similar conflict between the "interest-yielding" and the "national-investment" objectives of the fund has been experienced in some European countries which in- vested their social insurance reserves in working-class housing or hospital construction.

in the years ahead; and to the extent to which the present generation is having to cut current consumption to invest in armaments, partly in the interests of future generations. Others have held that the effort to avoid shifting the cost to future generations is unfair to the present generation, for it imposes upon the generation now living and working a double burden: first the burden of taking care of those who are already old and without means of support; and second, the burden of building up out of current revenues a reserve sufficient to provide for themselves when they too become old.

Still other uses have been claimed for the Reserve. Some feel that if a substantial reserve is built up from the contributions of future beneficiaries, it will serve as a bulwark against any tendency of future legislatures to refuse needed appropriations. Since the Fund is part of the national debt, the safety of the future income of the system is bound up with that of all national debt holders, and it is held to be unlikely that any Congress would default on national debt interest payments. This argument, which had some force when the system was new and its advantages to beneficiaries not fully appreciated, becomes steadily less powerful as the number of actual and potential beneficiaries increases, i.e., as the system approaches universality of coverage and offers substantial benefits on which the voting population as a whole has begun to count. The necessity for an earmarked reserve then turns on judgments as to the likelihood that any future Congress would run the risk of disappointing the expectations of so many million voters.

One other purpose of a reserve may be mentioned, though today relatively little importance is attached to it. But it has sometimes been held, on the analogy of private insurance, that a social insurance system should accumulate reserves so as to be able to meet its accrued liabilities in the event of its termination. The accrued liability of a system at any time is the dollar amount which would enable it to meet all commitments as of that moment. At the end of 1953, for example, the accrued liability of OASI was about $200 billion. This sum would have enabled the system to pay all beneficiaries in current payment status and to make payment to all others who had contributed, on the basis of their "rights" as of the year 1953.[27] Since as of that date the Trust Fund amounted to only $19 billion,[28] some critics have claimed that the system is badly underfinanced and is indeed "a fraud."

In fact, however, the analogy to private insurance is misleading: public

[27] If the purpose were only to continue payments to all those on the beneficiary rolls at the time the system terminated, the accrued liability (i.e., the present value of benefits on the rolls) would have been $23 billion at the end of 1953.

[28] On the basis of the 1953 estimates, the disparity would continue indefinitely. By 2050, on the intermediate-cost estimates, the present value of benefits then on the rolls would be $200 billion, but at that time the reserve would be exhausted.

programs do not need to accumulate reserves for this purpose.[29] In private insurance such reserves are required because an individual firm may go out of business due to competitive pressures or for other reasons (e.g., people in general might become less "insurance-minded"). Public programs are not thus menaced: the government has a monopoly and is unaffected by changes in attitudes toward the worth-whileness of purchasing insurance since it can exercise compulsion. A regular influx of new insured persons can thus be depended on to continue indefinitely. The real safeguard of the accrued rights of the contributors is thus the continued willingness of the population to tax itself for the purpose of paying old-age benefits.

In fact, it is doubtful whether any public old-age security system has been fully funded in the strict actuarial sense, and there are good reasons for this. For if the reason for building up a fund which would suffice to pay off accrued liabilities should the system at any time be terminated is a fear that future generations will be unwilling to tax themselves to meet their obligations to the contributors, there would seem to be no certainty that this same irresponsibility could not also extend to the reserves in an earmarked fund. A generation that was prepared to scrap its obligations to past contributors would hardly hesitate to raid the fund if this seemed expedient.

Finally it should be noted that a formal and earmarked reserve is not inevitable in a contributory system. It has sometimes been held that because such a system requires beneficiaries to pay all or part of the costs of their own old-age security, and excludes from benefits those who have already retired or are close to retirement, a reserve is unavoidable because in the early years income will inevitably exceed benefit costs. It is true that in such circumstances there will be a surplus, but whether this should be identified in a separate earmarked reserve fund is another matter. It would be quite possible for the government of the day to use the surplus for current governmental purposes in return for a promise, express or implied, to make good from the general revenues in subsequent years the deficit attributable to the loss of interest earnings on the reserve which the system would otherwise have had. This is the arrangement which was adopted in Great Britain for the contributory pensions system inaugurated in 1925 and continued after 1946. Whether or not such an arrangement would be acceptable would in part depend upon public confidence in government itself.[30]

---

[29] For a definitive discussion of the issues raised and the position adopted by actuaries in America and elsewhere, see Reinhard A. Hohaus, "Reserves for National Old Age Pensions," *Transactions of the Actuarial Society of America*, October, 1936, pp. 338ff.

[30] Even in Great Britain provision was made for small annual payments from general

Before reaching a final judgment on reserve policies, some of the other disadvantages of large public reserve accumulations must be evaluated. It has been claimed that because its purposes are not clearly understood, there is a tendency for large reserves to be used as an argument in support of unjustifiable liberalizations,[31] and it is true that during the 1940s, Congress, in refusing to raise social security taxes as scheduled, was impressed by the absolute size of the Reserve.[32]

It has also been claimed that the availability of an annual surplus for investment in the Reserve (amounting in the case of OASI to around $1.2 billions) makes it all too easy for governments to borrow in a protected market instead of having to raise a similar sum from a competitive market that reflects public attitudes to further government borrowing [33] or adopting the even more painful course of increasing current taxation to meet current expenditures.

UNEMPLOYMENT INSURANCE

The case for the adoption of long-period financing in unemployment insurance rests upon different considerations from those applicable to old-age security systems. It is possible to discern two lines of thought which have led to the view that the financing of this program should be based upon a period of accounting longer than a year. The first of these derives from the theory that in periods of serious unemployment and general recession of business it is desirable, in the interests of the economy as a whole, to maintain or expand the flow of purchasing power throughout the community. Although at such times the institution of unemployment insurance ensures automatically a flow of income to the unemployed (even though, as was shown in Chapter 4, this flow is far short of

revenues to what was in effect a contingency fund as a token of the government's permanent involvement in the scheme.

[31] "The illusory situation produced by the apparent excess of receipts over expenditures formed the basis for demanding increased benefits. In 1952, Congress immediately prior to the political conventions approved a 12½ per cent increase in benefits without hearings. . . . Proposals, based on the same argument that the 'trust fund' was in a favorable position, were made for medical benefits and hospital care for the aged." (*Proposed Policy Declaration: Federal Social Security Program for the Aged,* U.S. Chamber of Commerce Referendum 93, Washington, D.C., 1952, p. 6.)

[32] Similarly, President Eisenhower in proposing to postpone the scheduled tax increase due in January, 1954 gave as his reason the fact that the "fund has now reached $18 billion and receipts at present tax rates are in excess of current expenditures." (Television message, May 19, 1953.)

[33] On the bearing of social security funds on government control of interest rates, see Alan T. Peacock, *The Economics of National Insurance,* William Hodge and Co., Ltd., London, 1952, chap. VI.

replacing the purchasing power lost because of unemployment), the nature and timing of economic fluctuations will limit the impact of this built-in stabilizer if the financing of the program is on a year-to-year basis. For since the general upward or downward movements of economic activity usually do not occur normally and regularly within the compass of a year but are characterized by cyclical or irregular appearances over a period of years, the effort to balance the books of the system at the end of each year will have one of two consequences. Either, in a year when outpayments are heavy because of widespread unemployment, it will be necessary to raise current tax rates, thereby eliminating the net stimulus to the economy since the taxes will be drawn either from consumers (where workers contribute to the cost of the program) or from investors (where the taxes are paid by employers); or, in the effort to balance the books the benefits will be cut, thereby preventing the system from performing the desired stabilizing function, as well as causing it to fail to carry out its major social purpose, namely to pay benefits to unemployed workers when they need them.[34]

The second consideration which has led to financing unemployment insurance over periods longer than a year has also been concerned with the impact of the system upon employment levels but stresses rather the psychological effect of tax payments on employers at different levels of economic activity. Since, it is argued, the effect of tax payments is generally depressive of initiative, it would be highly undesirable to increase the burden of taxes during a period when employers are in any case pessimistic as to market prospects and particularly sensitive to the burden of costs. Yet this would occur if, in a year when outpayments were heavy due to widespread unemployment, the necessity of annually balancing the books involved a simultaneous increase in taxes.

These considerations have led to the adoption, or proposals for the adoption, of two types of unemployment insurance accounting. Both involve the effort to estimate the range of costs over a period of years under what are deemed to be the most probable set of assumptions. In the one type, an effort is then made to set a level rate of contributions over the entire period which is expected to keep the fund in balance not in any one year but over the period as a whole. In this way, it is held, there will be no necessity to reduce benefits precisely at the time when their payment is most needed by workers and by the economy as a whole. At

---

[34] Rather more than half the American unemployment insurance laws by the mid-1950s required the state agency to inform the governor and legislature whenever it was believed that a change in contribution or benefit rates would become necessary to ensure the solvency of the fund and to make recommendations therefor. About ten states had specific provisions for reducing benefits in one or more respects when the fund falls below a certain amount or a defined ratio to benefits for a specified period.

the same time, employers will be able to count upon a predetermined level of tax payments in good years and bad and make their commitments with no danger of an increase in tax rates precisely at the time when their concern about costs is greatest. In depressions the fund will be paying out more than it receives, thereby stimulating the economy as a whole. In good times the fund will be replenished in relatively painless fashion, for higher employment spells more income even with unchanged tax rates, and benefit payments will automatically decline.

The second approach would go further and vary the tax rate with fluctuations in the general level of economic activity. In periods of depression taxes would be cut both to maximize the net flow of purchasing power injected into the economy and to give a stimulus to employers by lowering their costs. In high employment, taxes would be raised, since at such times their deterrent effect on enterprise is likely to be minimized, while the slight deflationary effect of the excess tax payments over benefit outflows is to be welcomed. But on the average and over a period that included high and low economic activity the sums collected would be such as to cover the benefits payments. Great Britain has, indeed, made legislative provision for varying contribution rates for all social insurance programs, and not only unemployment insurance, in accordance with changing employment levels. The high employment that has prevailed since the principle was adopted in 1946 has rendered unnecessary any effort to apply it.

It will be seen that this second approach merely carries the logic of the arguments in favor of long-period financing one stage further than the plans which provide for a level rate of tax over a period of several years. But in so doing it creates problems additional to those common to all attempts to adopt a period of accounting running over several years (to be discussed below). For if rates are to be changed by reference to the general level of economic activity, some agreed measure, such as employment or unemployment indices or indices of national income and the like, must be adopted, and these indices must be available promptly in order that the change in tax rate may take effect at the time when it is most needed. Otherwise, if, for example, the tax rate at any given time depends on the employment levels in some previous period, the economic situation may have changed by the time the new rate is payable.[35] Indeed, the objectives of this kind of tax adjustment can be attained with certainty only if the index used is a forecast of future levels of economic activity. Despite the progress that has been made in economic forecasting in recent decades, it is doubtful whether the science is as yet so exact as to offer real assurance that tax rates set in accordance with such esti-

[35] This is a danger that is run by many American experience-rating systems, as will be indicated below. See also Chap. 9.

mates would in fact operate in precisely the countercyclical manner in-tended. Furthermore, some have objected that this kind of flexibility in tax rates would introduce an element of uncertainty into business calculations that might more than offset any expected stimulus due to a well-timed tax reduction. Others have pointed to the psychological obstacles to raising taxes even when employment is high and have feared that once tax reductions were granted, there would be great difficulties in raising the necessary additional revenue to recoup the fund once industry revived. Finally, those who see in the contributory system an instrument for emphasizing the relationship between benefits and costs have feared that this kind of variation in tax rates would weaken the connection between the two in the public mind.

Some employers, who attach great importance to the psychological considerations mentioned above, would go even farther than this and have urged that the rate of tax should be varied with the business ex-perience of the individual employer. According to this view, what mat-ters to the employer is the state of his own level of activity, and while this may often coincide with that of the economy as a whole, it will not always do so. It is true that more recent business-cycle theory has indicated that there may be "hidden cycles" within the general upward and down-ward swings of business activity, so that there may be some contractions in the face of a general upswing and vice versa [36] and to the extent that this happens the setting of tax rates by reference to the general level of employment or economic activity may be of little help to the employer whose experience departs from the general trend. However, so individual-ized a structure of tax rates has many difficulties of application. Not the least of these would be the difficulty of knowing how far the employer's lack of success was due to general economic factors over which he per-sonally could exercise no control and how far it was due to controllable factors. To the extent that an employer's inability to give continuous employment was due to careless personnel policies or failure to take rea-sonable steps to regularize employment, a policy of permitting him to pay lower taxes would run counter to the theories underlying experience-rating, which would suggest higher penalty rates in such circumstances. To the extent that his poor business experience was due to inefficiency or failure to anticipate demand correctly, lowered tax rates would act as a subsidy to keep the inefficient in business.

It is not surprising therefore that no countries have as yet attempted

[36] ". . . business cycles consist not only of roughly synchronous expansions in many activities, followed by roughly synchronous contractions . . . ; they consist also of nu-merous contractions while expansion is dominant." Wesley C. Mitchell, quoted in Arthur F. Burns, *New Facts on Business Cycles*, National Bureau of Economic Re-search, New York, May, 1950, p. 10.

to vary the rate of tax by reference to each individual employer's state of business at the time he pays the tax. However, most unemployment insurance systems adopt a period of accounting longer than a year and aim to set an average rate of tax that will cover costs over the period. Provision for the possibility of upward or downward revision of the tax rates for all employers and workers as the index of unemployment falls or rises is more rare.

It is, however, undeniable that the adoption of long periods of accounting for unemployment insurance presents many difficult technical problems. The first of these concerns the selection of the appropriate period. Prior to World War II policy in general reflected a view of economic fluctuations that presumed fairly regular cycles of high and low activity, so that the problem appeared to be primarily one of determining the precise length of the "typical cycle" over which the system was to be kept in balance. Even this did not prove an easy task, as the experience of the British Unemployment Insurance Statutory Committee, under the chairmanship of Sir William Beveridge, showed.[37] But increasingly the usefulness of this simple view of economic oscillation has come to be questioned, and the long period of relatively high employment and the absence of prolonged departures of great amplitude from the average level since the beginning of the 1940s have raised many doubts as to the appropriate length of the balancing period.

Closely related is the question of what average level of employment is to be assumed for the period as a whole. The British system, after the change in 1934, had, on the basis of past experience, postulated an oscillation around an average percentage of unemployment of 8. The National Insurance Act of 1946 assumed an 8½ per cent unemployment in setting contributions. In fact, this proved to be far too high, and even the much lower average of 4 per cent assumed in the actuarial calculations for the Amending Acts of 1951 and 1954 also appears high in relation to current experience. Similarly, in the United States, the original estimates as to the average levels of unemployment and the amplitude of swings above and below the average proved to be unduly pessimistic. Increasingly since 1940 both countries have been faced with a problem of "excess reserves," in relation to the benefit liabilities of the funds.[38]

A third problem raised by efforts to adopt a period of accounting in

[37] See Eveline M. Burns, *British Unemployment Programs, 1920–38,* Social Science Research Council, Washington, D.C., 1941, pp. 160–166.

[38] For the British experience, see Eveline M. Burns, "Social Security in a Period of Full Employment," *Proceedings of the Fourth Annual Meeting,* Industrial Relations Research Association, 1951. For America, see *Unemployment Insurance Financial Experience, 1946–1950,* and *Supplements,* U.S. Department of Labor, Bureau of Employment Security, July, 1951, *et seq.* For the problems created in the United States by the absence of a single national fund, see Chap. 11.

excess of one year in unemployment insurance in order to achieve the objectives outlined at the beginning of this section is psychological in character and has been more evident in the United States than in European countries. It concerns the willingness of a people to live with a deficit. In the case of long-period risks, such as old age, the persistence of a deficit for several years is indeed a serious matter since in such programs all the evidence points to a secular upward trend in expenditures. But if countercyclical policies are applied to the financing of unemployment insurance, the appearance of a deficit for some years may merely mean that the system began to operate in a period of heavy benefit outpayments and, if the estimates on which the tax structure was based are reliable, this deficit will be repaid during the next upswing of economic activity. It would thus be a matter of chance whether such a system began by accumulating a surplus, to be subsequently drawn down in a depression, or began with a deficit, which would be subsequently repaid when industry revived. In fact, however, the American people appear to be unwilling to contemplate even temporary deficits in their unemployment insurance systems, and the greatest pains have been taken to ensure that these never occur.[39]

This almost morbid desire that at no time should the system ever show a deficit reveals a lack of appreciation of the real purposes of long-period financing in unemployment insurance and raises acute questions as to the purposes served by the reserves currently held. For if at no time can deficits be contemplated, and if the reserves cannot even be reduced below the "danger point" without immediate impact upon benefits or tax rates, their only function could be to carry on the system during the period of time that would have to elapse before the new benefits or taxes could come into effect, and this would seem to call for much smaller reserves than most states appear to consider "safe." [40]

[39] These are shown in the original provision that no benefits were to be paid out until taxes had been collected for two years (despite the fact that the taxes were first imposed in a period of low economic activity where the effect of such deflationary policies would be most harmful), by the provisions already noted for cutting benefits when the fund falls below a certain level, and in the so-called fund-solvency protective devices found in most state laws. Among these are provisions for the suspension or modification of experience-rating when state reserve funds fall below a specified danger level, and much time and effort have been devoted to selecting an appropriate danger signal. In addition, in the original plans suggested by the Committee on Economic Security, financial considerations appear to have determined benefit provisions rather than vice versa. The question was what level of benefits could safely (i.e., with no risk of incurring even a temporary deficit) be financed by a given level of payroll tax and the meager benefits proposed reflected this extreme caution. (Cf. Harry Malisoff, "The Emergence of Unemployment Compensation, III," *Political Science Quarterly*, vol. 54, 1939, pp. 577–599.)

[40] Even if a reserve is accumulated as a safeguard against errors in estimating, or

The American attitude to unemployment reserves appears to be explicable only as an accident of history but is interesting as illustrating the variety of forces that bear upon policy determination. At the time when unemployment insurance was first under discussion as a possible form of social security in the United States, the only long-established system whose experience could be studied was the British. As a result of the British decision to use unemployment insurance as the major instrument for meeting income needs created by the long-period unemployment of the 1920s it had incurred a substantial deficit. Because of the expectation that this deficit would never be repaid (and hence public subsidies would be involved) the British unemployment benefit came to be referred to in America as "the dole" [41] and pointed to as an example to avoid, by the opponents of social insurance. Proponents of unemployment insurance in the United States were at pains to show that their proposals were in no sense a dole, and specifically that the provisions of the suggested scheme were well calculated to avoid a deficit at any time. In fact, the British experience has belied the pessimists. The debt, which amounted to £115 million by 1931, was funded and repaid in full by 1941, and by the time the new National Insurance system went into effect in 1948, the system had accumulated a surplus of £546 million which continued to grow at an almost embarrassing rate. The influence of the earlier debt on the American attitude to debt accumulation as part of the technique of long-period financing, however, remains.

A final difficulty faced by efforts to effectuate countercyclical financing in unemployment insurance is also peculiar to the United States. This is the difficulty of reconciling this objective with the operation of experience-rating systems. Where, as is the case in a large number of state experience-rating plans, the rate paid by any employer in a given year is affected by his experience with employment in previous years, a period of high employment succeeded by a year or more of recession will mean that most employers will have qualified for tax reductions during economic prosperity and will find, if low employment persists for more than a year, that precisely at the time they are less prosperous their tax rates will be increased, either because their own accounts need replenishing or because the balance of the state fund has fallen.[42] That this situation

---

against short-period and unanticipated declines in revenue, the unwillingness to draw down reserves without simultaneously changing tax or benefit provisions makes little sense.

[41] In Britain the same term was applied to the same payment but had a different meaning, for it related to the meager amount of the benefit.

[42] It will be recalled that many states provide for variable rating schedules whereby the precise rate of tax that corresponds to any given index of stability of employment on the part of the individual firm changes with changes in the state fund. The

has not led to greater difficulties in the United States as yet is due to the fortunate accident that since the almost universal reductions in tax rates which resulted from the high employment of the war and postwar years the country has experienced only short-lived periods of recession, and to the fact that for the reasons given above, almost all the systems had accumulated embarrassingly large reserves.[43] Although it has been claimed by exponents of the reserve-ratio formula for experience-rating that this method avoids the difficulty of raising taxes in periods of depression and reducing them in periods of prosperity, the economic condition of the country has as yet precluded a rigorous testing of this claim.

In these circumstances, it is not surprising that in the United States, at least, the objectives of long-period financing appear to have changed from a concern about the system as a major technique for countercyclical measures, toward short-period solvency through the development of contingency reserves, although the contingency which is taken into account covers a period of several years. Thus the typical state "solvency study" (and the use of the term is itself significant) by the mid-1950s had come to take the form of an attempt to estimate costs over some future period, usually about five years in length. It consisted of a comprehensive analysis of the state's economy leading up to a series of alternative projections for the future, an account of the benefit and other relevant provisions of the state law, often with indications of possible changes to be anticipated during the period in question, and actuarial estimates of costs for each set of economic and legal assumptions, as well as a reserve valuation and an indication of the tax requirements under each formula.[44] Moreover, such studies had come to be thought of as periodic in character: it was considered sound policy to revise the five-year estimates every two years or so.

This virtual abandonment of the countercyclical objective and the adoption of a strictly pragmatic "solvency" approach may, however, be defended as rational in view of the very limited character of the American unemployment insurance systems. As we have seen, they aim to pro-

---

less money in the fund, the higher will be the rate of tax corresponding to any given stability index (see Note to Chap. 9).

[43] By 1950 for the country as a whole, reserves equalled 5.7 times the average annual cost rate during the period 1946–1950, and in almost half the states they exceeded ten times these costs, while in three states they exceeded twenty times these benefit costs. During this period the average annual contribution rate for the country as a whole was 1.4 per cent of payroll, and in almost a fifth of the states it was less than 1 per cent, instead of the standard 2.7 per cent. (*Unemployment Insurance Financial Experience, 1946–1950*, pp. 9, 22.)

[44] For a bibliography of such studies, see *State Studies in Unemployment Insurance Financing*, U.S. Department of Labor, Bureau of Employment Security, October, 1954.

vide only against short-period unemployment, and the limited duration provisions in particular virtually insulate them from benefit drains due to long-continued depressions. Indeed, it will be recalled that it is this very feature, namely the existence of an effective limit to benefit liability in serious depressions, that has made it at all feasible to estimate long-range costs in this program. Were the country to experience any prolonged and heavy unemployment, the unemployment insurance systems would soon cease to have real significance as a device for assuring alternative income, and some other measures would have to be devised. At such times the possibility of financing such measures by accumulating deficits would always be available to the Federal government, which would be the inevitable residuary legatee for unemployment relief. Even if the country were to decide to follow the British example and grant extraordinary extensions of benefit duration at the expense of the Federal government, this too could also be financed by Federal borrowing, and the sums involved would be so significant in relation to the "normal" payments from the state systems that the objectives of countercyclical financing could in fact be thus achieved.

CHAPTER 11

The Distribution of Financial Responsibility among Different Levels of Government

QUESTIONS as to the respective financial responsibilities of different levels of government give rise to some of the most perplexing of contemporary social security issues. One of the most significant trends in social security financing in the United States, as in most other countries during the last half century, has been the increasing financial participation of larger units of government.[1] By 1949 to 1950 a comparative study of five English-speaking countries showed that the national or federal government had assumed entire financial responsibility for income-maintenance services in two countries (Great Britain and New Zealand), while in Australia the Commonwealth carried 92.7 per cent of the burden. For Canada and the United States, the corresponding figures were 85.0 per cent and 56.8 per cent.[2] This is a far cry from the situation in the nineteenth century and even the early years of the twentieth century, when except for war veterans public responsibility for income maintenance was typically a function only of the local governments. A variety of forces has brought about this situation, and the precise distribution of financial responsibilities among levels of government at different times and in different countries reflects their relative strength.

[1] In this chapter a program is regarded as being "federally financed" when the taxes by which it is supported are levied by the Federal government. "Federal support" does not necessarily imply a subsidy from the general Federal taxpayer, i.e., the social security wage and payroll taxes are treated as Federal taxes.

[2] It should be noted that these distributions relate to income-maintenance programs as defined in this book. Inclusion of other services sometimes classified as social security services, such as health and rehabilitation programs, institutional care, child welfare, school lunches, and the like, reduces the proportionate share carried by the national or Federal government. For all social security expenditures in this wide sense, the proportions in 1949 to 1950 were as follows: Australia, 74 per cent; Canada, 66.5 per cent; Great Britain, 90.9 per cent; New Zealand, 97.6 per cent; United States, 49.5 per cent. (*Social Security Expenditures in Australia, etc., 1949–50: A Comparative Study*, Department of National Health and Welfare, Research Division, Ottawa, February, 1954, p. 14. For the sources of expenditures on income maintenance alone, see *ibid.*, Appendixes A1, B1, C1, D1, E1.)

THE TECHNICAL NATURE OF THE PROGRAM

In part the increased financial participation of the larger units of government is due to the adoption of specific types of social security benefit for certain kinds of risks. An old-age insurance program, for example, where benefit rights are based upon a lifetime of earnings, can hardly be financed except through the largest unit of government, especially in a country in which people move about like ants and may well have worked in several states before deciding to retire in yet a different part of the country. Both security for the potential beneficiary and the desire to minimize obstacles to mobility point to central or federal financing. It is not surprising, therefore, that in the United States, as elsewhere, such measures are a central government responsibility, supported by taxes levied only by that government (or by authorities to whom the central authority in effect delegates its powers).

Similarly, in unemployment insurance systems technical considerations point to the desirability of spreading the risk over as large a group as possible and assessing the costs over an area which as nearly as possible is a self-contained economic unit. In most countries unemployment insurance is a national system or, if smaller and separate systems operate, provision is made for reinsurance or the meeting by the national government of deficits attributable to the uneven incidence of unemployment.

In the United States, the decision was made in 1935 that unemployment insurance was essentially a state responsibility. Even at that time there was a strong minority who believed that unemployment should be nationally financed, pointing to the essential economic unity of the country and the fact that unemployment in any one state was often due to factors entirely beyond its control. This group also urged that a single reserve for the country as a whole would be more satisfactory and useful than fifty-one different state reserves. These views are still held by substantial sections of the population, notably organized labor. On the other hand, employers in general and state legislatures are equally firmly in favor of separate state systems.

From the financial point of view, the ability of states to operate independent systems has not as yet been definitively tested because of the high employment that has in general characterized the years since the systems began paying benefits. However, more recently, the financial position of one or two state systems, and in particular Rhode Island, has raised the question in more acute form. Opinions differ as to whether the Federal government should take any action to assist such states, and if so, whether this should take the form of loans or of nonrepayable grants to the states in difficulties.[3]

[3] See Chap. 12 for a discussion of these issues.

The weight of technical considerations arising from the nature of the program in other types of social security systems is much less easy to determine. Indeed, one of the least explored aspects of the problems associated with public income security measures concerns the precise extent to which the nature of any given program technically demands for its most effective operation a unit of government of any specific size. The need for more precise analysis in the light of factual investigation is particularly acute in the field of disability insurance and public assistance. Meanwhile it should be observed that decisions on the location of administrative responsibility will often influence those concerning the allocation of costs, and vice versa, for it is generally held to be undesirable for one unit of government to administer a program for which it carries no financial responsibility.[4]

In any case, technical reasons are not compelling or decisive and cannot be the sole explanation of the prevailing distribution of financial responsibility for income-maintenance programs as between central and state and/or local authorities. For on the one hand, in some countries the central government has assumed the financial burden of programs for which no very obvious technical argument in favor of centralization can be adduced. In Great Britain, for example, since 1948 public assistance has been financed and administered solely by the central government, and even in the United States since 1935 the Federal government has carried a share of the costs of special public assistance and played some role in its administration.[5] And on the other hand, even in regard to social insurance programs, where technical considerations might seem to point to extending financial responsibility to the largest political unit, some countries have decided to organize their systems on the basis of smaller political units. Thus in the United States, as we have seen, despite the national character of the labor market, the high mobility of the labor force, and the economic interdependence of various parts of the country, all of which would seem to point to a single national unemployment insurance system, the programs are nonetheless operated on a state basis. It is evident, therefore, that technical considerations have to be weighed against other factors.

[4] This rule is, however, not always observed, and as will be seen in Chap. 12 one of the crucial questions faced by those who advocate variable grants-in-aid concerns the extent to which a relatively generous grant approximating 100 per cent fosters extravagance and irresponsible administration on the part of the recipient unit.

[5] On an emergency basis the Federal government's financial participation in public assistance costs dates from the Federal Emergency Relief Administration of 1933.

The Nature of the Fiscal Resources of Different Levels of Government

One such factor is the nature of the relative financial resources of the different levels of government, and it is, indeed, the fiscal limitations of the small units of government which have in large measure accounted for the trend to financial support by the larger units to which reference was made above. As compared with the states and localities, the federal or national government has tax resources that are more richly yielding (for the federal government has in fact prior, if not exclusive, recourse to the productive personal and corporation income taxes as well as customs and excises) and more flexible than those, like the property tax, which form the backbone of the local tax system, or the excise and sales taxes of state governments. Furthermore, only the federal government can tax income wherever it originates.[6] Finally, the borrowing powers of the federal government are vastly greater than those of the other levels of government.

In these circumstances, it was inevitable that as the total volume of social security financial commitments has increased, the search for adequate sources of revenue brought both states and federal governments into the financial picture. This was seen dramatically in the United States in the 1930s when the growing cost of supporting millions of unemployed workers forced a sharp break with traditional methods of financing public assistance. First, some of the states came to the support of the localities, and from 1933 the Federal government shared the burden. After 1935 the Federal government carried the lion's share of the costs of the WPA program for the employable unemployed while Federal and state financial participation in public assistance costs was continued under the Social Security Act. By 1954 the Federal government was carrying 50.6 per cent and the states 37.4 per cent of all public assistance payments, while the share of the localities had fallen to 12.0 per cent.

In other countries too the depression of the 1930s led to the assumption, or increase, of financial responsibilities by the larger units of government. And this is not surprising, for it is precisely in regard to threats

---

[6] For a brief discussion of the relative tax resources and structures of the different levels of government, see "Government Finance in a Stable and Growing Economy," *The Annals of the American Academy of Political and Social Science*, November, 1949, *passim*. See also, *Security, Work and Relief Policies*, National Resources Planning Board, 1942, Chaps. 3, 10. For state revenue sources see "State Collections by Major Sources, Selected Years 1902–53," *State Government*, June, 1954, pp. 126–127; and *Federal-State-Local Tax Coordination*, U.S. Treasury Department, 1952. See also The Commission on Intergovernmental Relations, *A Report to the President for Transmittal to the Congress*, Government Printing Office, Washington, D.C., June, 1955, Chapter 4 and pp. 297–299.

to income due to general depressions that the fiscal inadequacy of the smaller units of government is most apparent. The inflexibility of property taxes, the inability greatly to increase sales and even income taxes without stimulating an exodus of taxpayers, and the limited borrowing powers of local and even some state governments all make these units peculiarly ill equipped to carry a burden that is sporadic but extremely heavy when it occurs. In general, the more sharply social security costs fluctuate with general economic conditions (e.g., costs of maintaining the long-period unemployed), the more likely will it be that recourse will be had to the financial resources and borrowing powers of the largest unit of government.

But even fiscal consideration alone cannot account for the allocation of financial responsibilities between levels of government typically found in most highly developed countries today. If the differing revenue-raising resources of different levels of government were the only consideration, it might have been expected that, once the problem of the fiscal limitations of smaller political units became acute because of the mounting totals of income security expenditures, efforts would have been made to redistribute tax resources and program responsibilities so as to secure a more reasonable relationship between them. In this connection, it must not be forgotten that the problem with which we are now concerned is not peculiar to income security programs but is of much broader import. As the citizens have demanded more and more services of their governments, these have been assumed by one level of government or another with little consideration of the relationship between the total financial burden to which these services give rise and the fiscal resources of each governmental level. In countries such as the United States, with a historical bias in favor of local administration of welfare programs (including education) the tendency has been to assign major responsibility for these newer and growing services to the states and localities.

One solution, therefore, would seem to be a reallocation of fiscal resources between the central government and its political subdivisions, and this has often been proposed. From time to time suggestions have been made in the United States that the Federal government should cede certain taxes to the states and even that it should forego full exploitation of the income tax in order to give more leeway to states desiring to utilize this richly yielding source of revenue,[7] and a Presidential

[7] Thus the Chamber of Commerce proposed in 1954 that the following taxes should be turned over to the states: admissions, club dues, initiation fees, various taxes on amusements, taxes on safe deposit boxes, the Federal employment tax, and estate and gift taxes. (*Federal Grant-in-Aid Programs*, Report of the Committee on Social Legislation, U.S. Chamber of Commerce, Washington, D.C., 1954.) Similarly the meeting

Commission on Intergovernmental Relations was appointed in 1953 to explore these possibilities. The Commission did not favor such radical proposals and preferred a continuation and improvement of existing grants-in-aid.[7a] Similarly in Canada shortly before World War II, a Royal Commission, the Rowell-Sirois Commission, undertook an exhaustive investigation of the desirability and feasibility of reallocating program responsibilities and sources of revenue as between the Dominion government and the provinces. Its recommendations have, however, not been carried into effect.[8] It would be far from easy to resolve the technical problems of such reallocations of revenue sources and to select for exclusive state exploitation a group of taxes whose yield closely corresponded to the total revenues needed by those programs which for technical or other considerations should be operated and financed by the states and localities. Even so, such a division of the field between the different levels of government would not be a complete solution. For tax redistribution would merely mean that each state would have free access to certain methods of collecting revenue, but the yield of these taxes would still be affected by the size of the tax base, i.e., by the wealth and income of the population in each state. Where there are wide differences between the political subdivisions in this respect, a disproportion between functions to be performed by government and the financial resources for their support would still remain, though it would be a difference as between similar units of government rather than between different levels of government. The result would be differences in levels of service or in burdens on state taxpayers, as between the states. One of the limitations of proposals for redistribution of tax resources, therefore, is that it fails to resolve this latter problem, concern over which has contributed significantly to the growing financial involvement of the larger units of government.

---

of the Council of State Governors in 1954 called for relinquishing or reduction of such Federal taxes as those on gasoline, payrolls, telephones and telegraphs, admissions, transportation, alcohol, tobacco, and estates and gifts. (See *State Government*, August, 1954, pp. 166–168; and for resolutions adopted in previous years, *State Government*, January, 1953, p. 33.)

[7a] For the recommendation of the Commission, see The Commission on Intergovernmental Relations, *A Report to the President for Transmittal to the Congress*, Government Printing Office, Washington, D.C., June, 1955, *passim*. See also the supplementary Study Committee Reports issued by the Commission.

[8] For a brief account of the Commission and the aftermath, see James A. Maxwell, *Recent Developments in Dominion-Provincial Relations in Canada*, National Bureau of Economic Research Occasional Paper 25, New York, March, 1948; and A. H. Birch, *Federalism, Finance and Social Legislation in Canada, Australia, and the United States*, Oxford University Press, New York, 1955, chap. 7.

The Intensity of the Desire to Assure Equality of Access to Minimum Security

A third influence upon the allocation of financial responsibility between different levels of government has thus been the strength or weakness of a sense of national unity and an extension of this concept to include assurance of equality of access to some minimum of security for all members of the nation wherever they reside.[9] The influence of this factor can be very clearly seen in countries with federal governments in which social welfare activities have been traditionally exercised by the smaller political subdivisions and where there is marked geographical inequality of income. If the costs of income security programs are then thrown exclusively on these smaller units, great differences in the provision for the economically insecure will result. For the poorer state or locality is doubly disadvantaged: not only are its economic, and therefore its fiscal, resources limited, but the poorer it is, the relatively larger will be the numbers of people with incomes below what at any given time is accepted as a general standard of minimum adequacy. Thus the problem of financing income security measures is intensified by the fact that there tends to be an inverse relationship between need and capacity.

In the United States, for example, there is a great difference between the states in per capita income. The richest states have a per capita income that is over 30 per cent higher than the national average, while the two states at the bottom of the scale have per capita incomes that are around half of this national average.[10] Although the degree of inequality between the states appears to have diminished over recent decades and to have been somewhat narrowed by the differential impact of Federal taxation,[11] the average per capita income of the three richest states by 1952 was still 2.4 times that of the three poorest, and the richest state of all (Delaware at that time) had an income per capita that was 2.8 times that of Mississippi, then, as in all previous years, the poorest.

It is not therefore surprising that there should have been pressure from the poorer states to secure financial aid from the Federal government, on the ground that only so could they afford to make adequate provision for the income security needs of their residents. The extent to which such

[9] Attitudes toward equality of access to some minimum of security also play a role within the states and affect the allocation of financial responsibilities between the states and the localities.

[10] For detailed figures for individual states and for different years, see *Survey of Current Business*, U.S. Department of Commerce, August, 1952, 1953, and 1954.

[11] Selma J. Mushkin and Beatrice Crowther, *Federal Taxes and the Measurement of State Capacity*, U.S. Public Health Service, May, 1954, Appendix E, "Relative Change in Economic Position of Regions and States, 1890–1910 and 1929–52."

demands are acceded to reflects the relative voting strength of the voters in the wealthier states and the intensity both of their belief that it is desirable to assure some uniform minimum of security to all Americans wherever they reside and of their willingness to undergo financial sacrifices to make this possible. For all such grants from the national government to the poorer states involve a redistribution of incomes in favor of the latter, and the more clearly this is perceived, the more the richer states may oppose such proposals.[12]

THE IMPORTANCE ATTACHED TO FREE MOBILITY

The actual allocation of financial responsibilities between levels of government is also affected by a variety of other attitudes and social values. Among these is the strength or weakness of the desire to prevent the method of financing the security program from distorting the geographical distribution of labor and of capital and enterprise.

Worker Mobility

Where financial responsibility is carried wholly or largely by the smaller governmental units, it is understandable that these tend to protect their own taxpayers by limiting their responsibilities for income security to persons who reside or work within their own boundaries. Thus residence requirements have been a familiar feature in public assistance programs. Where this status can be secured only by many years of residence within a given state,[13] mobility may be deterred.[14] Similarly, when unemployment insurance systems are operated on a state basis, benefit rights may be lost by employment in, or movement to, another state. In American systems these dangers, which may have some effect upon mobility, have been partially offset by agreements between the states for the handling of interstate claims.

[12] As will be seen in Chap. 12, the unwillingness of the richer states to countenance a real geographical redistribution of incomes has led to the adoption of formulas for the public assistance grants which greatly weaken the relative gain of the poorer states.

[13] At the beginning of 1935 two-thirds of the American states required fifteen years of residence for old-age assistance, and many also required a specified period of county residence. By 1953 only three states had no residence requirement. By 1946 there were only seven states which did not limit legal settlement for general assistance eligibility to persons who had resided there for defined periods which ranged from six months to five years. For an account of state residence requirements, see *The Public Welfare Directory, 1955*, American Public Welfare Association, Chicago, 1955, pp. 367–382.

[14] It is significant that when in 1935 the Federal government began to share in the costs of special public assistance, one of the conditions of Federal aid was that the states should not have residence requirements of more than a defined degree of severity.

Although far too little is known about the precise effects on worker mobility of these restrictions (such studies as have been made having usually concentrated upon the extent to which they result in denial of aid to needy persons), it is evident that they cannot be disregarded. For a society which places a high value on worker mobility will count among the advantages of financing by larger units of government the fact that such arrangements eliminate or reduce to a minimum adverse effects upon worker mobility.[15]

Business Location and Tax Competition

If a community which is in all other respects an economic unit finances costly social welfare services on a state and local basis, those units of government which maintain relatively high levels of service may find themselves at an economic disadvantage, more particularly if they finance these measures by taxes, such as payroll taxes, that fall at least in the first instance on producers. For to the extent that these levies enter into costs they adversely affect the competitive situation of firms located in states where such taxes are relatively high.

The charge that the high cost of workmen's compensation premiums in certain American states has been "driving industry away" has been a perennial feature of the history of this legislation. Similarly, prior to 1935 it was thought that states would be inhibited from enacting unemployment insurance laws by the fear that the competitive position of their own employers would be prejudiced by the imposition of the payroll taxes. If, as a matter of policy, it is desired that income security programs of this type shall be put into effect, but that impediments to interstate competition shall be avoided, financial participation by larger units of government becomes inevitable.

One such solution has been the assumption by the national government of exclusive responsibility for the operation of programs of this type, as occurred in Canada where unemployment insurance (though not workmen's compensation) is a Dominion responsibility. If importance is attached to state operation, other types of action are necessary. Thus in the United States, it was this concern to avoid interstate competition while at the same time making it possible for all states to enact unemployment insurance laws that brought the Federal government into the financial picture in 1935. By the tax-offset provisions included in the Social Security Act of that year, the Federal government levied a uniform

---

[15] Similarly, many European countries have concluded a series of international agreements protecting the social security rights of foreign workers domestically employed, in the interests of fostering worker mobility. For an account of these arrangements and their problems, see Pierre Laroque, "International Problems of Social Security," *International Labour Review,* July and August, 1952, pp. 1–29, 113–141.

tax on specified categories of employers in all states but allowed the individual taxpayer to offset against 90 per cent of the Federal tax such taxes as he paid to his state under an unemployment insurance law. In this way, the competitive position of firms in different states was protected: the same rate of tax was paid by all employers. The firm in a state with an unemployment insurance law divided his tax obligation between the Federal government and his state; the firm in a state which did not enact such legislation would have to pay the identical total rate of tax wholly to the Federal government.[16]

THE IMPORTANCE ATTACHED TO SPECIFIC FISCAL POLICIES

Attitudes toward certain broad fiscal policies also play a role in determining the allocation of income security costs as between different levels of government. Societies which lay great stress on progressivity in the general tax system will lean toward financing by larger units of government. For another of the differences between the sources of revenue available to the central government and to the political subdivisions is that the tax resources of the former, and notably the income tax, are more amenable to the application of progressive tax policies than the property, gross revenue, or receipts and sales taxes which figure prominently in the revenue sources most readily available to the latter.[17] Broadly speaking, therefore, shifts of financial responsibility between central and state or local authorities mean shifts between relatively progressive and relatively regressive methods of raising revenue.

A second type of fiscal consideration, which becomes more important as the volume of social security expenditures assumes an increasingly large place in total government expenditures, is the desirability of coordinating the collection of revenues and the administration of reserves with the general fiscal policies of the national government. It was this consideration, among others, which led in 1935 to the arrangement whereby the unemployment insurance funds collected by the states were deposited in the Federal Unemployment Trust Fund, the management of which was vested in the Federal Secretary of the Treasury.

Finally, societies which desire their governments to play an active role in employment stabilization, and which attach importance in that connection to compensatory public spending and fiscal policies, are more likely to favor federal financing of income security programs. For these

16 For the effect of experience-rating on the achievement of this objective, see Chap. 9.

17 As was shown in Chap. 9, however, national governments do not always avail themselves of this possibility. One of the major taxes used by central governments for social security financing is the "workers' contribution" or wage tax, which is definitely regressive.

programs can function as a highly effective means of reducing spending when demand is excessive and prices rising and increasing spending when demand is deficient and prices falling and employment contracting. This happens because the beneficiaries are unlikely to save the publicly supplied income channeled to them and because the volume of benefit payments will automatically fall and rise with the general improvement or deterioration of business conditions. This use of income security guarantees has long been noted, unemployment insurance, for example, frequently being referred to as a "built-in stabilizer." It is less frequently noted that OASI and the public assistance programs also operate in the same way, for their beneficiary or caseloads also fluctuate inversely with levels of employment.[18] But if increased income security payments are to serve the purpose of maintaining or increasing purchasing power in periods of depression, they must, once accumulated reserves are exhausted, be financed by borrowing, and as already stated, the borrowing powers of the localities and states are restricted relative to those of the central government.

GENERAL ATTITUDES TOWARD CENTRAL AND LOCAL GOVERNMENTS

All of the considerations hitherto discussed operate, of course, against the general background of prevailing attitudes to central and local governments as such. In the United States, a sharp cleavage of opinion is evident and exerts a real influence on the distribution of financial responsibilities. On the one hand are those who hold that "no function which can be effectively performed by a lower authority should be assumed by a higher authority" [19] and who regard almost every new activity of the Federal government as a dangerous incursion on the rights of the states. And on the other hand, although it would probably be difficult to find any convinced exponent of the reverse doctrine, that "no function which can be effectively performed by a higher authority should be assumed by a lower authority," it is undeniable that a sizable body of opinion fails to share the concern about states rights.

While it would be inappropriate here to explore in detail the many

[18] It must be emphasized that these favorable effects are attributable to fluctuations in the volume of benefit payments. The net effect of the system as a whole will depend on the methods of financing the program. For the simultaneous collection of taxes to accumulate an old-age reserve fund will, during a recession, exercise a deflationary effect. Even so, the adverse consequences of these tax collections will be mitigated in some degree by the automatic increase in benefit payments that typically occurs when employment declines.

[19] Henry D. Allen, "The Proper Federal Function in Security for the Aged," *American Economic Security,* Conference Issue, 1953, p. 51.

implications or the factual basis of the opposing schools of thought, one or two comments are in order if the influence of these attitudes on methods of financing income security programs is to be properly appreciated. Far too little is known as to the precise facts regarding the effect of administration (and therefore at least in part of financing) by different levels of government. It is, for example, as difficult to establish the validity of the assumption that local government is essentially more democratic than central [20] as to determine the precise respects in which one type of administration is inherently superior, or inferior, to the other. It is often difficult to tell whether the advantages claimed for any given level of government relate to protection of the interests of those for whom the program was devised or of those who foot the bill. Similarly, far too little is known about the relative freedom from graft of the different levels of government.

In these circumstances it is not surprising that, faced with specific issues, the position taken by individuals tends to be influenced less by a general philosophic viewpoint than by the intensity of their desire for some specific end and their beliefs as to the relative prospects of obtaining it from one level of government rather than another.[21] Nevertheless in the United States, the considerations influencing decisions as to the distribution of financial responsibilities between levels of government, which have been outlined in the preceding pages, operate against a historical "anti-Federal" tradition in the welfare field. Although the last quarter of a century has witnessed major extensions of Federal responsibility, it still remains true that politically the burden of proof is on those who favor further Federal action.

[20] Important labor groups have claimed that because of the unrepresentative character of American state legislatures, organized labor feels that the national government is much more truly representative of the majority than are state governments, and that "truly democratic" government is ensured by Federal action. ("How the Minority Rules in the States," *Economic Outlook*, CIO Department of Education and Research, August, 1953, reproduced in *Unemployment Insurance*, Hearings before the House Committee on Ways and Means on H.R. 6537, 6539, 7054, 8857, and 8858, 83d Cong., 2d Sess., June, 1954.)

[21] It is significant, for example, that many large employers and some state administrators who in other respects are strongly, and in principle, against Federal action or standards in unemployment insurance have nonetheless insisted on retention of those Federal standards which have the effect of forcing a state to adopt experience-rating if it desires to reduce its average tax level below 2.7 per cent. Similarly, social workers as a group, despite their emphasis on individualization and on participation of individuals in decision-making processes, a point of view which might have been expected to lead them to prefer small units of government, nonetheless became in general strongly pro-Federal after 1933, when it appeared that the Federal government was, on the whole, more liberal than the states and that certain social policies could be achieved by embodying them in the standards of a grant-in-aid program. (Cf. Eveline M. Burns, "The Role of Government in Social Welfare," *Social Work Journal*, July, 1954, p. 124.)

CHAPTER 12

Methods of Implementing Intergovernmental Cost Sharing

THE ASSUMPTION of financial responsibility by larger units of government has taken various forms. Sometimes, as we have seen, the larger units accept complete responsibility for financing a given program. In the United States the Federal government is solely responsible for OASI, for the Railroad income security systems, and, in effect, for benefits to veterans.[1] Similarly the states have exclusive responsibility for workmen's compensation (other than for Federal employees and longshoremen and harbor workers) and temporary disability insurance (other than for railroad workers). In about a quarter of the states, general assistance is wholly a local financial responsibility, and in almost another quarter it is wholly a state responsibility.

The same kind of division of costs occurs in other countries. In Canada the Dominion government exclusively finances old-age pensions (after age 70), unemployment insurance, veterans' benefits and children's allowances. In Australia the Commonwealth finances all income security programs except workmen's compensation and minor expenditures for supplementary relief, which are financed by the states. In some unitary forms of government, such as New Zealand and Great Britain, the central government, as we have seen, assumes one hundred per cent responsibility for financing all income security measures whatever their type.

Sometimes, however, the larger authority shares the cost with the smaller by some type of grant-in-aid arrangement. Thus in the United States the Federal government and the states both share the costs of all forms of special assistance (i.e., OAA, ADC, AB, and APTD), and in many states the localities also provide financial support for one or more of these programs.[2] Most states share with their localities the cost of general assistance (which receives no Federal subsidy). In unemployment insur-

[1] Most of the states operate small assistance programs for veterans, but these are insignificant in relation to the income security and medical benefits administered by the Federal government.

[2] In 1954 the local share of expenditures for assistance and administration was: OAA, 6.8 per cent; ADC, 11.5 per cent; AB, 8.1 per cent; and APTD, 13.9 per cent. For details of the situation in individual states, see *Social Security Bulletin*, September, 1955, p. 76.

ance, although benefit payments are wholly a state responsibility, the Federal government pays all of the costs of administration.

In Canada the Dominion government helps to finance old-age benefits payable to aged persons between 65 and 69 years of age and also shares with the provinces the cost of pensions to the blind. In Great Britain before 1948, when the National Insurance Act of 1946 came into effect, the national government had given financial aid to the counties and boroughs through a block grant, some portion of which was used by the recipient governments for public assistance.

Even, therefore, when a decision has been reached in favor of financial participation by larger units of government, a choice still has to be made between methods.

DIVISION OF THE FIELD ON A PROGRAM BASIS

At first sight the method of dividing the field between levels of government on a program basis would seem to have many advantages. Each government can operate its own program without interference from the other, and the many difficulties arising out of joint administration are avoided.[3] But it is not always possible so to divide programs between different governmental units as to result in a division of the over-all costs which precisely corresponds to the total burdens to be incurred by each and to their respective capacities to bear them.

Technical and other considerations which were discussed in the preceding chapter have in general promoted a division of programs whereby the nondiscretionary non-means-test systems are the responsibility of the larger units of government. But, as we saw in Part One, the scope and coverage of these programs may be restricted because of technical administrative considerations or because of a desire to hold the taxes by which they are financed down to some specified level, or for other reasons. From the point of view of the requirements of the centrally or federally administered program, these limitations may be wholly justifiable, but their effect is to throw all residual responsibilities, which may sometimes be very large, on the smaller units of government. This fact tends to limit the extent to which exclusive operation of income security programs by the different levels of government can solve the problem of the disproportion between fiscal resources and responsibilities to be carried.

When the Social Security Act was passed, for example, it was anticipated that by the creation of a national OASI program the burden, both absolute and differential, falling on the states for the support of the needy aged would be greatly reduced and over a foreseeable period of years completely removed. But quite apart from the fact that the technical

---

[3] For the nature of these administrative difficulties, see Chap. 13.

requirements of OASI caused the system to mature very slowly, so that in the early years its impact on the total problem of need for income in old age was relatively small, the exclusion of agriculture intensified rather than ameliorated state disparities in resources in relation to needs for old-age support. This happened because some states are much more heavily agricultural than others and because on the whole the agricultural states rank comparatively low in terms of per capita income. Hence by mid-1953 in such wealthy and highly industrialized states as Connecticut, Massachusetts, New Jersey, and Rhode Island over 40 per cent of the population 65 and over were eligible for and received OASI benefits, while in agricultural states, such as Mississippi, South Dakota, Nebraska, South Carolina, and Arkansas, OASI beneficiaries amounted to only between 13.3 and 19.7 per cent of the population 65 and over.[4] In other words, the poorer states received the least benefit, in terms of a reduction of their burden of old-age support, from the Federal government's assumption of responsibility for an old-age insurance program. The consequence has been that recipient rates for old-age assistance have tended to be relatively high in such states and correspondingly low in the states where a large proportion of the aged population can qualify for OASI.[5] The Amendments of 1950 and 1954, which extended coverage to agricultural workers, will in time eliminate this disadvantage of the agricultural states.

The shortcomings of the method of allocation of programs to the exclusive responsibility of one level of government or another are evident in another respect also. As we have seen, the assumption by the largest unit of government of the nondiscretionary non-needs-test systems means in effect that the smaller units of government are allocated the residual role, and the size of this burden varies from time to time, and notably with changing economic conditions and changes in price levels.

Thus unemployment insurance programs typically pay benefits only for a limited period of time. With relatively high employment, therefore, assumption of financial responsibility for this program by the national government might relieve subordinate governments of all, or almost all, of the costs of unemployment relief. But in serious depressions, the num-

---

[4] At the time the average percentage receiving OASI in the nation as a whole was 31.8. There were 6 states in which the percentage was 40 or more, 18 in which it was between 30 and 40, 20 between 20 and 30, and 9 in which it was less than 20 per cent. For the position of individual states, see *Analysis of the Social Security System*, part 3, p. 287; and for a chart comparing recipient rates on OASI and OAA, see *Social Security Amendments of 1954*, p. 101.

[5] As against an average OAA recipient rate of 18.9 per 100 aged persons in June, 1953, the rates in some of the agricultural states were as follows: Arkansas, 34.1; Mississippi, 36.4; South Carolina, 32.7. Not all of the differences in recipient rates however can be thus explained, as will be shown below. Nevertheless, in general, the highest OAA rates are found in the agricultural states and the lowest, in the industrialized.

ber of unemployed exhausting benefit rights may be very large, and the burden of their support which will fall on the lower levels of government may be entirely disproportionate to their fiscal capacities.[6]

Similarly the over-all division of financial responsibility between levels of government independently operating separate programs will be affected by changes in the general price level. Rising prices will lessen the adequacy of the benefits payable under the non-needs-test, nondiscretionary programs, which are those typically allocated to the larger units of government. If supplementation is needed, this will be sought from the residual programs, which adjust payments to demonstrated need, i.e., from those which are often financed by the smaller political units. Thus in the United States the increasing inadequacy of OASI benefits in the light of rising prices led to a growing volume of supplementation from OAA prior to the Amendments of 1950,[7] and to charges that the Federal government was throwing back to the states and localities an undue share of the burden of old-age support. On the other hand, in Great Britain, where by 1955 the extent of subsidization of insurance benefits by National Assistance had become a major public issue,[8] as assistance was also financed by the national government, it did not involve intergovernmental financial recriminations.

GRANTS-IN-AID

In view of the inadequacies of the device of assigning exclusive responsibility for individual programs to different levels of government, many countries have adopted some method whereby the central government shares in the costs of some or most of their income security programs. This usually takes the form of some kind of grant-in-aid. By fiscal 1951

[6] Even when, as in the United States between 1935 and 1941, the central government in principle accepted major financial responsibility through the WPA for work relief for the "employable unemployed," financial pressures led to important restrictions on eligibility. At no time did the program provide work for as many as 40 per cent of the estimated numbers of unemployed, and the resulting burdens upon the residual state and local unemployment relief systems led to charges that the Federal government was evading its responsibilities. (*Security, Work and Relief Policies,* National Resources Planning Board, Government Printing Office, Washington, D.C., 1942, pp. 234–240.) For an account of British efforts to divide the burden of unemployment relief on a program basis (in this case the central government utilized a greatly expanded unemployment insurance system with at times almost unlimited duration), see Eveline M. Burns, *British Unemployment Programs, 1920–38,* Social Science Research Council, Washington, D.C., 1941, *passim.*

[7] Ruth White, "Concurrent Receipt of Public Assistance and OASI," *Social Security Bulletin,* August, 1954, pp. 12ff.

[8] By December, 1953, 26.2 per cent of all old-age pension beneficiaries in Great Britain were receiving supplementation from National Assistance. (*Ministry of Labour Gazette,* July, 1954, p. 229.) See also "Pensions in Perspective," *The Economist* [London], Dec. 11, 1954, pp. 883ff.

Federal grants-in-aid in the United States accounted for about 5 per cent of Federal expenditures from general revenues.

The use of the grant-in-aid long antedates the widespread development of income security measures.[9] By the mid-century there were some forty different grant programs in the United States. Of these only five were for income security purposes (four public assistance grants and one for employment security administration), around fifteen being for health and welfare and some half dozen for education, while the remainder were distributed among a variety of purposes.[10] But the income security grants are by far the most important, accounting for rather more than half of the $2.95 billion of Federal grants in 1953 to 1954.

It should be noted also that the use of this device is not peculiar to federal systems. In unitary countries, such as Great Britain, the national government makes grants to the counties or other political subdivisions. Also in the United States, the state governments make grants-in-aid to localities, and these grants are not only a very substantial part of states' expenditures (about 31 per cent in 1951), but also state grants to local units of government are larger in amount than the Federal grants to the states. Therefore, although in this chapter the problems of grants-in-aid will be discussed primarily in the context of the Federal grant system, it must not be forgotten that similar issues arise also in regard to state grants to localities.

When one level of government decides to share in the costs of programs which are essentially administered by, and within the control of, some other level of government, two major problems, a positive and a negative, are faced in determining the form and nature of the grant: How can attainment of the major purposes of the grant be assured? How can the financial interests of the grant-making authority be protected? In the search for solutions to these problems a wide variety of methods and grant formulas has been developed, although not all of them are as yet found in the income security grants.

Precise Definition of the Purpose of the Grant

At first sight, it would seem as if the obvious answer which would both achieve the objectives of the grant-giving authority and protect its

[9] For an account of the growth of the Federal grant system in the United States, see James A. Maxwell, *Federal Grants and the Business Cycle*, National Bureau of Economic Research, New York, 1952, chap. I. For a briefer description, see Ida C. Merriam, *Social Security Financing*, Federal Security Agency, Social Security Administration, Division of Research and Statistics, Bureau Report no. 17, 1952, pp. 86–88.

[10] For details by purpose of Federal grants 1935 to 1951 and by state in 1951, see Merriam, *op. cit.*, Appendix Table 14. For later years see "Federal Grants to State and Local Governments, 1953–54," *Social Security Bulletin*, July, 1955, pp. 13–17; September, 1955, p. 31.

financial interest would be to define very specifically the purposes for which financial aid is being made available. Where it is possible to define the purpose in exact and measurable terms, or to adopt standards which are broadly recognized as having scientific validity or have already gained widespread acceptance, this may indeed be the answer. The Federal grants for highway construction or for hospital surveys and construction can define with considerable precision the types of project which qualify for grant aid and the satisfaction of the requirements by the recipient unit can be determined by objective tests and relatively simply.

Somewhat the same is true of the growing system of Federal grants to assist in the control of various specific diseases, such as tuberculosis, cancer, or heart disease. Here, there is a considerable measure of professional agreement as to definitions. Mental health, which is also grant-aided, however, is a less precise and accepted concept where there is more room for genuine difference of opinion among professionals and between them and others as to the scope of phenomena and activities embraced by the term. In any case, when all or part of the grant is used to foster research, precise definition which would limit the use of the grant to specific purposes becomes much more difficult, and differences of opinion as to whether a given undertaking is or is not eligible for grant support inevitably arise from time to time. Here the utilization of advisory bodies consisting of outstanding professional personnel often serves as a safeguard for the grant-making government. But as the general purposes of the grant move away from material objectives or areas where the nature of the service is standardized (either by recognized professional criteria or by general public acceptance), it becomes much more difficult both to define the specific purpose of the grant and to ensure compliance with its terms. This is notably the case in the social services, including even the apparently more objectively definable public assistance programs.

It might have been supposed that the Federal grants-in-aid for public assistance, which are admittedly special-purpose grants, would be very specific in the definition of the purpose for which they are available. It is true that under the Social Security Act the Federal government shares in the cost of cash public assistance payments to individuals, and this would seem specific enough. It also defines, by reference to the nature of the risk, the categories of persons in whom the Federal government is interested. Furthermore, the Federal Act requires that as a condition of aid the states must not impose citizenship or residence requirements of more than a certain degree of harshness. Also, the state must make public assistance payments available to all eligible people in all parts of the state, must make payments promptly, and must give applicants appeal rights.

And yet in two of the major essentials in a program of this type, the terms of the Federal Act are not specific. The states are free to define the most crucial factor affecting the financial commitment of the Federal government, namely the criteria of need, and they are not required to reach any defined standard of performance, in terms of a specific minimum level of living to be assured the recipient.

The Federal Act does indeed state that in determining eligibility the states must take into account the income and resources of the applicant, but, with one exception, they are left free to define income and resources as they wish.[11] As was shown in Chapter IV, there is great diversity in the standards of need adopted by the various states. These differences are reflected in the widely varying recipient rates of the public assistance programs. And these differences have increased over the years. By the end of 1951, state recipient rates for old-age assistance showed an average deviation of 45.7 per cent from the United States median, whereas in 1940 the range was 29.8 per cent. Similar trends are observable in the other federally aided programs.[12] By mid-1953, whereas the average old-age assistance recipient rate was 18.9 per 100 persons 65 and over, it was 30 or more in thirteen states (and in Louisiana as high as 59.9, in Oklahoma 45.0, and in Colorado 41.6) while in nine it was under 10.0. Even though, as was pointed out in the preceding section, some range is to be expected because of the differences in the amount of poverty as between the states and because of the differential impact of the OASI program, the range of recipient rates cannot be wholly thus explained. There is thus much truth in the charge often made against the public assistance grants, namely that the Federal taxpayer has given a blank check to the states: he stands ready to share in the costs of a program in which what is perhaps the major item determining the total bill, namely the number of recipients, lies entirely within the control of the states.

On the equally vital question of the level of public assistance payments, the Federal Act also has little to say. It is true that from the beginning the Federal government has always set a maximum to the payment to any individual in which it would share. But this is a device merely to protect the Federal taxpayer and to limit the volume of Federal aid going to the states which are willing and able to afford high payments. As a method of ensuring that the Federal grant results in the receipt by all needy persons of a standard of living of some minimum level of adequacy, the Federal matching maximum is of no help at all. The failure to include in the public assistance grant standards any require-

[11] After 1952 the states were required to disregard, up to $50 a month, earned income of blind persons, in determining their need. Between 1943 and 1949, also, the states were permitted to disregard earnings from agriculture (and from 1945 to 1949, earnings from nursing) in determining need for old-age assistance.

[12] For ADC, 41.4 per cent (1951) and 33.3 per cent (1940). (Merriam, *op. cit.*, p. 100.)

ment as to the minimum standard of living to be assured persons eligible for aid thus raises real questions about the purpose of the Federal grants. It seems not unreasonable to suppose that the original and probably also the continuing motivation has been a desire to make it possible for needy people to receive adequate public aid wherever they reside. And, in general, the availability of Federal funds has led to some increase in the level of monthly payments, although when allowance is made for changing price levels, the increase is relatively modest.[13] Yet the facts that as late as 1954 in old-age assistance there were still nine states where the average monthly grant was below $35 a person, that for aid to dependent children there were five where the average monthly payment was below $15 per recipient, while for the country as a whole the average ADC payment per recipient was only $23.73 a month, suggest that if the purpose of the Federal grant was to ensure more adequate payments to needy people, that result has not been wholly achieved.

Public assistance is indeed a good example of the difficulty of ensuring both attainment of an objective and protection of the financial interests of the granting authority by defining with precision the purpose for which the grant is made in the grant conditions. It seems doubtful whether there is in fact any agreed "American minimum standard" despite frequent reference to this concept in general discussion. In any case, the difficulties of spelling out a money equivalent in so economically heterogeneous a country as the United States are obvious. Even more fundamentally, to prescribe in the Federal Act both the standards of need which determine eligibility and the minimum level of living to be assured all eligible applicants raises major issues regarding Federal interference in an area which traditionally has been thought of as peculiarly a matter for local determination. To this issue we shall return later. Meanwhile, the fact remains that so long as the Federal grant contains no standards either as to how need is to be determined or as to the minimum standard of living to be assured, the question of the extent to which it achieves its objective will remain unanswered, for that objective will remain undefined, and the Federal taxpayer will continue to underwrite a bill whose size is largely beyond his control.

The arrangements for financing unemployment insurance illustrate the same broad problem, though here Federal financial participation does not involve subsidies at the expense of the Federal general taxpayer.[14]

---

[13] In 1936 the average payment for OAA was $18.79 a month. In 1953 it was around $51. In the same period the consumer price index rose from 59.3 to 114.4. When adjusted for price changes since 1940, average OAA payments in the lowest state increased 28 per cent between 1940 and 1951 and in the highest state by 1.1 per cent.

[14] In fact, the Federal general taxpayer has been subsidized at the expense of state payroll taxpayers (see Chap. 13).

Nevertheless, the Federal taxing power was invoked, in the tax-offset provisions, to make it possible for all states to operate unemployment insurance programs, and the fiscal consequence is that the Federal government has in effect ceded to the states access to the payroll tax, to the level of 2.7 per cent, for this purpose. Remembering this, the innocent student who assumes that the Federal government would have defined what it meant by unemployment insurance will search in vain for any definition in the Federal legislation. He will indeed learn that the proceeds of the tax collected by the states must be used for the payment of "unemployment benefits" and that these must be paid through public employment offices. He will find that there must be rights of appeal for claimants and that the states may not deny benefits for refusal of allegedly suitable work under three sets of circumstances. But as to the crucial features of an unemployment insurance system, the principles on which the benefits are to be determined, the conditions of eligibility therefor, and the duration of benefit payment, there are no Federal standards at all. The omission of any minimum standards regarding duration is particularly surprising since, if the experience of the 1930s be any guide, the Federal government is in the position of the residuary legatee for unemployment relief, and the shorter the duration of unemployment insurance benefit, the greater in a period of depression is the burden falling on the Federal taxpayer.

For two other reasons it might have been supposed that the Federal government would, by requiring certain standards as to benefits and eligibility, have defined the purposes it hoped to achieve by ceding to the states, via the tax-offset provisions, access to a 2.7 per cent payroll tax. First, as was shown in Chapter 9 there has been some tendency, under experience-rating systems, for the states to cut tax rates by restrictive benefit, eligibility, and disqualification conditions rather than in response to genuine employment-stabilizing activities by employers. This not merely defeats the general purpose of the tax-offset, which was to enable the states to operate comparable programs without prejudicing the competitive position of their own employers, but also, by opening the door to competitive rate reductions, exerts a general pressure for deliberalization of all such programs. Were this process carried to an extreme, the Federal government might find that it had foregone access to the 2.7 per cent payroll tax only to be left with responsibility for a sizable unemployment relief problem because of the limited and restrictive character of state unemployment insurance laws. Minimum Federal standards relating to benefits, duration and certain disqualifications would seem to be an essential safeguard when experience-rating is an integral part of all state systems.

Second, the necessity for Federal standards is evident when efforts are made to come to grips with the inability of a state or states to meet unemployment insurance costs without raising the tax on employers above the 2.7 per cent level. From 1952 onwards proposals were introduced with increasing frequency into the Congress to provide for loans or grants to states in financial difficulties. The proposal to make Federal loans available was vulnerable to the criticism that where the financial difficulty of the state was not merely temporary in character but attributable to a persistent high level of unemployment, or where the excess costs were extremely heavy in relation to the state's anticipated long-run payroll levels, a loan was hardly a realistic answer to the state's need, since the likelihood of repayment was remote. On the other hand, either an outright Federal grant or a Federal reinsurance system whereby all states would insure themselves against excess costs would, in the absence of any uniform maximum standards, make it possible for individual states to exercise undue liberality in both benefit provisions and administration at the expense of the Federal taxpayer or of employers in other states.[15]

The desirability or otherwise of Federal minimum standards relating to benefits, eligibility and duration is indeed one of the most hotly contested issues in unemployment insurance in the United States and reveals profound differences of opinion as to the purposes of unemployment insurance and the concern of the Federal government with this program.[16] Those who most strongly support state rather than Federal systems fear any new Federal standards, even though these might set limits to the risks of irresponsible state action. They would go so far as to argue that if a state is in financial difficulty, that is no concern of the Federal government. The state should either tighten up its administration, lower its benefits, or be

15 In 1954 the pressure to provide some form of aid for financially embarrassed states plus the opposition to any Federal standards led to the adoption of a device which is rationally hard to defend. A small loan fund was established from which states in financial difficulties could obtain interest-free loans. Repayment could be made at any time, but if not completed within four years, the Federal government would collect directly from individual employers in that state. Instead of receiving a 90 per cent credit against the Federal tax, employers would get only 85 per cent, and each year the loan remained unpaid the creditable offset would fall by another 5 per cent. It was expected that this provision would put pressure on the borrowing state to exercise economy and to collect taxes at least equal to the 2.7 per cent level, and be an effective substitute for specific Federal standards. However, if the failure of the state to make repayment were due to a continuing high level of unemployment, this provision for automatic repayment would either curtail the operation of the program within the state (by reducing the revenue of the state fund) or force the state to raise employers' taxes above the national level, thereby still further prejudicing their competitive position.

16 For a concise statement of the two viewpoints, see the "Statements on Benefit Standards of the Public Members of the Federal Advisory Council on Employment Security" (concurred in by the labor members), in *Unemployment Insurance*, Hearings before the House Committee on Ways and Means on H.R. 6537, 6539, 7054, 8857, and 8858, 83d Cong., 2d Sess., June, 1954, pp. 258–260; and for the employers, the reference cited in the following footnote.

prepared to tax its employers above the national level. As against this, it is held that unless the difficulty is due to lax administration, to cut benefits is to fail to use the system for the very purpose and at the very time when it is most needed, while to raise taxes when industry in the state is at a low ebb is to add still further to the competitive disadvantages of employers in that state.

However, it is undeniable that any standards which would appear to be necessary in the light of the problems discussed above would involve a significant measure of Federal control of the substantive provisions of state laws, and as such are regarded by those who attach major importance to state action as at best a dangerous entering wedge and at worst a complete removal of any control over the nature of unemployment insurance laws from the hands of the states.[17] And it is true that some of those who would accept the necessity for Federal standards hold that such arrangements are a clumsy and inadequate substitute for the wholly Federal system they would in principle prefer. So long as such sharp differences of opinion prevail, it seems unlikely that the purposes of the Federal tax concessions for unemployment insurance will be precisely defined.

Up to this point we have considered efforts to define the purpose of a Federal grant by reference to the characteristics of a particular institution or program (e.g., public assistance or unemployment insurance). A different attempt to focus more precisely the purposes of Federal grants while at the same time leading to reductions in Federal controls and the opportunity for the assumption of greater initiative or responsibility on the part of the states and local communities can be illustrated by the health and welfare proposals of the Republican administration in 1954. In place of a series of fourteen major and specific grant-in-aid programs (excluding hospital construction), it was proposed to substitute a threefold grouping: grants whose purpose was to support already existing programs in health, education, and welfare; grants for extension and improvement to assist the states in initiating and carrying out, through a developmental period, needed improvements and extensions of services in these areas; and finally grants for special research and development projects on the basis of unique problems and opportunities of regional or national significance.[18]

---

[17] "It appears ridiculous for the Federal Government to prescribe (1) the formula by which weekly benefits are to be determined for each individual, (2) the maximum and minimum amounts thereof, (3) the duration, (4) the conditions of eligibility or disqualification, and still to go through the motion of having the program operate under the legislation of separate states. To do so would preserve all the complexities of joint Federal-State operations without reserving to the individual states any of the rights of self-determination or flexibility in meeting the industrial, economic and employment conditions that are peculiar to the state." (Excerpt from letter from the U.S. Chamber of Commerce in *Unemployment Insurance*, p. 133.)

[18] In fact, this new basis for Federal financial participation was enacted only for

Yet analysis suggests that even this effort to define the objectives of the Federal grant will not avoid some of the problems we have already discussed. The differentiation between support, extension and improvement, and special projects admittedly clarifies policy and would permit more rational determination of the amount of Federal funds to be devoted annually to each broad purpose. But in two respects the Federal government would be involved in essentially the same kind of problems of program control as has been experienced in public assistance and unemployment insurance. First, although the number of grant categories would be reduced, not all would be eliminated: the proposals would have only reduced the ten health and welfare grants to four.[19] The grants would still have been special-purpose grants although the individual categories would have been larger.[20] Second, in all cases to secure the grant the state would have had to submit a plan for approval by the Federal government. In the last resort, therefore, as with most special-purpose grants, the granting authority would have been in a position to exercise considerable control over the nature and extent of the aided service.

It will be evident from the preceding discussion that the use of the special-purpose grant as an instrument for achieving the objectives and protecting the financial interests of the granting authority faces a fundamental difficulty. The more detailed and exact the defining standards it adopts, the more it removes from the recipient government control over the programs for which the latter is nominally responsible.[21] Yet the very purpose of the grant-in-aid device is to permit a high degree of state and local autonomy and initiative by removing or minimizing state and local financial limitations and differences.

Furthermore, the development of a multiplicity of special-purpose grants, each perhaps justifiable when considered in isolation but bearing

---

Vocational Rehabilitation. For the precise arrangements adopted, see "Vocational Rehabilitation Act Amendments," *Social Security Bulletin,* October, 1954, pp. 16–17.

[19] The proposals would have grouped together the previously separate categories of child welfare, maternal and child health, and programs for crippled children. The Vocational Rehabilitation grants would have remained as a separate category. The six separate health grants would have been merged into a general public health grant.

[20] However, the proposal in the maternal and child health and welfare services contained a proviso apportioning specific percentages of the total grant among the three types of program. This would seem largely to abandon the advantages of the block grant in this area. Only 20 per cent of the funds allocated to each state would have been free of this control.

[21] For a statement of the view that Federal grants have already dangerously trespassed upon states' rights, see Frank Carlson, "The Growth of Federal Control," *American Economic Security,* August–September, 1953; and Second Report, Temporary State Commission to Study Federally Aided Welfare Programs, New York State, Albany, 1954, *passim.*

no rational relationship to the already existing grant structure, enormously adds to the complexities of administration.[22] The problem is intensified when, as often happens in the public welfare field, there also exists a complicated system of special-purpose grants from the states to the localities.[23] The numerous special-purpose grants greatly multiply the number of instances in which the states are compelled to share responsibility with the Federal government in carrying out what are in principle regarded as state functions, thus multiplying the occasions for friction between the two governmental levels. These relationships are likely to be the more strained if, as tends to happen when a complicated grant structure develops on a piecemeal basis over a period of years, there are differences in the grant terms for closely related functions, if the functional organization for their administration differs at the different levels of government, and if there is less than perfect coordination of policy between related departments at any one level.[24]

It is also alleged that the highly categorized special-purpose grants have

[22] In 1953 the Commissioner of Welfare of New York State asserted that the Federal, state, and local governments "have promulgated so many policies, regulations and other controls that the federally dominated, State-supervised and locally administered public assistance system has become the most complex public service in the United States, and the key job in the system, that of the public assistance worker, has become one of the most difficult—if not the most difficult—in all public service." (*Public Welfare in New York State,* 86th and 87th Annual Reports, New York State Department of Welfare, Legislative Document (1954) no. 8, March 1, 1954, p. 3. This report contains on pp. 4–6 an illuminating account of how this tripartite control affects the task of the public assistance investigator.)

[23] Until 1954, for example, New York State gave financial aid to the localities through a series of categorical grants which involved, for the federally aided public assistance programs, paying the difference between the Federal grant and 20 per cent of the cost of this assistance. However, for general relief the state paid 80 per cent. Child care in institutions, care of adults in public homes and infirmaries carried no state grant, nor did hospital care given to home-relief recipients, children being cared for away from their homes, and persons not in receipt of public assistance but receiving hospital care at public expense. On the other hand, the state did share in the cost of hospital care given to the recipients of special public assistance, paid 80 per cent of medical (but not hospital) care of general relief recipients and 100 per cent of both hospital and medical care given to persons without residence in the state and to Indians.

[24] For a discussion of some of these broader consequences of the system of special-purpose grants, see George C. S. Benson, "Federal-State Relations—A Challenge," *American Economic Security,* June–July, 1954, pp. 9–15; George Bigge, "Federal Grants-in-aid: A Bulwark of State Governments," *Social Security Bulletin,* November, 1950; Eveline M. Burns, "Wanted: More Thought about Grants-in-aid," *Social Work Journal,* January, 1954; Paul Studenski and E. J. Baikie, "Federal Grants-in-aid," *National Tax Journal,* September, 1949, pp. 193–214; and *Federal Grants-in-aid,* Report of the Committee on Grants-in-aid of the Council of State Governments, Chicago, 1949. See also: The Commission on Intergovernmental Relations, *A Report to the President for Transmittal to the Congress,* Government Printing Office, Washington, D.C., June, 1955, Chapter 5.

another disadvantage: because of the lure of Federal funds, states may be tempted to channel a disproportionate share of state revenues into the federally aided service to the disadvantage of other state functions which receive no Federal grants.

The charge that Federal aid tends thus to distort state expenditure patterns has often been made in regard to the public assistance grants. It is claimed both that the states overexpand total public assistance as compared to other state functions and that within the public assistance field they favor the federally aided categories, at the expense of general assistance. The precise effects of the Federal subsidies are difficult to determine. However, there appears to be some evidence that when Federal grants are available for aid given to four special categories of needy people, but no subsidy is given for aid to all other needy persons (the general relief clientele), states which face difficulties in raising adequate revenues will tend to favor the services where a dollar of state expenditure brings in some Federal money.[25] Similarly, it seems likely that the relatively low levels of payments to ADC recipients are not unrelated to the relatively less generous Federal grants for this program which have led some states to neglect ADC financially.

For these reasons many authorities would prefer a single Federal grant for the total public assistance function related to the numbers of persons aided regardless of the reason for their dependency. But it is doubtful whether in comparison with other disadvantages of special-purpose grants, the possible distortion of state expenditure patterns by Federal subsidies can be cited among the more powerful arguments supporting proposals to merge all special-purpose grants into a single-purpose block grant. From one point of view, the very objective of the Federal grant is a distortion of state expenditures. Federal money is made available precisely because the national legislature believes that certain services are underdeveloped and that more money should be spent on them.

In view of the many problems created by the complex system of special-purpose grants, it is not surprising that there is considerable support for proposals to replace the more than twenty separate welfare grants by some type of block or general-purpose grant, such as exists in certain other countries.[26] Under such an arrangement each state would receive from the

[25] The relative neglect of the general assistance programs as evidenced by the disproportionately small recipient rates in some of the poorer states, the relatively low monthly payments as compared to those for OAA and AB, and the tendency, when financial stringency enforces percentage reductions in allowances, for these to be greater for general assistance recipients than for other categories has often been commented upon. See Eveline M. Burns, *The American Social Security System*, Houghton Mifflin Company, Boston, 1951, pp. 345–356, 364–365; and Merriam, *op. cit.*, p. 105.

[26] Thus the Committee on Federal-State Relations appointed by the Hoover Commission recommended in 1949 that "all . . . separate grants be rescinded and that a

Federal government a lump-sum contribution toward its total expenditures and be left considerable discretion as to the purposes for which it was to be employed. But it seems doubtful whether American Federal taxpayers would be prepared to support substantial grants to individual states leaving the decision as to their use entirely up to the states. For it must not be forgotten that this freedom implies the freedom to use the funds for relief of the state and local taxpayer instead of for the operation or development of social services.[27] Unless this leeway is to be permitted, some type of control over the use of the funds must be devised. Even if it takes the form merely of an annual accounting of how the money was spent, some categories of appropriate or acceptable objects of expenditure would have to be developed. In fact, it seems likely that many Federal taxpayers would raise objections to footing a bill for Federal grants unless they were in favor of the purposes of the grant.[28] Similarly, proponents of relatively new, or generally underdeveloped services, have expressed fears that the block grant would lead to still further neglect of those services whose value is not generally appreciated or whose clienteles possess no strong political influence.[29]

---

single comprehensive grant for [social, educational, public health services and housing] activities in general be substituted." For an account of the British system of block grants, see D. N. Chester, *Central and Local Government: Financial and Administrative Relations,* Macmillan & Co., Ltd., London, 1951.

[27] The Canadian Rowell-Sirois Commission frankly adopted this position with all its implications in proposing a series of Dominion adjustment grants of an amount which would enable a province to maintain the average Canadian level of public service without taxing its inhabitants more heavily than those in other provinces. In refusing to recommend any requirement that the grant must be used for certain specified services, the Commission admitted that some provinces might use the funds for the relief of taxpayers. But it held that this was the logical implication of a federal form of government. If local residents were not sufficiently active to insist that the available funds be used for public services, this was their concern. The function of the federal government was merely to remove the financial obstacle to the attainment of the accepted national level of service.

[28] Thus the congressional committee considering the proposed public Health Grants in 1954 amended even the modest block grant for special projects in order "more clearly to define the types of projects for which grants may be made." (*Public Health Grant-in-aid Amendments of 1954,* 83d Cong., 2d Sess., H. Rept. 1543, 1954, p. 14.)

[29] It is significant that in 1954 the congressional committee which considered the administration's proposals for unifying the public health grants into a single block grant recommended an amendment which would have retained, until 1959, the categorical grant for mental health, "in order to assure that mental health programs can be established on a firm footing. These programs have been in existence in many instances only for such a limited period of time that the Committee feels justified in singling out these programs as a special category." (*Ibid.,* pp. 9–10.) Similarly an editorial in the *Social Service Review* discussing the administration's proposal that 20 per cent of the child health and welfare funds should be distributed between the services at the dis-

In the last resort decisions as to the desirability of a block grant versus a series of special-purpose grants and, if the latter, determination of the extent to which the Federal government is to prescribe standards will reflect majority opinion on some of the major issues discussed in Chapter 11. Among these, the most crucial are the importance attached to ensuring some minimum level of service or income security for all Americans wherever they reside, the strength of the feeling attached to local autonomy as such, and the confidence of the mass of the voters in the representative character of the respective levels of government.

The Terms of the Financial Arrangements

Grant-making authorities have made use of a second device, the formula governing the amount of the grant, in their efforts to attain certain social objectives while yet protecting their own financial interests.

Open- versus Closed-end Grants. There is always a possibility that the response of the states to the offer of the Federal grant may exceed even the most rationally determined estimates, and the Federal taxpayer may find himself carrying a burden far larger than he had anticipated. One safeguard against this situation is provided by the closed-end grant.

Under this arrangement, the granting authority determines, by statute or annual appropriation acts, the total amount of Federal money which will be available for the aided service in any fiscal year. This system is used for example in the Federal grants for child and maternal welfare services, for hospital construction, school lunch programs, and several other purposes. It is in sharp contrast to the "open-end" grants in public assistance, where there is no absolute dollar ceiling, and the total amount of the Federal grant in any year depends upon the amounts spent by the states. Many people who take a dim view of the steady upward trend of Federal public assistance grants and the high recipient rates in some states have urged that closed-end grants should be used also for public assistance.

As a protection to the financial interests of the granting authority the closed-end grant is, of course, highly effective. In principle, it allows the Federal government to determine, by more or less rational considerations, precisely how much of its revenues it desires to devote to the fostering of any given service in the country as a whole. Yet for such a service as public assistance, where the need varies from year to year and is not always pre-

cretion of the state governor expressed fears "that the child welfare services would stand little chance of getting a fair share of the 20 per cent, as the value of health services is more easily understood and the groups interested in these services are more powerful politically than those interested in child welfare." And in stressing the importance of the previous education stipends, the editorial continued, "If the federal allotment were a lump sum for all purposes, we fear that many states would not use funds for educational stipends." (*Social Service Review,* June, 1954, pp. 206–209.)

dictable, the closed-end grant has real disadvantages. A period of economic depression or even recession will cause a sharp expansion in the rolls of the residual public assistance program. Where the poverty of a state precludes the raising of additional revenues and no further Federal aid is available because the maximum allocation has been received, the consequences will be the denial of aid to eligible needy people or a reduction in the amount of already modest grants. Furthermore, the determination of the amount of the closed-end grant may place the Federal government in an awkward position. It would be difficult to justify total allocations of any given size without public explanation of the Federal government's assumptions as to the extent of need and the level of monthly payments to recipients. Both of these are delicate matters for Federal commitment. The first involves specific forecasts of economic conditions for a substantial future period, and the central government may well be reluctant, however pessimistic the views of its economic consultants, to introduce specific legislative proposals which openly assume a sharp drop in economic activity. The second exposes the Federal government to charges either that it is adopting an unduly low estimate of the standard of living that is good enough for the poorer citizen or that it is pampering the poor, and, as we have seen, the Federal government has hitherto successfully avoided giving any precise definition of a minimum standard of adequacy for public assistance payments.

Furthermore, the closed-end grant is useful primarily as a control on excessive total expenditures: there remain still to be decided the questions of the relation between total Federal and total state expenditures on the service in question, and the precise allocation of the funds as between states. In fact, all Federal closed-end grants contain allotment formulas [30] dealing with these two issues, which are faced by all types of grant formulas, and to which we shall now turn.

The Matching Principle. A very usual device is to require the recipient body to match from its own financial resources all, or some proportion, of the grant received. Thus all the public assistance grants have, since their inception in 1935, required some financial contribution from the states. The obvious purpose of this requirement is to enlist the interest of the states in the aided programs and to ensure more responsible and economical program development and administration. The disadvantages of a system of 100 per cent grants have long been evident in the unemployment insurance program, where the Federal government pays all of the costs of administration of programs over whose nature and content it has little or no control. Here differences of opinion between the two levels of government have inevitably prevailed as to the sums needed for "proper

[30] For details, see Francis G. Cornell, "Grant-in-Aid Apportionment Formulas," *Journal of the American Statistical Association,* March, 1947, pp. 92–104.

and efficient administration," and the states have no financial incentive to moderate their requests or to give appropriate weight to the administrative costs of various proposed changes in the law, because these costs are met by the Federal government. In the public assistance programs, where the largest part of the money granted takes the form of cash payments to individuals living in the states concerned, the desirability of imposing some check on efforts by the states to be generous to their own citizens at the expense of the Federal taxpayer is even more evident.

In addition to assuring more responsible administration by the grantee, the matching grant appears also to be an effective method of inducing the states to act in areas which it is the purpose of the grant to develop, though its influence varies with the size of the Federal share. The rapid growth of special public assistance programs after 1935 is attributable in large measure to the knowledge that every dollar a state invested in these programs brought into the state at least another Federal dollar.[31] Nevertheless, for services whose value is not everywhere appreciated, the requirement that the recipient state match in some degree the Federal grant sometimes results in failure by certain states to take full advantage of the Federal offer, and to that extent, the objective of the grant is not attained. Thus each year some of the states have failed to utilize portions of their child welfare allotments and of one part of the available grants (Part A) for maternal and child health services because they were unable or unwilling to put up the necessary state funds. This possibility has suggested the desirability of eliminating the matching requirement in the case of developmental grants, where the object of the granting authority is to encourage experimentation or development of services hitherto nonexistent or embryonic. It is undoubtedly for this reason that part (Part B) of the Federal grant for maternal and child health carries no matching requirement. Similarly, when in 1954 it was proposed that the public health grants be reclassified by objective, the grants for extension and improvement of services, in contrast to those for support of established ongoing services, offered very generous Federal subsidies for the first two years and thereafter declined until, at the end of six years, the states were expected to carry the entire burden.

Although the degree of stimulus offered will of course depend in large measure on the proportion which the Federal grant forms of total expenditures, relatively little is known of the reasons which led to the adoption of any given proportion in individual grants. It is difficult, if not impossible, for example, to explain why 50 per cent of payments up to a certain amount was selected in 1935 as the appropriate share of the Federal

[31] For the influence of grants in another area, see Joseph W. Mountin and Clifford H. Greve, *The Role of Grants-in-aid in Financing Public Health Programs*, Public Health Bulletin 303, Government Printing Office, Washington, D.C., 1949.

government for OAA and AB; why the share was subsequently changed to a range of 80 per cent of payments up to $25, to 64 per cent of payments of $55 monthly, rather than some other percentages; or why in the initial ADC grant the Federal government reimbursed only 33⅓ per cent of payments up to a low maximum, while for OAA and AB the grant was 50 per cent up to a higher maximum. The reasons for the selection of precise percentages contributed by the Federal government in other programs such as the health grants or those for maternal and child health grants are equally shrouded in mystery.

The point is not merely academic. The different influences exerted by different percentages can be tremendous, and failure to consider all their implications may lead to unfortunate, and unexpected, results. When, for example, as has been the case in public assistance since 1946, the proportion of Federal aid is much higher for a low payment to recipients than for one at the maximum matchable amounts,[32] there is at least a psychological barrier against making payments at levels where the proportion of Federal aid is less. The poorer states, or states where social attitudes toward those in need are relatively illiberal, may be particularly sensitive to this kind of consideration. Thus the grant formula may operate so as to place a premium on making a large number of low grants.

Furthermore, any given percentage, once adopted, is difficult to change, except in an upward direction. The fact that 50 per cent was selected in 1935 as the Federal matching share has placed a real barrier in the way of subsequent proposals to vary the grants in favor of the poorer states. For thereafter any such plan which would have had the result of lowering the matching proportion received by some states in order to increase the proportion of others met resistance from the former on the ground that funds were being taken away from them. Hence after 1935 all proposals for variable grants had to assume that variation could only be from 50 per cent upwards, and in view of the disadvantages stemming from grants approximating 100 per cent the range of possible variation was necessarily narrowed. A variable grants system ranging from 33⅓ per cent for the richest to 66⅔ per cent for the poorest states, which was provided from the first in some other grant programs, became unthinkable in public assistance.

It is this fact which in part explains the adoption of the 1946 grant formula, which had the effect of giving additional money to all states in-

---

[32] By 1955 the formula provided that the Federal government would pay four-fifths of the first $25 average payment plus one-half of the balance up to $55, per individual payment. For Aid to Dependent Children, the formula was four-fifths of the first $15 average payment plus one-half the balance up to $30 for the first child and one adult and $21 for each additional child. For a detailed account of procedures in determining the Federal share for any state, see *Analysis of the Social Security System*, pp. 384–387.

cluding the very richest, and every amendment of the formula since that date has served only to increase still further the degree of subsidization of all states.[33] It was presumably thought that the 1946 formula, while giving aid to all states, would give relatively most to the poorer states since it is in these that the average grant is typically low. But two important facts were overlooked: (1) some very rich states (e.g., Delaware, the richest state in the Union) also give low grants as a matter of policy, so the formula gives relative advantage both to states which are unwilling and to those which are unable to finance high monthly payments; (2) such additional aid as was given to the poorer states involved a substantial increase in the total Federal commitment because precisely the same additional percentage was granted for the first $25 of each payment in the richer states.

Nor in devising the form of the grant was there apparently adequate consideration of the question whether the purpose of the grant was to encourage the making of higher payments to recipients or to benefit state and local taxpayers. One consequence of this type of formula is that whenever the terms of the grant are liberalized (as happened periodically after 1946, by increases of the Federal percentages and raising the maximum matchable), uncertainty always prevails as to whether the states will use the extra Federal money to raise grants (presumably the Federal objective) or to reduce state and local tax burdens.[34]

Equal-Matching versus Variable [35] *Grants.* Whatever decision is reached as to the proportion of total cost to be carried by the Federal government, a further question has to be faced in any grant-in-aid program that calls for some matching by the recipient: shall all states be required to match

[33] The share of the Federal government increased from around 20 per cent of all public assistance payments in the years immediately following the 1935 Act to 51.9 in 1953. During the same period, the share of the localities had fallen from around 30 per cent to 10.2 per cent. The state share fell from around 50 per cent to 37.9 per cent. (*Social Security Bulletin*, September, 1954, p. 77.) For assistance and administration of all programs excluding general assistance the Federal share had increased to approximately 54 per cent by the fiscal year 1953. For OAA alone in that year Federal aid was 55 per cent of total expenditures of assistance and administration. (*Annual Report of the U.S. Department of Health, Education and Welfare, 1953*, 1954, p. 80.) During the calendar year 1954 the Federal share of the individual programs was: OAA, 55.8; ADC, 57.0; AB, 49.5; APTD, 50.8 (*Social Security Bulletin*, September, 1955, p. 76.) In fact, the Federal share is even larger than these figures suggest, for the state taxpayer deducts his state taxes from income reportable for Federal tax.

[34] For a discussion of the situation following the liberalized matching formula of 1952, see *Analysis of the Social Security System*, pp. 378–380.

[35] This terminology is preferred to the frequent use of the term "equalization" in this connection because of the ambiguity of the term "equalization." It is variously used to cover both equalization of service and equalization of tax burdens, and often a grant may "equalize" in one sense and not in the other. Furthermore, as will be evident from the discussion in the text, many of the issues in selecting grant-in-aid formulas turn around the question of precisely what is to be equalized.

in the same proportion, or shall there be differences between the states? The very common arrangement of an equal-matching grant, for example, may serve as a general stimulus to desired action, but it is no solution to a major problem which many people hold to be the prime justification for Federal grants. This is the effect upon levels of service and on local tax burdens of the unequal wealth and resources of the different states. With an equal-matching grant, the poor state must raise precisely as many dollars as a rich state to provide any given level of income or service to any defined caseload. The consequence is that if the poorer state attains the same standards of service as the richer state, it does so at the cost of a disproportionate burden upon its own taxpayers. Alternatively, if it is concerned about tax burdens, relative to those of other states, it will not take full advantage of the grant, because it cannot raise the necessary matching sums, and levels of service will continue to be below the national average.

The equal-matching grant formula embodied in the 1935 Social Security Act has long been criticized for this very reason. The greatest advantage of the Federal offer could be taken by the richest states, which could afford to match, from state dollars, the Federal maximum. The Amendments made in 1946, and thereafter continued in principle with some liberalization, did not go to the root of this problem. For the formula, which, as we have seen, gives a larger Federal grant for payments below a certain sum to needy people and a smaller percentage grant for payments over this amount but less than the fixed matching maximum, still requires of all states, rich and poor alike, the same tax effort if any defined level of income payment to the needy is to be assured. Indeed, since the poorer states typically have relatively larger numbers of people with incomes below any given level, resulting in higher recipient rates, their tax efforts will have to be greater than those of the richer states if they are to maintain the same level of payments to each recipient.[36] It is therefore not surprising that after nearly twenty years of Federal assistance grants, wide disparities still remain between the states in both the level of average grants [37] and in tax burdens or that the average monthly payments still fall below the maximum sum for which Federal matching is available (i.e., not all states take full advantage of the Federal offer).

As late as March, 1954, for example, the average OAA monthly payment was only $51.32, in spite of the Federal government's willingness to share in the cost of payments up to $55.[38] It is highly significant that of the

[36] Nor must it be forgotten that taxpayers in the richer states which put up more state money also get relatively more tax relief from the Federal government since state taxes are deductible from income reported for Federal taxes.

[37] As shown above between 1940 and 1951 differences among the states in the size of the average monthly payment for ADC cases even increased.

[38] Old-age assistance payments have been selected for illustrative purposes because

25 states with payments below $55, all but 8 fell in the lower two quartiles of states ranked by per capita income, and the group included all but one of the states in the lowest quartile. Moreover, of the 25 states with payments above $55, only 6 were in the two lower quartiles when ranked by per capita income, and of these, in all save one, the fiscal burden of public assistance was substantially in excess of the national average.[39]

Thus if the purpose of the Federal assistance grants was to make possible some agreed minimum level of income for needy persons even in the poorest states, they certainly have not succeeded. Nor do they appear to have resulted in an equalization of tax burdens, even for states making monthly payments of approximately the same level, though here the evidence is less conclusive, because the state tax burden for public assistance is affected by the extent to which it is willing to make payments in excess of the Federal matchable maximum [40] and by its eligibility policies, which affect recipient rates and which, as was pointed out in the previous section, are subject to practically no Federal controls. In general, comparisons of the fiscal burdens attributable to public assistance with the recipient rates and average monthly payments in the individual states suggest that many states faced with the dilemma of increasing tax rates substantially above the average or providing less than average grants for eligible needy persons have given the benefit of the doubt to the taxpayer, though there are notable exceptions.[41]

To overcome the deficiencies of the equal-matching grant as a device for solving the problems attributable to the unequal needs, income, and fiscal resources of the various states, it has often been proposed that the formula should be scrapped for one that would provide variable or differential grants. Under such arrangements, the proportion of state and local money that would be required to match any given Federal grant would vary from state to state. Thus the matching proportion might

---

they are financially the most significant (in 1953 they accounted for $1.69 billion out of a total of $2.51 billion of federally aided assistance) and because this is the program which appears to have responded most sensitively to the stimulus of Federal grants.

[39] *Social Security Bulletin,* June, 1954, p. 14; and *Analysis of the Social Security System,* p. 406.

[40] For state practices and proportions of payments in excess of the matchable maximum, see *Analysis of the Social Security System,* p. 1160 (for OAA), pp. 1149–1152 (for ADC).

[41] In 1952 in 2 states, California and Oklahoma, state and local assistance expenditures equalled over 1.6 per cent of state per capita income. In Louisiana they were 1.13 per cent, the national average being 0.48 per cent. At the other extreme, there were 5 states (all except Virginia being in the highest per capita income quartile) where the percentage was 0.18 per cent or less. In 18 states the ratio was 0.40 to 0.59 per cent of income payments. For details of public assistance burdens in the states, see Charles J. Lopes and Ellen J. Perkins, "State and Local Fiscal Effort for Public Assistance," *Social Security Bulletin,* May, 1954, pp. 3–6.

range from one-third to two-thirds, with the proportion required of any given state being determined by the proportion which its per capita income bears to the national average. This type of formula has been adopted in many Federal grants, such as those for school lunches, and for hospital construction, and has been frequently proposed for the public assistance programs by the Federal agency and other groups.

The logic behind the variable grant is unassailable. If the object of the Federal government is to make possible the maintenance of any level of service or assured income to all citizens regardless of the wealth or poverty of the state in which they reside, and to do so with the minimum burden upon the Federal taxpayer, then Federal aid should be proportioned to the needs and resources of the individual states. But quite apart from the fact, noted earlier in the preceding chapter, that this policy may face political objection from the richer states precisely because it so clearly reveals that the real purpose of Federal aid is an interstate redistribution of wealth, the selection of appropriate indices of need and resources presents formidable, though not necessarily insuperable, problems.

Much research has been undertaken to discover an appropriate index of state capacity.[42] Technical opinion has increasingly come to accept state income payments or personal income as the most readily available objective measure of state capacity. This position has been adopted for a number of reasons. Comparison of the results achieved by combining a number of indices into a multiple index with those secured by the index of state per capita income indicates a high degree of correlation. Being based on a single index, the use of per capita income avoids difficult value judgments involved in the weighting of items in a composite index. The index of income payments is also available on a relatively current basis,[43] whereas the necessary data for many of the other items that would logically find a place in a composite index are often not available until after a considerable time lag. Furthermore, being prepared by an agency not involved in the administration of grants, the income index is less susceptible to charges of manipulation. As against alternative indexes of fiscal capacity measured by the amount of revenue which each state could raise by a uniform plan of taxation, the proponents of the use of the per capita income series hold that in the last resort the amount of money which could be raised from such a uniform tax plan would be determined by the state's income. Hence the effort to determine the relative yields of

---

[42] For a convenient summary and critique of the various measures that have been suggested, see Selma J. Mushkin and Beatrice Crowther, *Federal Taxes and the Measurement of State Capacity*, U.S. Public Health Service, May, 1954, pp. 1–7.

[43] The Department of Commerce prepares annual estimates of state income payments (personal income from 1955 onwards) which are available by the middle of the following year.

a uniform tax system is viewed as an unnecessary and highly complicated additional step.

Two shortcomings of the index of per capita income as a measure of state capacity have often been pointed to: the failure to allow for the difference made by Federal taxation [44] and for the unequal distribution of incomes within the states. Because of the unequal incidence of Federal taxation and its relatively progressive character, it cannot be assumed that the income accruing to the residents of any given state is an accurate measure of its relative capacity to support public services. A comparison of the years 1941 and 1954,[45] while establishing that the differences between the states in per capita incomes and Federal tax severity had narrowed over the period and that the relative position of the individual states would be affected relatively little by an adjustment for Federal tax withdrawals, nonetheless confirmed previous findings that Federal tax incidence is higher in wealthier states. Hence adjustment of the per capita income figures for such withdrawals would reduce the absolute income differences among the states. This is an important consideration in view of the fact that grant formulas which use the income index as a measure of capacity typically determine a state's matching proportion by relating its dollar per capita income to the average for the country as a whole. Unfortunately, however, the great practical difficulties which are faced in determining the incidence of most types of Federal taxes other than the income tax probably preclude for some time any complete refinement of the index. An allowance for income-tax withdrawals alone is more practical, although one investigation has suggested that the effect of this refinement on the matching percentages required of states may be relatively slight.[46]

The differences as between the states in the equality or inequality of distribution of incomes also may limit the precision of the index of income per capita as a measure of relative state capacity. For if it is assumed

[44] It appears also that in certain years veterans' payments have modified the distribution of incomes as between the states. Thus in 1949, it has been estimated that veterans' transfers combined to reduce the relative differences in state per capita incomes by 5 per cent (as against 1 per cent in 1929 and 1939). The reduction in the relative differences appeared to be due not to any relatively larger proportion of veterans in the poorer states but to the larger proportion of veterans therein taking advantage of the G.I. Bill and receiving relatively larger subsistence payments presumably because of differences in family responsibilities. (Howard G. Schaller, "Veterans Transfer Payments and State per Capita Incomes, 1929, 1939 and 1949," *Review of Economics and Statistics*, November, 1953, pp. 325–332.)

[45] Mushkin and Crowther, *op. cit., passim*.

[46] A comparison of state matching percentages required under a formula similar to that in the Hospital Survey and Construction Act, with and without an adjustment for net Federal income taxes, indicated that the actual matching percentage would be changed in seventeen states, but in only one instance (New York) would the difference be more than 1 per cent. (*Ibid.*, p. 38.)

that there is to be any measure of progression at all in state tax systems, then of two states with equal average per capita incomes the one with the greater degree of income inequality will have a relatively greater capacity to raise revenues.

Difficult as are the technical problems associated with efforts to adjust Federal grants to the relative financial capacity of the different states, they are probably exceeded by those faced when an attempt is made to vary the grants also by reference to relative need. For some types of program, population (total or some subgroup) may be an appropriate index, for it can be assumed that the need for service is equally felt by all individuals. Thus relative population has long been used successfully as a measure of need for certain health services (e.g., hospital surveys and construction), while for educational grants or programs of special importance for children, the relative number of children below a given age has generally been accepted as a measure of need.

But with income security programs the situation is different. Here population is not an infallible guide. The poorer states are likely to have a larger proportion of needy persons than the richer. In addition, they have in general a larger ratio of young and old to the population aged 18 to 64 than the richer states.[47] The adoption of relative wealth as an index of need as well as of capacity implies the existence of some national minimum of income as the test of need, and as we have repeatedly seen, it is doubtful whether any specific figure would secure general approval. Need for income security programs is also affected by other less measurable forces. The ADC programs, for example, suggest that there may be some differences between the states in the incidence of desertion by the breadwinner, divorces, or the extent of illegitimacy.[48] An allowance for such differences would not be easy to introduce into the grant formula. On the other hand, to the extent that need is affected by differences in employment levels it would not be impossible to use state unemployment percentages as one element in an index of need. The devising of appropriate measures of need remains a major area for productive research.

[47] In the country as a whole the ratio of young and old to persons 18 to 64 is 72 per hundred. With very few exceptions the ratio is far higher in the states with per capita income below the national average than in those above. Thus the proportions in the District of Columbia, New York, New Jersey, and Rhode Island are 56.6, 60.5, 61.5, and 65.6, respectively, while in Mississippi, South Carolina, New Mexico, and Utah they are, respectively, 91.8, 90.8, 91.6, and 89.9. ("Age of Population and per Capita Income, by State, 1953," *Social Security Bulletin*, December, 1954, pp. 20–22.)

[48] For an analysis by states in 1948, see *Analysis of the Social Security System*, pp. 118–119.

PART FOUR

Decisions Regarding the Structure and Character of Administrtaion

THIS BOOK is not concerned with administration per se. Yet, as will have been clear from the preceding chapters, consideration of the policy issues involved in the development of public income security programs cannot neglect problems of administration. As we have seen, in some cases the benefit formulas and eligibility conditions have had to be modified in the interests of administrative feasibility. Similarly, administrative difficulties have from time to time been the decisive influence in determining the coverage of certain types of program. Again, the nature of entire systems, such as unemployment insurance, has been radically affected by choices in favor of administration by one level of government rather than another.

It is a truism, too, that the effectiveness of any law is determined by the quality and nature of its administration. Despite the efforts of legislatures to define with increasing precision over the years the terms of rights to income security payments, many undefined areas calling for administrative interpretation remain, and are likely to remain. How the administrators interpret the law vitally affects not only the people whose benefit rights are involved but also taxpayers and the wider community. The sheer technical competence or incompetence of administrators can make a world of difference to the costs and effectiveness of any program, as the experience of some workmen's compensation and public assistance systems has shown.

Delays in service, or even a failure to attain stated objectives, may occur if administrators concerned with different aspects of some one social security system, or in charge of programs that are closely related functionally to others, fail to develop harmonious and cooperative working relationships or take too narrow or too wide a view of their own responsibilities.

Above all, the impact of a service that deals so directly with people who, almost by definition, at the time of contact with the administration are undergoing some kind of emotional disturbance (whether due to economic insufficiency, unemployment, bereavement, or illness) will have positive or negative social and personal effects according as the administrators are or are not able to establish understanding and constructive relationships with their clienteles, whether applicants for public assistance or social insurance claimants.

Finally, with a group of social services that affect so large a proportion of the population, involve the expenditures of such sizable proportions of the national income, and have such wide economic and social repercussions, administration that is in the hands of even the most devoted and capable professional administrators may, if these are wholly insulated from the body of citizens as a whole, develop bureaucratic tendencies and foster policies that are out of step with prevailing public opinion.

In the following chapter, therefore, some of the more important administrative issues, as they bear upon the functioning of social security measures, will be briefly examined.

CHAPTER 13

Administrative Issues

TO A SIGNIFICANT DEGREE, the structure of administration reflects decisions made by the people of any country regarding the policy issues discussed in the preceding chapters. Prominent among these are the decisions made about the respective financial roles of the various levels of government and the kinds of benefits it is desired to pay. As a result of such decisions the American people by the mid-century had saddled themselves with an administrative structure that was highly complex. For the American social security system is characterized by the existence of three types of benefits (based, respectively, on the beneficiary's previous earnings, on demonstrated individual need, and on assumed average need); separate programs for different risks, sometimes the same risk being covered by more than one type of benefit system (e.g., OASI and OAA); preferential treatment of some groups of people in respect of certain risks (e.g., the favored and separate position of the veterans and railroad workers); and involvement of two and often three levels of government in the financing of the same program (e.g., Federal and state governments in unemployment insurance, Federal, State and, in the majority of cases, local governments also in special public assistance, state and local governments in general assistance). In addition, private enterprise is involved in the administration of some programs (e.g., workmen's compensation, and disability insurance where employers can contract out of the system or insure their liabilities with private insurance companies), thus introducing a new range of administrative relationships into an already complex structure. Furthermore, this series of governmental protective measures was built up over a long series of years on a piecemeal basis, each being developed with little relationship to what existed before.

So long as these substantive decisions remain in force, the administrative structure is likely to remain complex even though there may be major redistributions of program responsibility between units of government or some regrouping of agencies at any one level of government. Indeed, the administrative picture may become even more complicated if certain proposals in the field of disability and health care should materialize. Proposals that would involve government subsidies or public reinsurance for private insurance plans would extend still further the range of authorities

251

involved in social security administration by utilizing private organizations which, since they would be spending public funds, would have to be held to public accountability.

Many proposals have been made for the simplification of this unwieldy structure, in the interests both of economy and of better service. While some changes for the better could undoubtedly be made, decisions about program content and financing set obvious limits to what can be thus achieved. And even a simplified structure would still have to grapple with the problems of staffing and ensuring truly democratic administration.

ORGANIZATIONAL STRUCTURE

Some countries (such as Great Britain) have grouped all income security programs under a single administrative agency and, at least at the national level, have allocated health and other social service programs to another. Such a division has many advantages, not the least of which is the greater likelihood of consistency of policy and greater certainty that similar treatment will be afforded persons in similar circumstances. It also eliminates frictions between a variety of independent agencies. But as income security measures have become more all-embracing (as to both risks and persons covered) this simple division into income security and other social service agencies leads to the development of agencies that may become unwieldy in size and exhibit rigidities of large-scale organization which may be deemed inappropriate in a service so intimately concerned with the needs of people.

Furthermore, many would question whether income security programs and service programs can or should be thus sharply divorced. Thus, for example, it is sometimes held that in health programs better results would be achieved by having the agency which is in charge of health, and notably rehabilitation services, also administer whatever income security system exists for making cash payments in the event of disability.

In the United States there has been much discussion, more particularly since the Federal government began to share in the costs of medical care given to public assistance recipients, as to whether at the state or local level administrative responsibility for such a service should be vested in the public welfare or in the public health agencies. The former claim the field as the authorities already providing not only cash payments but also a variety of consulting and casework services to their clients and as the agencies which have to foot the bill (minus the Federal share) for medical services rendered their clients. On the other hand, the health authorities can claim to be the logical administrators in view of their special knowledge of the health field and health problems and their existing close relationships with the medical profession.[1]

[1] For a discussion of these viewpoints, see W. Palmer Dearing, "Medical Care for

Some have held that administrative structure should be developed on the basis of clientele. This principle has been applied from the first in regard to veterans and railroad workers, for whom all Federal social security and health measures are administered by one Federal agency (the Veterans Administration and the Railroad Retirement Board, respectively). The principle of structural organization on the basis of clientele has also been applied to programs for children.[2]

The strongest argument in favor of the principle of organization by clientele is, of course, the allegation that in this way the maximum of service can be rendered to the defined group. Since people do not consist of a bundle of separate and watertight needs, a single agency which can plan for the needs of "the whole child," "the whole aged or veteran," etc., is more likely, it is held, to develop appropriate and needed services, and the beneficiary, instead of being served by a variety of agencies with possibly conflicting or overlapping objectives, will have the convenience of dealing with only one.

Thus some public assistance agencies have held that the welfare department should operate its own employment service for its clients, on the ground that these, being often marginal workers, need special counseling or unusual care in placement, which only the welfare agency is likely to give. For it is held that the placement problems of the unemployed public assistance recipients are likely to be neglected in a public employment service, anxious to make a good placement record, intent on impressing employers with the high quality of labor it can supply, and, as an administrative arm of the unemployment insurance system, prone to give preference to unemployment insurance beneficiaries over public assistance recipients when openings occur.

But as against these claims for organization by clientele there are disadvantages. Many of the functions to be performed for the different client groups are similar in character, and if maximum quality service is to be rendered, call for a high degree of technical or professional skill and frequently for much specialization. Such standards, it is held, can best be met by a grouping of responsibilities on the basis of function; only thus will the scale of organization be sufficiently large to permit specialization, the appropriate technical division of labor, and adequate resources for research. There is also a danger of much duplication of technical functions

---

Public Assistance Recipients," *Public Health Reports,* Jan. 25, 1951, pp. 89ff.; and Selma J. Mushkin, "Medical Services and the Social Security Act Amendments of 1950," *Public Health Reports,* Jan. 25, 1951, pp. 98ff.

[2] Health and welfare services under the Social Security Act (other than ADC) were administered by the Children's Bureau, which was originally in the Department of Labor and was concerned with other programs for children, such as hours and employment legislation. More recently the Bureau has been transferred to the Department of Health, Education and Welfare.

if a large number of client-oriented agencies come into existence, each maintaining its own cluster of frequently similar services for its own clientele.

Furthermore, the adoption of the client basis of organization fosters the growth of interest groups and an administration that is likely to be, at the worst, unduly subservient to its organized clients and, at the best, unduly zealous in pushing the claims of its clientele, to the exclusion of wider interests. Indeed, this function of the administrative agency as a pressure and propagandizing group has even been urged as a major advantage of the client-oriented basis of organization in the case of the Children's Bureau, where it has been held that because children exercise no vote, some public agency should act on their behalf and promote their interests. Whatever may be felt about this theory in the case of children, more doubts have been raised when the principle is applied to the organization of services and income-maintenance systems for veterans and railroad workers. Nevertheless, so long as there is a disposition to countenance favored treatment of some categories of workers, for whatever reason, such separate administrative organization as is represented by the Railroad Retirement Board or the Veterans Administration is likely to persist.[3]

In view of the disadvantages of an administrative structure that groups all income-maintenance or all service programs in a single giant agency, or of using the clientele as the basis of organization, some have urged that administrative organization should mirror the nature of the risk. In fact, this principle is often found. One agency administers old-age programs, another unemployment or disability measures. In such a plan both temporary and permanent disability insurance would be in one agency: both long- and short-period unemployment programs would be administered by another.

From many points of view the principle of organization by risk has much to commend it. The long-period disabled or unemployed person has usually been a short-period disabled or unemployed individual first, and there is obviously a convenience to the beneficiary in dealing with one administration instead of being shifted to another at some arbitrary point of time. Furthermore, if constructive and rehabilitative measures are contemplated, everything points to the commencement of these services at as early a date as possible and to the desirability of their being undertaken by a single agency which can plan comprehensively for the needs of the unemployed or disabled worker.

[3] The success with which these two client groups have opposed proposals, made with increasing frequency after 1950, to, for example, transfer hospital care and some other medical services from the Veterans Administration to a new, comprehensive health agency or to integrate the Railroad Retirement system into OASI illustrates the influence that can be exerted by the combination of a powerful lobby of interested beneficiaries and a client-oriented agency.

Some, however, hold that the allocation of administrative responsibilities should reflect rather the nature of the administrative problems created by the different programs. According to this view, long-period disability should be administratively grouped with the other long-period risk program (old-age insurance), while temporary disability should be grouped with the agency administering short-period unemployment insurance.[4] But the principle of functional similarity has difficulties of its own, as the history of the U.S. Employment Service well illustrates. Originally the Employment Service was, logically enough, placed in the Department of Labor. With the coming of unemployment insurance, it was transferred to the then Social Security Board because of the integral relationship of this service to unemployment insurance administration. When the war elevated labor-market organization to a major national problem, the service became part of the independent War Manpower Commission, was later transferred to the Department of Labor and then back again to the Social Security Administration. Finally, in 1949, it returned to the Department of Labor together with the Bureau of Unemployment Insurance. It will be noted, however, that this solution of the problem created another: for while the employment service and unemployment insurance were now brought together, the social insurances were in consequence separated, with OASI remaining in the Social Security Administration and unemployment insurance lodged in the Department of Labor. Some advocates of the functional principle deplore this division of social insurance programs between two Federal agencies.

Enough has been said to indicate the nature of the problems faced when efforts are made to regroup the administrative organization of social security programs along more rational lines. In the United States probably the principle commanding the most general support is that which holds that the nature of the benefit system should influence administrative organization, and in particular that there should be separate administrations for the social insurances and for public assistance. However, even here, there are some who point to the integral relationship between the two types of measure and who fear that administrative separation would make it all too easy for policy decisions affecting one program to be made without taking into account the repercussions on the other.

INTERGOVERNMENTAL COOPERATION

In very few countries is administration of social security programs concentrated solely in the hands of one level of government. Even in unitary

---

[4] This view was reflected in many proposals of the administration prior to 1952 and in the publications of the Bureau of Employment Security on disability insurance. Cf. *Temporary Disability Insurance: Problems in Formulating a Program Administered by a State Employment Security Agency,* U.S. Department of Labor, Bureau of Employment Security, 1953.

countries, such as Sweden, the local authorities have been involved in several phases of administration or carry major responsibility for such measures as public assistance. And even in Great Britain, which has a highly centralized income security system wholly financed and administered by the national government, important responsibilities for the health service are still carried by the local authorities, which also administer many welfare programs intimately related to the income security services. In fact, the typical administrative structure of the social security services in most countries is one that involves at least two, and sometimes several, levels of government.

The reasons for this situation will have been clear from Chapter 11. Predominant among these, as we have seen, have been financial requirements which have fostered recourse to the fiscal resources of the larger units of government, for financial participation has inevitably been accompanied by the assumption of some measure of administrative responsibility. At the same time considerations relevant to the nature of the service rendered and the desire to avoid too great a concentration of power in the hands of a single central government have led to the adoption of a series of arrangements running from a division of the field giving exclusive responsibility for the administration of individual programs to different levels of government, to a system of shared administration. Yet whatever the current allocations of responsibility, the programs involved will have very different consequences according as certain problems of a specifically administrative character are, or are not, effectively grappled with.

In the first place, where the largest unit of government administers one or more programs and where the area over which it exercises authority is large and diversified in character, the functioning of the program will be greatly influenced by the extent to which the central office finds it possible to devolve responsibilities upon regional and district offices. This is important not only in the interest of speedy service to clients but also to ensure that, wherever possible, program operation and development may reflect the diversity of local conditions and that the average citizen may feel less remote from, and impotent in regard to, the agency administering the social service in which he is interested. Obviously the extent to which devolution is possible will vary with the nature of the program: the more the terms and conditions of benefit rights are minutely prescribed in law, the fewer will be the policy decisions which can be delegated to regional and district units of the central administration. Yet even so, as we have seen, there are practically no programs where the application of the law to the individual case does not give rise to differences of opinion between the claimant and the administrator or where there is no need for on-the-spot interpretation and explanation. Even more important is the fact that in the last resort all the income security measures are not only interrelated but also involve administrative relationships with the agencies responsible for other social services if the results are to be of maximum benefit to the individuals concerned and the community as a whole. And typically, many of these related services are administered by other levels of government. The necessary cooperation between Federal and state agencies is likely to be hindered if all local issues and working arrangements have to be negotiated through a remote central office, or if the central administration keeps a very tight hold over its regional or field units.

Difficult as it is to believe that administrative inventiveness has yet exhausted all the possibilities of modifying the rigidities of large-scale administration by a single government authority, the problems faced are perhaps less serious and difficult than those which arise when two or more levels of government share in the administration of a given program.[5] In part the extent to which joint administration proceeds harmoniously and smoothly with maximum service to those for whom the program was devised and with the minimum expenditure of the taxpayer's money will depend on whether the statutory division of functions between the partners has been clearly defined and well devised in that each is given authority commensurate with its responsibilities. It was suggested in the previous chapter, for example, that the division of functions in unemployment insurance in the United States is one well calculated to promote friction between the Federal government and the states. For not only is the Federal government charged with meeting 100 per cent of the administrative costs of a program over whose content it can exercise practically no control, but the Federal agency is also required to certify that the state laws meet the Federal requirements for employer eligibility for the tax-offset. These requirements are, however, couched in such general terms that it is understandable if, from time to time, the Federal administrators, adhering to what they believe to be the ultimate purposes of the Federal off-set provisions and calling attention to provisions of state laws which

---

[5] For further detail regarding intergovernmental administrative relationships in American social security programs, see Eveline M. Burns, *The American Social Security System*, Houghton Mifflin Company, Boston, 1951, pp. 174–184, 383–393. The proceedings of the annual meetings of the Interstate Conference of Employment Security Agencies and the American Public Welfare Association throw valuable light upon the point of view of state administrators. For some of the methods developed by the Federal government in the Federal-state public assistance programs, see *The Regional Conference: A Method in Group Consultation*, Social Security Administration, Bureau of Public Assistance, 1950; Mark P. Hale, "Some Aspects of Federal-State Relations," *Social Service Review*, June, 1954, pp. 126ff.; and Anne E. Geddes, "Federal-State Fact-finding and Research," *Social Service Review*, pp. 146ff. See also the Study Committee Reports on Federal Aid to Welfare and on Unemployment Compensation and Employment Service, issued by the Commission on Intergovernmental Relations in June, 1955.

would seem to be at variance with these purposes, find themselves charged with invading a sphere which the law has formally reserved to the states or with attempting to exercise an undue influence on the course of state legislation.[6]

But even where the allocation of the respective functions is more rational, the effectiveness of joint administration will depend on a second factor, namely the skill with which the administrators concerned can devise and operate harmonious working relationships. This is an acute problem in all grant-aided programs. The granting agency has to develop methods of control of the use of funds which protect the interests of the taxpayer, ensure the attainment of the objectives for which the grants were made, and yet do so without intruding upon the proper spheres of activity of the recipient government. Even here the outcome will in some degree be influenced by the extent to which the legislature has defined standards with specificity. Where general language is used, or important aspects of program content or administration are passed over by the authorizing legislation in silence, the agency administering the grant must issue administrative interpretations.[7] The experience of the United States with public assistance programs and unemployment insurance suggests that vigorous efforts to associate the grant-receiving administrators with the formulation of these major policies would not only be conducive to sounder program development, but also would make for more harmonious relationships between the administrators concerned.[8] The existence of

[6] Until 1954 the arrangements for Federal financing of unemployment insurance administration were calculated to promote friction in yet another way. The final determination of the amount of the administrative appropriation rests with Congress. The budget request is presented by the Federal Department of Labor on the basis of budgets prepared by the state administrators, usually after clearance with their own state budget directors. Not only do the states feel that the Federal bureau adopts an unduly restrictive attitude toward acceptance of their proposals, but until 1954 they had a real grievance in that for many years the Congress had appropriated less even than the agreed budget presented by the Secretary of Labor. Their sense of grievance was enhanced by the fact that it has generally been held that the 0.3 per cent of the employment tax retained by the Federal government was to be used to finance administrative costs, and apart from the first few years, the congressional appropriations have been consistently less than the yield of these taxes, thereby yielding a "profit" to the general Federal taxpayer at the expense of the state payroll taxpayers. In 1954 an amending act provided that from 1953 the 0.3 per cent tax would be earmarked for employment security purposes. Any excess of the yield over the appropriations for administration was to be placed in a reserve, and when this exceeded $200 million further excesses were to be credited to the state funds in proportion to the taxes their employers had paid.

[7] The experience of the Bureau of Public Assistance in the United States has also suggested that the supervisory agency has to differentiate very sharply in its interpretations between what it regards as "required" and what as "desirable" policies.

[8] In certain grant programs, such as some of those administered by the Public Health Service, the Federal administrator is required by law to consult with the appropriate state authorities.

such organizations of recipient agencies as the American Public Welfare Association and the Interstate Conference of Employment Security Agencies provides a channel through which such cooperative determination of the broad lines of policy can be implemented. At the same time, as the activities of the Interstate Conference have on occasion shown, a willingness for joint action with the federal agency must exist on the part of the recipient agencies if fruitful use is to be made of the availability of such organizations.

But even when the two levels of government successfully cooperate in the setting or interpretation of standards, the problem of ensuring compliance remains. The undesirability of ex post facto determinations of noncompliance and the social and political disadvantages of relying solely on the ultimate sanction, which usually takes the form of denial of the grants, are so obvious that supervising agencies have sought rather to develop techniques for continuous contacts between the two groups and to search for methods of control by advice and consultation rather than by fiat. The device of the administrative review, which associates the grant-receiving agency with the process of determining compliance and which aims to stress the joint interest in improving program content rather than formal compliance with each and every detailed requirement, is an example of an administrative invention which has had an important influence on the nature and quality of the program. Nevertheless, when account is taken of the fact that, at least in the United States, joint operation is so peculiarly characteristic of the social services, and when the nature of the administrative relationships between the various governmental levels involved so directly affects not only the functioning of the program but also its cost, it is surprising that more attention has not been devoted by students to the nature and effects of the administrative relationships found in the various grant-aided programs and to the search for the most effective administrative devices. It is probably not too much to say that one of the most challenging administrative problems of the future will be the discovery of ways and means of improving joint administration.

THE ADEQUACY AND QUALITY OF ADMINISTRATIVE PERSONNEL

A major problem facing all countries embarking upon extensive social security systems is that of attracting and retaining a supply of properly trained and incorruptible administrators. In the United States, the vast majority of administrative positions are held on a merit basis, but it is doubtful whether the social security services are as yet adequately staffed or offer salaries which attract a sufficient number of administrators with the necessary training and of the high caliber called for in a service which affects so intimately the lives of millions of citizens and which accounts for almost 5 per cent of personal incomes.⁹ Whether or not the social security services will in the future be adequately and appropriately staffed depends upon several factors.

The first of these is the importance attached by the community as a whole to constructive social service. If emphasis is placed solely upon assurance of income, this can, it is true, be accomplished by relatively automatic methods calling for little more than accurate record keeping and the devising of machinery for the distribution of payments and verification of formal eligibility requirements. Such conditions would be satisfied by a universal pension system, such as the Canadian over-70 pension. The social insurances, however, make greater demands on administrative personnel, for as was shown in Part One, it has proved impossible wholly to eliminate from these programs all elements of administrative discretion. Furthermore, these programs are complex and technical in character and at the policy-making levels in particular call for highly trained and intelligent administrators. The public assistances, dealing as they do with applicants on an individual basis and involving a high degree of administrative discretion, would seem to need for their administration persons not only well trained in methods of establishing constructive human relationships with applicants for assistance but also aware of the broader social and economic implications of day-to-day policy decisions on individual cases.

Many communities are, however, not content to equip themselves merely with institutions for assuring continuity of income. Both economic self-interest and a concern for the well-being of people have pointed to the desirability of restoring to self-support as many as possible of the recipients of socially provided income. Social services with this object in view cannot be staffed by untrained persons. The services of medical men, psychologists, social workers, vocational rehabilitation experts, employment counselors, to mention only a few professions, then become essential. Furthermore, the proportion of administrators per case treated inevitably rises. The caseworker carrying a caseload of 200 to 300 cannot give his clients the

⁹ The salary level is higher at the Federal level than in most states and localities. In 1950, for the country as a whole, the median salary of social workers was $2,950, and in the public assistance agencies throughout the nation, the average salary of directors of offices was only $3,550. Director-workers, who ran offices alone or with a staff of less than six, averaged only $2,742, while supervisors averaged $3,383. For further details, see Ellen J. Perkins and Charles J. Lopes, "Public Assistance Employees: Their Salaries," *Social Security Bulletin*, March, 1952. In workmen's compensation "low salaries, lack of tenure and absence of bona fide merit systems for hiring and retention of personnel combine to give the administrative agencies their poor reputations. The problem is aggravated by the extraordinary range and complexity of technical competence required in compensation administration. Except in a handful of states, even top officials and technicians are paid notoriously low salaries." (Herman Miles Somers and Anne Ramsay Somers, *Workmen's Compensation*, John Wiley & Sons, Inc., New York, 1954, pp. 147–148.)

supportive and constructive services likely to be needed if a return to self-support is to be achieved. The restoration of the disabled worker to some degree of capacity to work often takes months or years during which he receives services from a variety of experts. So long as the community attaches little value to these more constructive social services, there will be an unwillingness to allocate the resources necessary to proper staffing. It seems likely that to some extent public attitudes, and hence the willingness to pay the necessary price for proper administration, reflect the extent of knowledge or ignorance of what is comprised in the administration of the social services. So long as the view prevails that this involves little more than automatic record keeping and expeditious handling on a routine basis of large numbers of applicants or claimants, the taxpayers are unlikely to provide for the administration of the social services sums commensurate with the importance of these programs to the individuals directly affected and to the community as a whole. How to secure wider public understanding of the potentialities of effective administration remains in many countries an unsolved problem.

In the second place, however, the likelihood that the social services will be adequately staffed will be influenced by the behavior and attitudes of the professions involved and their willingness to consider the public interest in establishing staffing requirements and in their demands for remuneration and other conditions of employment. As Professor Titmuss has stated, "Professional associations are not the only repositories of knowledge, but they are the repositories of a very special kind of knowledge; and the establishment of proper relations between them and the democratic state is, today, one of the urgent problems affecting the future of the social services." [10] Two aspects of professional behavior call for comment. One is the need for a continuing appraisal by the professions concerned of the types of service or administration that call for highly and expensively trained personnel as against those which, under appropriate professional supervision, could be carried out by less well-trained auxiliary workers. More than one government has had differences of opinion with professional organizations regarding the nature of the services which could appropriately be carried out by, for example, dental assistants or nurses rather than fully trained dentists. Similarly, social workers, in their eagerness to protect their professional status, have sometimes made too far-reaching demands for the staffing of the social services solely by graduate social workers. Yet the public interest requires of the professions, notably when they function as part of a public service, an eternal vigilance to ensure that no service that could, under appropriate supervision, be rendered effectively by a less well-trained worker shall be re-

[10] Richard M. Titmuss, "Social Administration in a Changing Society," *The British Journal of Sociology,* September, 1951, p. 193.

served by professional rigidities for the fully qualified professional.[11]

The second challenge to the professionals participating in the administration of a public program is to refrain from exploiting their monopoly position when pressing demands for remuneration and working conditions. For here, too, if the taxpayers believe that advantage is being taken of the professional monopoly to extort conditions for employment that are felt to be out of line with those of other differently but equally highly qualified workers, the social services may well experience difficulty in securing adequate appropriations for administration.[12]

BUREAUCRACY AND DEMOCRATIC ADMINISTRATION

The last, and perhaps the most important, of all the major administrative problems confronting countries operating extensive social security systems is how to ensure a truly democratic administration of these programs. For as we have seen, the general tendency is toward the development of large administrative agencies staffed by professional administrators or at least by civil servants protected by tenure rights. This situation gives rise to two dangers: first that the administration may become out of touch with the needs and wishes of those whom it was brought into being to serve; second, that the public may come to rely too heavily upon its professional or civil servants and to concern itself so little with what is done in its name as to be poorly prepared to make intelligent and balanced decisions when the need for policy changes becomes evident.

Hitherto, in the United States, public interest in the nature and operation of social security programs has tended to be concentrated and intense during brief periods of legislative activity or has been evident mainly on the part of self-interested pressure groups anxious to mold existing programs to their own interests. There has been much less evidence of continuing concern over the day-to-day operation of the programs or

[11] "Each profession makes progress, but it is progress in its own groove. . . . The fixed person for the fixed duties, who in older societies was such a godsend, in the future will be a public menace. The dangers arising from this aspect of professionalism are particularly great in democratic societies. . . ." (A. N. Whitehead, quoted in *ibid.*)

[12] Thus Professor Titmuss has drawn attention to the favored position of professional workers under the health services in Great Britain. "The great expansion of the social services in recent years has been accompanied by the introduction and extension of some of the most generous public superannuation schemes in the world. . . . At a time when men and women are urged to continue in work up to the age of seventy the State is committed to the payment of superannuation at a lower age to some 1,500,000 professional and technical workers and administrators." (*Ibid.*, p. 191.) The disproportionate space devoted to the sections on conditions of employment in the interest of protecting the professional status of the social worker in the Code of Ethics of the American Association of Social Workers may indicate a similar tendency to subordinate efficient and economical rendering of service to the interests of the professional group.

the reasons for the results achieved or not achieved. In part the problem is one for which the voters have themselves to blame: namely a lack of information about what is in fact happening. Legislators, presumably reflecting what they believe to be the views of their constituents, tend to take a dim view of appropriations for research by operating agencies and are especially suspicious of appropriations for information departments. While it can be admitted that it is not always easy to draw the line between the giving of necessary information and propaganda looking toward the aggrandizement of the agency concerned, it seems difficult not to conclude that the sums devoted to research and dissemination of information are far out of line with the importance of contemporary social security programs in the social and economic life of the people who have enacted them.

It is also true that even when appropriations have been available, not all administrators have realized the importance of presenting information about their program in a form that assures wide publicity and an interested audience, nor have they always had the courage to take the public into their confidence. And unfortunately the lack of reliable and relevant information from public sources has not in general been compensated for by the devotion by the private welfare agencies or the large private foundations of substantial sums for research in this important area of social policy.

In part, however, the problem of how to ensure truly democratic administration of social security programs is one of devising techniques for enlisting lay participation in appropriate phases of administration and policy formation. A number of devices has been experimented with in the United States and other countries. One of the most widely used is the advisory council which is attached to the headquarters of the administration and which may either consider issues on reference from the legislature or the administrator or do so on its own motion. But the device of the advisory council raises many unsolved problems. One of these concerns its composition. In most countries such councils consist of representatives of employers, workers, and the general public. Yet it seems likely that this tripartite principle is increasingly out of keeping with the realities of modern social security systems which cover also independent workers and provide benefits for some people, such as widowed mothers, who may not be involved in employment relationships as such, or parents who in many countries benefit from children's allowances regardless of their employment status. Furthermore, where representation is based on such highly organized groups as employers and workers, there appears to be a tendency for the council members representing the two groups to consist more and more of the technical or expert bureaucracy of the organizations concerned. Such individuals will bring to the council

a high degree of technical knowledge (which may, however, have the disadvantage of causing major policy issues to be submerged in discussion of
technical detail), and their position as representatives of their organizations may enlighten the administrator as to the viewpoints of the groups
concerned if he does not already know them. But such a council will
hardly serve the purpose of diffusing among the wider citizenry a better
understanding of the fundamental problems at issue and of the character
of the administration, or even of resolving differences of point of view, for
the technical official is seldom free to commit his organization or firm.
There is sometimes a tendency, too, to select as public representatives persons who are notable rather for their professional competence in the fields
concerned than for the influence they exert with particular segments of
the lay public.

The composition of such councils, however, is not the only problem
which challenges ingenuity. Perhaps even more important is the discovery of ways and means whereby their deliberations can influence public thinking and legislative action. In this, some countries have been
notably more successful than others. While part of the difference in
influence may be due to formal legal provisions (e.g., some countries
require the administrator to present the views of his council in making
legislative proposals and where he differs from them to state his reasons),
the more important determinants still evade analysis.[13]

In public assistance systems administrative boards of lay persons with
varying powers are very common. Here again, their effectiveness is in large
measure dependent on the character of their membership and in particular on the extent to which it truly reflects the various interests in the
community. In the United States there is some evidence of excessive
representation of the more solid citizens and the relatively well-to-do to
the neglect of representatives either of workers or of groups able to speak
for the beneficiaries. The crucial, and as yet unsolved, problems to which
the use of lay boards gives rise are (1) how to draw the line between those
matters which are appropriate for lay, as opposed to technical or professional, consideration and determination and (2) how to ensure that each
group respects the line as drawn. Because the units of administration of
public assistance are often small and because, as we have seen, decisions
as to eligibility and payments in the individual case are less precisely
defined by law than in social insurance systems, there appears to have
been some tendency for such bodies to take over some of the functions of
the administrator in dealing with individual cases, to the neglect of con-

[13] A study of the different status, authority, and influence of the British Statutory
Committee on Unemployment Insurance and of the American Federal Advisory Council
on Employment Security might yield some suggestive clues.

sideration of the wider policy issues or evaluation of the operation of the program as a whole.

Another type of effort to secure lay participation is seen in the care with which some social security systems, such as the British, enlist the cooperation of employers and workers, on a decentralized basis, in appeals procedures for unemployment insurance or for advising on certain policies of the employment service. Such arrangements have at least the advantage of acquainting a considerable number of individuals with the problems faced by the administrator and serve to keep administration in line with prevailing industrial practices and standards.

The method adopted in France, and some other European countries, of entrusting administration to a semiautonomous body governed by lay persons representative of employers and workers (or beneficiaries), with the latter usually in the majority, is another type of attempt at democratizing administration. The degree of popular interest in social security programs thereby aroused is, however, inevitably limited by the restricted range of responsibilities necessarily permitted to such organizations in a public system where rates of benefit, eligibility conditions, and amount of contributions are in any case fixed by law and for the nation as a whole. In France elections for board membership appear to reflect political party affiliations rather than viewpoints on social security issues.[14] Such a system undoubtedly permits more lay participation in the day-to-day dealing with individual cases and, in the French system at least, gives considerable leeway for the expenditure of certain funds available for auxiliary services according to locally expressed needs. Some have, however, asserted that being so largely controlled by workers and in effect by organized workers, positions in the administration are filled on the basis of union service or membership, to the detriment of quality. And in any event, such a system is administratively very complex.

The device of the legislative, and notably the congressional, hearing, as developed in the United States, is undoubtedly a valuable method of keeping legislators in touch with the views of the more vocal and highly organized groups. It is more questionable whether it secures adequate representation of public opinion in general: the organized group and the one able to devote large resources to the preparation of an effective brief is at a big advantage. Furthermore, a study of the amount of time allocated to the different groups at the average hearing raises real questions as to the basis on which allocations of time are often made. Professional

[14] For a brief account of the French system, see Barbara Rodgers, "Social Security in France: Part I," *Public Administration* [London], Spring, 1954, pp. 390ff.; and for a fuller account, "Elections sociales et élections politiques," a colloquium, *Revue française de science politique,* Paris, April–June, 1953, pp. 221–297.

and other well-organized groups frequently appear to be given an opportunity to present their views that is excessive in proportion to their numbers in the total population. In any case, the congressional hearing can at best acquaint the legislator with the viewpoint of his organized constituents. It does little to enlighten the average voter regarding the facts and the real issues involved unless he is sufficiently patient to attempt to distill the truth from the welter of assertions and counter-assertions as to the effect of measures actual or proposed. Nor, as a general rule, does the sober, fact-laden hearing command a high priority in the columns of the daily press.

By the mid-century social security programs had come to be so common a feature of contemporary societies that they affected directly and indirectly the life or the pocketbook of almost every member of the population. No problem created by this situation is more challenging than that of devising ways and means of giving a larger number of citizens a knowledge of what is and is not being achieved by these measures, some understanding of the range of issues at stake, and some opportunity of participating, in appropriate ways, in the continuing operation and, in the widest sense, in the administration of their social security institutions.

PART FIVE

Conclusion

CHAPTER 14

The Choice of Social Security Policies

IT WILL HAVE BEEN OBVIOUS from the preceding chapters that societies seeking to assure a greater measure of economic security for their members through the enactment of social security legislation have available to them a variety of instruments, in the form of social inventions or techniques, such as social insurance, public assistance, the income-conditioned pension, or the statutory payment. Furthermore, each of these systems is capable of considerable diversification. The social and economic effects of a social insurance system that pays benefits related to the previous earnings of those covered will be very different from those of one which pays flat rates of benefit. And as we have seen, different results are also achieved by different types of eligibility conditions, different levels of benefits, different methods of financing, and different kinds or standards of administration even in systems that belong in the same general category. But what makes the study of the efforts of societies to achieve social security even more fascinating and challenging is the fact that the effects of any particular system with all its detailed provisions will be greatly influenced at any given time by the character of the prevailing economic and social environment.

The Underlying Determinants

Some of these features of contemporary societies which are of especial relevance to social security planning can be identified without too much difficulty. Thus it is clear that the general level of productivity in a country will greatly influence the form of social security system which will be favored and feasible. A high-level economy is likely both to stimulate a concern about the plight of those who do not share in the general prosperity and also to make it more possible to do something about it. For, on the one hand, the difference between the well-being of those who are fully employed or securing income from property and those who because of old age, sickness, unemployment, or loss of a breadwinner are deprived of such income becomes ever more pronounced and increasingly challenges the public conscience. Furthermore, it is clear from the experience of most countries which have enacted social security systems that the idea of what is an appropriate standard of living to be assured those who are less fortunate tends to be affected by the standard of living of the rest of the population. But on the other hand the highly productive economy is better equipped to handle the problem and has available to it a wider choice of techniques. It is, for example, much easier for the high-level economy to assure social security benefits that are both adequate for maintenance and provide differentials above the maintenance minimum, because the relatively high level of wages leaves room for a considerable margin between the income to be secured from "adequate" security benefits and that to be obtained by active participation in production. And at the same time, the burden of supporting any given number of nonproducers will be less onerous the higher are the incomes of the vast mass of the current producers. With a rising standard of output, indeed, it may be possible greatly to improve the economic circumstances of current nonproducers and still to permit an upward trend in the disposable income of the taxpayers. The poor society, however, faces many more difficulties, and may well have to forego some of the types of social security system that are available to the richer.

Economic conditions also influence the development of social security systems in other ways. The extent of irregularity of operation of industry and the character of the resulting unemployment will directly affect the types of risk for which a society will feel it important to plan. It is no accident that since World War II, despite the great expansion and development of social security systems all over the world, relatively little attention has been paid to creating unemployment insurance schemes, and even in the United States, as we have seen, no formal program or policy has been developed for providing income for those who have exhausted unemployment insurance benefits.

In another sphere, the attitude of, for example, the disabled worker to undergoing rehabilitation which, while increasing his employability, will deprive him of an assured pension will be very different according as he lives in an economy of high employment or makes his decision at a time of widespread unemployment. Societies which have an excess labor supply or which countenance discrimination against the employment of the aged or elderly are scarcely likely to look with much favor on proposals for a high age of eligibility for old-age benefits or for measures which would put pressure on the aged to remain in the labor market.

The types of employment relationships characteristic of society at any given time also influence the economic impact of specific provisions of the social security laws. Where arrangements exist which cause value to be attached by the worker to as continuous a contact as possible with his customary employer (such as fringe benefits, seniority rights, prospects of promotion from within, and the like), the risk that guaranteed benefit payments may cause some to prefer benefit status to employment if available will be less than if the job carries no rights or advantages beyond the payment of a weekly wage.

The level of employment affects too the specific problems faced in operating social security systems. The problem of the "voluntary quit" in unemployment insurance, for instance, is likely to arise primarily in a high-employment economy when workers believe in the reality of full employment and are no longer afraid to sacrifice the security of the job they hold for the chance of bettering their economic position elsewhere. Similarly, the effectiveness of controls designed to protect society against malingering varies with employment conditions. In high employment the requirement to register at an employment office may serve as an efficient protection against the work-shy; when the demand for labor is less intense, other controls may have to be devised.

The socioeconomic configuration of societies also has a direct bearing upon the nature and extent of the social security programs likely to be favored and upon the effects of whatever measures are selected. The influence of a change in the age composition of the population has been noted at various points in the preceding chapters. An increase in the proportion of the aged affects both the intensity of the pressure to make some provision for this group and also the real economic cost of doing so. If long continued, it may initiate a growing concern about the birth rate and lead to reconsiderations of social policy, including social security measures, with a view to improving the relative economic position of the age groups who today are at a relative disadvantage economically, namely married people with children. Similarly the increasing tendency of married women to engage in gainful employment even when they have young children and the development of day nurseries compel reconsideration of certain social security programs which have been developed on the theory that the normal life for a child is in a home in which the mother is not employed.

In the same way, the changing role of the family system inevitably affects social security policy. If other social and economic developments conspire to weaken the sense of family economic solidarity, a social security program that presupposes a degree of mutual support which no longer corresponds to economic realities and current mores will prove difficult to administer and enforce.

The state of technical knowledge and administrative inventiveness also directly influences the ways in which societies will find it possible to provide for the economic security of their members and the results of whatever measures are selected at any given time. Reference has been made at a number of points throughout this book to the influence of administrative skills on program content. The state of these techniques influences not only coverage of social insurance plans but also the nature of the benefit provisions. It would hardly have been possible, for example, so economically to operate a program, such as OASI, which calls for maintaining detailed records of a highly mobile working population over a forty- or fifty-year period had it not been for the development of business machines of a high degree of specialization and efficiency. Nor, in the absence of such aids, might the complicated experience-rating systems adopted in some states have proved feasible. The effects of joint operation of social security programs by several levels of government are in large measure dependent on administrative inventions: in this case the development of effective and acceptable controls and methods of supervision and cooperation. The rigors of a federal program may be greatly modified by administrative ingenuity in devising methods of decentralization. And at all times the efficient operation of social security programs is dependent upon the extent to which any country can devise methods of recruiting and maintaining a civil service that is both generally competent and honest and free from political influence.

Even more broadly, human ingenuity directly influences the way in which countries solve their social security problems, through the invention of specific social forms or structures or techniques which provide a convenient instrument for implementing certain objectives. Two such social inventions have been of great importance in the field of social security during this century, namely the invention of social insurance and the invention of the children's allowance. Both can be said to be truly revolutionary in that once these social institutions were conceived, their availability became a potent influence toward social change.

Social attitudes and values form a further readily identifiable feature of societies. They profoundly affect both the type of system likely to be favored at any given time and the social and economic effects of the programs adopted. Among them the more relevant to social security policies seem to be the value attached by the members of the community to economic welfare and a high standard of living for themselves and their families; the prevailing attitudes toward conformity with certain patterns of behavior, such as assuming responsibility for the support of oneself and one's family; attitudes toward status and the precise attributes which are held to confer status; attitudes toward the use of means tests; attitudes toward the desirability in principle of greater or lesser inequality of incomes; and attitudes toward government activity as such.

The society whose members place great value on attainment of a high and constantly rising standard of living will experience less difficulty in connection with the possible impact on initiative of income security programs that assure everyone a modest competence than will one where the desire for individual economic advancement is less developed or nonexistent. From this point of view it might be said that a society such as the American, which through its highly developed advertising institutions strives constantly to condition its members to desire ever more goods and services, is in a peculiarly advantageous position to develop social security systems of a high degree of liberality. Attitudes toward conformity with certain norms of behavior are also important in this connection. Where the individual who does not conform to the accepted pattern of economic behavior, such as undertaking productive employment, suffers a loss of status or develops feelings of inferiority and a sense of exclusion from free participation in the usual activities of his fellows, where, in short, he develops a sense of inadequacy if he does not conform to the generally approved pattern, such pressures reinforce other stimuli to self-support and render much easier the task of assuring an adequate minimum of security without adverse effects on the total volume of output.

But status feelings have other impacts also on the form and effects of social security systems. A society which attaches importance to money income as an indicator of status and which further believes that income differentials should extend over the whole of a man's life will hardly look with favor on a social security system paying uniform benefits to all eligible persons. For many years and in many countries dependence on a particular type of social security system, namely public assistance, has been held to involve a loss of social status. So long as this is so, it is to be expected that if the economically disadvantaged are in a position to exercise political influence, they will press for the substitution of this system by some other. And it may even be possible to offer on the alternative system benefits that yield less to the beneficiary than would public assistance, precisely because recourse to it is not held to involve a loss of social status. But a change in certain features of public assistance and vigorous propaganda directed to enhancing the status of recipients of public assistance may change public attitudes and lead to a reevaluation of the relative merits of the two programs.

Attitudes toward the necessity of undergoing a test of need or a means test have been especially significant in molding social security policies in many countries. It would hardly be possible, for example, to explain the evolution of the British social security system, with its effort to provide through social insurance for as many types of interruption of incomes as possible, unless account was taken of the extremely strong dislike of submitting to a test of need, which had come to symbolize for the average worker the repressive poor law of the previous century. Something of the same attitude to a needs test as such seems to prevail in the United States and, as we have seen, has been invoked as a reason for a preference for the social insurance technique. On the other hand, in both New Zealand and Australia, where a precisely defined income test has replaced a more general and discretionary test of need, extensive social security systems have developed which utilize hardly at all the social insurance principle.

Of particular importance in influencing the nature and provisions of social security systems has been the prevailing attitude toward inequality of incomes. In the absence of any strong democratic tendency even the existence of large incomes which can be tapped to support public programs is no guarantee that there will be an adequate social security system, as the experience of several Latin American and Eastern countries has shown. Conversely, in the event of a conflict between attainment of a relatively high degree of assured income for all citizens and other objectives, such as maximizing output or maintaining the highest possible degree of independence for the smallest units of government, the society which regards greater equality of incomes as a positive good may well select the former and regard the sacrifice of other values as a small price to pay for attainment of the goal to which it attaches a high priority. Similarly, as we have seen, attitudes toward inequality of incomes have directly influenced the types of taxes selected for the financing of social security programs.

Finally, attitudes toward government activity as such play an important role. The society that regards its organized government as a dangerous and uncontrollable authority whose powers and activities must be kept to a minimum or which holds governmental agencies to be inherently inefficient or corrupt will display much more resistance to proposals for extensions of public action, such as the various social security measures which have been discussed in the preceding pages. In contrast to those countries, such as Great Britain, which appear to regard government merely as the most effective of several possible institutions for the administration of income security programs or for the provision of services and which believe that the public agency can be kept under control and made responsive to the wishes of the citizenry, a society that distrusts its government is likely to seek to organize its social security services in such a way as to keep government activity to a minimum. It will be likely to favor methods which allow the maximum participation in financing and administration of private organizations and agencies (such as trade unions and organized beneficiaries in France or private insurance companies and private health insurance concerns in the United States) and will probably make use of the instrument of government only if long experience with other methods demonstrates that the desired results can be achieved in no other way.

One other but extremely important determinant of the effect of given social security measures must be noted. This is the extent to which they do or do not form part of a comprehensive and constructive attack upon the evils of which income interruption or the need for medical care are but symptoms. A public assistance program limited to paying cash benefits which does not simultaneously provide medical and social services designed to restore as many recipients as possible to self-support may be properly charged with perpetuating the social ills attributable to poverty. Experience of many countries has shown that a disability insurance program can be a positive force assisting in the recovery of earning power or a perpetuation of a state of dependence on community support according as it is or is not developed as part of a network of constructive services directed primarily to the rehabilitation of the disabled person. In unemployment insurance the implications of this situation have been recognized in principle from the first. Efforts have always been made, in part as a by-product of administrative controls, to put the unemployed worker in touch with employment opportunities. Yet even here, in too many instances an undesirably limited view has prevailed of the responsibilities of the employment service, and inadequate resources have been devoted to constructive services to increase the employability of certain categories of workers, marginal by reference to prevailing employer specifications, such as the aged, the long-period unemployed, or the disabled. Similarly the effects and costs of a health service will be in large measure influenced by the extent to which it is conceived of merely as a curative service or is envisaged as concerned fundamentally with prevention, and curative only in so far as the preventive objective is not achieved. Even more broadly, the economic effects of income security systems are directly influenced by the degree of success attending efforts to maintain a high level of employment.

Although there is considerable difference between countries in the extent to which they thus conceive of income security measures as an integral part of a broader attack upon the problem of interruptions of income (and hence a difference in the social and economic impact of their specific income security programs), it is probably true to say that in general over the last half century public policy has tended to concentrate on amelioration of the situation of individuals and families suffering from interruption of income (in itself a major social challenge) to the relative neglect of the broader problem of prevention. The mounting costs of income security programs may, however, in the years ahead act as a spur to the development of constructive and preventive programs, even though for a time their operation will involve a further extension of government activity. From this point of view the increasing attention paid in recent years to measures for maintaining high employment and the expansion of public health activities are encouraging signs.

The Implications for Policy

These facts suggest certain conclusions important both for the study of social security problems and for the formation of policy in this increasingly significant area of social legislation. The first of these is the unreliability, and indeed the danger, of facile generalizations as to the social and economic effects of social security programs. Assertions as to the effect of "social security" on freedom, on initiative, on mobility are meaningless unless related to a specific program and a specific environment. For, as we have seen, at any given time the different types of social security program will have very different effects, and their precise nature can be ascertained only by detailed analysis of the specific provisions regarding benefits, eligibility conditions, methods of financing, and nature of administration of each individual program. In addition, the same program will have different effects if there are changes in the social and economic environment. It is this fact which suggests caution in too facile a use of the experience of other countries: such comparisons are relevant to domestic policy formation only if the utmost care is taken to ensure that the basic social and economic structure and the social values of the countries in question are approximately similar. It follows, too, as will be emphasized below, that the appropriateness of any set of social security institutions to the needs of any given country calls for periodic reassessment as the environment changes.

The second broad consideration which is suggested by the analysis of the preceding chapters is that it is unwise, and indeed both arrogant and undemocratic, to assume that any one set of considerations or values should prevail in the determination of policy. It may indeed be possible to show, for example, that the effect of certain social measures is to lower the general level of output. But, as has been abundantly clear from our analysis of the forces influencing public policy decisions, men attach value not only to economic considerations but to other ends as well. The willingness to sacrifice the maximum of economic output in order to ensure a distribution of income that commends itself to the majority as being more acceptable and socially stable can be condemned as "irrational" or "unwise" only if it is made without adequate knowledge of the *degree* of sacrifice of output accompanying the selected redistributional measures. Similarly it is often possible to show that certain administrative arrangements, and notably those which allocate administrative responsibility to one level of government or another on the basis of values attached to "local self-government" or "states rights," are ill adapted to secure the maximum of equality of access to minimum security or, to cite another type of objective, the maximum of labor mobility. Yet to assert that one set of values is inherently superior to another is to claim an omniscience or an authority that is perhaps understandable on the part of interested partisans in the heat of political argument but which cannot be reconciled with the practice of the democratic form of government. For in the last resort, in a democracy, the values which commend themselves to the majority must prevail.

In the third place, the analysis of the preceding chapters suggests an important and sobering consideration for policy formation. It is that policy can never be fixed once and for all. A program that is appropriate to the needs and circumstances of any given country at the time it is adopted may later prove to be highly inappropriate if needs and the environmental conditions change.[1] The selection of an appropriate age at which old-age benefits may be claimed will vary with the changing demographic configuration of a country. So will the decision as to the proportions of national income to be channeled via social security systems to the aged as a group as compared to the young or the population of working age. The state of the labor market will influence the extent to which unemployed workers are put under pressure to take unaccustomed jobs or to undertake retraining as a condition of eligibility for unemployment insurance. The use of an employer contribution may make sense when a program is first introduced if it is felt necessary to use the employer as a fiscal agent of the government, or to reconcile workers to the demand that they too help to pay for their own security, or because the program is new and it appears important to assure it a certain and earmarked source of revenue. But it may make much less sense if treasuries have as part of their general fiscal procedures developed methods (including the withholding tax) for collecting taxes from workers and small-income receivers, or if workers have accepted the desirability of paying something toward the costs of their social security benefits, or if the system has been in effect so long, covers the vast mass of the voting population, and is so generally accepted as being a "normal" function of government that the likelihood of a failure of the legislature to provide adequate funds for its support is minuscule.

In particular, it must not be forgotten that among the factors making for change is the very adoption and continuous functioning of social security systems over a period of years. Many social security programs contain provisions which were necessary and justifiable at a time when the programs were first introduced and when it was essential to embody certain safeguards to reassure those who feared the consequences of a

[1] Cf. Eveline M. Burns, "Social Insurance in Evolution," *American Economic Review Supplement*, March, 1944; and Richard M. Titmuss, "Social Administration in a Changing Society," *The British Journal of Sociology*, September, 1951, especially pp. 189ff.

new experiment in methods of providing for the economically insecure. Many features of contemporary programs mirror the degree of administrative inexperience that necessarily prevailed when these new social inventions were first adopted. But a country in which every worker has been born into a world in which it is as natural for his government to operate institutions guaranteeing him some minimum income in the event that he should, for various specified reasons, be unable to participate in production as it is that government should provide him with roads, police, and education has available to it a much greater range of alternative methods of providing this security than one introducing such measures for the first time. It is not only that greater administrative experience has been gained: more important is the fact that the members of the community have had an opportunity to live with such programs, to reach a more secure judgment of their social and economic effects, and to adjust their behavior patterns to the new circumstances. The experience of most countries with the income tax illustrates the same point. The effects upon enterprise of the high tax levels found in many countries by the mid-1950s would probably have been disastrous had they been imposed when income taxes were first introduced. Fortunately for governments, however, attitudes of taxpayers to what is reasonable or normal appear to be primarily influenced by what they have been accustomed to in the relatively recent past.

One of the more important by-products of the continuing operation of social security systems, which has a tremendous impact on future policy development, is that for the first time the community begins to obtain comprehensive and reliable data as to the extent of the social risks, concern about which led to the introduction of these measures in the first place. It also obtains data about the costs of the various programs and the manner in which their benefits are distributed. This information facilitates more rational policy formation. It may lead to the adoption of new programs for groups whose needs are for the first time identified and their extent known. It may result in more constructive efforts looking toward prevention of those interruptions to income whose true cost is for the first time accurately known. For so long as the costs of inability to work, and hence of lack of income, are diffused among the community in the form of a lowering of the living standard of the individuals and families concerned, or of burdens thrown upon relatives, or even of costs carried by thousands of small political subdivisions, their seriousness may not be appreciated by the community as a whole. A public commitment to provide alternative income on some standard basis and on satisfaction of specified eligibility conditions permits the accumulation of data on a unified and comparable basis and reveals for the first time the true extent of need and the cost of providing for it.

The Role of the Social Scientist

It is clear that the development of social security systems represents the search by the community for the best possible compromise between conflicting desires and social values. In the face of this search the question may well arise as to the role of the social scientist and more particularly the specialist in social security legislation and policy. In fact it would seem that he has an important part to play.

In the first place, intelligent policy formation, i.e., the attainment of the best possible compromise between conflicting objectives, can be expected only if people know what they are choosing between. And the choice is not of an "either-or" character but between relatively more and relatively less. There are no absolutes. In essence the process is one long familiar to the economist, namely the application of the marginal principle. Rational policy formation requires that the community should know *how much,* e.g., decline or gain, in national output will result from any specific proposal; *how much* diminution of insecurity is likely to result from adoption of any given measure; *what degree* of economic burden will be thrown on various categories of taxpayers by alternative methods of financing; *how much* stabilization of employment results from experience-rating; *to what degree* a contributory requirement induces more responsible use of the service; *what proportion* of workers are likely to malinger and to be deterred by what kinds of controls; and the like. Only with this more precise knowledge can rational choices be made.

Again and again throughout this book attention has been drawn to the many instances in which there is a disturbing lack of knowledge of the precise effects of the various provisions of the different types of social security systems. Again and again it has been shown that societies include provisions in their laws because of a belief that individuals are motivated to economic activity by certain desires or stimuli or because they believe that these legal provisions will have certain economic or social results. Yet many of these assumptions are untested, and until they are verified there can be no assurance that the social security institutions are well adapted to the needs and circumstances of the nation. Here, then, is one area where the expert can contribute fruitfully to policy formation, by tracing as precisely as possible the effects of the different programs and legal and administrative provisions and by subjecting to rigorous scrutiny the assumptions, both express and implied, as to human motivation, especially in the economic sphere, which underlie the specific provisions of the individual programs.

There is a second and even more challenging and difficult task for the social scientist. Precisely because the nature and structure of social institutions, including those concerned with social security, must in the last resort be adjusted to the values and social and economic characteristics of the society in which they function, it is desirable that changes in these underlying determinants be identified as speedily as possible. The alternative is a long period of friction during which efforts are made to operate programs embodying a social philosophy and a set of values which have ceased to command general support or which presume the existence of certain social and economic conditions which are no longer characteristic of the society. It is the social scientist who should be in a position to hasten the process of change and shorten the period of friction, by identifying those social and economic characteristics, including currently held values, of any given society which are peculiarly relevant for social security policy formation, by drawing attention to significant changes as and when they occur, and, even more helpfully, by establishing probable future trends.[2]

Even when armed with this much greater scientific knowledge, contemporary societies will, of course, face difficult choices between simultaneously held but competing values or objectives. Although the alleged conflict between security and freedom no longer appears on careful examination to be a real one,[3] there are other competing values. The precise balance between adequacy and equity in the determination of social insurance benefits, between equal access to minimum security and retention of the principle of local autonomy, between the interests of different social classes in allocating the costs of social security measures, or between the claims of family obligations and responsibilities to the wider community illustrate the nature of these ultimate and difficult value choices. Yet while there is no guarantee that democracies will act rationally in formulating their social policies, it is also abundantly clear that they cannot even be expected to do so unless they are made aware of the full implications of the choices available to them.

[2] For the role of social scientists in the development of the American social security system and the influence of contemporary value judgments and political considerations, see Edwin E. Witte, "Twenty Years of Social Security," *Social Security Bulletin,* October, 1955, pp. 15–21.

[3] Cf. the conclusions of the American Assembly in *Economic Security for Americans: Final Edition,* Third American Assembly, Columbia University Press, New York, 1954, pp. 7–11; and those of the Conference on Income Security for a Free People, in James E. Russell (ed.), *National Policies for Education, Health and Social Services,* Doubleday & Company, New York, 1955, pp. 244–409.

Name Index

Allen, Henry D., 222
Altmeyer, Arthur J., 65
Anderson, Odin W., 146
Arndt, Hilda C. M., 65, 88

Bachrach, Peter, 116
Baikie, E. J., 236
Ball, Robert M., 191, 197
Becker, Joseph M., 57, 58
Benson, George C. S., 236
Berlioz, Charles, 120
Beveridge, William H. (Lord), 91, 93, 157, 158, 207
Bickley, John S., 180, 181, 184
Bierman, Pearl, 128
Bigge, George, 236
Birch, A. H., 217
Blackwell, G., 86
Bond, Floyd, 20, 22, 23, 66, 82, 83
Brown, J. Douglas, 40
Brown, W. R., 83
Browning, P. R., 174
Burns, Arthur F., 206
Burns, Eveline M., 10, 22, 28, 29, 35, 37, 60, 74, 93, 115, 153, 207, 223, 236, 257, 277
Butler, Hugh, 24

Calhoun, Leonard J., 169
Campbell, R. R., 146
Campbell, W. W., 146
Carlson, Frank, 235
Chester, D. N., 238
Civic, Miriam, 29
Cohen, Wilbur J., 86, 197
Cornell, Francis G., 240
Corson, John J., 99
Crowther, Beatrice, 39, 162, 218, 246, 247
Cruickshank, Nelson H., 33, 40, 190
Curry, R. B., 90
Curtis, Carl, 35

Dahim, Margaret M., 118, 181
Davis, Joseph S., 105
Davis, Michael M., 127, 128, 146
Dawson, Marshall, 183
Dearing, W. Palmer, 252
Dejardin, Jerome, 122, 124
Deutsch, Albert, 88
Dickinson, Frank G., 146
Durand, Paul, 173, 190

Eberling, Ernest J., 170
Epler, Elizabeth, 81, 82

Falk, I. S., 135, 146
Farman, Carl H., 49
Friend, Howard S., 65

Geddes, Anne E., 257
Goldmann, Franz, 147
Gould, R. F., 86
Greenfield, Margaret, 118
Greve, Clifford H., 241

Haber, William, 170
Hale, Mark P., 257
Hall, Helen, 146
Hamovitch, Maurice B., 128
Harris, Seymour E., 153, 161
Hayden, Charles G., 146
Hayes, John H., 146
Hibbard, Russell L., 188
Hohaus, Reinhard A., 34–36, 202
Hohman, Helen Fisher, 55
Howard, Donald S., 9
Hoyt, Elizabeth E., 39

Jacoby, George A., 78
Johnson, Thomas F., 169

Killingworth, Charles G., 194
Kissler, Henry H., 122, 183
Kulp, A. C., 165

Laroque, Pierre, 220
Larson, Arthur, 33
Lester, Richard A., 62, 75–76
Linford, Alton A., 85
Lopes, Charles J., 245, 260

McCamman, Dorothy, 54
McConnell, John W., 99
McNary, William S., 146
Malisoff, Harry, 208
Marsh, L. C., 93
Marshall, A. D., 118
Maxwell, James A., 217, 228
Meriam, Lewis, 23–24
Merriam, Ida C., 152, 165, 175, 191, 228, 230
Miller, John H., 146
Mitchell, Wesley C., 206
Mountin, Joseph W., 241
Musgrave, R. A., 162
Mushkin, Selma J., 39, 162, 218, 246, 247, 253
Myers, Charles A., 57
Myers, Robert J., 103, 110, 190–197
Myrdal, Alva, 92

Newcomer, Mabel, 162
Niessen, Abraham M., 20
Nowacek, Charles G., 165

Osborn, Phyllis R., 86, 87

Parker, James S., 191
Peacock, Alan T., 172, 174, 203
Perkins, Ellen J., 86, 245, 260
Pohlmann, K., 125

Rasor, Eugene A., 191–197
Reed, Margaret G., 39
Roberts, Ffrangcon, 135
Rodgers, Barbara, 265
Ross, James Sterling, 130, 134, 140, 141
Russell, James E., 63, 89, 153, 280

Sanders, Paul H., 72
Schmidt, Emerson P., 146
Schroeder, Gertrude, 194
Schultz, George P., 57
Schultz, Theodore W., 4
Shoup, Carl, 161
Shyrock, Henry S., 105
Siegfried, Charles A., 189
Skolnik, Alfred M., 54, 118
Somers, Anne Ramsay, 63, 118, 121, 122, 124, 126, 165, 179, 182, 260
Somers, Herman Miles, 63, 118, 121, 122, 124, 126, 165, 179, 182, 260
Studenski, Paul, 236
Switzer, Mary E., 125

Teple, Edwin E., 165
Titmuss, Richard M., 137, 261, 262, 279
Towle, Charlotte, 21
Tuchmann, Emil, 145
Tucker, Rufus, 162

Wallace, Elizabeth, 29
Watson, A. D., 27
Weaver, Findley, 174
Weinberg, Nat, 60
Wentworth, Edna C., 109
White, Ruth, 227
Whitehead, A. N., 262
Whitton, Charlotte, 92
Williams, Jene S., 72
Williams, Lee G., 70
Wiltze, Kermit T., 88
Witte, Edwin E., 280
Woofter, T. J., Jr., 90
Wootton, Barbara, 89

Subject Index

AB (Aid to the Blind), 12, 13*n.*, 230*n.*
Abuse, as effect of controls, 73–74
  of public medical services, 144–145
  (*See also* Malingering)
Accountability with private underwriting, 183
Accounting periods, 189–211
ADC (*see* Aid to Dependent Children)
Additional credits, 170*n.*
Adequacy of Benefits under Unemployment Insurance, 42*n.*
Adequacy, of benefits, 31–32, 41–42, 52–54, 231
  (*See also* Supplementation)
  of incomes, costs of child rearing, 89–93
  measures to protect, 4
  medical-care costs, 127–149
Administration, citizen participation, 252–254
  costs, 178–180
  disability insurance, 119–120, 124–126
  by disqualifications, 70–78
  levels of government, 223
  personnel, 259–262
  problems, 248–266
  retirement tests, 106–109
  shared programs, 235–236, 240–241, 255–259
  unemployment insurance, 165*n.*, 257–258
  wage-related benefits, 42–47
  workmen's compensation, 182–183
Administrative organization, 252–254
Administrative review, 259
Administrative skills, influence on policy, 271–272
  (*See also* Administration)
Advisory councils, 263–264
Age of retirement, 97–111
Age-of-business formula in experience rating, 185*n.*

Age composition, influence on policy, 270–271
  state differences, 248
Aged, economic needs of, 101–102
  employment of, 99
  trends, 191*n.*
Agricultural workers, coverage problems, 43–44
Aid to the Blind (AB), 12, 13*n.*, 230*n.*
  (*See also* Public assistance)
Aid to Dependent Children (ADC), 86–89
  changing caseload, 86–87
  federal grant formula, 237, 242
  payments, 58–59
  recipient trends, 86*n.*
  (*See also* Public assistance)
Aid to the Permanently and Totally Disabled (APTD), 13*n.*, 118, 125
  (*See also* Public assistance)
Allocation formulas, 240
American Assembly, 35*n.*
American minimum standard, 231
American Public Welfare Association, 259
Analysis of the Social Security System, 20*n.*
Appeals procedures, 265
APTD, 13*n.*, 118, 125
Assigned risk plans, 182
Assistance in kind, 5–9, 64, 91–92
Assumed average need, 22–26
Australia, expenditures, 5*n.*, 212, 224
  income-conditioned pension, 23, 25
Availability for work, 70, 76, 77
Average earnings, in covered employment, 194
  by industry, 39
  in manufacturing, 59
Average monthly payments, 13*n.*, 58–59

Bank deposit insurance, 4
Base year, 48

283

Beneficiary taxes, 156–159
Benefit ceilings, 50–55
Benefit duration, 69–70, 112–117
Benefit exhaustions, 69, 113–114
Benefit formulas, maximums, 50–51
  modifications of, 44–45
  and price changes, 51–55
  (See also Old Age and Survivors Insurance; Unemployment insurance)
Benefit-ratio formula, 184n.
Benefit-wage differentials, 60–64, 93
Benefit-wage formula, 184–185
Benefit year, 48
Benefits, adequacy, 61–62
  based on assumed average need, 22–26, 59
  based on need, 19–26, 58–59
  of dependents, 42
  and family system, 42, 77, 80–93
  flat-rate, 24–26, 59–60
  and initiative, 56–79
  in kind, 5–9, 91–92
  and national income levels, 25–26, 152–154, 269–270
  nature and conditions, 17–93
  related to contributions, 27–37, 60
  related to earnings, 38–55, 60–64
  unearned, 29–34, 98, 172, 176–177
Beveridge Report, 157, 158n.
"Blanketing-in," 29, 177
Block grants, 237–239
Broken families, 86–89
Budgetary deficiency, 19–20
Bureau of Internal Revenue, 43
Bureau of OASI, 43–44

Canada, children's allowances, 90, 92–93
  expenditures, 5n., 211
  financing, 172, 211, 217, 224–225
  health programs, 136, 140
  needs-test pension, 99
  unemployment insurance, 113n., 220
  universal age benefit, 60, 70, 97, 99, 172
Capitation system, 141–142
Categorical assistance (see Public assistance)
Characteristics of the Low-Income Population and Related Federal Programs, 125n.
Chargeable employers, 186–187

Child welfare grants, 238n., 241
Children's allowances, 7–8, 89–93, 172
Children's Bureau, 253n., 254
Citizen participation, 262–266
City worker's family budget, 82
Civilian Conservation Corps, 87
Clientele basis of administration, 253–254
Closed-end grants, 239–240
Commission on Intergovernmental Relations, 217, 236n., 257n.
Comparison of State Unemployment Insurance Laws as of August, 1954, 68n.
Compensable-separations formula, 185n.
Compensatory fiscal policies, 206, 221–222
  (See also Economic stabilization)
Compulsory health insurance, 8, 11, 129, 139–145, 189–190
Confidentiality of records, 64–65
Congressional hearings, 265–266
Contracting-out in disability insurance, 178, 182
Contributory system, basis of financing, 156–159, 175, 202, 206
  and benefit determination, 27–37
  in medical programs, 133
Cost-of-living adjustments, in public assistance, 54
  in social insurance, 31–32, 54
  (See also Price changes)
Costs, disqualifications and, 77–79
  duration limits and, 114n.
  intergovernmental distributions, 211
  meaning of, 151–154
  medical care, 146–147
  per capita income and, 5, 152–154
  predictability of, 188–197
  prevention and, 278
  private underwriting and, 179
  public medical services, 134–135
  retirement age and, 102–103
Countercyclical financing, 203–206, 209–211, 221–222
  (See also Economic stabilization)
Coverage, 43–44, 51, 107n., 159
Credit unions, 4
Crop insurance, 3–4

Day-care nurseries, 89
Deferred pay, 40–41
Demographic trends, 104–105

Dependents' benefits, 41, 42, 59, 61, 62, 93
Desertion, 86–88
Deterrent conditions, 64–67
Devolution, 256–257
Disability, certification of, 118–120
    effect on benefit rights, 46–47
    income-maintenance programs, 117–126
    medical care programs, 127–149
    (See also Disability insurance)
Disability assistance, 117–118
Disability freeze, 47
Disability insurance, 11, 117–126, 177–184, 189–190
Discharge for misconduct, 70, 72, 167
Disposable income, 103–104, 154
Disqualifications, 70–79, 169
Divorce, 86–88
Dole, 209
Domestic workers, coverage of, 43–44

Earmarked taxes, 156–173
Earnings requirements, 67–69
Economic conditions, influence on policy, 270–271
Economic Measures in Favor of the Family, 7n.
Economic stabilization, 2–3, 61–62, 170, 203–206, 221–222
Eligibility, for public assistance, 64–67
    for social insurance, 29–31, 67–69, 73–74
Employer fault, 78, 123–124, 160–161, 178–179
Employment Act, 1946, 61
Employment discriminations, 102
Employment levels, forecasting problems, 207
    OASI costs and, 192
    tax rates and, 204–206
Employment Security Administrative Financing Act, 52n.
Equal-matching grants, 243–248
Equalization grants, 243n.
Equity, 31–33, 35–36
Evaluation of Invalidity, The, 122n.
Excess reserves, 207
Exclusive state funds, 178
Exhaustion of benefit, 69, 113–114
Expenditures, by country, 5
    by governmental level, 211

Experience rating, 78–79, 165–171, 184–188, 209–211, 223n.

Family solidarity, 84–85
Family system, 77, 80–93, 271
Federal Advisory Council on Employment Security, 78
Federal loans, unemployment insurance, 233
Federal share, public assistance costs, 243n.
Federal taxation, progressivity of, 221
    revenue sources, 215–217
    state per capita income and, 247
Federal standards, public assistance, 229–231, 258–259
    unemployment insurance, 232–234, 257–258
Fee for service, 139–140
Financing, intergovernmental cost sharing, 212–248
    periods of accounting, 189–211
    types of taxes, 155–188
Fiscal resources, Federal and state, 215–217
Flat-grant-minus system, 23
    (See also Income-conditioned pension)
Flat-rate benefits, 24–26, 49, 59–60
    (See also Great Britain; New Zealand)
Foreign Resident Claimant funds, 182
Foster homes, 87
France, administration, 265
    children's allowances, 92, 93
    health insurance, 129–131, 139
Free choice of doctor, 129
Freedom and social security, 5, 77, 276, 280
Fringe benefits, 57, 181
    (See also Guaranteed annual wage)
Full employment, public measures, 2–3
    (See also Economic stabilization)
Fund solvency provisions, 168, 188, 204n., 208n.
Funds for reopened cases, 182

General assistance, 5, 58, 65, 95n., 224
General relief (see General assistance)
General revenues, 171–177
General taxation, 171–177
Genuinely seeking work clause, 63, 73–74

Germany, health insurance, 129
Government, attitudes to, 147, 175, 201, 274
and economic security, 2–4
Grants-in-aid, 227–248
administration, 257–259
block, 237–239
closed-end, 239–240
equal-matching, 243–248
extent, 227–228
health (see Health grants-in-aid)
history, 14
open-end, 239–240
variable, 243–248
Great Britain, administration, 252, 256, 262n.
attitude to needs test, 66, 273
benefits, 24, 59
children's allowances, 90
consumption taxes, 174–175
credited contributions, 46n.
cyclical tax adjustment, 205
expenditures, 5n., 211
financing, 157n., 172, 175n., 176n., 177n., 197, 202, 209, 214, 224
health insurance, 129–131
industrial injuries insurance, 123, 177n.
National Health Service, 8, 11, 130–131, 133–142, 144–145, 157n., 175n., 262n.
National Insurance Act, 1946, 25–26
old-age pensions, 97, 99, 105n., 110, 176n.
periodic actuarial review, 197
relatives' responsibility, 85
reserve policies, 202
social insurance coverage, 95
supplementation, 19–20, 227
unemployment insurance, 113, 117, 172, 207, 209, 227n.
Unemployment Insurance Statutory Committee, 207
Guaranteed annual wage, 63n., 169–170

Health grants-in-aid, 229, 234–235, 238n., 241n., 248, 258n.
Health insurance, voluntary, 147
subsidized, 128–129
(See also Compulsory health insurance)
Health programs, 4, 8, 11–12, 127–149, 252
"High-cost" estimates, 195

Illegitimacy, 86–88
Incentive, benefits and, 58–64
deterrent conditions and, 64–65
duration limits and, 69–70
earnings requirements and, 67–69
needs test and, 64–67
social security and, 56–79, 270, 273, 276
taxation and, 153–154, 164–165
Incentive taxation, 164–165
(See also Experience rating)
Incidence of payroll taxes, 161–163
Income-conditioned pension, 22–26, 85–86, 97, 172
Income distribution, state variations, 39, 247–248
Income maintenance, administration, 252–255
attitudes to, 153, 218–219, 274, 276–277
definition, 4
disqualifications and, 276–277
expenditures, 5, 212
social insurance and, 29–33
wage-related benefits and, 41–55
Income payments by state, 38n.
(See also Per capita income)
Income redistribution, 152–153, 173–175, 218–219, 274
Income scales, 82
Income security, definition, 4
(See also Income maintenance)
Income tax, 172, 173, 175, 215–217, 278
Income-tax deductions, 89
Income test, 273–274
(See also Income-conditioned pension)
Incomes, farm, 39n.
Indemnification in health insurance, 129, 131–133
Individualization, disability insurance, 124
public assistance, 19–20
Inducements to retire, 109–110
Industrial injuries (see Great Britain, industrial injuries insurance; Workmen's compensation)
Inequality of incomes (see Income distribution; Income redistribution)
Inflation (see Price changes)
Initiative (see Incentive)
Institutional relief, 6–7, 64
Insurable interest, 60
Insurance concepts, 27–37, 60, 97–98, 113, 201–202

Interest rates and OASI costs, 193
Intergovernmental cooperation, administrative, 255–259
financial, 212–248
International agreements, 220n.
Interstate competition, 220–221
unemployment insurance, 232
workmen's compensation, 223
Interstate Conference of Employment Security Agencies, 259
Invalidity insurance, 121–122
(See also Disability insurance)
Investment of reserves, 198–200

Labor force, attachment tests of, 67–69
Lay boards, 264–265
Lay participation, 262–266
Legal fees in Workmen's Compensation, 183
Legal-support provision, 81, 85
Less-eligibility principle, 58
Level premium in OASI, 197n.
Level wage assumption and OASI costs, 193–195
Liens, 81
Local self-government, 276
(See also Intergovernmental cooperation)
Long-period disability, 121–122, 255
(See also Disability insurance)
Long-period financing, 189–211
Long-period unemployment, programs for, 8–9, 112–117
unemployment insurance and, 210–211
Long-range costs of OASI, 191–197
"Low-cost" estimates, 195

Malingering, administrative controls on, 70–78
benefits and, 58–64
social security and, 56–79
Marginal workers, 57–62
Matching grants, 240–248
(See also Grants-in-aid)
Matching maximum in public assistance, 230–231, 245
Maternal and child health grants, 241
Maximum benefits, 50–55, 60–64
Maximum creditable earnings, 50–55

Means test (see Needs test)
Medical care, costs, 127–149
indemnity system, 8, 129, 131–133
proposals, 11–12
public programs, 127–149
(See also Health grants-in-aid; Health insurance; Public medical services)
Medical profession, demands on, 147–149
and disability insurance, 118–121
and public medical programs, 131–132, 137–144
Medical secrecy, 120
Minimum benefits, 42
Minimum-wage laws, 3
Mobility, disqualifications and, 74–76
financing and, 213, 219–221
Money earnings test of retirement, 107–108

National Health Service (see Great Britain)
National health services (see Public medical services)
National income, and medical-care costs, 134–135
and retirement policies, 103–104
and security costs, 5n., 151–154
National output, benefits and, 56–58
disability insurance and, 121–123
retirement policies and, 98–101
security costs and, 152–154, 270, 272–274, 276
National Youth Administration, 87
Need, basis of benefits, 19–26
basis of grant-in-aid, 248
Needs test, 21–22, 64–67, 82, 117, 273–274
"New start," 47
New Zealand, benefits, 23, 59
expenditures, 5n., 211
financing, 163, 172, 224
health service, 131, 132, 139
relatives' responsibility, 85
supplementary system, 19
Noncharging in experience-rating, 167, 187

OAA (see Old Age Assistance)
OASI (see Old Age and Survivors Insurance)

Old Age Assistance (OAA), average
    monthly payments, 231, 244–245
  financing, 229–231, 241–245
  recipient rates, 226, 230
  relatives' responsibility, 81–86
  residence requirement, 219
  (*See also* Public assistance)
Old Age and Survivors Insurance (OASI),
    administrative costs, 179
  agricultural exclusions, 43–44, 226
  average monthly earnings, 46
  benefit amounts, 13
  benefit formula, 33n.
  benefit limits, 61
  benefit principles, 27
  benefits, 13, 27, 32–33, 39, 41–42, 46, 49–
    53, 61, 109n.
    adequacy of, 109n.
    of dependents, 42
    by dollar intervals, 39n.
    maximum, 50–53
    minimum, 42
    price changes and, 32, 49–51
    state variations, 39
    years of coverage and, 32–33
  cost estimates, 191–197
  current issues, 10
  disability freeze, 47
  earnings requirements, 67
  economic stabilization and, 222
  eligibility problems, 29–31
  financing, 156, 177, 189–203, 213
  insurance character, 28–33, 97–98, 201–
    202
  level premium contribution, 97, 197n.
  maximum creditable earnings, 50–53
  new start, 47
  purpose of reserves, 197–203
  recipient rates, 226
  reserves, 197–203
  retirement experience, 110
  retirement test, 97–98, 100, 102–103, 107–
    110
  supplementation by OAA, 227
  weighted benefit formula, 41–42
Old Age and Survivors Insurance Trust
    Fund, 197–203
Open-end grants, 239–240
Outdoor relief, 5
Overprescription, 144–145

Panel system, 141–142
Parental responsibility, 91
Patient-doctor relationships, 119, 142–143
Payroll taxes, 156, 160–171, 184–188, 220–
    221
Payroll-variations formula, 168, 185–186
Pensionable age, 98–99
  (*See also* Retirement)
Per capita income, and assistance ex-
    penditures, 245
  and state assistance payments, 244–245
  state differences, 38, 218
  and variable grants, 246–248
Permanent disability insurance, 121–126
  (*See also* Disability insurance)
Personal income, 38n.
  (*See also* Per capita income)
Personnel, 258–262
Poor law, 5, 6, 64–65, 80–81, 171
Population, age composition, 104–105
  children's allowances and, 92–93
  grant-in-aid basis, 248
  and OASI costs, 191–193
Population trends, 104–105
Postponed retirement, 103, 110, 111
Predictability of security costs and income,
    191–197, 207–208, 240
Preventive measures, 88, 135, 138–139, 141,
    164–165, 274–275
  (*See also* Rehabilitation)
Price changes, and earnings requirements,
    69
  and intergovernmental cost sharing,
    227
  and reserve financing, 190
  and retirement test, 107
  and security benefits, 25, 48–55, 231n.
Private insurance, concepts, 33–37, 97–98,
    113, 201–202
  and social security financing, 177–184
Private underwriting, 177–184
Productivity, influence on policy, 152–154,
    269–270
Professions, remuneration, 131–132, 139–
    142
  and social security programs, 118–121,
    137, 260–262
Progressive taxation, 173–175, 221
Public assistance, administration, 253
  benefits, 19–23
  cost-of-living adjustments, 54–55

Public assistance, costs, by level of government, 224n., 243n.
current issues, 12
deterrent features, 64–65
discretionary nature, 21–22
expenditures, 244–245
Federal standards, 219n., 229–231
financing, 171, 173, 214, 215, 224, 237, 241–245
lay boards, 264–265
mandatory standards, 20
maximum payments, 20
medical care, 127–128, 252
minimum living standard, 230–231
monthly payments, 13n., 58–59, 231, 244–245
needs test, 66–68, 230
recipient rates, 226, 230
residence requirements, 219–220
Public medical services, costs, 134–135
and health insurance, 130–134
nature of, 8, 11, 127–130
problems, 134–145
standards, 142–144
(See also Great Britain; New Zealand)
Public work programs, 8–9, 115–116
Works Progress Administration (WPA), 9n., 215, 227n.

Quarterly earnings formula, 44–45

Railroad Retirement Board, 253–254
Railroad workers, programs for, administration, 253–254
disability insurance, 119, 179–180
financing, 156, 157n.
retirement test, 106–107, 110
Ratio rule, 113
Recipient rates, Old Age and Survivors Insurance, 226
public assistance, 226, 230
Recovery provisions, 173n.
Regressive taxation, 159
Rehabilitation, 121–123, 183, 254, 274–275
Reimbursement, 129, 131–133
Relations between Social Security Institutions and the Medical Profession, 127n.
Relatives' responsibility, 80–86

Request reporting, 45
Reserve-ratio formula, 165–166, 184
Reserves, purposes, 197–203
in OASI, 189–203
in unemployment insurance, 189–190, 203–211, 213
Residence requirements, 219–220
Retirement, influences affecting, 101–102, 111
practices, 99, 110
tests, 98–111
Revenue Act, 1951, 64–65
Right to benefit, 157–158
Risk basis of administrative organization, 254
Risks, American programs, 95–96
coverage problems, 97–126
Rowell-Sirois Commission, 217, 238n.

Salaried service in medical programs, 140–141
Second-injury funds, 182
Self-employed, coverage problems, 43
Semiautonomous administration, 265
Senate Advisory Council, 1948, 120n., 121n., 126n., 164n.
Senate Finance Committee, 67
Seniority, 57
Shifting of taxes, 161–163
Sickness (see Disability)
Social attitudes, toward aged, 101–102, 105–106
toward deficits, 208–209
toward government, 41, 147, 175, 201, 274
influence on policy, 272–274
toward levels of government, 216, 222–223
toward medical care proposals, 145–147
toward minimum security, 153–154, 218–219, 274
toward mobility, 219–221
toward retirement, 104
Social insurance, administration, 252–259
benefits, 27–37
characteristics, 27–29
equity concepts, 31–33, 35–36
financing, 156–177, 189–211, 213–214
historical advantages, 27–29
modifications, 29–32

Social insurance, private insurance and, 29, 33–37
  weighted benefits, 31
  and years of coverage, 32–33
  (*See also* Contributory system; specific individual programs)
Social inventions, 271–272
Social security, expenditures, 5, 152n., 212
  programs and issues, 9–13
  scope, 4
Social Security Act, 1935, 6–7, 29, 41, 43, 51, 64–65, 100, 197n., 215, 225, 244
  amendments, 1939, 41n., 107, 194, 198
    1946, 242–244
    1950, 30, 32, 33, 42n., 43n., 47, 49, 51, 88, 98, 107, 194, 197n., 198, 226, 227
    1952, 32, 42n., 108n., 193n., 194, 197n., 230n.
    1954, 31n., 46, 50, 51, 107, 108n., 193n., 196n., 197n., 226
Social Security Administration, 20n., 103, 255
Social Security Board, 28n.
  (*See also* Social Security Administration)
Social status, 28–29, 57, 64–65, 89, 273
Social utilities, 92n.
Solvency of funds, 168, 188, 204n., 208n.
Solvency studies, 210
Special adjustment funds, 182
Special public assistance (*see* Aid to the Blind; Aid to Dependent Children; Aid to Permanently and Totally Disabled; Old age assistance; Public assistance)
Special-purpose grants, 228–239
Stabilization of employment (*see* Economic stabilization; Experience rating)
Standards of service in public medical programs, 142–144
State capacity, indices of, 246–248
State expenditure and Federal grants, 236–237
State-local tax resources, 174, 215–217, 221
Statutory cash payments, 24
  (*See also* Canada, universal age benefit)
Subsidized voluntary health insurance, 128–129
Suitable work, 70–71, 75–77
Supervisory relationships, 258–259
Supplementary benefits, 181
Supplementation, 19–20, 227

Sweden, administration, 256
  cost-of-living adjustment, 54
  financing, 172
  old-age pension, 25, 54, 98–99, 172
  standard-of-living adjustment, 25

Take-home pay, 63–64
Tax competition, 220–221
Tax offset, 170n., 220–221, 232
Tax reallocation, 216–217
Taxes, on employers (*see* Payroll taxes)
  and initiative, 204, 206
  selection of, 155–188
  on workers, 156–159
Technical knowledge, influence on policy, 271–272
Temporary disability insurance, administration, 118n., 255
  financing, 156, 177–184
Test of need (*see* Needs test)

Unearned benefits, 29–34, 98, 172, 176–177
Unemployment, and duration policy, 113–114
  effect of, on benefit rights, 46–47
    on workers, 8–9, 115
  and grants-in-aid, 240
  programs, 8–9, 112–117
  and retirement policies, 100–101
  (*See also* Long-period unemployment)
Unemployment compensation (*see* Unemployment insurance)
Unemployment insurance, abuse, 57, 58, 73–74
  administration, 165n., 257–258
  base year, 48–49
  benefit ceilings, 52–53
  benefit duration, 31, 69–70, 112–113, 226–227
  benefit exhaustion, 113–114
  benefit formulas, 42, 44–45, 51, 60–61
  benefit year, 48–49
  cost-of-living adjustments, 55
  coverage, 43
  current issues, 10–11
  disqualifications, 70–78
  and economic stability, 61–62, 203–211
  effect on wage levels, 75–76
  eligibility, 67–70

Unemployment insurance, Federal standards, 71, 232–234
  federalization proposals, 165n.
  financing, 156, 203–211, 213, 221, 224–225, 258n.
  loan provisions, 232–234, 258n.
  private insurance concepts, 27, 31
  and prolonged unemployment, 114–117
  request reporting, 45
  reserves, 203–211
  solvency of funds, 168, 188, 204n., 208n.
  (See also Experience rating)
Unemployment Insurance Legislative Policy: Benefits, Eligibility, 70n.
Unemployment Trust Fund, 221
  (See also Unemployment insurance, reserves)
U.S. Department of Labor, 255
U.S. Employment Service, 255
Universal free pensions, 24

Variable grants, 243–248
Veterans Administration, 253–254
Veterans' programs, administration, 125n., 253–254
  benefits, 24, 123–124
  cost trends, 176
  financing, 172
  medical care, 8, 127, 133, 140
  payments, 247n.

Vocational rehabilitation, 125–126, 234–235
Voluntary health insurance, 147
  subsidized, 128–129
Voluntary quit, 71–72, 77, 167

Wage levels and OASI costs, 193–195
Wage-related benefits, 38–55
Wage taxes, 156–159
Welfare grants-in-aid, 234–235, 238n.
Withheld benefits, 107, 110
Withholding tax, 158
Work programs, 8–9, 115–116
Workmen's compensation, administration, 125n., 179, 182–183, 260n.
  benefit ceilings, 53–54
  benefit provisions, 61
  coverage, 118
  dependents' benefits, 42
  duration limits, 121n.
  evaluation, 125n.
  financing, 177–184
  and malingering, 63n.
  objectives, 123–124
  and prevention, 164–165
  and rehabilitation, 126
Works Progress Administration (WPA), 9n., 215, 227n.
WPA (see Works Progress Administration)

SOCIAL PROBLEMS
AND
SOCIAL POLICY:
The American Experience

An Arno Press Collection

Bachman, George W. and Lewis Meriam. **The Issue of Compulsory Health Insurance.** 1948

Bishop, Ernest S. **The Narcotic Drug Problem.** 1920

Bosworth, Louise Marion. **The Living Wage of Women Workers.** 1911

[Brace, Emma, editor]. **The Life of Charles Loring Brace.** 1894

Brown, Esther Lucile. **Social Work as a Profession.** 4th Edition. 1942

Brown, Roy M. **Public Poor Relief in North Carolina.** 1928

Browning, Grace. **Rural Public Welfare.** 1941

Bruce, Isabel Campbell and Edith Eickhoff. **The Michigan Poor Law.** 1936

Burns, Eveline M. **Social Security and Public Policy.** 1956

Cahn, Frances and Valeska Bary. **Welfare Activities of Federal, State, and Local Governments in California, 1850-1934.** 1936

Campbell, Persia. **The Consumer Interest.** 1949

Davies, Stanley Powell. **Social Control of the Mentally Deficient.** 1930

Devine, Edward T. **The Spirit of Social Work.** 1911

Douglas, Paul H. and Aaron Director. **The Problem of Unemployment.** 1931

Eaton, Allen in Collaboration with Shelby M. Harrison. **A Bibliography of Social Surveys.** 1930

Epstein, Abraham. **The Challenge of the Aged.** 1928

Falk, I[sidore] S., Margaret C. Klem, and Nathan Sinai. **The Incidence of Illness and the Receipt and Costs of Medical Care Among Representative Families.** 1933

Fisher, Irving. **National Vitality, its Wastes and Conservation.** 1909

Freund, Ernst. **The Police Power:** Public Policy and Constitutional Rights. 1904

Gladden, Washington. **Applied Christianity:** Moral Aspects of Social Questions. 1886

Hartley, Isaac Smithson, editor. **Memorial of Robert Milham Hartley.** 1882

Hollander, Jacob H. **The Abolition of Poverty.** 1914

Kane, H[arry] H[ubbell]. **Opium-Smoking in America and China.** 1882

Klebaner, Benjamin Joseph. **Public Poor Relief in America, 1790-1860.** 1951

Knapp, Samuel L. **The Life of Thomas Eddy.** 1834

Lawrence, Charles. **History of the Philadelphia Almshouses and Hospitals from the Beginning of the Eighteenth to the Ending of the Nineteenth Centuries.** 1905

[Massachusetts Commission on the Cost of Living]. **Report of the Commission on the Cost of Living.** 1910

[Massachusetts Commission on Old Age Pensions, Annuities and Insurance]. **Report of the Commission on Old Age Pensions, Annuities and Insurance.** 1910

[New York State Commission to Investigate Provision for the Mentally Deficient]. **Report of the State Commission to Investigate Provision for the Mentally Deficient.** 1915

[Parker, Florence E., Estelle M. Stewart, and Mary Conymgton, compilers]. **Care of Aged Persons in the United States.** 1929

Pollock, Horatio M., editor. **Family Care of Mental Patients.** 1936

Pollock, Horatio M. **Mental Disease and Social Welfare.** 1941

Powell, Aaron M., editor. **The National Purity Congress;** Its Papers, Addresses, Portraits. 1896

The President's Commission on the Health Needs of the Nation. **Building America's Health.** [1952]. Five vols. in two

Prostitution in America: Three Investigations, 1902-1914. 1975

Rubinow, I[saac] M. **The Quest for Security.** 1934

Shaffer, Alice, Mary Wysor Keefer, and Sophonisba P. Breckinridge. **The Indiana Poor Law.** 1936

Shattuck, Lemuel. **Report to the Committee of the City Council Appointed to Obtain the Census of Boston for the Year 1845.** 1846

The State and Public Welfare in Nineteenth-Century America: Five Investigations, 1833-1877. 1975

Stewart, Estelle M. **The Cost of American Almshouses.** 1925

Taylor, Graham. **Pioneering on Social Frontiers.** 1930

[United States Senate Committee on Education and Labor]. **Report of the Committee of the Senate Upon the Relations Between Labor and Capital.** 1885. Four vols.

Walton, Robert P. **Marihuana, America's New Drug Problem.** 1938

Williams, Edward Huntington. **Opiate Addiction.** 1922

Williams, Pierce assisted by Isabel C. Chamberlain. **The Purchase of Medical Care Through Fixed Periodic Payment.** 1932

Willoughby, W[estal] W[oodbury]. **Opium as an International Problem.** 1925

Wisner, Elizabeth. **Public Welfare Administration in Louisiana.** 1930